SLOVAKIA

STUDIES OF NATIONALITIES
Wayne S. Vucinich, General Editor

The Crimean Tatars
Alan Fisher

The Volga Tatars: A Profile in National Resilience
Azade-Ayşe Rorlich

The Making of the Georgian Nation
Ronald Grigor Suny
(copublished with Indiana University Press)

The Modern Uzbeks: From the Fourteenth Century to the Present; A Cultural History
Edward A. Allworth

Estonia and the Estonians, second edition
Toivo U. Raun

The Azerbaijani Turks: Power and Identity under Russian Rule
Audrey L. Altstadt

The Kazakhs, second edition
Martha Brill Olcott

The Latvians: A Short History
Andrejs Plakans

The Moldovans: Romania, Russia, and the Politics of Culture
Charles King

Slovakia: From Samo to Dzurinda
Peter A. Toma and Dušan Kováč

SLOVAKIA

From Samo to Dzurinda

Peter A. Toma
and Dušan Kováč

HOOVER INSTITUTION PRESS
Stanford University
Stanford, California

Hoover Institution Press Publication No. 487

Copyright © 2001 by the Board of Trustees of the
Leland Stanford Junior University

First printing, 2001

Manufactured in the United States of America
09 08 07 06 05 04 03 02 01   9 8 7 6 5 4 3 2 1

The paper used in this publication meets the minimum
requirements of American National Standard for Information
Sciences—Permanence of Paper for Printed Library Materials,
ANSI Z39.48-1984. ⊗

Library of Congress Cataloging-in-Publication Data
  Toma, Peter A.
    Slovakia : from Samo to Dzurinda / Peter A. Toma and Dušan
Kováč.
        p.   cm. — (Studies of nationalities)
    Includes bibliographical references and index.
    ISBN 0-8179-9951-5 (alk. paper) — ISBN 0-8179-9952-3
      (pbk.: alk. paper)
    1. Slovakia—History.   I. Kováč, Dušan.   II. Title.   III. Series.
  DB2763.T66   2001
  943.73—dc21   00-054246

For the victims of prejudices, past and present

Contents

Maps

Tables

Foreword

We are delighted to see still another volume appear in the Studies of Nationalities series. The book will be welcomed in scholarly circles and among sophisticated readers in general. The Slovak Republic established with the dissolution of Czechoslovakia at the beginning of 1993 may be one of Europe's youngest states. For most of their history, with the dubious exception of the years of World War II, the Slovaks lived in larger states in which others controlled most of the political power. For centuries the territory of Slovakia was part of the Hungarian kingdom, and with it joined other territories in the Habsburg monarchy. After the Habsburg empire collapsed at the end of World War I, the Slovak lands became part of Czechoslovakia. With the ruin of Hitler's New Order in Europe, Czechoslovakia was again re-created, to endure until after the Velvet Revolution. Slovaks may be forgiven for feeling that they have been overlooked by history, and for not being better known both in Europe and beyond.

The political tempests of this century cast up on our shores émigré authors who have also produced works on Slovakia, but they frequently wrote in pursuit of one or another political position in a pietistic style. As Slovakia moves nearer to the desired goal of integration into European security and political structures, there is still a shortage of thorough, comprehensive, and objective studies of Slovak history and modern politics directed at a broad audience. The appearance of this volume will go a long way toward remedying that shortage. What is particularly impressive is the manner in which the authors, Peter Toma and Dusan Kovac, combine their scholarship to present the complexity of the Slovak history with maturity, sophistication, and objectivity.

Kovac, one of Slovakia's leading native historians, effectively sets the story of modern Slovakia in its historical context. He traces the lives of the inhabitants of the territory of today's Slovak state through the earliest Slavic settlement of the region, and then the centuries of development within the Hungarian kingdom. He demonstrates the ties between the ancestors of the modern Slovaks and the other inhabitants of Hungary, but also shows the contacts between the territory and its neighbors, especially the Czech to the west. This was the setting in which elements of Slovak society accepted and began to propagate a modern Slovak national identity. His account points out the historical experiences, patterns of political behavior, and levels of economic development that the Slovaks brought into their new political framework in 1918 when they joined the Czechoslovak state.

Within Czechoslovakia, Toma documents how Slovak society matured and the people gained more of the cultural, economic, and educational requirements for independence than they had been able to develop within old Hungary. Nevertheless, problems of Slovaks' relationship to Czechoslovakia persisted in different forms at different periods of the state's existence. Toma, a Slovak-born American political scientist, discusses the politics of Czechoslovakia during the interwar period. He brings to light new evidence about the weaknesses of Czechoslovak democracy (which had been exploited by the ambivalent leaders of the multiparty system who had dominated the political scene since 1918), Slovak nationalism, and the irredentist movements of national minorities. Persistent demands by the Slovak autonomist movement, spearheaded by the Hlinka Slovak People's Party, against the power holders in Prague, who believed in a common Czechoslovak political nationality, are scrutinized by Toma within the framework of Czechoslovak democracy. Toma's analysis of the Slovak parliamentary elections of the 1920s up to 1935 and the onset of the Great Depression introduces Kovac's discussion of the role of the Third Reich, the Munich Crisis of 1938–39, and World War II, when, from 1939 to 1945, after invasion by the Germans, Slovakia under Jozef Tiso became a puppet state, collaborating with the Germans even in a Holocaust of Slovak Jews.

Toma vividly describes the underground resistance of the last years of the war, which, with Soviet and Allied support, culminated in 1944 in a Slovak National Uprising and ended in 1945 in liberation from the Nazis and then, with the agreement of Benes's Czechoslovak government-in-exile, in a Soviet-backed new Czechoslovak government, known as a people's democracy. In a detailed analysis Toma then documents the communist power play, which in February 1948 resulted in a coup d'etat. In turn, Toma and Kovac discuss Slovakia's efforts to gain more autonomy in communist-controlled Czechoslovakia. Kovac relates the events of the Prague Spring of 1968, when for a brief period there was a possibility of a Czecho-Slovak federation that might eliminate old grievances.

The final two sections (Parts IV and V) bring the history of the Slovaks up to the present—starting with the Velvet Revolution of November 1989, which in three weeks ended the forty-year communist regime. Toma shows how this move toward a democratic system precipitated the breakup of the Czechoslovak federation and the emergence at midnight on December 31, 1992, of an independent Slovak Republic. Toma's account of independent Slovakia since 1993 makes up one of the work's most significant contributions. Without mincing words, Toma examines the record of the new country and its varying political fortunes under the charismatic populist leader Vladimir Meciar. He gives a detailed analysis of the elections of 1998 that replaced Meciar's rule of democratic tyranny with a coalition government that seems at the moment to be committed to bringing Slovakia successfully into NATO and the European Union. Like its neighbors, with whom it shares so much of its history, Slovakia faces daunting—but not insurmountable—challenges in the new century.

This new Slovak Republic will have to deal with the challenges posed to the majority's view of the state as their "Slovak" nation-state by the existence of Slovak citizens of Magyar and other ethnic groups (in 1991 some 15 percent of the total population). And it will have to convince its citizens that a future within the broader structures of European security and economic institutions will be better for it than going it bravely alone as a xenophobic nation-state. Whatever their interest in this process, readers of the present study will be able to grasp the historical context, political traditions, and "imagined" experience that Slovaks will take with them into the challenge of the coming decades.

The excellence of the Toma-Kovac work, based on their broad background of professional experience and diverse Czech, Slovak, and foreign sources, will have an enduring quality.

Wayne S. Vucinich

Preface

This book—a contribution to the history and politics of Slovakia as researched and told by a naturalized American from Slovakia with the assistance of a Slovak historian—is intended for readers in the English language who desire to acquire a more sophisticated understanding about past and present Slovakia. Events involving other than Slovak national are narrated in their scope and in some detail with emphasis on the Slovaks. To do full justice, these events are left to other countries' historians and their interpretations. I have tried to place Slovak history in its true setting without prejudice. The guiding and only reference to what happened and how it seemed at the time is my reliance on documentation. Libraries and archives in Bratislava or Prague are not known for easy access and reliable cataloging of research data; hence, to reconstruct past events after World War I, for example, was very often a frustrating experience. That disappointment was further compounded by contractual limits imposed on the size of the manuscript, which necessitated a reduction from 800 to 450 pages.

Perhaps the most bewildering experience for me was the discovery in late September 1999 that my coauthor, under the same contract, without informing me as senior coauthor and/or the publisher, had published his own book, *Dejiny Slovenska* (History of Slovakia); Prague: Naklada-telstvi Lidove noviny, 1988). I made this discovery while perusing the daily Slovak press for research data. A reading of the book soon revealed the shocking truth. Several chapters in the Prague publication were identical to the Slovak text in the manuscript chapters the coauthor submitted to me for this book on March 24 and May 12, 1997. However, because of the required shortening of the original manuscript and the editing of the submitted chapters, the present contribution by my coauthor only resembles and therefore is not identical to the Slovak version of some chapters in *Dejiny Slovenska*. In the course of translation—some of it done by Professor Emeritus Jan Simko—I was careful to retain the literary meaning of the Slovak text submitted by my coauthor; only factual corrections were made where scholarship was at issue.

Because my professional career is political science with an educational background primarily in the United States, whereas my coauthor's is modern history taught in Slovakia under the communist regime, the reader may detect a style of "two voices" or an emphasis on certain detailed events that reflect the interests or specialization of the coauthors. When a book of this dimension in scope is researched and written by more than one author, the difference in style and emphasis is almost inevitable.

As one might expect, both coauthors were assisted by a number of others in various capacities before this study appeared in print. I have been greatly assisted in the acquisition of bibliographic and research data by four of the many junior colleagues who also assisted my coauthor with the preparation of his chapters when he served as director of the Institute of History at the Slovak Academy of Sciences. They are Dr. Elena Londakova, Dr. Miroslav Londak, Dr. Xenia Suchova, and Dr. Jozef Zatkuliak. The Interlibrary Loan at the University of Arizona has aided me in obtaining more than a hundred journal articles utilized in my project. In the verification of the notes and references, I must make acknowledgments to the large number of librarians and students in Tucson, Bratislava, and Prague—in particular to Atifa Rawan, social sciences librarian, and to Luther Doyle and Courtney Southerland, my former students at the University of Arizona, who persevered in making a tedious search for references palatable.

In addition, I must express my gratitude to Linda Gregonis, Olga Markovich, Gregory McNamee, and Elizabeth Shaw, who assisted me in the reduction of the manuscript from its original to present size. Both manuscripts were typed in draft form by my dedicated and patient wife, Letty Ann, and then prepared for submission on word processor and diskette by our able administrative assistant in the Department of Political Science at the University of Arizona, Vickie Healey.

The initiative for writing this book belongs without any doubt to the general editor of the Studies of Nationalities Series published by the Hoover Institution Press, Wayne S. Vucinich, professor emeritus of history at Stanford University. It was Wayne's power of friendly persuasion that inspired me to search for a Slovak historian as a potential coauthor before commiting myself to this project. While I am willing to share any accolades of this study with its originator, the responsibility for all trials and tribulations leading to its completion is mine alone.

I acknowledge with gratitude the guidance and assistance received from the members of the editorial staff of the Hoover Institution Press— especially Patricia A. Baker, executive editor, for her encouragement to make the manuscript "more concise"; Ann Wood, senior editor, for her coordination efficiency; and Shirley Taylor for her thorough editing. Marshall Blanchard and Akiko Arakawa have also given me their invaluable aid in providing the design for this book.

Space and confidentiality would not allow me to express my thanks for the manuscript reviewers or others who aided me in making this publication a success. Nevertheless, I owe a debt of gratitude to all who labored on this project.

Peter A. Toma
March 2000

Introduction

This book is about the history of the Slovak people: their struggle for national identity, their aspiration for independence and economic development, their ambition to become a democratic state. In the recent past, the history of the Slovaks was presented in different languages, to different audiences, from different points of view. For example, during the Austro-Hungarian Dual Monarchy, it was the feudal Hungarian point of view that was spread around Europe and other areas of the world. During the time of Czechoslovakia, the Slovaks appeared more or less as "a postscript to Czech history."[1] After the Communist usurpation of power, Marxist historians again reinterpreted Slovak history within their own image of dialectical materialism. At different times, under different rulers, the Slovaks were cast in different roles and perspectives on the world stage of history in order to satisfy the interests of those who wrote about them.

In these various accounts, professional scholarship and scientific inquiry were often sacrificed for ideological interests or national prejudices. Several of the historical accounts written in the English language about the Slovaks and Slovakia were either sketchy, romanticized versions of a pastoral society or nationalistic exaltations of the Slovak past, presented in an exaggerated, unrealistic fashion. Thomas Capek's little book on *The Slovaks of Hungary*, published in 1906 by the Knickerbocker Press in New York, is a good example of the former.

As late as 1930, there was only one unscholarly monograph on Slovakia in English: Jozef Skultety's *Sketches from Slovak History*. Between the two world wars, the Slovaks and Slovakia were described almost exclusively in scholarly treatises dealing with Czechoslovakia—treatises that dealt more with Czech and less with Slovak history, and were in many cases marred by oversimplification, distortion, and even falsification of historical data.

Not only were there no reliable scholarly studies about the history of the Slovaks in English before World War II, but there were not, it appears, any interested Slovak-American scholars to undertake such studies, nor was there any interest even among Slovak émigrés in such publications.

The Slovak immigrant community in the United States prior to World War II was not inconsiderable, though figures are not at all precise. No separate records were kept for Slovakia, an integral part of the Kingdom of Hungary, but according to the 1910 U.S. Census there were 284,444 people who claimed Slovak origin. The same census also recorded over three million "Slavic or Lettic" people in the United States, many of whom could have been of Slovak origin because the census takers, like the immigration officers, probably created their own categories of people as a matter of convenience—the country of origin (the Kingdom of Hungary or Czechoslovakia after 1918) was probably more meaningful to the census takers than nationality. The 1920 census, which appears to have been more accurate, recorded 619,866 Slovaks in the United States.[2] But since few of the early Slovak immigrants could speak or understand English, communication was in any case a serious handicap.

In per capita emigration before 1914, the Slovak migration was second only to the Irish.[3] The overwhelming majority of émigrés were poor peasants, unskilled laborers, or so-called *drotari* (tinkers) who moved from place to place repairing household implements.[4] They came from small villages and had very little education, no special skills, and no knowledge of the English language. Usually, they were at the mercy of their sponsors—the company where they worked or the friends or relatives originating from the same village or general area in Slovakia. About half a million Slovaks worked as underpaid laborers in the mines, steel mills, and ironworks—from New York and New Jersey, where they landed, to Ohio, Illinois, Michigan, Minnesota, and Pennsylvania. Slovak émigrés established their own settlements around the Pittsburgh area after the men saved enough money to send for their families to come to the New World. They were émigrés eking out a living through hard labor. There were no scholars or intellectuals among them—only a few members of the clergy who had no interest in writing and publishing books on Slovak history.

About 90 percent of the Slovak immigrants were Roman Catholic; 15 percent were Lutheran; 4 percent Greek Orthodox, and about 1 percent Calvinist.[5] Their parishes also established their own schools, fraternal benefit societies, and newspapers. Yet all four religious denominations became independent of each other and in time even competed with one another in political-philosophical matters. Primarily because of the impact of the Reformation that began in the sixteenth century, the division between the Slovak Roman Catholics and Lutherans also acquired a political significance during the time of the creation of the Czechoslovak Republic in 1918. In general, though the Lutherans favored the new Czechoslovak state, the Catholics were skeptical because they opposed a unitary system of government. That controversy between the supporters, the "Czechoslovaks," and the opponents, the "separatists," continued to dominate the Slovak political scene at home and abroad until the beginning of World War II.[6]

Between 1920 and 1937, according to official records, some 430,000 people left Czechoslovakia. Because official statistics gave emigration figures for Czechoslovakia as a whole, without distinguishing between Czechs and Slovaks, we can only assume that at least half of them were of Slovak origin. As in Slovakia, the majority of Slovaks in the United States in 1939, especially those belonging to the Slovak League of America, were in full support of an independent Slovak state,[7] and they continued to support the Tiso regime in Slovakia until December 1941, when Congress declared war on Japan. A minority of Slovaks in the United States joined the Czech-Americans in their organizational support of the Czechoslovak government in exile led by former president Eduard Benes in London. Interestingly, in September 1939, the members of the Canadian Slovak League pledged their loyalty to Canada, and thus by implication renounced the Slovak state led by Josef Tiso.[8]

In the forty-five years after the end of World War II, three waves of Slovak immigrants left Czechoslovakia.[9] The first postwar wave of emigration consisted of Slovak political refugees who left the Slovak

state with the retreating German army in early 1945 and found temporary refuge in the western military zones of Austria and Germany. Most
of them eventually emigrated to Canada, the United States, Argentina,
and Australia. Many of these refugees were well-educated, former functionaries of the Slovak state, and in Canada, where they were more numerous, they soon rose to leadership positions in various Slovak organizations, journals, and newspapers.[10]

A second wave of Slovak émigrés arriving in the United States and
Canada were also mostly political refugees, who left Czechoslovakia
after the February 1948 communist coup d'état. This wave was much
larger than the first postwar wave, but not as large as the third wave. In
this group of displaced persons (or DPs), besides politicians, there were
professionals, academicians, and university students as well as businessmen and entrepreneurs whose property had been confiscated by the
communists. Although most of these Slovak political refugees were
strong defenders of Czech and Slovak unity, they were also strong proponents of a federal system of government based on the principle of two
equal nations. In addition, this second wave included a small group of
Slovak "separatists" who had joined forces with the Slovak émigrés
from the first wave still awaiting emigration in occupied West Germany.
Before the "separatists" (so called by the advocates of the Czechoslovak
state) and the "Czechoslovaks" (so called by the advocates of an independent state) emigrated from Germany to the United States, Canada,
and other countries, they had challenged each other in polemical
speeches before wide audiences in DP camps and in mimeographed
newspapers and pamphlets produced in those camps. After they were
resettled, the controversy between the two groups continued for a long
time in the ethnic press in the United States and Canada. They were
united only by their opposition to communism. However, the "Czechoslovaks" never failed to remind the "separatists" that they were cut from
the same cloth as the communists because of their past philosophical
orientation.

The third, and largest, postwar emigration wave of Slovaks followed
the Soviet-led invasion of communist Czechoslovakia in August 1968;
emigration continued until November 1989. During that period some
250,000 people left communist Czechoslovakia, most of them illegally.[11]
Altogether, the country lost more than 550,000 people—3.5 percent of
its population. The majority of the émigrés were Czechs, but a great
many were Slovaks—mostly well-educated professionals and entrepre-

neurs who felt constricted by communism and left not so much for political reasons as for greater economic opportunities and a better life available in the West. After resettlement in the United States or Canada, most of them, "much to the dismay of the [Slovak] nationalists, took little interest in the political agendas of postwar émigrés."[12]

This brief survey of the history of the American and Canadian Slovaks—who in 1991 numbered about 830,000 people—may at least partly explain why on the North American continent it took such a long time to write in English a scholarly study about Slovakia and the Slovaks. Josef Kirschbaum's approach to Slovak history is couched in a setting of a "struggle for survival," especially as seen through the prism of Czech-Slovak relations; our approach is to a large extent exogenic—recording events and analyzing situations as they developed and affected the Slovak population within the time frame of historical events taking place in Central Europe. We are concerned less with social Darwinism of the Spenglerian sort and more with the facts about *what actually happened in the past;* we are interested in identifying individuals and movements both for their contribution and for their responsibility for the decline of the intellectual, cultural, economic, and political advancement of the Slovaks. We have been particularly careful to maintain scholarly objectivity and to avoid personal prejudices, even though in some instances the discovery of "truth" through research has clashed head on with old beliefs and teachings of "historical facts" acquired since childhood. To tell the "truth," based on documentary evidence, was a guideline for the principal author, which he was taught in schools in the country where T. G. Masaryk was the "philosopher king," and is now, in his adopted country, where he considers it his duty to "tell it as it is."

We trust that our readers, regardless of ethnic origin or political or religious persuasion, will appreciate this factual historical survey of the Slovaks and Slovakia. It was written not from a Slovak but from a scholarly point of view for readers in the English-speaking world who desire to learn about the Slovaks, who, on account of the circumstances of history, lived for many years in obscurity. In 1914, just before the war that unleashed the destructive forces against Western civilization and plunged the entire world into disorder for almost a century, the British historian G. E. Mitton, quoting his colleague Mr. Drage, offered the following characterization of the Slovak in his book *Austria-Hungary:* "The Slovak, who lives chiefly in the north-west, is poor, hardworking, honest and superstitious, full of curious beliefs; but the epithet 'stupid' cannot be applied to a race which, apart from Pan-Slavist writers like Kollar and Stur, produced the great Magyar poet of the revolution, Alexander Petöfi, and the great Magyar national hero, Louis Kossuth."[13]

Of course, the Magyars could well take issue with Mitton's allegation that it was the "Slovak race" that produced the two great Magyar idols, Petöfi and Kossuth, since both disavowed their so-called racial heritage and proudly supported a strong Magyarization policy. Moreover, not even anthropologists would be simplistic enough to maintain that nations in Central Europe are a "race" with attributes distinguishable in any scientific way. As we glean from the past history of the Slovaks, from the early medieval period to the present, we can soon discover that on the relatively small piece of real estate in Europe called Slovakia, various hordes, tribes, clans, troops, and armies of non-Slovaks moved back and forth for centuries—including the long-lasting Turkish invasion—which brought about intermarriage, migration, and displacements of Slovaks. In our study, we do not advocate any Slovak racial purity and for this reason treat the Slovaks and Slovakia conceptually as members of the modern nation-states.

Frequently Used Abbreviations

AEPS	Association of Employees of the Piestany Spa
AM	Agricultural Movement
AMS	Association for Moravia and Silesia
AWS	Association of Workers of Slovakia
BC	[Slovak] Board of Commissioners
CACNF	Central Action Committee of the (Renewed) National Front
CC	Central Committee
CCSR	Constitutional Court of the Slovak Republic
CDM	Christian Democratic Movement
CDP	Christian Democratic Party

CDU	Civic Democratic Union
CEC	Central Election Commission
CF	Civic Forum
CIR	Civic Initiative of Romas
CM	Coexistence Movement
Cominform	Communist Information Bureau
CPC	Communist Party of Czechoslovakia
CPS	Communist Party of Slovakia
CPSU	Communist Party of the Soviet Union
CRC	Central Referendum Commission
CSCE	Conference on Security and Cooperation in Europe
CSD	Czechoslovak Social Democracy
CSEMADOK	Cultural Association of Hungarian Working People in Czechoslovakia
CSR	The Czechoslovak Republic
DB	Deutsche Bank
DNC	District National Committee
DO	Druha Obchodna [Banka]
DP	Democratic Party
DS	See DP
DU	Democratic Union
EBRD	European Bank for Reconstruction and Development
EU	European Union
FA	Federal Assembly
FHC	Forum of Hungarians in Czechoslovakia
FP	Freedom Party
FS	Freiwillige Schützstaffel

FSIC	First Slovak Investment Company
GDP	Gross domestic product
GDR	German Democratic Republic
GTS	Gremium of the Third Sector
H SIPO	Einsatzgruppe (Substitute Unit)
HC	Hungarian Coalition
HCDM	Hungarian Christian-Democratic Movement
HCP	Hungarian Civic Party
HG	Hlinka Guard
HSLS	Hlinka's Slovak People's Party
HSPO	General Staff of the Partisan Movement in Czechoslovakia
HZDS	See MDS
ICJ	International Court of Justice
ICNL	International Center for Not-for-Profit Law
ISP	Independent Slovak Party
KAN	Club of Active Nonpartisans
KdP	Carpatho-German Party
KSS	See CPS
MDS	Movement for a Democratic Slovakia
MPS	Minister Plenipotentiary for Slovakia
NATO	North Atlantic Treaty Organization
NBS	National Bank of Slovakia
NC	National Committees
NCSR	National Council of the Slovak Republic
NF	[Slovak] National Front
NG	Nafta Gbely

NGOs	Nongovernmental organizations
NPF	National Property Fund
NSP	National Socialist Party
OECD	Organization for Economic Cooperation and Development
OF	See CF
OSS	Organization of Strategic Services
PAV	Public Against Violence
PAV-DS	Public Against Violence—For a Democratic Slovakia
PCU	Party of Civic Understanding
PDC	Party of the Democratic Center
PDL	Party of the Democratic Left (the former CPS)
PFP	Partnership for Peace
PG	Party of the Greens
PHC	Party of the Hungarian Coalition
PP	People's Party
PPS	Peasants' Party of Slovakia
RII	Romany Independent Initiative
ROH	Revolucne odborove hnuti (Revolutionary Trade Union Movement)
RP	Revival Party
SCC	Slovak Constitutional Court
SCO	Special Control Organ
SD	Sicherheits Dienst (Security Services)
SDC	Slovak Democratic Coalition
SDCU	Slovak Democratic and Christian Union
SDK	See SDC

SDKU	See SDCU
SDL	See PDL
SdP	Sudeten German Party
SDP	Social Democratic Party
SDPS	Social Democratic Party of Slovakia
SIS	Slovak Information Service
Sk	Slovak Koruny
SLA	Slovak League of America
Smer	Direction Party
SMFA	Slovak Ministry of Foreign Affairs
SMK	See PHC
SNC	Slovak National Council
SNP	Slovak National Party
SNR	Slovenska narodna rada (See SNC)
SNU	See SNP
SOP	See PCU
SRO	Slovak Resettlement Office
SRSP	Slovak Rehabilitation Spa Piestany
SSDP	Slovak Social Democratic Party
StB	State Security
STV	Slovak Television
SVV	Slovak Underground Military Headquarters
UNRRA	United Nations Relief and Rehabilitation Administration
USPH	Ukrainian General Staff of Partisan Movement
VPS	See PAV
WAS	Workers Association of Slovakia
ZRS	See WAS

FROM EARLY MEDIEVAL HISTORY TO THE NINETEENTH CENTURY

PART ONE

1 From the Slovaks' Slavic Ancestors to National Renaissance

When, in the fifth century A.D., the Old Slavs migrated from the east into the Carpathian region, they found a country that had long been inhabited—and contested—by Celts, Romans, Germans, and other peoples. The region was attractive not only for its fertile soil and dense forests but also because several ancient roads and navigable rivers passed through it. In time, these routes—including the Danube, a highroad from Buda to Bohemia, and a north-south trade route that linked Slovakia to the Balkans and the Mediterranean—gave the region access to the larger world, as well as strategic importance.

The Old Slavs settled in abandoned towns like Gerulata, a Roman center whose ruins provided walls, stones, and tools for the newcomers. They lived there in monogamous families, observing the ancient customs of their people: they cremated their dead, placed them in urns, and buried them in shallow pits, and, according to the sixth-century Byzantine historian Procopius, they worshiped a god whom they called "creator of lightning and master of all things." The Old Slavs were farmers who required vast fertile plains to support their economies. Their settlements were relatively sparse, small hamlets that cultivated large areas. As time went on, they grew somewhat more prosperous, especially after they began trading extensively with their neighbors, the Wends.

This chapter is based on the Slovak text by Dusan Kovac.

The Slavs were also warriors, in constant battle with their enemies. They fought on foot, without armor but with shields and spears.[1] Their skill in warfare proved useful when they made contact with the Avars, a nomadic people who entered the Carpathian region at the beginning of the sixth century.[2] Expeditions of the nomadic Avars, who established the center of their empire between the Danube and Tisa rivers, tormented the Slavs. The Russian chronicler Nestor writes: "These Avars fought with the Slavs and abused their women. If an Avar wanted to travel, he did not allow a horse or a bull to be harnessed, but he let three, four, or five women be harnessed to a cart and in this way the Avar was pulled."[3]

The Avars' attacks forced the Slavs to unify and defend themselves. Thus, the first historically known tribal union of Slavs was founded under the leadership of a Frankish merchant, Samo. A contemporary, the Frankish chronicler Fredegar, witnessed this union:

> A man named Samo, a Frank, brought many merchants with him and intended to do business with those Slavs who are known as Wends. The Slavs had already started to rebel against the Avars and their ruler the Khagan. When the Slavs with their army attacked the Avars, the merchant Samo stepped forward at their side. And here he showed that great ability, which evoked admiration, and the Slavs' swords killed a countless number of the Avars. The Slavs, acknowledging Samo's leadership, pronounced him their king, and here he happily ruled for thirty-five years. Under his sovereignty the Slavs carried on many battles against the Avars, always defeating them. Samo had twelve women from the Slav tribe with whom he produced twenty-two sons and fifteen daughters.[4]

Samo's empire spread to the territory of present-day Moravia and western Slovakia. In time, it became a threat even to the Frankish empire, repelling a Frankish invasion led by King Dagobert. Yet Samo's empire lasted only a short period, from 623 until his death in 658, when the tribal union disintegrated.

Western Slovakia developed rapidly after the end of the eighth century, when the Avars were finally subdued. The town of Nitra became a principality under the rule of Pribina, and its confines extended to Spis and Gemer in central Slovakia. In 828, the first Christian church in Slovakia was erected in Nitra and consecrated by the Frankish archbishop Adalram of Salzburg. In 833, the principality of Moravia, led by Mojmir, subsumed Nitra and united both principalities into the Empire

Map 1. East Central Europe, seventh–eighth centuries

of Great Moravia;[5] Pribina and his entourage fled to the south and came
under the patronage of the Franks, who awarded the prince with land-
holdings in the province of Pannonia.

The most important rulers of the Great Moravian Empire were Rastislav (846–870) and Svatopluk (870–894). Rastislav enjoyed some success as a ruler, but when the Frankish armies invaded Great Moravia
in 870, his nephew Svatopluk allied himself with the Margrave of the
Ostmark, Carloman. Svatopluk captured Rastislav and handed him over
to Carolman, who sent Rastislav in chains to Bavaria, where his eyes
were publicly burned out. Svatopluk took power, and not only did he
strengthen the empire internally, but he also expanded it to Potisie, Little
Poland, Czech territories, and Lusatian Serbia. In 872, he defeated the
Durin and Saxon armies sent by King Louis the German, Carloman's
father; according to a chronicler, Slavic women fought against the invad-
ers, ambushing the enemy horsemen as they tried to escape. In 874,
Svatopluk signed a peace agreement with King Louis at Forchheim. Svatopluk promised to be loyal to the king and agreed to pay an annual fee,
but he insisted that the king let him "live in peace." Svatopluk used the
truce with the king to go on expeditions to conquer surrounding territories (from the present Czech Republic to the borders of contemporary
Bulgaria). The booty taken from the newly acquired territories was sufficient both to pay his duty to the king and to expand his holdings.

Great Moravia did not long outlive Svatopluk. But its short existence was significant. It coincided with the growth of Christianity
throughout the area. From the west—from the East Frankish empire—
the religion was an arm of Frankish expansion into the Danube basin.
Rastislav fought this by establishing the Slavic liturgy. He turned to the
Byzantine emperor Michael III and asked him to send missionaries who
could speak a Slavic language to Great Moravia. Michael complied by
sending two Greek monks, Constantine (Cyril) and Methodius. Their
accomplishments were many.[6] As missionaries, their task was to spread
Christianity. Because Rastislav requested that this task be accomplished
in a Slavic language, Constantine created the Slavic alphabet, which enabled them to translate parts of the Bible and other liturgical texts into
Slavic—which meant codifying the Old Slavonic language.

Constantine (827–869), called the Philosopher, belonged to the
most educated group of personalities of his era and had a profound
influence on the diplomatic-Christian missions. Methodius (815–885)
was educated in law and was good at organizing church and social life.

Both brothers defended their translations and their liturgies before the pope. In 867, Constantine decided to remain in Rome, entered a monastery, accepted Cyril as his name, and died soon after that. Methodius returned to Great Moravia and tried to continue the work the two had started. It was not easy. The fight for the Slavic liturgy became part of a political battle to govern Great Moravia and, later, the entire Danube basin. The Frankish priests considered the work of Constantine and Methodius an unacceptable intervention and tried to suppress their work. The battle between the followers of the Latin and the Slavic liturgies became a long-standing theme in the region's history, one that continues in the Balkans today.[7]

In 907, the Old Magyars defeated the army of the East Frankish Empire. Their victory meant continuous invasions and threats to neighboring countries, not only to Bavaria and Saxony but also to the Byzantine empire. Their defeat by Emperor Otto I at Lechfeld near Augsburg, in 955, forced them to concentrate more on the stabilization of their power in the central parts of the Danube basin, and, under the rule of the Arpad dynasty, the aggressive nomadic Magyars began to devote more time to the organization of their state.

Slavic inhabitants of the Carpathian region and the Danube lowland were gradually overtaken by the influential and growing Hungarian state. Great Moravia, because of its inner decline, was not able to face the attacks of the Old Magyars, and it fell under the hegemony of the Hungarian state. The Slavic inhabitants, with their skill of cultivating the soil, were on a higher level of development than the nomadic Magyars, and the Magyars, during their transition from a nomadic to a settled way of life, made use of the more developed agricultural tools and techniques of the Slavs and gradually adopted their Slavic names. It is also obvious that Slavic magnates—that is, the persons of rank and influence—entered the Arpads' service and played a role in the formation of the Hungarian state.[8]

Hungary was divided from the very beginning into parts that were managed by members of the ruling Arpad dynasty. One such part was Nitra. These parts remained intact even after the centralization attempts of the Magyar duke Gejza and the first Hungarian king, Stephen (997–1038). King Stephen was an educated Christian and a great proselytizer who enjoyed political support throughout Christian Europe. In the year 1001, he was crowned and proclaimed a saint. Subsequently, Stephen created a centralized, homogeneously organized state. The whole coun-

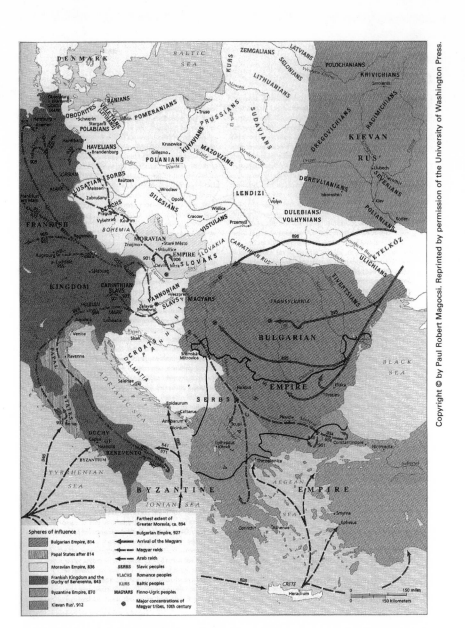

Map 2. East Central Europe, ninth century

try was administratively divided into royal counties (comitats), ruled by counts (Ispan) appointed by the king. The Nitra comitat consisted of the entire area of western and central Slovakia. In the second half of the eleventh century, during the rule of King Andrew I, this comitat contained almost all of present-day Slovakia.

The Tartar invasion in 1241 temporarily halted the development of the early Hungarian state. The Tartars conquered the weak army of King Bela IV and penetrated into the center of Hungary, and their plunder of the inhabited area of southwestern Slovakia resulted in poverty and famine that left many regions depopulated, as the inhabitants fled to the better-protected cities. In 1272, after these ravages, the Hungarian throne passed to ten-year-old Ladislas IV. His brief rule was disastrous, ending in his assassination. His successor, Andrew III, the last Arpad sovereign, died in 1301, probably after being poisoned. His death plunged the country into anarchy.

The feudal aristocracy used the monarchy's weakness to strengthen their own positions. In the early fourteenth century Hungary was a feudal country in which the magnates and bishops ruled as potentates, while the lower nobility, organized in the comitats, controlled the administration. In what is now Slovakia there were twelve provincial governments: Bratislava, Gemer, Hont, Liptov, Nitra, Orava, Spis, Saris, Tekov, Trencin, Turcin, and Zvolen. During the period of Hungarian control, there were only a few changes and shifts in the administration of these counties.

The growth of the nobility led to the empowering of influential upper-class families. The greatest magnates were Matus Cak (Matyas Csak, or Matthew Cak) of Trencin and the Amadeis of the Aba family in eastern Slovakia. The Caks, of Magyar origin, had begun their rise during the rules of Stephen V and Ladislas IV and consolidated their power during the reign of King Andrew III. At the end of the Arpad dynasty, Matus Cak took advantage of the succession struggle between Charles I (Charles Robert of Anjou) and the Czech royal prince, Wenceslas III, to obtain more properties and prestige from all quarters. When Charles I was made king, Matus Cak was appointed manager of the royal property. He conducted raids against rich monasteries, among them the Nitra diocese, and eventually controlled twelve administrative districts and thirty castles; thus, he was the real ruler of two-thirds of present-day Slovakia, a state within a state. Cak acted as a king and kept a court at the Trencin castle, signing international agreements as a self-appointed prince.

The rest of Slovakia found itself under the rule of a similar oligarchy, that of Amadei of the Aba family. Cak and Amadei allied against King Charles I, and for a time all of Slovakia slipped from royal control. In 1312, in the battle at Rozhanovce, Charles I convincingly defeated Amadei, but it meant only the end of the Aba rule in eastern Slovakia. It did not weaken the position of Matus Cak, who arrived on the battlefield after the combat was over; he continued to rule until his death, after which his domain disintegrated.

The fourteenth and fifteenth centuries were a golden era in the development of Hungary. The territory of Slovakia was a rich source of both gold and silver ore, especially in the area of Kremnica, where the annual production of gold was some 2,500 kilograms,[9] and this wealth, with mining and the rise of trades, contributed to the development of Slovak towns—Bratislava, Trnava, Kosice, Presov, and Bardejov, and the independent royal mining towns of Banska Stiavnica, Banska Bystrica, and Kremnica.

Much of the fourteenth century was a period of quiet development without any major foreign wars, invasions, epidemics, or famines. The population grew, augmented by the arrival of the Wallachs, sheepherders who used mountainous pastures that were unsuitable for cultivation. During this time, too, manifestations of the Slovak consciousness could be observed, especially where the Slovak ethnic groups interacted with other ethnic groups such as Germans and Magyars. In 1384 a royal document, *Privilegium pro Slavis,* addressed rising ethnic conflict in the region. In it, King Louis I guaranteed fair representation on the Bratislava city council for Slovak middle-class inhabitants, who had complained that Germans held disproportionate political power.

But this flowering ended with the death of Charles I's successor, King Louis I. Louis I did not have a male heir, and Sigismund of Luxembourg, son of the Czech king Charles IV and husband of Louis's older daughter, Mary of Anjou, sought the throne. The Hungarian nobility rejected his claims, and Sigismund had to fight for the throne against Louis's nephew, Charles of Durrazzo and Naples, as well as aspirants from the Polish Jagellon dynasty. Sigismund eventually prevailed, but it took him twenty years to strengthen his position on the throne. Nearly bankrupt, he began to give towns and castles as collateral for loans; in this way, his cousins, the Moravian marquis and earls, acquired Bratislava and Nitra. Sigismund also gave thirteen Spis royal towns to the Polish king. Sigismund's position weakened with his disastrous campaigns against the Osman founder of the Ottoman dynasty. Hungarian nobles eventually imprisoned Sigismund for four months in 1401.[10] Sigismund escaped, and after the death of his brother, the Bohemian king Wenceslas IV, he tried to seize the Czech throne, precipitating the Hussite wars in Bohemia—so named after the followers of the martyred scholar Jan Hus (1369–1415). The Hussites invaded Slovakia several times between 1428 and 1432, seizing castles and towns.

Sigismund finally secured the Czech throne in 1436, only to die after the battle at Lipany the following year. His death, followed by the death in 1439 of his son and heir, Albert of Habsburg, brought on a new struggle for the Hungarian throne. The Polish king, Vladislav VI, pitted himself against Albert's widow, Elizabeth, defending the interests of her infant son, Ladislas V. Though Vladislav prevailed, becoming king of Hungary in 1440, he died four years later at the battle of Varna against the Turks, and Ladislav V became king. The Hungarian parliament temporarily consigned the government of the country to seven captains, one of them being Jan Jiskra, a Czech warrior who had allied with Elizabeth. Jiskra became one of the most influential men in Hungary, residing with his soldiers, who called themselves "Brethren," in Slovakia from 1440 until his death in battle in 1462. The twenty-year Czech presence strengthened Slovak consciousness to a certain degree. The Czechs mingled with the Slovaks and passed on to them literature, mostly of a religious character and written in Czech, a language intelligible to Slovaks. The influence of Czech led in time to the establishment of Slovak as a written language, which was used along with Latin in royal documents in that part of multiethnic Hungary.

Ladislas V died a young man, whereupon the Hungarian parliament called a meeting on New Year's Day 1458 in Buda to elect Mathias Corvinus as king. The parliament charged Mathias with leading the country out of chaos and protecting it against Turkish incursions.[11] Mathias restrained the nobility, rallying the middle class in his cause. He was not as successful in his attempts to halt Turkish expansion in the Balkans, but he did conquer Silesia, Moravia, and lower Austria in 1485, increasing Hungary's territory and influence.

Mathias died at the age of forty-seven, in 1490, and is remembered as one of the greatest Hungarian kings. The Hungarian nobles took advantage of his death to install a weak and subordinate Czech king, Ladislas II of the Jagellon dynasty, on the throne. Ladislas did not disappoint: he has entered Hungarian history as "King Good" since he always sided with the nobles by nodding his head and saying "Good." Ladislas's most serious rival was Maximilian Habsburg, with whom, in 1491, Ladislas entered into an agreement signed in Bratislava. According to this pact, in the event of the death of a ruling Jagellon or Habsburg, a member of the opposite family would assume the throne. Through this agreement, a great Central European empire, that of the Habsburgs, would be established in the aftermath of the Jagellon king Louis's death at the Battle of Mohács in 1526, a decisive victory for the expanding Ottoman empire.[12]

THE SLOVAKS UNDER THE TURKS AND HABSBURGS

According to the agreement between Ladislas of the Jagellon dynasty and Maximilian of the Habsburg dynasty, the Habsburgs were to ascend to the Czech and Hungarian throne after the death of the last Jagellon. The same agreement stated that Ferdinand of Habsburg would succeed the king of Hungary, Louis II, who died at the Battle of Mohács.

This transition was not easy. With the support of Hungarian nobles, Transylvanian prince John Zapolya contested the Habsburg succession. He led an army in fierce battles against the Habsburgs, most of them waged on Slovak territory, for which reason John Zapolya was called the "Slovak King" by his contemporaries.

In 1538, by the Peace of Nagyvarad, Zapolya and Ferdinand split Hungary, with Ferdinand taking the western part and Zapolya Transylvania. Zapolya quickly became a vassal of the Turks, but Ferdinand continued the war against them and after Zapolya's death in 1540 claimed Transylvania for himself. So, however, did the Ottoman supporters of Zapolya's infant son. Ferdinand's army invaded eastern Hungary, which was under Turkish protection; the Turks counterattacked, and in 1541 Sultan Suleiman's soldiers marched into Buda. Six years later, Ferdinand accepted a humiliating peace, by which Hungary was divided into three parts. The majority of the country, including central Hungary and Buda, was under the direct control of the Turks. Transylvania, under John II (Sigismund) Zapolya, was a vassal state of the Turks but was left almost entirely autonomous. The Habsburgs retained only a narrow strip of western and northern Hungary, the region of Slovakia, for which they paid tribute to the Turks.

Ferdinand left Slovakia to the management of Italian and Spanish mercenaries under the leadership of John Katzianer, who was promoted to "captain of Upper Hungary." These soldiers plundered Slovakia with no mercy and differed from the Turks only in the appearance of their uniforms. To escape Turkish pressure, many nobles moved from Hungary proper to the territory of present Slovakia, establishing Bratislava as their capital. Under these displaced nobles, the Slovaks' burdens multiplied: the nobles obtained the rights of meat cutting, beer tapping, the selling of wine and alcohol; they prescribed how much the serfs had to drink; and if the quota for alcohol consumption was not fulfilled, villages were forced to pay "dry pub" taxes.

The nobles also had an effect on Slovakia's ethnic composition. The increased presence of Magyar nobility and other Magyar middle-class families meant that Slovak cities became trilingual (Slovak, German, and Magyar) and multiethnic. Hoping to escape the economic pressure, Slovaks and Germans joined forces, not only against the wave of Magyars but also against the arrival of several thousand Croatian families in southern Slovakia. Many Germans and Slovaks relocated to the western part of the country, where they came under Habsburg rule.

Slovak contacts with Moravians and Czechs thus grew, especially among the scholars. In 1571, a collection of poems called *Pisne nove na sedm zalum kajicich* (New Songs on Penitent Psalms) was published in Prague. It was written by John Sylvan, the most important Slovak poet of the sixteenth century. Other prominent Slovak writers and scholars, such as Martin Rakovsky, Paul Kyrmezer, and Jur Tesak Mosovsky, became active in the Kingdom of Bohemia. One of the prominent physicians of that time, the Slovak Jan Jesenius, was the chancellor at Prague University. He participated in a Czech class revolt and was decapitated along with the Czech rebels on the Old Town Square (Staromestske) of Prague. Another Slovak, Vavrinec Benedict, taught at the University of Prague, where he wrote and published a Czech grammar. He also encouraged his fellow countrymen to use the Czech language as well as their own.[13]

For those who remained in Slovakia, Turkish invasions were a constant threat. Until their final defeat at Vienna in 1683, the Turks frequently penetrated into the heartland of Slovakia through the valleys of the Vah, Hron, and Nitra rivers, raiding and taking many Slovaks captive. In 1552, the Turks gained control of Filakoo (Fülek) castle, an important fortress, and created four governing *sanjaks,* or counties: Esztergom, Novohrad, Secany, and Filakovo. This area, which included almost seven hundred villages, was placed under direct control of the Turks, who exacted heavy taxes that were often brutally collected.

In 1593, the army of Habsburg emperor Rudolph II attacked the Turks, opening a fifteen-year-long war. This army recaptured the Slovakian *sanjaks*; then Crimean Tartars invaded, destroying much of the region. At the beginning of the seventeenth century, the wars with the Turks were intermingled with anti-Habsburg rebellions and religious fights between the ongoing reformation and Counter-Reformation forces.

The Protestant Reformation had taken root among the Slovaks in the first half of the sixteenth century and had grown in strength in eastern Slovakia and in the mining towns, where Germans were numerous.[14] Slovak theologians, too, had traditionally acquired their training at German universities, mainly at Wittenberg. The *Katechismus Martina Luthera* (Catechism of Martin Luther, 1581) was written in Czech and published in Bardejov. Thus conditions for the spread of the Protestant Reformation in Slovakia were very favorable. In Slovakia, most people accepted a moderate form of Luther's teachings, while a small segment of the population in the southern and eastern parts of Slovakia accepted the teachings of John Calvin. Other Protestant proselytizers (Anabaptists, Czech Brethren, Sacraments) appeared on the scene. Increasingly, too—though for mixed reasons—the nobility joined the Reformation movement, and under their influence the serfs followed. The nobles had plenty of secular reasons, namely, the seizure of properties held by the Catholic Church, and in a short time, the Hungarian nobility became the chief supporter of the Reformation movement.

In the sixteenth century, the Catholic Church—with the support of the Catholic Habsburgs—initiated the Counter-Reformation, slowly at first, with the arrival of many Jesuits into Slovakia to preach Catholic doctrine, and then with such intensity that many Protestants began fleeing to Hungary. The nobles, to whom the Hungarian constitution had given great powers and privileges, were much opposed to the Habsburgs' attempts to establish absolute rule, and in 1604, when Emperor Rudolph II's army tried to take property belonging to the Transylvanian prince Stephen Bocskay, their patience ran out. Bocskay decided to defend his estate and started an open revolt.[15] Many nobles and townsmen joined the Bocskay army, which enlisted Turkish aid.

By October 1605, Bocskay's rebellious army ruled practically all of

Slovakia. In July 1606, Rudolph II was forced to sign a peace treaty with Prince Bocskay. The emperor promised to respect the Hungarian constitution of estates, agreed that the only high-ranked officials in the country were to be Hungarian nobles, and promised to grant religious freedom. The peace treaty with the Turks at Zsitva-Torok, which ended the Fifteen Years' War, did not change conditions, since the Turks still controlled most of Hungary. The Habsburgs also agreed to pay 200,000 ducats in gold to the Turks.

The Hungarian nobility immediately took advantage of the newly granted religious freedom and began to organize the Protestant Church. In 1610, Palatine George Thurzo called the evangelic representatives from the entire "Pre-Danube" region of western and central Slovakia to Zilina for an ecclesiastical synod. A strong Protestant organization was founded. The Pre-Danube region was divided into three municipalities with superintendents at their head. During the second synod in 1614, in Spisske Podhradie, a similar organization was established for the eastern Slovakia region. Because this area had a Slovak majority, the ecclesiastical organization was led by Slovaks.

These events forced the Habsburgs to accept far-reaching concessions, on which they immediately reneged while using every opportunity to strengthen the Counter-Reformation movement. By not keeping their promises, the Habsburgs provoked further discontent among the Hungarian nobility. When in 1618 an anti-Habsburg revolt broke out in Prague, the Hungarian nobility rose up. Led by Gabriel Bethlen, a Transylvanian prince, the nobles' army occupied the entire territory of Slovakia. In October 1618, Bethlen entered Bratislava and seized the castle and its crown jewels. In 1620, he was crowned king of Hungary. Emperor Ferdinand II, who was preparing for a war against the Bohemian estates, entered into a peace agreement with Bethlen.

After the Habsburg defeat of the Bohemians at the Battle of the White Mountain (Bila Hora), Slovakia became the destination of numerous Czech Protestant families. Among them were members of the intelligentsia, such as George Tranovsky and George Jakobeus, who contributed to the development of the Slovak culture and education. The Czech families that settled in Slovakia brought with them a rich and well-developed literature in the Czech language.

During the Thirty Years' War, Slovak areas were plundered by both Habsburg and Swedish armies. According to a peace agreement, the Turks were supposed to leave Slovakian territory, but they continued to stay because the dissatisfactions and upheavals on the estates gave them new opportunities for devastating raids. Prince Gabriel Bethlen entered this conflict, allied with the enemies of the Habsburgs, and made Transylvania a vital factor in European politics. During the course of the war, he repeatedly forced Emperor Ferdinand II to make promises to respect the Hungarian constitution, the privileges of the Hungarian nobles, and religious freedom. When the Thirty Years' War turned in the emperor's favor, Ferdinand forgot his promises, which led to renewed resistance among the nobility. In 1643, Prince George Rakoczi I, as an ally of Sweden, took his army across Slovakia from Transylvania through Moravia all the way to the gates of Vienna and forced the emperor to restore all the rights and privileges previously accorded.[16]

The Treaty of Westphalia, which ended the Thirty Years' War in 1648, though it prevented the Habsburgs (now under Emperor Leopold I) from penetrating into the colonies and therefore weakened their position on the European continent, placed them under almost no restrictions in their own dominion. Once again, the Habsburgs threatened the Hungarian nobility and Hungarian Protestants.

In March 1663, the Turks declared war on the Habsburg empire and headed toward Slovakia.[17] They crossed the Danube and at Parkan (now Sturovo) defeated a hastily organized army of the nobles. Next they conquered Nove Zamky and seized Nitra, Levice, and other cities. Though Leopold's army at first opposed the Turks and began to drive them out of Slovakia, a peace was arranged, granting Nove Zamky and its vicinity to the Turks.

This concession provoked significant dissatisfaction in Slovakia, chiefly among the serfs, who had suffered greatly under the Turkish raids. Their discontent showed up in numerous local revolts throughout the seventeenth century.[18] The nobility was again disenchanted with the Habsburgs, both because of their refusal to fight the Turks and because of the broken promises concerning constitutional guarantees and recatholicization policies. A group of nobles headed by Francis Wesselenyi began to plot against the Habsburgs, but the conspiracy was uncovered, and its main organizers were executed in 1671. The country was ruled by mercenaries led by a General Spork, who initiated a reign of terror, suspended the Hungarian constitution, and started a new wave of recatholicization.

Government terror brought in new resistance. In the eastern Slovak section of the country, groups of soldiers, known as crusaders or *kuruc,* were organized. One such group, headed by Gaspar Pika, conquered the Orava region in 1672. General Spork succeeded in recapturing the castle and punished the rebels in a most cruel way: Gaspar Pika and twenty-five rebellious mayors were impaled on poles and left to die slowly.

Spork's cruelty, far from deterring the serfs, aroused new hatred. In 1678, a young nobleman from Kezmarok, Imre Thokoli, organized the people, eager for revenge, and in a short time took over eastern and central Slovakia and forced Emperor Leopold I to promise, again, to renew the Hungarian constitution, restore the office of the Hungarian palatine, and give the rebels the right to have two churches in each section. Thokoli did not trust the emperor's promises and, with his army, retook all of eastern and central Slovakia. Just as the emperor was ready to withdraw, the Turkish sultan, Kara Mustafa, entered the conflict; he promised Thokoli the emperor's crown if he would surrender to him and promptly also declared war on Leopold. Thokoli joined the sultan.

After the siege of Vienna in 1683, the imperial generals, Charles of Lorraine and Louis of Baden, beat the Turks back and advanced into Hungary. Their forces took Buda in 1686 and, after the victory at Mohács in 1687, drove the Turks beyond the Danube, thereby ending Turkish rule in Hungary.[19] But the defeat of the Turks also ended the Thokoli uprising and marked new waves of terror and oppression against the Protestants.

In 1707, Protestant rebels proclaimed the Habsburgs a monarchy without a throne. In retaliation, the new Habsburg emperor, Joseph I, organized a large army and, in 1708, defeated Francis II Rakoczi at Trencin. The Turks, who had hoped to take advantage of the uprising in Slovakia to reestablish themselves in Hungary, had lost. On May 1, 1711, Rakoczi's followers accepted the Peace of Szatmar, by which the emperor promised to respect the Hungarian constitution and redress the grievances. Rakoczi refused these terms and took refuge in Turkey. Thus, the Habsburgs still held the Hungarian crown.

Charles VI, the next Habsburg emperor, strove for internal consolidation and the strengthening of his position within the Central European monarchies. He tried to revive the faltering economy by raising taxes, sometimes in ingenious ways; in some counties, for example records of smokers were kept, and these smokers had to pay a smokers' tax.

Emperor Charles lacked a male heir, and in an effort to save the

Habsburg throne and the breakup of the empire, he endeavored to secure the various lands that were united under the scepter of Austria. In 1713, he established an order of succession under the Pragmatic Sanction, according to which a female could also succeed to the throne. The most important part of the decree was the provision that the lands belonging to the empire should be indivisible. This served the double purpose of strengthening the ruler's power and signaling the need for centralization.

Reforms of this time, which included census taking and the compilation of property records, afford historians relatively reliable demographic data. These indicate that in the early eighteenth century about two million people lived on the territory of Slovakia, the majority ethnic Slovaks. There were many cities, but they were very small, devastated by wars, and partly depopulated. The biggest city was Bratislava, with 10,000 inhabitants.[20] Almost as large was Komarno (Komarom), followed by Banska Stiavnica, with a population of 7,000. The majority of the Hungarian nobility also lived in Slovakia, in palatial residences in the baroque and rococo styles in cities, the suburbs, and the country. Their luxurious way of life came at heavy cost to the serfs, whose tax rates and work obligations increased. This, plus several years of crop failures and famines, brought about great discontent and social upheaval.[21] Many serfs fled the estates and hid in Slovakia's dense forests; some became highwaymen, among them Juraj Janosik, a Robin Hood–like figure in the Slovak folk tradition.

After the Peace of Szatmar, a great migration took place within the Kingdom of Hungary. The main stream of this migration was from the northern territories to the south. It proceeded gradually and was supported by some of the nobles. In central and northern Hungary, which had been liberated from the Turks, entire areas were depopulated and the fertile earth lay uncultivated. The Slovak inhabitants of the northern mountainous regions gradually moved into the Danube basin—around not only Pest but also farther south into the Tisa basin and mainly in the Bekes area. Gradually, Slovaks moved into the fertile areas of Backa, Banat, and Szeged, where the estates of the nobles were in need of manpower. A few cities were inhabited by Germans. Farther south were Magyars who had fled from the Turks. In the east, in the Zemplin and Saris areas of the northern tier, lived the Rusins. More than twenty thousand nomadic Gypsies were registered in Slovakia in 1770. And during the eighteenth century, Jews joined the population.

The Pragmatic Sanction opened the way to the throne to the eldest daughter of Charles VI, Maria Theresa.[22] From the very beginning the young empress had to deal with complicated, mainly international conflicts since Prussian king Frederick II the Great claimed part of Silesia. Even though the queen received full support from the deputies of the Hungarian Diet in Bratislava, she was not able to win the war and had to cede the territory to Prussia. With her astute diplomacy, she enabled her husband, Francis Stephen of the House of Lorraine, to be elected German emperor and thus was able to centralize the western part of her empire. However, she was unable to subordinate the Hungarian nobles to her wishes. Her fight with them reached a climax in 1765, when the queen, now the empress, dismissed the Hungarian Diet.

During the reign of Maria Theresa, Slovakia remained the economic and cultural center of Hungary. Living in Bratislava, the empress surrounded herself with many advisers and started the reform of the country with the aim of centralizing and modernizing the entire state and bringing her empire closer in line with the other, more developed, Western European countries. She was well educated and familiar with the ideas of an enlightened Europe, and her skillful program of reform affected all areas of the monarchy, touching the lives of both urban and village dwellers. A program of land regulation equalized the obligations of the serfs in Hungary and settled their relations with the landowners. Though the extent of these obligations was still extensive and great, a feudal lord could not indiscriminately raise them.

A very important part of the reform movement initiated by Maria Theresa and her son Joseph II was school reform, based on the Enlightenment principle that a school has to educate not only good Christians but also good citizens and that education has to be open to everyone regardless of origin. As early as 1753, the University of Trnava was reformed along the lines of the University of Vienna. Natural science was introduced in 1774. A well-known astronomer, Maximilian Hell from Banska Bystrica, proposed an astronomical observatory for the university. A medical faculty was also opened, and the law faculty was reformed. The University of Trnava, with a largely Slovak faculty, became the center of scientific life in Hungary. When the university relocated to Buda in 1777, the cultural and scientific life of the Slovaks was weakened considerably.

Another important school in Slovakia was the Mining Academy in Banska Stiavnica, established in 1735. Many great professors taught there, including the mathematician and cartographer Samuel Mikovini. A second academy for miners, established in Banska Stiavnica in 1762 and called the Berg Akademie, became world famous and a model for technical colleges throughout Europe.[23] Among the renowned professors of this academy were the chemist Anthony Rupprecht, who was among the first to develop the European method of amalgamation, and the Italian physicist Alessandro Volta.

Maria Theresa's education reforms culminated in the *Ratio Educationis* of 1777, which proposed a reorganization of the Catholic school system into a unified system of schools from the elementary level to the university level that for the first time gave non-Catholics access to the education system. One of the leaders of the reform program was the Slovak scholar Adam Francis Kollar, and it is significant that the reformed school system was of great importance to the Slovaks. From the eighteenth century on, the level of education in the cities was quite high; almost all city dwellers had a basic education and were multilingual, and many households acquired books, mainly religious. Education also spread among the villagers. A pioneer in this endeavor was Samuel Tesedik (1742–1820), an educator and promoter of the Enlightenment among his people.

The Enlightenment movement developed only in the second half of the eighteenth century in Hungary (the first half of the century is known as the Baroque period). With Jansenism and Pietism, more modern ideas were also noticeable among the Slovaks. Although the preceding battles of Reformation and Counter-Reformation had increased the overall culture of the population, especially in the cities, by broadening education and preparing the people to accept the ideas of the Enlightenment, the Enlightenment culture itself was barely felt among the Slovaks. To a large measure, its ideas emanated from the court and were promoted by members of the intelligentsia, members of the lower nobility, and bureaucrats in the state administration.

Kollar (1718–1783), the most important Slovak Enlightenment follower, a native of Terchova, had studied under the Jesuits but left the order and became the custodian, and later director, of the court library in Vienna.[24] He was a proud Slovak and Slavophile who urged Slovaks to love and take pride in their language. A philosopher and linguist, he developed far-reaching plans for the revival of scientific life in Hungary, earning the nickname "the Slovak Socrates" for his efforts. Kollar's treatise *De originibus et usu perpetuo potestatis legislatoriae* (About the Origin and Permanent Use of Legislative Power), published in 1764 and probably written with the agreement and support of Maria Theresa, targeted the privileges of the nobles and supported the powers of the central ruler. Not surprisingly, it provoked strong reaction from the Hungarian nobles, who confiscated copies of the book and burned them in the main square in Bratislava.

Joseph II, who succeeded Maria Theresa at her death in 1780, was already coregent for the Austrian lands and German emperor. He was a well-educated and well-rounded man brought up under the influence of Enlightenment and Empiricism, and he continued his mother's reformation efforts, issuing the Patent of Tolerance of 1781 and abolishing serfdom in 1785.[25]

The Patent of Tolerance proclaimed the equality of citizenship for all Christian faiths and allowed all Christians to perform religious services publicly.[26] Although non-Catholic Christians were not completely equal to Catholics, they were nevertheless now allowed to build churches—without towers—and to worship. Joseph II also published decrees that improved the legal position of the Jews. The abolition of serfdom meant the removal of personal peasant dependency on the feudal landlords. The preamble of the Patent of Tolerance stated that the emperor's aim was to improve the situation in the country and the condition of all its inhabitants without class differentiation.

Joseph II's reforms, more clearly than those of his mother, led to the centralization of the monarchy, which the Hungarian nobles strongly opposed. His effort to make German the official language of the entire country as well as the universal language of education also met Hungarian nationalist resistance, and with good reason, for not only did Joseph refuse to be crowned king of Hungary, but also during his ten-year rule he never called the Hungarian parliament into session, and he ordered the crown jewels to be moved from the tower of the Bratislava castle to the court museum in Vienna. Still, he single-handedly carried out a unified, centralized reform of the Hungarian administrative system and abolished the regional self-government of nobles, dividing the country into ten districts headed by commissioners appointed by and directly responsible to the emperor. In the territory of Slovakia there were three such districts: Nitra, Banska Bystrica, and Kosice.

Joseph's reforms also had a great impact on the Church. Although he was a Catholic, Joseph II tried to coordinate church affairs and religious beliefs with the ideas of the Enlightenment. He therefore renewed the *Placetum Regium*, which mandated that papal bulls be read in the country only with the ruler's approval. He voided the beggar monk's orders and used their properties for educational and charitable purposes. In spite of all of this, he had many supporters among the Catholic priests.

Though the French Revolution, which erupted in 1789—the year before Joseph's death at the age of forty-nine—was filled with exactly the same ideas as the Enlightenment that Joseph used during his rule, its antimonarchical and antireligious ideals threatened not only Joseph's position but also the life of his sister, Marie Antoinette, the queen of France. Before he died, Joseph revoked all his reforms except for the Patent of Tolerance and the abolition of serfdom. Legend has it that the dying emperor ordered that his grave be marked with the words "Here lies Joseph, one who wanted so much, but accomplished nothing."

The uncertainty and inner turmoil caused by the French Revolution also marked the short rule of Joseph's brother, Leopold II (1790–1792). Only with Leopold's son, Francis II (1792–1835), was a new and open antirevolutionary and antireform course followed. Francis II involved himself in an interventionist war against France and severely crushed all revolutionary movements in the country.

Some of the chief victims of Francis II's reign of terror were the Hungarian Jacobins, led by Ignatius Martinovics, who, like their French counterparts, sought an egalitarian democratic reform. Their views were summarized in a catechism in which, through a method of simple questions and answers, they offered basic instructions on how to organize civil disobedience against absolutism: "What should one do when bad people ignore his natural rights and threaten his liberty and possessions? —To preserve his rights, one should oppose such oppression. —When one does not have the power to oppose such oppression, what means should he employ? —In such a case, it is necessary for oppressed people to gather together and create a large common union and civil society. —What are the names of the members of such a society? —Citizens. Any other title or privilege such as king, count, baron, aristocrat, priest, etc., is against the law and punishable and heavily offends the social compact."[27]

Although the Hungarian Jacobins tried to reform the empire, they were the first in history to come up with a relatively complete plan for the national federation of Hungary. In such a federal empire, Slovakia, as the province of Slavonica, was supposed to form an independent ad-

ministrative unit. Some Slovaks were also active in the Hungarian Jacobins movement. The movement's ideologue was a highly educated lawyer from Modra, Joseph Hajnoczy. The activities of the Hungarian
Jacobins were uncovered. The execution of the main organizers was almost a symbolic end to the century of the Enlightenment in Hungary.

2 The Emergence of a Modern Slovak Nation

Ideas of the Enlightenment and the Reformation had a more lasting impact on the Slovak people than they did on their sovereign rulers. Even under adverse conditions, these ideas continued to influence the future development of society. The belief in the natural equality and rights of humans found a parallel in a belief in the natural equality of linguistically based nations. This view, which originated with the German philosopher Johann Gottfried von Herder, gave the Slovak intelligentsia the ammunition needed for continuing and expanding the Slovak national movement—the "national revival," which shaped the modern Slovak nation and its ideology.

Already by the middle of the eighteenth century, though Latin was still the official and scientific language, several living languages were in wide use. Maria Theresa and Joseph II used German as part of their centralization policies; administrators and clerics used the languages of local ethnic groups, the cause of conflict between loyalist speakers of Slovak, Magyar, and other tongues. Protestant Slovaks, and many members of the intelligentsia, also used classical Czech, the language of their Bible (also known as the Kralic Bible language) and of much literature.

Even the Catholic Church—the church of the majority of the Slovak population—began using Slovak dialects in addition to Latin; during the

This chapter is based on the Slovak text by Dusan Kovac.

liturgy, the clergy delivered sermons in different local Slovak dialects, and they began to work toward establishing a Slovak literary language.

The heart of the Catholic national movement was southwestern Slovakia. Here, in the cultural centers of Bratislava (Pressburg) and Trnava, the Catholic intelligentsia began intensive studies of the national past and the Slovak language as an expression of Slovak legitimacy. The most active institution was the Catholic seminary established by Joseph II in 1784 at Bratislava castle. The Pressburg general seminary emphasized Slovak language studies, and there Jozef Ignac Bajza wrote the first Slovak novel in verse. This language was rich and flexible, but it lacked a systematic grammar or orthography until Anton Bernolak (1762–1813) undertook the challenge of creating one.

Born in Orava in northern Slovakia, Bernolak joined the Pressburg general seminary shortly after its opening in 1784. Before his studies in Trnava and Vienna, Bernolak specialized in linguistics and studied the Slovak language. His major work, *Dissertatio philologico-critica de literis slavorum* (A Critical-Philological Discussion of Slovak Letters), was published in 1787.[1] In a short period, Bernolak finished several other linguistic studies, among them a Slovak grammar and etymology and an extensive Slovak-Czech-Latin-German-Magyar dictionary.

Credit for the popularization of Bernolak's Slovak language belongs above all to the Slovak Learned Brotherhood, founded in 1792 at Trnava. The association came into existence at a time when antirevolutionary and anti-Enlightenment sentiment was dominant in Vienna. In the Kingdom of Hungary, the main exponents of this course were members of the Magyar nobility, who adhered to the new laws giving the Magyar language preference over other languages. It was in this climate that the Slovak Learned Brotherhood, headed by Anton Bernolak, set itself a goal to disseminate the literary Slovak language. The most active member of the Brotherhood and its secretary was Juraj Fandly (1750–1811), a Catholic priest. For all practical purposes, the Bernolakian movement lasted for only one generation of the Catholic intelligentsia and only sporadically enticed other followers. Following the execution of the Hungarian Jacobins and the return of reactionary rule, and amid difficult economic as well as social conditions, the Brotherhood lost its vitality. Nevertheless, the Bernolakian movement has a special significance in Slovak development, for it formulated the concept of the Slovaks as a self-sustaining independent member of the Slavic family.

The Slovak Protestant intelligentsia advanced another view of the

Slovak language. Their proposal was an outgrowth of the idea of Czecho-Slovak national and linguistic unity. Although the Catholics made up the majority of the Slovak population, the Protestant minority was exceptionally active in national life, encouraged by Joseph II's Patent of Tolerance of 1781. Both national religions, Roman Catholicism and Lutheranism, vivified the national character, instigated historical inquiry, and contributed to the creation of a national tradition and a national awareness. They were, however, divided on the language issue: the leadership of the Catholic intelligentsia, united by Bernolak's Slovak Learned Brotherhood, advocated a Slovak literary language; the Protestant intelligentsia insisted on using classical Czech.

The center of the Protestant intelligentsia, like that of the Catholic, was located in Bratislava (Pressburg).[2] The nucleus of the group was an association called Societas Slavica, founded in 1785 at the initiative of Ondrej Plachy (1755–1810), a writer and educator. The association published a monthly, *Stare noviny literarniho umeni* (Old Gazette of Literary Art), and its members included many intellectuals and writers such as Juraj Ribay and Jan Hrdlicka, who continued to be active in the national movement even after the organization itself ceased to exist. Proponents of classical Czech and Czechoslovak national unity defended their concept against the followers of Anton Bernolak and Magyarization alike. They focused their arguments primarily on the necessity to create a broader base for the national movement. While doing so, they were in close collaboration with Josef Dobrovsky and the first generation of Czech patriots.

The Protestant national movement in Slovak society acquired a more pronounced character at the beginning of the nineteenth century. Credit for that belongs to the Institute for Czechoslovak Languages and Literature at the Evangelical Lyceum in Bratislava, where, in November 1801, a manifesto extolled the need to establish an institution for the study of Czecho-Slovak language and literature:

> Let us raise our eyes to the sky of the Hungarian literature and we shall see what a beautiful light glows from it. Let us look at our Czech brothers. We shall see with what passion their learned bodies reach out for the already forgotten paternal tongue and the badly shaken frightened Muse calling to one another. And must we, like some of those among our neighbors, walk in shameful languor toward the disgrace of our progeny? Slovaks, let us have feelings! Let us take care of ourselves and of our good name left to us by our forefathers, let us pull

ourselves and our language out of infamy, let us create an Association, let us join together with the Czechs and let us give to our melodious language . . . and to our glorious nation as a sacrifice at least a small part of our effort.[3]

A dominant personality at the Lyceum was Professor Juraj Palkovic (1763–1835). He was an active writer but, more importantly, an organizer of national life. In 1812, after many years of great effort, he published the first issue of a newspaper that he named *Tydennik, aneb cisarske kralovske narodni noviny* (The Weekly, or the Empire's Royal National Gazette). Another important personality of the Protestant national movement was Bohuslav Tablic (1769–1823), the inspiration for the Learned Association of Mining Society (1810), which, as the name implies, was active in the mining areas of central Slovakia. Tablic emphasized the need for studying language, literature, and history: "The greater the number of zealous intelligent patriots filled with reason and heart in our country, the sooner the homeland will reach its desired goal—the more zealous will be the patriots in defending the throne and country, and the more they will support useful institutions designed for the general welfare."[4]

Nationalists found a hero in the French emperor Napoleon, who defeated the armies of the German emperor Francis II in several engagements. Napoleon's troops occupied Vienna and a part of western Slovakia, including Bratislava and Trnava, and on December 2, 1805, they defeated the combined Austrian and Russian armies in a major battle in southern Moravia near Austerlitz or Slavkov. The Austrians hastily agreed to a truce, the Russians retreated, and, soon thereafter, Francis II was forced to relinquish his title of German emperor. Francis, however, quickly established the Austrian empire and proclaimed himself Francis I. In 1809, his forces fought Napoleon's armies in Bavaria and were again defeated. The French retook Vienna and part of western Slovakia, laying siege to Bratislava. The city suffered great losses: many houses were burned or heavily damaged, Devin castle was destroyed, and Bratislava castle was burned to the ground. (It remained in ruins until the 1960s.)

Francis I had no choice but to become Napoleon's ally, and in April 1810 his daughter, the archduchess Marie Louise, became Napoleon's second wife. But after Napoleon's unsuccessful invasion of Russia in 1812, Francis I, taking advantage of the situation, joined the anti-Napoleonic coalition and on August 12, 1813, declared war on France. During the Napoleonic wars the Russian army passed through Slovak territory several times.

Following the final defeat of Napoleon's armies in 1814, the major powers of the anti-Napoleonic coalition—Austria, Russia, and Prussia (the Holy Alliance)—at the Congress of Vienna (September 1814–June 1815), sought agreement on ways of preventing unrest and revolution while preserving the stability of the European continent. The influence of Austria and its chancellor, Prince Metternich, reached a new zenith in Europe. Metternich concentrated state power in the Viennese court and an omnipotent chancellor. In the political arena, the country was saturated with conservatism.

The century of the Enlightenment had brought Hungary technological and economic progress: in 1818, the first steamer on the Danube river entered the Bratislava harbor in front of amazed spectators, and the first horse-drawn railroad in the Kingdom of Hungary, built during the years 1838–1846, went from Bratislava to Trnava. Still, the country lagged behind other more advanced areas of Europe, in great part because of its reliance on an outmoded and cumbersome feudal system.

Feudalism hindered expansion of industrial development, even though there were favorable natural conditions for such development in Slovak territory. While the need for weaponry during the Napoleonic wars had a positive influence on the expansion of ironworks, the mining of precious metals and copper gradually declined. In the meantime, the production of traditional goods, such as linen and lace, expanded. This type of work enabled the peasants, mostly in the poorer areas of northern Slovakia, to eke out a living. At the same time, a new layer of predominately Slovak businessmen who sold these homemade products at home and abroad came into existence; the house-to-house salesmen of perfumed oils and rare spices, especially saffron, who came from the Turec area were well known in Europe. But this was not enough to induce further industrial development and enable competition with more advanced countries.

These economic conditions created a long-lasting crisis that resulted in frequent social unrest. Strikes and boycotts in the mines around Banska Stiavnica and the ironworks in 1820 were only a prelude to mass upheavals by the subjugated peasantry. During the same year, the serfs from Zahorie rose up against the feudal landlords, and in 1831 peasants from eastern Slovakia did the same.

The year 1830 was very unproductive, and in many areas famine set in. A small landowner, Jan Tasnady, from Male Raskovce in Zemplin, began to organize the peasants into the Peasant Confederacy of Upper Hungary and made preparations for an uprising that spread from Russia to Poland. In spite of all precautions taken by the government, the uprising penetrated into eastern Slovak territory and from there to the rest of the land. It erupted at the end of July 1831 in Zemplin, around the towns of Trebisov and Vranov nad Toplou, and spread to the Spis area, where miners joined the peasants. Their dissatisfaction and hatred turned into plundering, expulsion of the landowners from their homes, killing, and tyranny. Military units suppressed the uprising, and 119 revolutionaries were hanged.

The authorities failed to eliminate the dissatisfaction and tension between the serfs and the feudal authorities. Some of the intelligent and enlightened aristocrats, however, were moved by the social upheavals to contemplate possible reforms. At their head stood Count Istvan Szechenyi, who envisioned an independent, modern Hungary that would encompass many ethnic groups.[5] The events of the time also influenced the Slovak national movement. The center of attention continued to be the issue of language, but also the growing Pan-Slavic movement, which came to include many leaders of the Slovak national movement.

In the meantime, a new generation of Evangelical intelligentsia came up through the educational system of the lyceums. Among them were Pavol Jozef Safarik (1795–1861) and Jan Kollar (1793–1852), who established close contacts with the Czech national movement, especially with its leading personality, Josef Jungmann. Kollar held that a nation was a community of people united by a common language with the same habits, customs, and culture. According to this concept, all Slavs constituted one large nation, divided by tribes. In the entire Slavic nation Kollar saw four main tribes: Russian, Polish, Czechoslovak, and Illyrian. Thus, he considered the Czechs and Slovaks as one—the Czechoslovak tribe. Kollar viewed the further division of tribes as a weakening of the Slavic nation, and he envisioned a gradual coalescence of the Slavic tribes and finally a repeated linguistic and national unification. Kollar imagined a powerful future of the Slavs spread all over Europe, not as a result of military struggle but through natural Slavic development.[6]

The idea of Slavic reciprocity and the creation of a united Slavic nation was a product of its time—European politics after the Congress of Vienna and European romanticism in its Slavic image.[7] These ideas found a fertile soil among the Slovaks, who felt the weakness of their own national association and above all the absence of the leading layers of society—the aristocracy and middle class, which had become pro-Magyar. Yet the most severe blow to Jan Kollar's idea of a Slavic world came from Russia. In 1831, czarist armies suppressed a Polish uprising. The Magyar movement, leaning on the united aristocracy, middle class, and intelligentsia, began more intensively and openly to advocate the idea of a Magyar Hungary, and the Slovaks, who lived in Hungary, could no longer ignore this fact. In this situation, the idea of national unity with the Czechs was also losing its allure because the Slovaks were now compelled to define their national and political program based on the conditions prevailing in the Kingdom of Hungary.

The impact of Magyarization brought Slovak Catholics and Protestants closer together. In 1834, a new Association of Lovers of the Slovak Language and Literature was established. The association began publishing an almanac, called *Zora*, by means of which it propagated the unification of the Slovak movement. Contributions appeared in both Czech and Bernolak's Slovak languages. The president of the association was Jan Kollar, but the movement's most effective activists were Ludovit Stur (1815–1856), Josef Milaslav Hurban (1817–1888), and Michal Miloslav Hodza (1811–1870), a clergyman in Liptovsky Svaty Mikulas, somewhat distant from the centers of the national movement on western Slovak territory. Hodza began his work by rousing speeches and literary activities in the Czecho-Slovak Association and in the academic world, and he also made contacts with loyal Slovaks in the Kingdom of Hungary and with representatives of other Slavic nations. His work gradually led to the formulation of the first Slovak political program.

Meanwhile, the Magyar national movement, headed by radical leader Lajos Kossuth, became increasingly active. Kossuth was the most fanatical supporter of the theory of a united Hungarian nation of uniform ethnicity. In response to Kossuth's activism and other Magyarization efforts, members of the Slovak intelligentsia delivered a document, *Slovensky prestolny prosbopis* (Slovak Regional Written Request), to Chancellor Metternich on June 4, 1842. This document asked the emperor to protect the Slovak language and to introduce a separate censor for Slovak books, and it further requested the creation of a chair for the Slovak language at the university in Pest, the protection of the Slovak schools, and the use of Latin instead of Magyar in church registries. The request was ignored, and it enraged the Magyar camp.

Undaunted, Slovak nationalists pressed ahead in their efforts to create a literary Slovak language to replace the "Slovakized" Czech language, which they considered artificial and outdated. The followers of Ludovit Stur, a champion of Slovak unity, believed that the most important reason for developing a literary Slovak language was to come close to the Slovak people, especially the Slovak peasant: a new literary Slovak language must derive from the living language of the Slovak peasants and not the artificial language of the intellectuals. Stur therefore decided to use the central Slovak dialect as the foundation for creating a literary base of the Slovak language. His first treatise, *Narecja slovenskuo alebo potreba pisanja v tomto nareci* (Slovak Dialects or the Need to Write in This Dialect), appeared in 1846 and was closely followed by his *Slovenska gramatika* (Slovak Grammar). This codified literary language was later subjected to several reforms, but the principles established by Ludovit Stur remain to this day.

The new literary language made it possible for the followers of Stur and Bernolak to unite. Slovaks with various points of view at last felt they were part of an independent Slavic nation. The acceptance of a literary Slovak language became not only a festive literary occasion but also a significant political declaration, although some, including Jan Kollar, continued to argue for a language more closely tied to Czech. Stur and his compatriots rejected Kollar's arguments that the creation of a literary Slovak language was an affront to the Czechs that weakened any collaboration between Czechs and Slovaks; on the contrary, they considered collaboration with the Czechs as well as other Slavs a necessity.[8]

It was clear that the development of national movements in the multiethnic Kingdom of Hungary required some resolution of the nationality issue. The nascent nation-states were raising their language, school, and cultural requirements, and the nationality issue was showing its political side. The Magyar nationalist movement's idea of one state, a Magyar one, not only was wholly unacceptable to the other nations, including the Slovaks, but, within the Kingdom of Hungary, it was a romantic and even fantastic idea, inasmuch as the size of the Magyar ethnic group in the kingdom constituted less than half of the population. Still, Magyar opposition to the Slovak national movement caused the Slovak leaders to draw closer together, adopting a Slovak folk song with lyrics by Janko Matusek, *Nad Tatrou sa blyska* (Over the Tatra Mountains Is Lightning), which later became the Slovak national anthem.

The relationship between proponents of Magyarization and Slovaks became increasingly antagonistic and political. Ludovit Stur founded *Slovenskje narondnje novini* (Slovak National Gazette), a semiweekly newspaper, to argue the Slovak cause. In the developing revolutionary atmosphere, a young man named Janko Francisci-Rimavsky spurred Stur to prepare himself, via his newspaper, for great social upheavals: "We, on Slovak territory, need free ideas and free thinking to prepare our people with all possible means for a great catastrophe that we cannot avoid. Its praiseworthy or infamous, liberating or oppressive results will be determined by our own ability and whether or not we have missed the opportunities and means for preparing the road to Freedom."[9] Stur and his followers began to work among the Slovak population. They founded several agricultural and home savings and loan associations, and they promoted literature and enlightenment among the population. They captured the support not only of the intelligentsia and segments of the city population but also of the oppressed masses. In 1847, Stur was elected as a representative of the city of Zvolen to the Hungarian parliament. There he called for the abolition of feudalism and pressed the Slovak cause.[10]

In 1848, all Europe was engulfed in revolution, brought on by nationalist movements and an economic crisis aggravated by crop failures and famine the previous year. In the Habsburg empire there was general discontent with Metternich's absolutism, aristocratic privileges, and the oppression of the peasants. On March 11, at the St. Wenceslas spa in Prague, representatives of the Czech national movement met to draw up a list of their national and social demands to the attention of Ferdinand V. Two days later, revolution broke out in Vienna. The frightened emperor dismissed the despised Metternich and promised to introduce a new constitution. When news of the revolution reached Bratislava, the intimidated parliament adopted laws, proposed by Lajos Kossuth, to abolish serfdom and declare the creation of an independent Hungary, which hereafter was to be connected with Austria only in the name of the ruler. These two laws were the most significant ones of the so-called "March Laws," which Ferdinand V accepted on April 7.[11]

The Hungarian declaration of independence was accompanied by Magyarization tendencies carried out in the name of one Hungarian nation, which, far from guaranteeing national rights to the non-Magyar nationalities, was intended to be a unified Hungarian state dominated by the Magyar liberal aristocracy headed by Lajos Kossuth. Having achieved their chief aims—the abolishment of serfdom and a declared independence—the Magyar aristocratic revolutionaries had no further interest in democratic reforms that would weaken their position.

The Slovak national program thus found itself in conflict with the Magyar program concerning nationality and social issues as well as with the entire question of democratization of the political system. Ludovit Stur's radicalization of the Slovak political camp was based on the social construction of Slovak society. The majority of the Slovak nobility was more loyal to Magyar than to Slovak interests, and the top layer of Slovak society was made up of the intelligentsia who came from a lower-middle-class or folk background. But most Slovaks were peasants, and it was only natural that they would oppose not only Magyar national hegemony but also the class and socially motivated hegemony of the Magyar aristocracy.

After a stormy spring in 1848, Slovak revolutionary activity culminated with a public declaration of an all-Slovak revolutionary and national program, which was adopted on May 11 at a general gathering in Litovsky Sv. Mikulas. This declaration, known as *Ziadosti slovenskeho naroda* (Demands of the Slovak Nation), is one of the most important documents of Slovak history. It contained fourteen points. First, the Slovaks sought the recognition and guarantee of Slovak legitimacy. Hungary was asked to change into a country of equal nations with each having its own parliament. In the all-Hungarian Diet the nations and nationalities were to have equal representation. Slovak was to become the official language of the Slovak regions. In addition to these demands, the document also contained demands for the reform of the political system, general and direct voting rights, abolition of servitude for all peasants, and the return of land unjustifiably taken from the farmers by the nobility during the previous period.

The Hungarian revolutionary government responded with a declaration of martial law in the upper regions of Hungary and orders for the arrest of Ludovit Stur, Jozef Miloslav Hurban, Michal Miloslav Hodza, and other Slovak leaders. These activists eluded the police and escaped to revolutionary Prague.

Hardly a month later, on June 12, the wife of the Austrian general and prince, Alfred Windischgratz, was accidentally shot and killed during a demonstration. General Windischgratz seized the opportunity to bring in reinforcements. The Slovak leaders, joined by other Slovaks who had attended an important Pan-Slavic Congress, entered the fight.

On June 17, Windischgratz crushed the Czech revolutionary movement and established a military dictatorship in Bohemia. This was the first serious defeat of the revolutionary forces in the Habsburg monarchy.

Undeterred, the Slovaks shifted their activities to Vienna, where they established close contacts with the Croats and Serbs from Vojvodina in order to organize a common armed rebellion that could force the Magyar government to respect their rightful national demands. On September 16, 1848, in Vienna, the Slovak National Council came into being as the highest Slovak political and military organization. At the helm were Stur, Hurban, and Hodza. The leadership decided to create an armed expedition of Slovak volunteers on Slovak territory to coincide with Baron Jellachich's revolt against the Magyars in Croatia, which was countenanced by the emperor.[12] The Slovak volunteers were soon joined by volunteers from Bohemia and Moravia, and after crossing the Hungarian border, these forces were swelled by many peasant volunteers from the area of Myjava and other western Slovak regions.

On September 19, at Myjava, the Slovak National Council declared the separation of Slovakia from Hungary and called upon the entire Slovak population to take up arms. By the end of October, however, after several clashes, Magyar guardsmen had driven the Slovak volunteers into Moravia, and the Hungarian government instituted a reign of terror. Stur, Hurban, and Hodza were pronounced traitors and deprived of their Hungarian citizenship, and mass persecutions, arrests, and executions of Slovak patriots followed.

In the fall of 1948, the Magyar revolution was rapidly advancing. The revolutionaries and their guards controlled not only Pest, the center of the rebellion, but other Magyar cities. The government in Vienna decided to meet the Magyar revolutionaries head-on with brutal force and to nullify its previous sanction of Hungarian independence. On October 6, after news spread that the government had sent the army to fight the Magyars, the people in Vienna rose up in protest, and two weeks later, the emperor and the assembly left the city for the Moravian town of Kremsier (Kromeriz). Loyal General Windischgratz bombarded Vienna into submission, and the government stabilized, but the weak and shaken Emperor Ferdinand V abdicated, and Francis Joseph I ascended the throne. Windischgratz then turned his forces against Hungary, occupying Budapest on January 5, 1849.

Three months later, the representatives of the Slovak National Council petitioned the new emperor to create an independent Slovak territory within the Habsburg empire, removing Slovakia from Hungarian control. The petition stated: "We demand only the land we have lived on since ancient times, where our own language is native to us and is being used in every day life, which was at one time the cradle of our historical existence and which, from time unknown, in spite of being politically united with other countries, has never stopped being called Slovak territory—Slovakia."[13]

FROM NEO-ABSOLUTISM TO WORLD WAR I (1849–1914)

On April 13, 1849, at Debreczen, the Hungarian Diet proclaimed the Hungarian Republic, dethroning the Habsburgs. The next day, the Diet elected Lajos Kossuth "responsible governor-president." Kossuth declared that the newly created Magyar-dominated Hungary would not recognize the equal rights of other nations or nationalities in the country. In early June, Francis Joseph I accepted Czar Nicholas of Russia's offer of aid in suppressing the Hungarian revolution. On June 17 the Russian general Paskievich invaded Hungary from the north, while the Austrian general Haynau led the invasion from the west, and on August 9 the Magyars were decisively defeated in the battle of Temesvar. The government in Vienna took advantage of the Magyar defeat to strengthen and centralize its power in the state, inaugurating a brief period of neo-absolutism. A military dictatorship was installed in Hungary, with German declared the official language.

In spite of this, the emperor granted the Slovaks a few privileges. In Slovak counties, the use of the Slovak language was permitted in official dealings, and Slovak was introduced as the language of instruction in elementary and some middle schools. Jan Kollar was granted permission to publish the *Slovenske noviny* (Slovak Newspaper), and he became a court counselor for Slovak affairs.

In the Slovak political camp, especially among the uprising's active participants, the prevailing feeling was still one of disappointment and discouragement.[14] The essence of the Slovak program lay in the recognition of the Slovaks as a sovereign nation, and language rights were only minor gains. Even so, many of the activists met in October 1851 at a conference in Bratislava that codified literary Slovak and introduced a new orthography, closer to that of Czech. Martin Hattala (1821–1903) was placed in charge of compiling a new Slovak grammar, *Kratka mluvnica slovenska* (1852). The reformed Slovak language again unified the majority of the Slovak intelligentsia.

This success in the sphere of linguistics did not succeed in removing feelings of bitterness and disappointment brought about by political failure. Offered insignificant bureaucratic positions in the state administration, Ludovit Stur and Jozef Miloslav Hurban withdrew from public life. The idea of federalism, dormant for a time, was revived in 1859, when Austria suffered a defeat at the hands of Italian national-liberation armies fighting for the unification of Italy and the separation of Italian territories from under Austrian supremacy. In the political crisis that ensued in Austria, Emperor Francis Joseph dismissed Alexander Bach, the hated interior minister, and the government expressed its willingness to accept further concessions. Throughout the empire the goals of ethnic nationhood took on renewed vigor as representatives set out formulating and resubmitting the unfulfilled demands of the revolutionary years.

Slovaks followed the conflict closely. Jozef Miloslav Hurban openly expressed his view that the conflict could grow into a European war, in the course of which the Slovaks could again come forward with their demands. He drafted a petition that reiterated the demands of the 1848 revolution: the constitutional separation of Slovakia from Hungary and the safeguarding of separate Slovak rights within the frame of the monarchy.

The emperor seemed willing to accept certain Slovak demands. By an imperial decree of July 1860 he granted the use of Slovak, alongside German and Hungarian, in twenty-three Hungarian counties. Before the decree could be implemented, however, the emperor yielded to Hungarian pressure and instituted fundamental reforms for the benefit of the Hungarians. He also re-created a parliament in Hungary, placing internal matters in its hands. The Hungarian government took this as a signal to revive the idea of a united Hungarian nation with all its consequences, including the Magyarization, for the non-Hungarian nations.[15]

But Slovak leaders did not give up. They decided to organize a great Slovak gathering that would vote on Slovak demands. The *Pestbudinske vedomosti,* a Slovak newspaper in Budapest, publicized the assembly, and five thousand people showed up at Turciansky Svaty Martin on July 6–7, 1861. The new Slovak political program included demands for the recognition of the Slovaks as a sovereign nation and the establishment of a Slovak parliament. A Slovak delegation submitted the memorandum to the Hungarian Diet, but it went nowhere.

In the latter part of August 1861, as disputes between Vienna and the Hungarians escalated, Emperor Francis Joseph dissolved the Hungarian Diet and showed signs of being more amenable in considering the language rights of the nations of Hungary. The Slovak representatives then submitted a revised memorandum directly to the ruler demanding a Slovak parliament and Slovak legislative and executive organs. Vienna reacted in the spirit of its usual policy—making vague promises to all nations of Hungary as a means of exercising pressure on the Hungarian government.

This new failure caused a conceptual split in the Slovak movement. All parties were dissatisfied and disappointed—for not receiving understanding on the part of the Vienna government and its ruler and for the failure of the memorandum—but whereas some, headed by Stefan Marko Daxner (1822–1892), still believed in the contents of the memorandum, another group, centered around Jan Palarik (1822–1870) and critical of the exceeding trust placed in Vienna and the emperor, demanded that the Slovaks pursue a policy both within the frame of Hungary and in concert with the Hungarians. Though disunity remained, it was not long before the latter group realized that efforts to reach an understanding with the Hungarians would not yield positive results, even concerning language and school rights.

Another general assembly took place in 1863, the year in which Slovakia commemorated the one-thousandth anniversary of the arrival of saints Cyril and Methodius in Great Moravia. These celebrations turned into manifestations of Slovak national awareness and self-confidence, culminating on August 4 in the founding of the Matica Slovenska (Slovak Heritage Foundation). It was one of the high points of the Slovak movement during the nineteenth century.

As an institution created and organized by Slovaks, Matica Slovenska played a significant role in increasing Slovak national awareness. The first president was the Catholic bishop Stefan Moyzes (1796–1869); the acting vice president was the Lutheran minister Karol Kuzmany (1806–1866). The Matica immediately began to publish the *Letopis Matice slovenskej* (The Chronicle of the Matica Slovenska), which influenced research in many aspects of national culture—language, history, and ethnography. Annual national festivities commemorating the founding of Matica are still observed today.

Following the loss of the Italian territories, Austria faced another rival: Prussia, which competed with Austria for the leading position among German states. This rivalry culminated in the Prusso-Austrian War of 1866, in which Austria suffered another crushing defeat. Prussia completed Germany's unification and proclaimed the German empire in 1871. Austria ceased to play any role in German affairs. The defeat triggered a domestic crisis when Vienna decided to yield to Hungarian pressure and accept a settlement with Budapest. The settlement divided the empire into two independent parts: Hungary and Austria, which were equally represented in the imperial parliament of the new Austria-Hungary. The settlement had one ruler and three ministries in common: those of foreign affairs, war, and finance. All other matters were subject to independent governments.

In Austria, the political system was more liberal and more accommodating toward other nations. In Hungary, the Hungarian aristocracy kept their political and economic privileges, and the majority of the population was excluded from political life. Even those who were entitled to vote (and this was a minority) could elect only one-half of the parliament, the county, or city councils. The other half was filled, without any election, with the richest landowners and, later, with representatives of the industrial and banking interests.[16]

Under this new arrangement, as they well understood, the Slovaks could not expect any fulfillment of their national demands from the Hungarian government, which pressed for continued Magyarization. In 1868, after offering special concessions only to Croatia, the Hungarian government began preparing a nationality bill, the chief aim of which was to deny the other nations and nationalities in Hungary any national-political rights. Two drafts of the nationality bill were submitted to the Hungarian Diet. One safeguarded the respective individuality and equality of all nations in Hungary; the other did not, and it was this one that Francis Joseph I signed into law on December 6. Hungarian became the sole official language in all offices and institutions. The Slovak nation, along with the other nations in Hungary, was degraded to the status of a mere ethnic group, permitted by law to use Slovak in lower-level offices and elementary schools and to organize its own cultural and economic associations but otherwise forbidden any recognition as a political and national entity.

Hungarian policy pushed the Slovaks into a defensive position. The main substance of the Slovak national movement was simply its basic

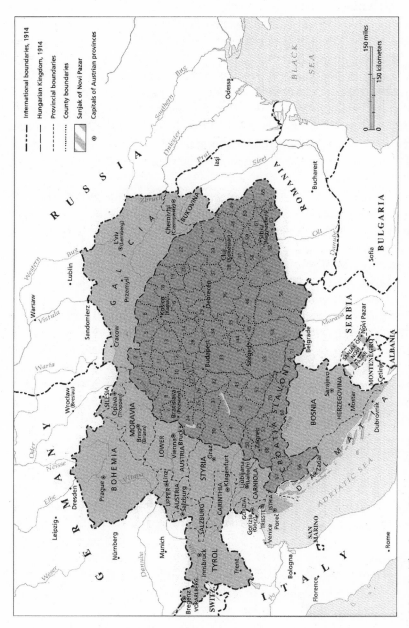

Map 3. The Austro-Hungarian Empire, 1867–1914

rights. Once again, efforts were made to seek support in the Slavic world,[17] Much of this work was directed by Viliam Pauliny-Toth (1826–1877), a Slovak deputy in the Hungarian Diet and acting vice president of the Matica Slovenska. The headquarters of the Matica, Turciansky Sv. Martin, became the main center of the Slovak movement, and the *Pest budinske vedomosti* moved its editorial offices there and changed its name to *Narodne noviny* (National Newspaper). Gradually, a political party of the Slovaks began to form under the name Slovenska Narodna Strana (Slovak National Party). It adopted the Memorandum of the Slovak Nation of 1861 as its main program and remained the principal political party of the Slovaks until the formation of Czecho-Slovakia in 1918.

Still, the last quarter of the nineteenth century was a period of the greatest stagnation in the evolution of a Slovak national society. The period saw modernization throughout Europe, brought about primarily by an unprecedented expansion of industrial production. Hungary built a new network of rail systems, most of it on Slovak territory, and next to Budapest, Slovakia soon became the most important industrial area of the Kingdom of Hungary.[18]

But industrialization did little to lighten the burdens of the Slovak people. Slovak workers in cities toiled sixteen hours a day in grim conditions, but their lot was perhaps better than that of Slovak farmers. As the Slovak population grew, the shortage of land and crop failures brought mass misery and starvation. Many families migrated south during the harvest season to work in the more fertile areas on large estates. Some Slovaks became door-to-door salesmen and tinkers; some families moved to the southern parts of the Hungarian kingdom or to Galicia, the Balkans, and even Russia. At the beginning of the twentieth century, there were as many as 100,000 Slovaks in Budapest; about 70,000 Slovaks lived in the Austrian part of the Dual Monarchy. The end of the nineteenth century was also the period of mass emigrations from the northern and eastern territories of present-day Slovakia into the United States and Canada, which became distant centers of Slovak nationalism.

At home, the center of this movement remained Turciansky Sv. Martin, where the Slovak National Party was headquartered. After the death of Pauliny-Toth in 1877, Pavol Mudron became the new party chairman. While in the cultural field the Slovaks were in general making progress, in the political area they were falling behind. Not one Slovak was able to win back Pauliny-Toth's seat in the Hungarian Diet. The Slovak National Party lodged a protest against the "manipulated" election results and in 1884 declared its abstention from future parliamentary elections in the Kingdom of Hungary. The party maintained that position until the end of the century.

During the Russian-Turkish War (1875–1878), Slovaks keenly followed the liberation movement of the southern Slavs, the Serbs and Bulgarians, with whom they felt empathy. A symbolic expression of this feeling can be found in a collection of poems, *Tatry a More* (The Tatras and the Sea), written and published by Svetozar Hurban Vajansky in 1880. Vajansky (1847–1916) was considered the major ideologue of the national movement. He was one of the most prolific poets and writers of his time, and, as a politician, he advocated strong ties with Russia and a kind of traditional Slovak Russophile philosophy.

His thinking captured the imagination of many Slovaks, but many others resisted Vajansky's ideas. Younger Slovak intellectuals rallied against the leaders of the Slovak National Party and the editors of the *Narodne noviny,* accusing the leadership of Russophile "politicking." Their criticism came from two different ideological positions: one that of young Catholics, the other that of the liberals. The young Catholic intelligentsia based their philosophical beliefs on the writings of the papal bull entitled *De Rerum Novarum* and the activities of Count Zichy's Hungarian People's Party. They founded economic associations, promoted education, fought alcoholism, and strove to elevate the economic and moral level of the Slovaks, especially the farmers. These programs were coordinated by the *Ludove noviny* (People's Gazette) published by Anton Bielek and Andrej Hlinka.

Another group of young Slovaks influencing the Slovak public at the turn of the century were the members of the Prague association known as Detvan. Their source of inspiration came from the Czech liberal camp and the teachings and practice of the main representative of Czech realism, Professor Thomas Garrigue Masaryk (1850–1937) of Prague University. Inspired by Masaryk's ideas about modest labor and moral revival, the young Slovak liberals operated in a similar spirit as the Catholic intelligentsia, and very often in close cooperation with them. The most active among them were Vavro Srobar (1867–1950) and Pavol Blaho (1867–1927), publishers of the journal *Hlas* (Voice). This group's political orientation was closely tied to intensive Czecho-Slovak cooperation and interdependence.

The Slovak workers were also organized. Though they belonged to and followed the rules of the Social Democratic Party, at the same time they cultivated a national awareness among their fellow workers and cooperated with the labor movement in the Czech Lands. The involvement of the young generation in the political arena signaled their restlessness and dissatisfaction with the stagnation and passivity of Slovak politics.

The unfavorable situation also contributed to the slowdown of the development of Slovak culture and science, though in contrast to politics, cultural activities required only minimal space. The political conditions were very unfavorable. The Hungarian governmental policy, supported by German emperor Wilhelm, concentrated its efforts on increased governmental centralization and speedy achievement of its goal—the creation of a one-nation, Magyar-dominated Kingdom of Hungary.[19] After the fall of Kalman Tisza's government, the nationality policy of the Hungarian government remained as before. Kalman Szell delivered a few complimentary speeches about the Slovaks, but during his regime the government held significant trials against twenty-three representatives of the Slovak national movement. The leaders of the Slovak National Party were aware that the nonparticipation in the elections caused stagnation in the national movement. Under the pressures of the young generation and its cultural activities, it was finally decided that the party would participate in the parliamentary elections in 1901. The platform of the Slovak National Party demanded universal suffrage rights and democratic freedom, including freedom of national languages. Newly structured by the time of the elections and organized like any other modern political party with party rules and discipline, the remodeled Slovak National Party succeeded in electing four representatives to the Hungarian Diet.

Further vitalization of Slovak politics occurred in 1905 with the outbreak of the Russian Revolution. The largest ascent in that period was registered by the labor movement and the Social Democratic Party, which included the Slovak workers. But because the All-Hungarian Social Democratic Party expressed little interest in the national demands of the Slovak workers, the Slovaks began to search for a way to have their own organization. In 1904, with the assistance of the Czech Social Democrats, Slovak workers established their own newspaper, which under its editor Emanuel Lehocky (1876–1930) attracted many nationally motivated Slovak workers. A year later (June 1905), these workers organized the Slovak Social Democratic Party. Though this soon merged organizationally with the All-Hungarian Social Democratic Party, the Slovak faction retained a certain autonomy on nationality issues and was able to publish its own *Robotnicke noviny* (Labor Gazette).

Hungary's most timely political issue at the beginning of the twentieth century was the demand for universal suffrage. Because the Magyars represented only about half the population, universal suffrage would have deprived them of their dominant role in the country.[20] Recognizing this, Slovaks joined other ethnic groups in demanding universal suffrage and democratization of the Kingdom of Hungary. At that time, the leading personality in Slovak politics was the politician and journalist Milan Hodza (1878–1944). Hodza joined the struggle for universal suffrage: "Our needs drive us toward democracy," Hodza declared.[21] In the 1905 elections, the long-lasting hegemony of the Liberal Party ended with the victory of the Independent Party, precipitating a deep, if short-level, crisis in the dual system of monarchy. The following year, new elections, marked by corruption, deceit, and violence, threw out the Independents, but the Slovaks gained seven deputies in the Hungarian Diet.

Not only the Slovaks but also the Romanians and Serbs were successful. The Hungarian government, however, did not take lightly the increase of non-Hungarian deputies in the Hungarian Diet and the renewed impetus in the nationalities movement. The coalition government of Alexander Wekerle, led by the Independent Party, initiated a new wave of terror against the politicians of non-Hungarian nationalities. At the end of 1906, trials began against Andrej Hlinka and Vavro Srobar for their participation in protests and demonstrations. Several other Slovaks were subsequently tried and imprisoned.[22]

The height of brutality carried out by the Hungarian authorities occurred in 1907 at Cernova near Ruzomberok. The devout Catholics in Cernova, through the initiative of their priest, Andrej Hlinka (1864–1938), had built a new church out of their meager collections and desired Hlinka to consecrate the church. But Hlinka was not just the local priest; he was the leading Slovak politician, orator, and organizer of the national movement and one of the most energetic representatives of the Catholic people's wing of the Slovak National Party. For his agitation during the 1906 elections, Bishop Alexander Parvy, an ardent supporter of Magyarization, suspended Hlinka and forbade him to officiate at church services. Thanks to the Moravian Catholics, especially Alojz Koliska, Hlinka's case was appealed to the pope in Rome. The pope decided in Hlinka's favor, but too late for Hlinka to perform the consecration ceremonies. The local citizens requested a postponement, and when Hungarian church and civil authorities ordered them to proceed with the consecration as previously scheduled, the inhabitants of Cernova staged a protest; the gendarmes began to shoot into the crowd, and fifteen protestors lost their lives. The brutality committed by the Hungarian authorities angered all Europe.[23]

The leaders of the Slovak national movement had, of course, been trying to bring the Slovak issue to the attention of European and world public opinion. Ironically, the events in Cernova contributed to this effort, but the real support came from the Czech intelligentsia as well as politicians and journalists, and from the small circle of French Slavicists. The Slovaks in America tried to inform the people there about the oppression of Slovaks in the Kingdom of Hungary. Support for Slovaks from abroad had a great moral significance, but it failed to stop the oppression. After the defeat in the 1905 elections, the Liberal Party quickly recovered. Under the leadership of Istvan Tisza, the liberals reorganized under the name National Labor Party. In the Hungarian political camp suddenly appeared new, democratically oriented movements, represented by the intelligentsia around the journals *Huszadik Szazad* (Twentieth Century) and *Nyugat* (The West). Democratic ideas appeared in a new political party organized in 1903 by Count Mihaly Karolyi. Nevertheless, democracy remained only a marginal political movement in Hungary until the war. The mainstream of Hungarian politics was still moving toward state centralization and Magyarization— that is, a state-supported assimilation of non-Magyar nationalities.

Owing to the initiative of the Czechoslovak organization Jednota and the event at Cernova, from 1908 until the beginning of World War I, Czecho-Slovak meetings were held annually in the Moravia spa city of Luhacovice. Here Czech and Slovak political, cultural, and economic functionaries came together to search for possibilities of deeper cooperation and new avenues for bringing the Czechs and Slovaks together. The most productive cooperation took place in the field of culture. Jednota was responsible for transporting entire libraries from Bohemia to Slovakia, and it helped Slovak scientists and artists find jobs in the Czech Lands. At Luhacovice there were already talks about political perspectives and economic cooperation, though conditions for economic cooperation were not very promising because of the Hungarian government's opposition to the inflow of Czech investments into Slovak territory. In the given international situation, the political perspectives were very unclear, and they offered no optional expectations.

Before World War I Slovak politics constantly oscillated between the need for unity and a defense of factional differences. Alongside the conservative national intellectual elite centered around the newspaper *Narodne noviny*, a special clerical wing emerged, which in 1913 founded its own political party, the Slovenska Ludova Strana (Slovak People's Party). In Turciansky Sv. Martin, a young liberal-democratic intelligentsia emerged in a certain opposition to the center of the Slovak National Party; these Slovak Social Democrats started to lay the foundations for the Slovak agrarian movement. There were also different perceptions of the international situation.[24] Whereas the center of the Slovak National Party depended on Russia, and expected changes in the international arena as a result of Russian influence in central Europe, the liberal segment of the party depended more on cooperation with the Czechs and joint Czecho-Slovak contacts with the Western Allies. Social Democrat leader Milan Hodza's concept was based on a plan calling for the federalization of Austria-Hungary. Hodza was included among the collaborators of the successor to the throne of Archduke Francis Ferdinand, and up until the outbreak of war he was the spokesman for the Slovaks in a federalized monarchy.

Nonetheless, these factorial differences remained subordinate to the primary Slovak goal, the basic national demands, which under the difficult conditions of national opposition prevented any serious split. All political currents were aware of the fact that polemics in the press and ideological disputes only tended to weaken the Slovak position within the framework of the Kingdom of Hungary. This was evident from the elections of 1910, when the Slovaks could place only three deputies in the Hungarian Diet. Compared with the results of the 1906 elections, 1910 was a complete fiasco. The hope placed in the nonpartisan government of Khuen Hedervary proved also to be unsubstantiated. A memorandum handed to the prime minister in June 1911 by the Slovak delegation contained only humble demands based on the existing law on nationalities dating from the year 1868. It was dismissed by Budapest as frivolous. Shortly before the outbreak of the war, Slovak political leaders felt the need to unite their political movements based on pressing national demands. The incentive for unification came on the occasion of the death of the chairman of the Slovak National Party, Pavol Mudron, in March 1914. At his funeral, followers of all orientations, wings, and beliefs of the Slovak political and cultural scene came together and listened to the appeal by Mudron's successor, Matus Dula, to form an all-national representative body. In order to formulate a unified program, a meeting was held in Budapest on May 26, 1914, in which the leaders of all political orientations, including the Social Democrats, agreed that in August 1914, during the traditional national festivities, a Slovak National Council would be established as the highest representative organ for the Slovaks. The outbreak of the war prevented the fulfillment of this plan.

THE RISE AND FALL OF THE CZECHOSLOVAK REPUBLIC

PART TWO

3 The Struggle for the Creation of Czechoslovakia (1914–1918)

In the Kingdom of Hungary the outbreak of war was hailed with great enthusiasm by most of the populace. Among the Magyars the war aroused a wave of chauvinism and pseudopatriotic excitement. But the Slovak population and their men, recruited into Austro-Hungarian uniforms, were less enthusiastic about going to fight for an alien cause. Some Slovak activists became victims of the enraged crowds, and several others ended up in jail the very first day of their opposition to the war. Some Slovak newspapers were closed down; others were subjected to censorship. Among the Slovaks the war against their Slavic brothers in Serbia and Czarist Russia could not have been popular. A feeling of Slavic brotherhood was well expressed by the poet Pavol Orszagh Hviezdoslav, who in August 1914 began writing his passionate attack on the war in a collection of poems entitled *Bloody Sonnets*, which could be published only after the war.

From the beginning, Slovak politicians were convinced that this war would determine the fate both of the world at large and of the Slovak people. During the early part of the war, a time of martial law and military rule and censorship, Slovak politicos decided to remain politi-

---

The first three sections of this chapter, "The First Steps of Czecho-Slovak Resistance," "Czech and Slovak Politics at Home and Abroad," and "Emergence of the Czechoslovak State," are based on the Slovak text by Dusan Kovac.

cally detached and thus prevent a clash with the government in case it demanded a public acknowledgment of loyalty.

In early summer 1914, Count Mihaly Karolyi, the Magyar political opposition leader, arrived in the United States on a lecture tour. Although he was quite critical of the contemporary monarchical government, he maintained that in the Kingdom of Hungary there was no persecution of minorities and that all nations and nationalities had their rights guaranteed by law. This provoked the Slovak League of America (SLA) into action. What the Slovaks could not express at home they freely voiced in their opinions abroad. The SLA reacted critically in the press to Karolyi's misleading statements and at the same time decided to publish a memorandum (on September 10, 1914) about the true situation of Slovaks in the Kingdom of Hungary and their demands for self-determination and complete self-rule. At that time the league secretary was Ivan Daxner, who was, coincidentally, the son of Stefan Marko Daxner, author of the first self-determination memorandum, published in 1861. There was a great resemblance between the two documents; in the memorandum of 1914, as in the earlier one, although self-determination was demanded, the exact way of achieving it was left open. The representatives of the SLA considered several possibilities while they were conducting negotiations and consultations with other national communities in the United States.[1]

THE FIRST STEPS OF CZECHO-SLOVAK RESISTANCE

War had the potential to change the entire world. If the Central Powers lost the war, the Slovaks might bring the Slovak issue before a world forum and demand a solution. The Slovaks considered several courses of action. They could stick with the memorandum of 1861 and demand Slovak autonomy within the Kingdom of Hungary, or—another possibility—they could seek a confederation of a Polish-Czecho-Slovak, or Polish-Slovak state; and there was also the possibility of uniting Slovakia in some form with Russia. But the most logical solution was to merge the Slovaks with the Czechs in a mutual Czecho-Slovak state. This solution was gradually embraced by the Slovaks at home and abroad, although it meant a separation from Hungary, where the Slovaks had lived for one thousand years.

The idea of a Czecho-Slovak state emerged early and was closely tied to the progress of the war. One important outside impetus in this calculation was the offensive of the Russian army in the Carpathian Mountains. In mid-November 1914, Russian units crossed the ridges of the Carpathians and penetrated into the eastern part of Slovakia. The Russian Eighth Army, under the command of A. A. Brusilov, crossed Lupkov Pass and moved into the valley of the Cirochy and Laborec rivers, and on November 23 it occupied the city of Humenne. After five days of fighting the Austro-Hungarian units pushed them back, but the Russians penetrated farther west in Slovak territory, where they captured the city of Bardejov. From there, too, the Russians were expelled by the Austro-Hungarian army. But the battles in the mountains continued, with the front lines changing positions back and forth until May 1915, when the German army succeeded in breaking through the defense lines in the north near Gorlica. The Russian army could no longer hold the line and was pushed deep into the Ukraine and Belorussia. This military episode also had political significance. It was assumed that since the Russian army could penetrate through the Carpathian Mountains, it could easily move through the Hungarian plains to Budapest and Vienna, and if they crossed the Moravian Gate, they could then move into Moravia and Bohemia.

Following such thinking, many Slovak politicians were under the impression that Slovakia would soon be occupied by the Russian army and began to plot plans for the creation of a Czecho-Slovak state. Very active in this respect was Vavro Srobar, the foremost representative of the group called *hlasisti*. The Hungarian officials discovered a "conspiracy" involving a priest from Donovaly, Jozef Kacka, and a notary, Josef Messerschmidt, who were agitating for Russian occupation and the creation of a Czecho-Slovak-Polish state; both men were sentenced to long prison terms. At the same time, under the auspices of the SLA, the Czechoslovak Unity movement formed and began mapping out the future state of Czecho-Slovakia.[2]

In October 1914, while traveling abroad, Prague University professor and Realist Party representative Thomas Garrigue Masaryk formulated the first memorandum about the future Czecho-Slovak state; it was sent to the British government through British reporter and historian R. W. Seton-Watson.[3] By the end of April 1915, Masaryk—who in the meantime had emigrated to Great Britain and resided in London—prepared another expanded memorandum, entitled "Independent Bohemia."[4] This program for the creation of the Czecho-Slovak state, which was in many ways a spontaneous response to the success of the Russian army in the Carpathians, was somewhat curious, coming from someone who had always been a staunch critic of czarist absolutism. Now Masaryk found himself in the position of having to acknowledge that the Russian army and the Russian empire could be of great assistance in the creation of a Czecho-Slovak state. Contrary to his strong beliefs in a democratic and republican form of government, Masaryk mentioned in his memorandum the possibility that the Czecho-Slovak state could become a monarchy with the Romanovs at its helm. On the other side of the coin, Masaryk tried to persuade the British and French politicians that by creating Czecho-Slovak and Yugoslav states and reviving Poland, a "Slavic barrier" would be erected against a potential German march to Constantinople-Baghdad: "By forming the Serbo-Bohemian corridor the Allies would prevent Germany from colonizing the Balkans and Asia Minor, and they would prevent the Magyars from being the obedient advance guard for Berlin."[5]

The idea of a Czecho-Slovak state received meaningful support from Czechs and Slovaks in the United States via the Slovak League, whose members in October 1915 signed the Cleveland Agreement, according to which Bohemia, Moravia, Czech Silesia, and Slovakia would form one state. The plan for the creation of a Czecho-Slovak state was also supported by Czech and Slovak associations in Russia, France, Switzerland, and other countries in Europe and elsewhere abroad. Masaryk began to gather and coordinate all efforts taking place abroad, first of all to organize a Czecho-Slovak army to join in the war against the Central Powers, and, second, through agitation and propaganda, somehow to persuade skeptical Allied politicians that the Austro-Hungarian state must be dismantled and smaller states like Czecho-Slovakia formed.

The success of Czecho-Slovak resistance to a great extent depended on its organization. The person who most distinguished himself in this regard, however, did not receive all the credit he deserved because of his untimely death. This Slovak, Milan Rastislav Stefanik (1880–1919), finished his university education in 1904 at the University of Prague, where he studied astronomy, and then worked at the renowned Meudon Observatory in Paris. He soon gained recognition as a scientist and as an able diplomat in the French service, moving in the highest cultural and political circles. When war broke out, Stefanik became a pilot in the

French air force. He had a very successful career: during the span of the war he rose in rank from corporal to general. At the end of 1915, after being wounded on the Serbian front and convalescing, Stefanik returned to Paris, already prepared with complete plans on how to organize the struggle for the Czecho-Slovak state. Stefanik's conceptualization was in basic agreement with that of Masaryk (a former professor of his at Prague University) and also with that of Eduard Benes (also a former student and protégé of Masaryk's who before the war had also studied at the Sorbonne and at the Dijon Law School).[6] Stefanik invited Masaryk to come to Paris and arranged for a meeting with French premier Aristide Briand and meetings also with influential French journalists.

In February 1916, during Masaryk's stay in Paris, Masaryk, Stefanik, and Benes decided to establish the Czecho-Slovak National Council (Conseil National des pays Tcheques). This became the main organizational center of the Czecho-Slovak resistance movement, led by Masaryk as its president, Stefanik and Josef Durich (a representative of the Agrarian Party) as vice presidents, and Benes as general secretary.

One of the key aims of the council was to organize an army (legions) abroad. Good prospects for army recruitment appeared to be in the United States but were even better in Russia, where, in addition to large numbers of countrymen and women, there were many Czech and Slovak prisoners of war. Durich, who had the task of organizing the units in Russia, ran into great opposition from czarists who disliked Masaryk and his democratic ideas. Frustrated by his experience, Durich gave up.

Still determined to organize a Czecho-Slovak army, Stefanik took on the job of rousing the patriotic zeal of Czech and Slovak countrymen and women residing in Russia. He, too, encountered opposition from numerous groups of Slovaks who had their own opinions about solutions for the Slovak issue. A particularly difficult figure was Professor Jan Kvacala, a renowned scientist at Yuriev (Tartu) University and Stefanik's former professor from his early studies at the Pressburg Lyceum. Kvacala was an advocate of Slovakia's annexation to Russia and supported it by preparing a detailed memorandum. The meeting of the two men in Russia was very emotional, but Stefanik failed to gain Kvacala's support, and they parted as enemies. With enormous effort and determination Stefanik eventually succeeded in overcoming the differences among the various Slovak camps, thus mobilizing them for the support of the Czecho-Slovak National Council in Paris. The culmination of this effort was reached on August 29, 1916, with Stefanik's Kiev Agreement, which was signed by the Czechs and Slovaks living in Russia.

Stefanik also met opposition among representatives of the czarist government, especially at the ministry of foreign affairs, but he did have the support of General Maurice Janin, the French military aide to the Russian general staff, and through him he succeeded in securing the affection of the czar and some of his military officers.[7] Yet Stefanik was not able to secure permission to recruit into a newly formed Czecho-Slovak army not only Czechs and Slovaks in Russia but also prisoners of war—the main reason being that Durich's previous effort in Russia to organize his own (anti-Masaryk-oriented) council had gained considerable support from a different group of czarist politicians and diplomats. Finally, Stefanik, with endorsements from Masaryk and Benes, officially expelled Durich from the Czecho-Slovak National Council.

The overthrow of Czar Nicholas I in March 1917 altered the situation for organizing a Czecho-Slovak army in Russia. Stefanik wasted no time in making preparations for Masaryk's arrival, and with the aid of the new government Masaryk succeeded in obtaining approval to recruit Czech and Slovak residents as well as prisoners of war in Russia for a Czecho-Slovak army. The result was a well-equipped army of about seventy thousand men, organized by the Czecho-Slovak National Council. The Czecho-Slovak Legion, as it was called, achieved its first success in July 1917 in a battle against the units of the Dual Monarchy near the Ukrainian village Zborov. Less successful were Czecho-Slovak dealings with the Allies, who still looked upon the idea of a Czecho-Slovak state with suspicion.

The greatest opposition to Czecho-Slovak aspirations came from Italy, the only Allied country that had direct territorial claims against the Austro-Hungarian monarchy. Italian politicians were reluctant to support the creation of new states in central-eastern Europe because Italy was threatened by the possible enlargement of Serbia into the new state of Yugoslavia, which might become a dangerous enemy in the Adriatic Sea. Italian authorities were also opposed to permitting the organization of Czech and Slovak prisoners of war in Italy into independent Czecho-Slovak legions. Changes in Italian attitudes did not occur until the end of 1917, when the Italian units suffered convincing defeats near Caporetto. In March of the following year, Italian-Yugoslav relations became much more cordial, and Stefanik immediately took advantage of the situation. On April 21, 1918, he signed a two-page agreement with the Italian premier, Vittorio Emanuele Orlando, creating an independent Czecho-Slovak army in Italy. This army, of almost 75,000 well-equipped and well-trained men, was the largest Czecho-Slovak army.

This was a much needed victory for the Czechoslovak political movement in exile because after the signing of the Brest-Litovsk Treaty, on March 3, 1918, Masaryk's program entered a critical time. The Allied powers had been inclined to enter into separate peace negotiations with Austria-Hungary, but it soon became evident that the Dual Monarchy was no longer in a position to negotiate independently without Germany's consent. After the fiasco of peace offers of Austria in 1917, transmitted through Prince Sixtus of Bourbon-Parma, it became clear that Austria-Hungary would first have to be defeated on the battlefield. Even so, a military defeat of the monarchy did not necessarily mean its liquidation and dismemberment.

The Allies did not show any significant change in their position until the summer of 1918, when Czecho-Slovak legions were fighting in Siberia.[8] After the Bolshevik Revolution in November 1917, Czecho-Slovak military units continued their battle against Germany and Austria-Hungary, but with the signing of the Brest-Litovsk Treaty the Czecho-Slovak military in Russia lost its enemy. A new idea surfaced among Czecho-Slovak political leaders in exile to have the troops transferred from Russia to the western front, where they could face the German offensive. Germany desperately tried to prevent such a transfer, insisting that the Brest-Litovsk Treaty called for the Soviet Revolutionary government to disarm all Allied military units on its territory. Under pressure, the Soviet Revolutionary government issued a command to disarm the Czecho-Slovak legions. The legionnaires were willing to obey the command, provided that they be given free and secure passage from Russia—which, under the chaotic conditions, the Soviet Revolutionary government could hardly guarantee. In certain areas the Bolsheviks provoked fighting between the Czecho-Slovak legionnaires and Bolshevik units. Soon the Czecho-Slovak legions seized the Trans-Siberian Railway, thus controlling a very important Russian transport connection between Asian and European Russia, which was used extensively in July and August 1918 for Allied intervention. In a short time news about the fighting morale and the successful Czecho-Slovak military operations against the Red Guard in Siberia captured the attention of the entire world.

These successes roused the interest of the Allies, and in the summer of 1918, primarily at the instigation of the French, they asked the Czecho-Slovak legions to attack the Bolsheviks from the rear in return for recognition and assistance. On June 30, 1918, the French government was the first among the Allies to recognize the Czecho-Slovak National Council as the de facto Czecho-Slovak government and the Czecho-Slovak army as an Allied army. The British government followed suit on August 13, the United States on September 2, and the Italian government on October 3.

CZECH AND SLOVAK POLITICS
AT HOME AND ABROAD

While the struggle for an independent Czecho-Slovakia was successfully moving forward abroad, at home there was no visible activity. The Slovaks had no burning desire to go to war, and Slovak men found clever ways of avoiding conscription. Yet the news from the front described the Slovak soldiers as courageous and motivated, especially during the first two years of the war. In other words, Slovak soldiers fought for their king and for Austria-Hungary. The fighting morale of the Slovaks was praised in military reports and in the press: "Even though a small segment of the Czechs, blinded by the Slavic frenzy, shows inclination toward treason, the Slovenes and Croats, Dalmatians and Ruthenians, but above all the Slovaks are showing their homeland an unshakable loyalty."[9] Like all clichés, this one was only partly true. Among the Slovaks there were no spectacular desertions such as, for example, the defection of the Twenty-eighth Prague Regiment to the Russian side during the Russian offensive in the Carpathian Mountains. When Slovak soldiers defected they did so in small groups not worthy of headline news. It is also important to point out that the position of the Slovak soldiers changed through time. They started out as obedient soldiers, but toward the end of the war some Slovaks became great rebels, as proved during the rebellion in Kragujevac, Serbia, in June 1918. One should also keep in mind that there were great differences in attitudes between the common segments of Slovak society and the political and cultural elite.

At the outset of the war, Slovak political representatives took a position of wait and see, with the understanding that at the right time they would start a revolt. By then they had abandoned the idea of resolving the Slovak issue within a framework of the Kingdom of Hungary, and therefore politicians of all interests had decided to seek the creation of a Czecho-Slovak state. Systematically and with great concern they followed the development of the war.

Slovak politicians were active in several cities. In Turciansky, Sv. Martin was the headquarters of the Slovak National Party; in the Liptov region at Ruzomberok, Vavro Srobar was carrying out his political activities. In Budapest, Emil Stodola (1862–1945), a lawyer and economist, was in charge of Slovak political interests. The only active Slovak representative in the Hungarian parliament at that time was Ferdis Juriga (1874–1950), who assisted Stodola in his work. In Presporok (Bratislava), the Slovak Social Democrats were chaired by Emanuel Lehocky.

The most important Slovak center was established in Vienna, outside the supervision of the Hungarian authorities. A Slovak by the name of Kornel Stodola (1866–1946) became head of the censorship division of the high command of the Royal Army in charge of screening and evaluating all military correspondence. Through the Free Masons, Stodola had very good contacts in the highest circles of the military. He was successful enough to gain employment in Vienna in the censorship office for such prewar active Slovak politicians as Ivan Derer (1884–1973), Jan Cablka, and Milan Hodza. The last named became the chief *spiritus movens* of the entire group. The Vienna center was important in that it maintained contact with the Czech representatives of the Imperial Diet and also arranged contacts with the secret organization called Maffia, which was subordinated to the Czecho-Slovak National Council. In this way it was possible to coordinate the resistance abroad with domestic politics.[10] Both Hodza and Stodola had supported pro-Habsburg and federalist policies before the war, but because the assassination of the Austrian Archduke, Francis Ferdinand, and the outbreak of the war had made these policies meaningless—federalization of the monarchy only being possible in case of a defeat or a serious weakening of the Central Powers—they were free to change orientation. Accordingly, the Slovak followers of the idea of a central European federation, in anticipation of an Allied victory, became the most active supporters of the revolution carried out in exile under the leadership of T. G. Masaryk.

At the end of 1916, whereas the situation for the Central Powers on the eastern and western fronts looked favorable, in Austria-Hungary there were already signs of weariness. The situation worsened after the death of Francis Joseph I, emperor of Austria, who in November 1916 was succeeded by his grandnephew, Charles—also known as Charles IV, king of Hungary. Shortly after Charles became emperor and king, he appointed Count Ottakar Czernin as Austro-Hungarian foreign minister. Czernin was a former close collaborator of Archduke Francis Ferdinand from the so-called Belvedere circle. His first undertaking was a thorough analysis of the political, economic, and military situation. The conclusion of this analysis was unanimous: Austria-Hungary needed peace.[11] Though there were separate efforts to negotiate a peace settlement with the Allies, they failed to bring about positive results.

In Russia, the revolution had further weakened the already militarily weak state. Furthermore, the Russian Bolsheviks, after taking power in November 1917, began separate negotiations with the Central Powers that culminated in the Brest-Litovsk peace dictate and thus ended warfare on the eastern front. This weakening impact on the Allies was counterbalanced by the official entry of the United States into the war (April 6, 1917) and the economic stability of the Allied camp.

The changes in the international arena had an immediate effect on the political movement of the Czechs and Slovaks in their homeland. The Czechs took advantage of the meeting of the Imperial Diet in Vienna at its session in May 1917 by submitting a basic political declaration that, at the urging of Slovak politicians, especially Vavro Srobar and his associates in Vienna, incorporated a demand for the merger of the Czech territories and Slovakia into one integral unit: "In this historic moment, we base our claim on the precedence of natural law for all nations to enjoy self-determination and a free development, strengthened in our case by unfulfilled historical rights fully acknowledged state acts, to strive for uniting all branches of the Czechoslovak nation into a democratic Czech state, including the Slovak branch of the nation, which lives in contiguous unison with the Czech historical land."[12] This declaration did not signify a separation from the Habsburgs, although the demand for uniting the Czech Lands (Bohemia, Moravia, and Silesia) with Slovakia presumed a full-fledged federalization of the empire, including its Hungarian part. The Hungarian government immediately responded with sharp condemnation, but by then the declaration had made its way through the press agencies into world headlines and as a result significantly boosted Masaryk's campaign abroad.

Just as the Czecho-Slovak National Council in Paris referred to the concept of the Czechoslovak nation as one nation with different branches, so did the pronouncements issued by the politicians at home. It was a deliberate tactical move on their part. The complicated question of the creation of the Czecho-Slovak state, which was looked upon by Allied politicians with great skepticism, was supposed to have been presented to these politicians as simply and clearly as possible. There is one nation that wants its own state; this was the main argument. The historical explanation for this oversimplified argument was the example of the ninth-century entity of Great Moravia, which declared itself to be a state of Czechs and Slovaks, a "Czechoslovak" state revisited in this new historical moment by the Czechoslovak nation. Though the acceptance of such an argument revealed the naïveté of the Allied politicians, many of those who dealt with Masaryk and Stefanik believed in the possibility of creating a political Czechoslovak nation. The issue of language was fairly insignificant; what mattered most was the acceptance of a mutual state and with it the creation of a united political nation. All these calculations were arrived at from a very unrealistic analysis of the existing conditions of Slovak society and the measure of its national awareness.

From the very beginning of the resistance, contacts between the revolutionaries at home and abroad were very effective because they were organized by the Maffia. Thanks to its activities, the politicians at home who saw the success of Masaryk's action abroad readily accepted his program and actions as well as his method of argumentation to the demands of the resistance carried out at home. This coordination was imperative for the success of the entire movement.

In the Tri-Royal Declaration passed in January 1918, Czech representatives subscribed to the creation of an independent Czecho-Slovak state. Their actions not only radicalized domestic political activism but also helped to remove some of the distrust Allied politicians harbored against the domestic activists. It was in this same spirit in April 1918 that the Czech oath was administered.

Although still under Magyar dependency, the Slovaks also became more active. During the celebration of May Day, 1918, at Liptovsky Sv. Mikulas, through the initiative of Vavro Srobar, a resolution was issued demanding a joint state with the Czechs. The second point of the resolution stated: "As a natural consequence of inalienable rights, we demand the unconditional recognition of the right to self-determination of all nations not only outside the boundaries of our monarchy but also for the nations within Austria-Hungary, that is, also the Hungarian branch of the Czechoslovak tribe."[13] Although the formulation of the resolution was cautious and written in an oblique style, it was an agreed cue for the overseas resistance movement that the Slovaks also support Masaryk's action. Here again the contact between the movement in the homeland and abroad was carried out through the Maffia. However, Masaryk and his activities faced the problem of legitimacy of his Czecho-Slovak National Council. Masaryk was a member of the Imperial Diet, but if he represented only a small and powerless political party, the other officers of the council had no mandate whatsoever. The Austro-Hungarian propaganda machine, of course, tried to discredit Masaryk's activities as nothing more than the whim of a group of adventurers who had no support in their homeland. The legitimacy of the council was indeed very questionable, especially as far as Slovakia was concerned—Milan R. Stefanik, the leading Slovak representative, was, after all, a French citizen. Thus, it was very important for domestic politicians to express their views in meaningful political action and to send signals to the exiles that they supported the concept of a Czecho-Slovak state. To comply with Masaryk's coordinated strategy, Srobar included the right to self-determination for the "Hungarian branch of the Czechoslovak tribe" in the resolution of the worker's gathering at Liptovsky Sv. Mikulas, which also spoke to social demands, cessation of the war, and the reinstatement of democratic rights. Srobar was arrested and jailed by the Hungarian imperial government shortly after the May Day festivities.

The definitive and programmatic separation between Slovakia and the Kingdom of Hungary, as well as the Slovak announcement to support the creation of the Czecho-Slovak state, took place on May 24, 1918, when politicians met at a confidential gathering of the Slovak National Party. The programmatic orientation at that conference was etched in stone by Msgr. Andrej Hlinka when he stated: "Let us not evade the issue, let us say openly that we are for the Czecho-Slovak orientation. The thousand-year marriage with the Magyars did not work out. We must go our separate ways."[14] It was a program supported by all important Slovak personages, from the representatives of the Slovak National Party in Turciansky Sv. Martin to the Liberals and Catholics, as well as the Slovak Social Democrats.

As a demonstration of Czecho-Slovak reciprocity, in May 1918, the fiftieth anniversary of the Prague National Theater was celebrated in the presence of a Slovak delegation led by the poet Pavol Orszagh Hviezdoslav. The following July 14, in commemoration of Bastille Day, the Czechoslovak National Committee was established. It was to become the leading organ of Czecho-Slovak resistance in the homeland. The declaration announcing the creation of the committee sounded abroad more like a matter of fact than a great surprise. It referred to the future independent Czechoslovak state as a fait accompli, which had the support of the entire "Czechoslovak" nation: "We know that behind the Czechoslovak National Committee stands our entire nation like a wall of galvanized steel. Overwhelmed with happiness for the political deed that gave the National Council life and work, filled with confidence in the victory of our mutual goal, we turn today to the entire Czechoslovak nation with the ardent appeal to give our work support with all its strength and to obey all commands with mutual discipline and go steadfastly and resolutely after our common goal."[15]

The Czech politicians had decided that the concept of the independent Czecho-Slovak state would gain support from all quarters as soon as it became public. Early in September 1918, at a session of the Austrian Imperial Diet, Frantisek Stanek declared in the name of Czech politicians that the Czechs had separated from the Austrians and that the issue would be placed before the international forum for a solution. On October 19, the Slovak representative in the Hungarian Diet, Ferdis Juriga, threatened a similar action. He declared that the Hungarian Diet had no right to represent Slovak interests—only the Slovak National Council had that right; furthermore, the Slovaks had a natural right to decide for themselves about their statehood.[16] Juriga's speech was long, somewhat rambling, and frequently interrupted by his Hungarian colleagues. But its message was clear: to declare the separation of the Slovaks from the Kingdom of Hungary and to let the Hungarian Diet know that the Slovaks were determined to decide their own fate independently of other nations. In that respect, this speech was also part of the programmatic scheme of Czecho-Slovak tactics aimed at Allied acceptance of the Czecho-Slovak state.

EMERGENCE OF THE CZECHOSLOVAK STATE AND THE DECLARATION OF TURCIANSKY SV. MARTIN

Juriga's speech in the Hungarian Imperial Diet openly revealed the existence of the Slovak National Council, which until that point had worked in secret. Although there were plans to create such an organization shortly before the outbreak of World War I, the organizers had had to postpone their plans because of martial law and other restrictions during the war.[17] At the urging of other Slovak politicians, the chairman of the Slovak National Party, Matus Dula, gathered a meeting of Slovak politicians in Budapest on September 12, 1918. It was here that the Slovak National Council was established and that participants agreed that the Slovak National Party would soon call for an official public gathering to proclaim the creation of the Slovak National Council. Such a gathering was not allowed by the Hungarian government until October 30, 1918.

Under the pressures of war and because of the deteriorating conditions in the homeland, on October 16, 1918, the Austro-Hungarian emperor, Charles I, proclaimed the reorganization of the non-Hungarian part of the monarchy as a federal state, with complete self-government for subject nationalities. Like most of the preceding political moves, this one was also patently belated. The proposal of federalization of the Austrian part of the monarchy may have been of interest in 1917, but by mid-October 1918 the nationalities (from the Austro-Hungarian point of view) had decided to leave the monarchy and create their own states.

The Czech politicians rejected the emperor's plan outright; they were already preparing for state independence. The proclaimed reorganization plan had still another weakness that compelled Czech and Slovak politicians to reject it. The proposed federal system applied only to the Austrian part of the monarchy, while Imperial Hungary was supposed to have remained a centralized state. The Magyar politicians were opposed to such a drastic step. They continued to keep alive the unrealistic hope that the Kingdom of Hungary could stay together as one unit.[18] In any case, the emperor's proposal was ill conceived because the Czech and Slovak politicians demanded that their territories be united, which would have meant a breach of integrity of the historical part of Hungary. Similar opposition against the proposal was waged by the representatives of other ethnic groups, and Emperor Charles's efforts failed.

Serious negotiations were taking place between Czech and Slovak politicians. Josef Rotnagl, president of the Czechoslovak Union, visited Slovakia in the summer of 1918, and in October of the same year Matus Dula visited Prague. The Slovak group in Vienna met regularly with representatives of the Czech parliament. There was general agreement that the resistance movement in the homeland would take full action on the day Austria-Hungary capitulated to the Allies. The negotiators, of course, were not aware of how near that day was.

The recognition of the Czechoslovak National Council as the de facto government and of the Czecho-Slovak army as a belligerent force were two important historical events in Allied politics vis-à-vis Austria-Hungary.[19] Recognition enabled the Czechoslovak National Council to transform itself into a provisional government, with Masaryk as president, Benes as foreign minister, and Stefanik as minister of defense. The date for the establishment of this temporary three-member government was October 14, 1918. There was, however, always the possibility that the Allies might revoke their decisions, especially the president of the United States, Woodrow Wilson, who tenaciously insisted on his January 1918 program, according to which the nationalities (or nations) of the Austro-Hungarian monarchy were to be satisfied only with autonomy. To head off such a possibility, Masaryk had gone to the United States in April 1918 to launch a campaign to influence American politics on statehood for Czecho-Slovakia.[20] For any possible success, Masaryk needed, first of all, a clear and publicly declared statement about the support for his cause and program. With this aim in mind, he initiated a new agreement between the American Czechs and Slovaks. This document, signed on May 30, 1918, by both parties in Pittsburgh, demanded the creation of a mutual, democratic Czecho-Slovak state in which Slovakia would have autonomy. The Pittsburgh Agreement gave to the movement in the United States a new impetus and to Masaryk a new, convincing argument to persuade the American government about the utility of his cause for Czecho-Slovak independence.[21]

The peak of Masaryk's political activity was reached on October 18, 1918, when the Czechoslovak National Council declared the independence of Czechoslovakia. The declaration was prepared for and published in the American press.[22] This declaration, also known as the Washington Declaration, contained several main principles of the new state, which was supposed to become a democratic republic. The text and style were purposely modeled after the American Declaration of Independence—presumably to influence U.S. public opinion in favor of Czecho-Slovak independence. About the merger of the Czech Lands with Slovakia, the declaration stated: "We demand for the Czechs the right to be united with their Slovak brothers from Slovakia, which at one time was part of our nation state, later torn off from our national body and fifty years ago incorporated into the Hungarian Kingdom of

Magyars who in an indescribable manner of violence and cruel oppression of subjugated vassals have lost whatever moral and human rights to rule over anyone except themselves."[23] This argument was historically incorrect, but to the Allied politicians at that time it was understandable. The declaration also sketched out the main principles guiding the internal arrangement of the state:

> The Czechoslovak state will be a republic. Our constant effort for progress will guarantee full freedom of conscience, religion and science, literature and arts, speech, the press and the right to assembly and petition. The church will be separated from the state. Our democracy will be based on universal suffrage. Women will be politically, socially, and culturally equal to men. Minority rights will be protected by proportional representation, national minorities will have equal rights. The form of the government will be parliamentary and will recognize the principles of initiative and referendum. The regular army will be replaced by the militia.[24]

The Czechoslovak Declaration of Independence, received with great enthusiasm by the U.S. public, was the final impetus President Wilson needed to respond to the Austro-Hungarian peace proposal with a statement that the fate of the monarchy must be decided by its nations. It was an explicit decision about the future abolition of Austria-Hungary.

At the end of October 1918, the government in Vienna was so liberal that it allowed the representatives of the Czechoslovak National Committee to travel to Geneva to a meeting with representatives of the resistance in exile. Before arriving in Geneva, the delegation stopped in Vienna to consult with Milan Hodza. At the meeting in Geneva, the delegation of the Czechoslovak National Committee from Prague recognized everything the Czecho-Slovak National Council in Paris had accomplished: "We fully approve the politics and all the activities—military as well as diplomatic—of the Czechoslovak National Council which was transferred into the provisional government of the Czechoslovak Lands with headquarters in Paris. We also approve the commitments it made in the name of the Czechoslovak nation with the Allies and its friendly powers. At the same time we are expressing our thanks for the great deeds which it had shown to our nation."[25] The key point of negotiations for both delegations was the creation of the Czechoslovak government. They agreed that Thomas Garrigue Masaryk would become the president of Czechoslovakia, Karel Kramar the premier,

Eduard Benes the minister of foreign affairs, and Milan Rastislav Stefanik the minister of war. Stefanik at that time was in Siberia with the Czecho-Slovak legionnaires. Simultaneously with the ministry of war, the ministry of national defense was created, assigned to the National Socialist Vaclav Klofac.

During the time the two delegations were negotiating in Geneva, the world press announced that Austria-Hungary had accepted the terms of unconditional surrender. The Czechoslovak National Committee reacted to this news by taking power into its own hands and on October 28, 1918, adopted the law declaring the existence of the Czechoslovak Republic.

What the government in Vienna promised the Czechs, the Hungarian government in Budapest emulated toward the Slovaks. After all, it was no secret that the war had been lost—Count Istvan Tisza, the former premier, had stated so publicly. For the Slovaks it was also clear that all the threats and pressuring would soon come to an end. In order to influence the Slovaks toward a favorable attitude to remain in the fold of larger Hungary, the Hungarian government had decided to allow the Slovak National Party to hold a public gathering. Thus on October 30, 1918, the Slovak representatives met in Turciansky Sv. Martin. Their original plan was officially to establish the Slovak National Council as the representative organ of all the Slovaks and in its name to seek the rights to self-determination and the declaration of a common state with the Czechs. In other words, it was supposed to satisfy the demands for a public testimony about the political representation of the Slovaks in an independent Czecho-Slovak state. When the delegates gathered in Turciansky Sv. Martin, they were unaware that a Czecho-Slovak state had already been declared in Prague. Though the Hungarian newspapers carried headlines about the unrest there, they omitted the most significant political news about what had actually taken place. Therefore, the delegates at the gathering went about their business as planned. They elected the Slovak National Council and adopted a declaration that stated the following: "In the name of the Slovak nation in Slovakia only the Slovak National Council is authorized to speak. The National Council of the Czechoslovak nation, living within the Kingdom of Hungary, certifies that (1) The Slovak nation is part in language and in cultural history of one Czechoslovak nation. In all cultural struggles, which the Czech nation carried out in the past and which made it famous around the world, the Slovak branch also had a part in. (2) For this Czechoslovak nation we also demand unrestricted self-determination of rights based on full independence."[26]

On the evening of the gathering, when a segment of the delegation was already on its way home, Milan Hodza arrived in Turciansky Sv. Martin bearing news of the Prague declaration of the Czecho-Slovak state. In accordance with the new situation, the delegates who still remained amended the text of the declaration, deleting the passage about Slovak representation at the Paris Peace Conference, which could have been interpreted as a mistrust by the Slovaks toward the new state and its official representation. The delegates also added a sentence to point two of the declaration: "On the basis of this principle, we express our agreement with this newly created international situation which on October 18, 1918, was formulated by President Wilson and which on October 27, 1918, was recognized by the Austro-Hungarian foreign minister" (Count Julius Andrassy).[27]

With the Martin Declaration (as it was referred to), Slovakia accepted the independent Czecho-Slovak state as its own. The Martin Declaration exemplified a decision for the Slovaks to leave the Kingdom of Hungary and begin a new stage in its existence within the framework of the Czecho-Slovak Republic. For the Slovaks it was truly a revolutionary event—the end of their thousand-year existence in the Kingdom of Hungary and the beginning of a new era.

THE STRUGGLE FOR SLOVAKIA AND ITS BORDERS

Slovakia did not become part of the new common state called Czecho-Slovakia immediately after the declaration by Czech and Slovak political representatives on October 28 and 30, 1918. Slovak territory remained in and out of the hands of Hungarian authorities until June 4, 1920, when the Hungarian representatives signed the Treaty of Trianon, by which the old Kingdom of Hungary was shorn of almost three-quarters of its territory and two-thirds of its inhabitants. Czechoslovakia was given Slovakia, Austria received western Hungary, Yugoslavia took Croatia-Slovenia and part of the Banat, and Romania received the rest of the Banat-Transylvania and part of the Hungarian plain.

On November 6, 1918, three days after the establishment of an independent Hungarian government under Count Mihaly Karolyi, the Allied

Powers concluded an armistice with Austria-Hungary. As a result, several Magyar military units withdrawing from the Italian front moved into Upper Hungary or Slovakia. The armistice left this territory under Magyar military and civilian control until the convening and determination of the Peace Conference. Newly declared Czecho-Slovakia had no established or even provisional boundaries with Hungary. In spite of diplomatic efforts by the Czecho-Slovak National Council in Paris before December 24, 1918, there was not even a temporary demarcation line between the newly created republics.

In this situation the new liberal Magyar government made great efforts to retain Slovakia within the future Hungarian borders. The new Hungarian Republic did not recognize Czecho-Slovak sovereignty over the territory of former Upper Hungary and tried to win over the representatives of the Slovak National Council in Turciansky Sv. Martin by offering them autonomy within the framework of a Hungarian federal state à la Switzerland (the idea of a so-called "Slovak Empire").[28] In particular, it made overtures to Slovak irredentists who proposed the separation of Slovakia from Bohemia and Moravia and on December 11, 1918, declared a so-called "Slovak Peoples' Republic." The Hungarian Republic also instigated feelings of discontentment and resentment toward Czecho-Slovak institutions. For instance, in February 1919, it was instrumental in causing a general strike of railroad workers. Finally, Budapest advocated that a plebiscite be held on the issue of Slovak autonomy.

But at the same time that it engaged in massive pro-Slovak autonomy and anti-Czech propaganda, the new Magyar government was applying old techniques of duress and oppressive force by the military, the police, and the bureaucracy. By government edict, the Magyars began to dismantle several industrial factories and move them with supplies of food and raw materials by rail—which they controlled—into the plains of new Hungary. In addition to pressure and diplomacy, the Karolyi government also relied, justifiably, on the Magyar sentiments of the overwhelming majority of its population, which was alienated under the Habsburgs.[29]

After the signing of the Treaty of Brest-Litovsk, on March 3, 1918, between the Germans and the Bolshevik government and the failure of Austria-Hungary to secure a separate peace agreement, it was not only France but also England and the United States who supported the creation of small states in Eastern Europe—among them, of course, the independent state for the Czechs and Slovaks. At the end of 1918, the United States proposed a Czecho-Slovakian-Hungarian border that was ten to twenty kilometers farther north (into Slovak territory) than the one later approved in the Treaty of Trianon.[30] At about the same time, three weeks before the commencement of the Paris Peace Conference, the new Czecho-Slovak government began a systematic annexation of territories designated by Foreign Minister Eduard Benes as indispensable for the future size of the state and its economic and military stability. Benes's conceptualization of the borders was to a great degree supported by the commander-in-chief of the Allied armies in France, Marshal Ferdinand Foch, and the French foreign ministry because it corresponded to the French security and power interests in Europe. To France, Czecho-Slovakia represented a barrier against future German expansion, Magyar revisionism, and Bolshevik threats.[31]

On December 6, 1918, probably with the knowledge of the Slovak National Council in Turciansky Sv. Martin, Milan Hodza, the former Slovak representative in Budapest, and the Hungarian minister of war, Albert Bartho, made the first attempt to agree on the Czecho-Slovak-Hungarian borders. They decided on a demarcation line that would have permitted large enclaves of a predominately Magyar population along the Trianon borders to stay in Hungary. As soon as Prague learned about this agreement, Premier Karel Kramar immediately disavowed his ambassador and instructed Benes to take necessary countermeasures. After consulting with his friends in the French ministry of foreign affairs, Benes managed to persuade the preparatory commission of the Paris Peace Conference to deal with Czecho-Slovak presence on Slovak territory. Thus in a note dated December 24, 1918, a new demarcation line was declared by Colonel Vyx, a member of the French military high command in Belgrade. From the west, the line followed the Danube to the mouth of the river Ipel, then along the river Ipel directly to the mouth of the river Uh, and along the river Uh all the way to the Uzok pass.[32] This demarcation line was to be settled at the Peace Conference.

In order to strengthen the Czecho-Slovak position at the Paris Peace Conference, the Ministry of National Defense in Prague dispatched units of the Italian Legion and Czecho-Slovak volunteers to take possession of Slovak territory.[33] By the end of January 1919, they had completed this mission. At the same time the government in Prague made an attempt to fill several higher administrative positions with Slovaks, though the situation in Slovakia was discouraging. In eastern Slovakia, for in-

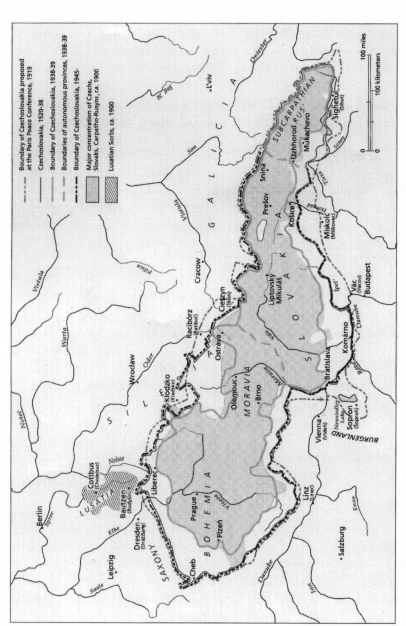

Map 4. Czechoslovakia in the twentieth century

Copyright © by Paul Robert Magocsi. Reprinted by permission of the University of Washington Press.

stance, the Eastern Slovak National Council, headed by a pro-Magyar exponent, Viktor Dvortsak, advocated a differentiation between the population of eastern Slovakia and the rest of the Slovaks, which on December 11, 1918, at Kosice, led to the declaration of a Slovak Peoples' Republic. In north-central Slovakia, on November 9, 1918, the German minority declared the independent Spis Republic but two days later joined the Slovak National Council in Turciansky Sv. Martin. In Ruthenia (Carpatho-Russia), one segment of the population attempted to join the Soviet Ukraine by proclaiming a Russian National Council on November 8, 1918, at Stara Lubovna, while the other segment of the population opted for continuation with Hungary under the People's Council of pro-Hungarian Ruthenians established on December 9, 1918, at Uzhorod (Ungvar). These atomizing efforts and movements ended with the arrival of the Czecho-Slovak army in January 1919, but their leaders and followers became a part of the irredentist movement against the Czecho-Slovak state.

Five days after the Peace Conference convened in Paris, on January 23, 1919, the Supreme Council, also known as the Big Ten (composed of President Wilson and the prime ministers and foreign ministers of the five major powers), decided that states with territorial demands must present a written request within ten days. To this end, Benes and his team prepared eleven memoranda, which were presented to the council by Benes himself. According to the Czech historian Rudolf Kucera, "All of Benes' memoranda can be without exaggeration classified as a compilation of half-truths or even lies."[34] Benes delivered his proposal for the Czechoslovak-Hungarian borders in a meeting with the Big Ten on February 5. The idea was supported by his Memorandum no. 2, on territorial demands, which deviated considerably from that proposed a few weeks earlier by the United States but was in full harmony with the French endorsement. Because of the magnitude in scope and coverage of the eleven memoranda, the council decided to set up a special Committee for Czecho-Slovak Affairs, consisting of two representatives from the United States, Great Britain, France, and Italy, with Jules Martin Cambon (former French ambassador at Berlin) at its head. On February 27, this committee accepted the U.S. proposal to annex Ruthenia into Czechoslovakia and to provide it with considerable autonomy. The borders between Czecho-Slovakia and Hungary proved to be much more complicated, and the issue was postponed for further study. There were no historical precedents or natural configurations to follow; in the end, strategic political and economic factors played the determining role.

After several debates in the committee, the so-called Trianon borders between Slovakia and Hungary were announced on March 8. The compromise failed to satisfy Eduard Benes, and he turned to the French General Staff to seek a more favorable solution. Shortly after that, a major crisis developed in the new Hungarian Republic. On March 21, the president of the republic, Mihaly Karolyi, tendered his resignation in protest of the Allied decision to assign Transylvania to Romania and Ruthenia and southern Slovakia to Czecho-Slovakia. The same evening, the republican government was overthrown by a socialist-communist government, with Alexander Garbai acting as president and Bela Kun as commissar of foreign affairs. Almost immediately Bela Kun established telephone contact with V. I. Lenin, seeking instructions for the Hungarian communists to follow. The two leaders soon developed a strategy that would become part of the Leninist world communist movement.[35]

The events in the Hungarian Republic caught the Allies in Paris by surprise. Several leaders of the major powers blamed the creation of the Hungarian Soviet Republic on unsuccessful aggressive French politics.[36] In spite of the enormous efforts and French support, Benes failed to achieve his goals. There were no changes in the proposals originally recommended by the Committee for Czecho-Slovak Affairs on March 8, 1919. While on the same day the French Senate committee approved a proposal—sent to the Peace Conference the following day—that the Allies without delay begin a military campaign against the newly declared Hungarian Soviet Republic, the British were opposed to the extension of French influence in the area, and the Americans would not approve any costly and drastic military action. The conference decided to deal with the problem diplomatically rather than militarily. In early April, after the decision of the Commission of Experts of the Peace Conference, President Masaryk of Czecho-Slovakia was selected to render a more just demarcation line between Czecho-Slovakia and Hungary. Masaryk proposed that the Czecho-Slovak borders be moved well north of the Danube so that all ethnic Magyars could remain territorially in Hungary. As a compensation for this, Masaryk would provide Czecho-Slovakia with river access directly opposite Bratislava on the southern bank of the Danube.[37]

In the meantime, the Czecho-Slovak Ministry of National Defense authorized Generals Piccione and Hennocque to proceed with the occupation of Ruthenia and southern Slovakia, which were assigned to Czecho-Slovakia by the Paris Peace Conference on February 15 and March 20, 1919. But on March 28 the Hungarian Soviet Republic declared war on Czecho-Slovakia, with the goal of obtaining Slovakia and Ruthenia. On April 6 the Hungarian Red Army entered Uzhorod (Ungvar), the capital of Ruthenia, and various communist attacks were reported along the southeastern border of Slovakia. On the following day the minister of the Czecho-Slovak National Defense, Vaclav Klofac, informed his army commanders that they should stand by for orders to make an assault on the Hungarian Red Army, which would be accompanied by a similar attack from the south led by the Romanian army.[38] On April 27 minister Klofac issued an order to attack the Hungarian Red Army at once and to occupy territory in Ruthenia and Slovakia in accordance with the decision of the Paris Peace Conference. During the implementation, however, the Czecho-Slovak army went beyond the demarcation lines prescribed by the Peace Conference: on May 2, some army units penetrated through Miskolc and threatened Salgotarjan. Bela Kun's quite justified accusation that by these actions the Czecho-Slovak army violated the Paris Agreement was heard all over the world. Lloyd George, Clemenceau, and even Benes had to condemn the Czech military operations, thus enabling Bela Kun to launch a military counterattack under the pretense of defense.[39]

The Hungarian Red Army began its counteroffensive on May 20, sending at least four well-equipped army corps north into Slovakia. The Czech army, consisting of just two divisions, retreated so rapidly that its movements resembled an escape. Prague tried to deal with the demoralization in the army and the ineptitude in the command with personnel changes; for example, the highest-ranking Italian officers were replaced with French officers. When on June 5 the Big Four (Woodrow Wilson, David Lloyd George, Georges Clemenceau, and Vittorio Orlando) learned that two-thirds of Slovakia already had fallen into the hands of the Hungarian Red Army, they were surprised but not alarmed because by then the Allies were more concerned about the signing of a peace treaty with Germany and the border issue between Czecho-Slovakia and Hungary did not figure prominently on their agenda. A German refusal to sign a peace treaty could have meant a prolongation of the military conflict, which was hardly in the interest of any one of the major powers. The Peace Conference in Paris therefore decided to settle the border issue through diplomatic means.

On June 6 Clemenceau dispatched a wire communique to Bela Kun demanding that the Hungarian Soviet Republic cease military operations on Czechoslovak territory. While at the same time Clemenceau had extended invitations to the Hungarian delegation to come to Paris and learn about the conditions for peace, he also expressed a threat of reprisals in the form of coordinated military retaliation in case the Hungarian Red Army continued its offensive.[40] Kun's reply to Clemenceau on June 9 was intentionally evasive, obviously to give the Hungarian Soviet Republic time to strengthen its bargaining position. On June 9, on the orders of General Pelle, the Czecho-Slovak units in northern Slovakia stopped their military action—but only for one day. The Hungarian Red Army, however, responded with its same determination to repel Czech units and continue its drive to the northeast in order to achieve a joint corridor with the Bolshevik units. The Red Army had already established local soviets for the purpose of exchanging currency, rationing food, communitizing private property, applying price controls, abolishing liquor trafficking, and so on in such cities as Nove Zamky (Esek Ujvar), Lucenec (Losonc), Rimavska Sobota (Rima Szombat), Roznava (Rozsnyo), Kosice (Kassa), Presov (Eperjes), Mukacevo (Munkacs), and Uzhorod (Ungvar). Probably because of the advance of the Hungarian Red Army deeper into Slovakia and Ruthenia, the Supreme Council of the Paris Peace Conference on June 11 arrived at agreement on a demarcation line between Czecho-Slovakia and Hungary. It rejected General Pelle's recommendation, which strongly resembled the proposal submitted by the Czecho-Slovak delegation, and instead approved a binding demarcation line showing a definite border between Hungary and Czechoslovakia similar to the one submitted in December 1918 by the French foreign minister, Stephen Jean-Marie Pichon. The final demarcation line was made known to Prague and Budapest by Paris on June 15, and the Hungarian Red Army withdrew its troops from Slovak territory on July 4 so that two days later the Czecho-Slovak army, which in April had commenced the attack against the Hungarian Soviet Republic, could regain its position on the prescribed demarcation line. The only meaningful border correction subsequently arrived at between the two countries occurred on September 14, 1919, when Petrzalka, a town opposite Bratislava on the south side of the Danube, was added to Czecho-Slovakia. The final adjustments of the border were stipulated in the Treaty of Trianon signed on June 4, 1920.

On June 3, 1919, during the peak of the offensive into Slovak territory by the Hungarian Red Army, the Slovak newspaper *Cervene Noviny* (The Red Gazette) carried the headline "Dictatorship of the Proletariat in Slovakia and Bohemia" and stated that a dictatorship was being established in Slovakia. On June 16 at Presov, in the presence of thousands of people, including representatives of the Czech and Slovak section of the Social Democratic Party, a Slovak Soviet Republic was proclaimed.[41] The chief organizers of the event were Bela Domjan, the Bolshevik commander of the city, Julius Vondra, Ludvig Jakab, Gustav Fleischer, and most particularly Stefan Stehlik, a Slovak communist who read a resolution to the assembled masses. Among other things, Stehlik stated that "the newly-born Slovak Soviet Republic considers its victorious brothers, the Russian and Hungarian Soviet Republics, as natural allies and it stands under the protection of the entire international proletariat, under the protection of its united and responsible workers' international. Its first greetings belong to the Czech proletarian brothers who are still under the yoke of imperialism."[42]

Following the adoption of the resolution a Provisional Revolutionary Executive Committee was elected, consisting of Stefan Stehlik, Jan Vavrica, Josef Vavrecha, Gustav Fleischer, Szamu Csapo, Ludvig Jakab, Antonin Janousek, Stefan Mokran, Erno Por, Ferenc Feher, and Jozsef Czapai. The seat of the committee was transferred to Kosice. At its session four days later (June 20, 1919), the Provisional Revolutionary Executive Committee elected a twenty-member government of people's commissars called the Slovak Revolutionary Soviet government, with Antonin Janousek as chairman. His first move was to send a telegram to the Czecho-Slovak government at Prague:

> Today the proletariat in Slovakia established a Soviet government. . . . We explicitly declare that from now on Slovakia belongs exclusively to the Slovak working class. . . . The government of the Soviet Republic has no hostile intentions vis-à-vis your republic. We are aware of the fact that the head of your republic [T. G. Masaryk] is a man of worldwide reputation of a sound scholarly name, who is completely aware of the fact that the waves of social revolution will not pass by states destroyed by the war and capitalism. His as well as our only desire is to have a revolution without disorder so that it would not bring anarchy.[43]

The Slovak Revolutionary Soviet government went to work immediately. It issued a number of decrees nationalizing industrial plants, banks, large estates, and other private property. It ordered the payment of old age and disability benefits. Everybody who worked was eligible to vote. Farmers who owned less than one hundred acres of land were declared free from taxes; their old debts were annulled. A peculiar item was the decree stating that "all documents initiated by the Slovak [Revolutionary] Soviet government will be printed in dialects of the various regions."[44] The purpose of this law was to enable the Slovak masses (who could not understand the literary Slovak language) to read about the new social order initiated by the Slovak Soviet Republic. For that purpose the *Kosicke Cervene Noviny* (Kosice Red Gazette) and *Nasa Cervena Zastava* (Our Red Flag) were published in the Saris and Zemplin dialects; other newspapers appeared in the German dialect; and the *Cervene Noviny* (Red Gazette), printed in Budapest, appeared in the literary Slovak language. The Magyars in Slovakia published their own *Voros Ujsag* (Red Gazette) and, for a brief period, the *Felso Magyarorszag* (Upper Hungary). Slovak units of the Hungarian Red Army were being formed, and a constitution of the Slovak Soviet Republic was under consideration.[45]

The Bolsheviks tried to establish their political power in Slovakia by means of constant fear and persistent terror. The slightest suspicion was sufficient for communist organs to jail multitudes of people without due process of law. The death penalty was imposed for offenses considered to be misdemeanors in democracies. Even telling the truth was punishable if the facts were unfavorable to Bolshevik ethics.

By the end of June 1919 the morale of the Bolshevik soldiers had been undermined and their aggressiveness had dissipated. The Slovak population did not welcome the "liberating" Red Army. In central Slovakia, for example, advancing Hungarian Red Army units had to face local militias organized by patriots struggling for a Czecho-Slovak Republic. In towns such as Tisovec, Revuca, and Brezno nad Hronom, the Bolsheviks were attacked while asleep and driven south, defeated and disorganized.[46] The Bolsheviks also were short of food, clothing, and ammunition, and under the influence of the nationalistically oriented officers the proletarian momentum was becoming demoralized.

At this juncture the Allies interfered a second time. On June 22 Clemenceau sent another note to Budapest demanding the evacuation from Slovak territory of the Hungarian Red Army and promising that, in exchange, the Romanians would evacuate the Hungarian territory they still held. By this time the socialists (members of the Social Demo-

Map 5. East Central Europe, 1918–1923

cratic Party who formed the majority in the coalition in the government of the Hungarian Soviet Republic) favored peace at any price. Influenced by the leaders of the Social Democratic Party of Bohemia and the potential military threat from the seventeen Allied divisions surrounding Hungary, the socialists had to recognize the futility of their cause. The left-wing leader of the Czech Social Democratic Party, Dr. Bohumir Smeral, sent a special messenger to Bela Kun requesting that he withdraw his troops from Slovakia. Already on June 15 the right-wing leaders of the Social Democratic Party had issued a proclamation: "We are invaded: Slovakia . . . is supposed to be snatched away from us and subjected again to foreign rule. We appeal to you, working men and women, with the request to help defend our invaded country with all your means."[47] Faced with famine, Kun decided to accept Clemenceau's offer.

The Hungarian Red Army began its retreat from eastern Slovakia on June 28. Two days later, the core of the army marched through Kosice, and on July 2 the American Military Mission, under the command of Colonels Gosman and Bankhead, arrived in the city to supervise the departure of the Bolshevik soldiers. On July 4 the American Mission witnessed the departure of the Slovak Revolutionary Soviet government with the Hungarian Red Army and its Slovak units. While the Slovak Bolsheviks continued to fight with their Hungarian comrades against the Romanian army, the members of the government took refuge at Miskolcz. A few weeks later the Hungarian dictatorship was approaching its end. Romania did not evacuate the territory occupied by its army but instead, with the support of the Hungarian "white army," began to march on Budapest. Suddenly the Bolshevik soldiers were betrayed by their comrades-in-arms belonging to the Social Democratic Party. On August 1, 1919, Bela Kun and several of his associates fled to Vienna in face of the Romanian advance. The Soviet government fell, and the Hungarian Soviet Republic and the Slovak Soviet Republic ceased to exist.[48]

4 Slovakia in the Pre-Munich Czechoslovak Republic (1918–1939)

In contrast to the Czech Lands, where the transition from the old Austrian territorial administration to the new Czech republican administration was for all practical purposes a smooth process, in Slovakia the process was complicated and slow, requiring the dismantling of the old feudal administrative system and the erecting of a new, more democratic system from the bottom up. During the turbulent and uncertain period from October 1918 to August 1919, Slovakia was governed from Prague by a temporary political administration.

While all existing laws of the Kingdom of Hungary remained in effect and all state offices continued to conduct their business, they were now subjected to the Slovak National Council in Turciansky Sv. Martin, which became the highest representative of Czecho-Slovak state sovereignty on Slovak territory. During this revolutionary period a network of district and local councils were created as executive organs of the central Slovak National Council.

In the meantime, on November 4, 1918, the Czech National Committee in Prague named a Central Slovak Governing Board (a quasi "Slovak government") with broad powers as the first Slovak governing body. Vavro Srobar served as president, and Pavol Blaho, Ivan Derer, and A. Stefanek were members. Two days later the appointees returned to Slovakia accompanied by a small military and police security and set up their headquarters in Skalica. However, their effective administrative power was felt only on the western edge of Slovak territory.[1] Therefore, their first political task was to replace the Slovak National Council at Turciansky Sv. Martin and thereby assume the function of the most authoritative political organ in Slovakia. All members of the "Skalica government," followers of the idea of a single Czecho-Slovak nation, emphasized the obsolescence of the Slovak National Council, the reasoning being that a duality of power would be detrimental to the survival of the new republic. But in Slovakia the attempt to abolish the Slovak National Council, and after January 20, 1920, the dissolution of the local national councils, justifiably were felt as a purposeful design to liquidate all Slovak national organs.

The Skalica government ceased to exist on November 14, 1918, because on that day the Czech Revolutionary National Assembly in Prague confirmed the new republic, the presidency of Thomas Garrigue Masaryk, and the establishment of the first Czecho-Slovak government. In the first postrevolutionary central coalition government and until the elections of 1920, Slovakia was represented by ministers. Milan Rastislav Stefanik became minister of war (after his accidental death on May 4, 1919, this post remained vacant), Vavro Srobar served as minister of public health, Fedor Houdek was minister of food supply, and Milan Hodza became minister of public administration and law. On December 10, 1918, the Skalica government was replaced by the institution of the *Minister s plnou mocou pre spravu Slovenka* (Minister Plenipotentiary for Slovakia, MPS).[2] The position to carry out this function was given to Vavro Srobar.

The minister plenipotentiary held broad and unspecified powers, which Srobar applied through his fourteen fact-finding commissions. The office of MPS began its work on December 11, 1918, at Zilina, and on February 2, 1919, moved to Bratislava. As MPS, Srobar appointed the first *zupany* (area administrators), who swore their absolute loyalty to the republic, and Srobar insisted that all state officials and administrators take a loyalty oath to the Czecho-Slovak republic in his presence.

Srobar served in his post as MPS with great authority and determination. He already had the reputation from his previous post as "the dictator of Slovakia."[3] Because of the revolutionary conditions created by the Hungarian Red Army, on June 5, 1919, Srobar declared martial law and military rule in Slovakia.[4] However, he was not the only one to govern with an iron-clad fist; in 1920, for example, Srobar's successor, Ivan Derer (a Social Democrat), also used extraordinary measures as head of the office of the MPS. Although the office of the MPS was created only as a temporary administrative organ of the Czecho-Slovak government, it lasted for nine years until the definitive civil administration for Slovakia was established, though from 1922 on, its powers gradually diminished and its task-force function was transformed into Slovak sections that were absorbed by central ministries in Prague. Until the end of 1927 the office of the MPS was also headed by Martin Micura and J. Kallay.

On November 14, 1918, the Czech National Committee in Prague was renamed the Revolutionary National Assembly—a single-camera legislative body, which, according to the provisional constitution of November 13, 1918, held all the powers of the republic.[5] The Czech representatives in the Revolutionary National Assembly were chosen on the basis of the pre–World War I election results into the Austrian Diet. The first forty and later fifty-four Slovak representatives were appointed on the recommendation of the MPS, Vavro Srobar. They formed the Slovak Club, which until 1920 officially represented the entire political spectrum of Slovakia, though it did not accurately reflect Slovak society— Slovak Catholics, for example, had a relatively small representation both in the Slovak Club and in the Revolutionary National Assembly. The Slovak Club was dissolved before the first parliamentary elections in April 1920. After the election, the newly elected members of the assembly and senate from Slovakia joined different clubs organized by their own political parties.

THE STATUS OF SLOVAKIA AND THE SLOVAKS IN THE CONSTITUTION OF 1920

Following the Constitution of the Czechoslovak Republic, adopted on February 29, 1920, and in effect until October 1938, pre-Munich Czechoslovakia adhered to a system of parliamentary democracy closely modeled on the French system. The parliament consisted of a bicameral legislative system called the Czechoslovak National Assembly, with a Chamber of Representatives (300 members) and a Senate (150 members). Members of the government were simultaneously members of both the Chamber and the Senate, as long as there was no conflict of interest involved. The government was made up of political party leaders or a coalition of parties that gained a majority in parliament. According to this model, the head of the government was the premier (or prime minister), whose powers were much greater than those of his colleagues in the government or parliament. The constitution made the government and the parliament share the power of political decision making: parliament had the legislative power and the government the executive power. In other words, the parliament enacted legislation upon the initiative from the government. The constitution made it clear that the executive (government) was responsible to the National Assembly.

Though the two-chamber legislative system in Czechoslovakia would appear to be similar to a democratic system of checks and balances, the similarity was only superficial because the supremacy of power was vested in the hands of party leaders who controlled both the legislative and executive branches of the government. There was no secret about the fact that in both chambers key issues were decided in the executive committees of the political parties rather than in parliament or the government. Indeed, the ruling political parties gained almost dictatorial powers, and the party system was in many respects opposed to the ideas expressed in the constitution and the parliamentary rules. The constitution made an elected representative accountable to the nation (that is, the voters) and not to a political party; but in practice the multiparty system, representing different political, economic, nationality, and religious interests, was more centrifugal than centripetal. Ultimately, these strong party divisions and the creation of more and more splinter parties had a great deal to do with the disintegration of Czecho-Slovak society.

The practice of deferring political decision making to the political party leaders resulted in party autocracy, voter apathy, a decline in democratic standards, and even political paralysis. Frequent difficulties in creating a majority in the parliament shackled the government's ability to act, and the electoral system, dominated by party leaders, made it almost impossible to allow new voices in to reenergize the parliament. The party elite, who decided the state's affairs, stayed in power by circumventing the democratic process of electing functionaries legitimized by the electoral laws of the country. In other words, the party elite replaced the democratic method of elections with its own party machines controlled by party bosses from the top. Whenever democracy was discredited in the First Republic, it was for the simple reason that the people at large were unable to elect representatives with the qualifications they desired and had to settle for those handpicked by the party elite. Although the laws permitted government initiatives to be submitted to the voters for a referendum, the government never used the referendum during its twenty years of existence. Masaryk himself, however, had reservations about the use of referendum during the 1920s because he was reminded that during the first parliamentary election in 1920 it was necessary to use ballots of different colors in order to distinguish the many political parties, colored ballots being necessary because of the large number of illiterate voters in Slovakia.[6] It has also been suggested that the use of referendum could easily have been abused by demagoguery.[7]

The executive branch of the government in the First Czechoslovak Republic was as weak as the legislative branch. In the tradition of French parliamentarism, dating back to 1875, the dual powers of the executive—the president and the government (also referred to as the cabinet)—in time reduced the office of president to a symbolic position as head of a parliamentary state. Instead of being the representative of the people at large, the president was elected by the members of the parliament, and his impotence was guaranteed by the constitutional provision that exempted the power-holders from any accountability to him. The principal reason for this weakness in the executive—a president without power—was Masaryk himself. The political leaders in the soon-to-be new state who, in the final analysis, were responsible for framing the constitution, correctly perceived that Masaryk—then still abroad—would become their first president and would be willing to accept the party strategy responsible for representation in the National Assembly based on the power of the parties derived from the election results of 1911. The party leaders did not consider Masaryk to be a team player, and they therefore made certain that, as president, he would have no power over the legislative or executive branches of the government. His main function was to oversee the branches independent of political influence. He was responsible to no one and could only be persecuted for treason.

All executive powers not specified in the constitution were reserved for the government, not the president, although pro forma the government was named by the president in both the selection and removal of cabinet ministers. The cornerstone of the government during the two decades of the First Czechoslovak Republic was a series of four coalitions: the all-national, the red-green, the citizen parties, and the broad bureaucratic coalition. The "broad coalition," which held power from 1929 to March 1938, included every political loyal opposition in the government. Thus during the second half of the new state's existence, for all practical purposes, there was never a possibility of changing the government. The coalition system of government that had been considered open and vibrant during the 1920s turned into a closed and stagnant system in the 1930s.

In hindsight, it can be argued that the incompatibility of the multiple-state interests weakened the domestic rule of the government and the stability of the political regime. The easier the rotation of the representatives in the legislative and executive branches of the government, the more stable was the state political system. In other words, political stability in Czechoslovakia was determined by the ability to create parliamentary majorities, and owing to communist, Slovak separatist, and German political party opposition, stability was impossible.[8] In the last parliamentary election, held in May 1935, Czech political parties returned 167 deputies, and the other parties elected 133 deputies. It must be emphasized again that one of the major weaknesses of the pluralistic parliamentary democracy in Czechoslovakia was the existence of too many political parties (twenty-nine altogether, with fourteen parties represented in parliament), which were organized along narrow interests of diverse groups and thus contributed to numerous political tensions and conflicts.

Unlike most parliamentary democracies, the governments in Czechoslovakia were not created on the basis of unifying interests held by the parties participating in the coalition, nor did the premier choose cabinets to carry out programs prepared by his own party and endorsed by the majority of the electorate. Quite the contrary. The party leaders chose the cabinet members, and the cabinet members felt and acted like party members rather than representatives of the government. In all their actions they sought approval from their respective parties—which not only did not trust each other but disliked compromise. Coalitions with diverse political, economic, religious, and nationality interests, finding compromise as a tool to be either difficult or unsatisfactory, all too frequently left vital issues to be resolved by the bureaucracy in Prague, thereby strengthening centralism in government.

There were eleven cabinets after the founding of the republic in 1918, with three coalitions during the 1920s. This demonstrates the vitality of the new state, which was able to reorganize itself into new coalitions rather than tolerate stagnation. In the 1930s there was only one coalition and eight cabinets, a clear indication of a need for continuous renewal of the balance of power.

After 1929, the opposition within the Czechoslovak government turned into a disloyal opposition. If consensus in a democratic parliamentary system is built on the relationship between the government in power and the opposition out of power, then such a consensus never existed in Czechoslovakia during the 1930s. Not only was the opposition antigovernment, but it was opposed to the democratic regime. It was ironic that among the opposition obstructing the entire democratic system of government were not only national minorities, such as the Konrad Henlein party of German nationalists, but also a large portion of the "governing nation," namely, the Czech communists and a segment of the Slovak People's Party. The lack of loyal opposition and at the same time the determination to defend the government from a strong, and to a certain extent dangerous, opposition were symptomatic of a crisis-prone Czechoslovak democracy. These circumstances foreshadowed the self-destruction of Czechoslovak democracy from within, through a persistent struggle against an undemocratic opposition, and from the outside, via the totalitarian regimes of neighboring states who collaborated with a strong undemocratic opposition among the nationalities of Czechoslovakia.

In view of the complex structure of nationalities in the new republic, after World War I, the Czech politicians and the framers of the constitution insisted on making Czechoslovakia an indivisible unitary state. The issues at that time included not only the future status of Slovakia but to a greater extent, the question of how to prevent the early attempts of Sudeten-German provinces to break away from Bohemia and the decentralizing tendencies of other minorities in Silesia. Thus the politicos in Prague decided *against* self-rule and the creation of a democratic public administration and instead opted for continuity by revamping the old Austro-Hungarian system into a centrally controlled administrative system. The so-called experts who conceptualized the system of public administration and the framing of the constitution were, according to the Czech political economist Josef Macek, inexperienced in statecraft.[9] They applied the French idea of identical administration—*pouvoir fort*—to the new state that was to unite Czechs and Slovaks, the identity deriving from the mutual satisfaction of having achieved their own independent state. According to this concept, democratization of public administration and the guarantee of a certain autonomy in economic matters were supposed to have been carried out in such a way that state interests would not suffer.[10]

With the adoption of the Czechoslovak Constitution in February 1920, the National Assembly also passed laws about the creation of the offices of *zupa* (administrative area) and *okres* (district), also known as administrative area laws, which transferred the legislative power of the former Land Diet (parliament) to the central government.[11] The purpose of these laws was to curtail the Land autonomy and introduce a centralized system of administration that would also abolish the historical significance of the Lands and simultaneously bring about the establishment of a unitary state of Czechoslovakia. The new restriction favored the executive rather than the legislative branch of government. The new laws divided the state, with the exception of Ruthenia, into twenty-two *zupy* or administrative areas (six in Slovakia and sixteen in Bohemia and Moravia), each one encompassing a population of 511,000–800,000. At the helm of each *zupa* was a *zupan* (area governor), named by the minister of the interior in Prague and responsible to him. The *zupy* were divided into *okresy* (districts) headed by a district chief or *okresny nacelnik*.

When the *zupa* system became operational in Slovakia in 1923, the result was administrative dualism. In Bohemia and Moravia the administrations continued to carry out the functions of internal governance, whereas in Slovakia and Ruthenia administrations functioned as service offices. The law of 1920 did not respect the natural rights of the Slovaks to administer some of their own affairs. If these laws about the new system of public administration were intended to obstruct the emergence of Slovak national separatism, then the laws failed. In contrast to Czech Lands, Slovakia had not become a separate administrative unit nor had it acquired a legal subjectivity. The promised *zupny zvaz* (administrative area association), which was supposed to have represented a certain restricted administrative autonomy, was never realized. Because of the multitude of problems with the 1920 administrative laws, during the political crisis of 1925–1926, the minister of the interior declared that the laws relating to *zupy* could not be implemented because the *zupy* were financially unsound and lacked viability. In 1927, the government proposed administrative reforms, which resulted in dividing the Czechoslovak Republic into four Lands: Czech, Moravian-Silesian, Slovak, and Ruthenian.[12] Like the previous reform of public administration, however, this one, too, lacked the demanded attributes of self-government. In hindsight it is realistic to argue that in Czechoslovakia between the two world wars there was no self-rule but only a certain degree of decentralized state administration. From the standpoint of democratic theory, it is fair to point out that after the administrative reforms of 1927, the tendency in Czechoslovakia was toward bureaucratization, which also led to the restriction of general voting rights and, of course, self-rule.

For the Slovak separatists, the reference to the concept of "nation," written in the preamble of the 1920 Czechoslovak Constitution, was perhaps emotionally the most disturbing aspect of Czechoslovak centralism.[13] The intent in the constitution was to make clear that the Czechoslovak state had only *one* national character. The basic document made certain that the name Czechoslovak Republic expressed the unitary character of the state, and within the constitutional framework many similar concepts were made into laws, among them the very controversial language law.[14] Critics called this law a constitutional modification of the fictional "Czechoslovak language," which became the official and state language of a fictional "Czechoslovak nation."[15] It was a deliberate political concoction enacted into law because of the existing foreign policy situation and because it was supported by the Slovak Club in Prague.[16] The legislators who passed this law perceived the concept of "the language" as a complete equality between the Czech and Slovak languages.[17] Thus official explanation of the controversial formulation was that in Slovakia, as a rule, the official language was Slovak and in Bohemia and Moravia, Czech. In practice, however, Czech was favored over Slovak in state employment and in nonstate administrative offices, even in Slovakia, and this practice traumatized Slovak-Czech relations during the entire existence of the First Czechoslovak Republic. Still, largely because the new state was built on Masaryk's democratic idea of tolerance and cooperation among all nations on Czechoslovak territory, the Czechs and Slovaks built a closer relationship than before.[18] Slovak expectations for the new state were best characterized by J. Huska, signer of the Cleveland and Pittsburgh agreements, in his letter to O. Zlamal, a Czech Catholic priest, on February 12, 1919: "If the Czechs are sincere with us, then let them help us to build our own Slovak state with a Slovak constitution, a Slovak parliament and a Slovak government—a state that will be equal, of the same value and a legitimate part of the Czecho-Slovak Republic."[19] This idea turned into a general belief system among many Slovak and Czech statesmen and served as an impetus for launching a new democratic state in a spirit of great optimism.

After the withdrawal of the Hungarian Red Army from eastern Slovakia and the collapse of the Slovak Soviet Republic in July 1919, law and order and the common state with the Czechs and a large population of minorities were possible only with immediate and persistent Czech assistance in the areas of administration, education, and other key sectors. The Czech soldiers, public servants, teachers, and administrators who arrived in Slovakia in 1919 were welcomed as necessary to help Slovakia deal with numerous problems created by the sudden political and social changes.[20] The apathetic population, once resigned to existence within the Kingdom of Hungary, now had to be transformed into passionate patriots with national pride and self-awareness who welcomed union with the Czechs.

One of the measuring devices used for judging the accomplishments of Czecho-Slovak democracy after union was contained in the age-old question: Who were the rightful representatives of the Slovak Nation in the new republic? It is important to point out that before the Slovaks joined the Czech revolt against the Habsburg monarchy at home and abroad, there was only one representative in the Hungarian Diet, Dr. Ferdis Juriga, who sought independence for Slovakia before the end of World War I. It was the same Juriga who on November 13, 1918, while on the train to Prague, prepared the first proposal for Slovak autonomy, which he then submitted to the Slovak (Parliamentary) Club at Prague. In it, he emphasized that he supported the "unitary state of Czechoslovakia," but for the sake of the Slovak branch of the Czechoslovak family, he demanded Slovak self-rule and Slovak administration, Slovak schools and offices, independence of religion, and "equality of our language on the entire state territory."[21]

The first democratic parliamentary elections were held in Slovakia from April 18 to 25, 1920.[22] There were four all-state and a few smaller parties in the contest. The Czecho-Slovak Social Democratic Party gained 510,341 votes, more than twice the number received by the Slovak National and Agrarian Party (242,045) and the Czechoslovak People's party in Slovakia (235,389) (see Table 1).

The election results were more a reflection of postwar economic conditions and social chaos induced by the revolutionary provocations of the Hungarian Red Army than of Slovak political preferences or ideological convictions. The official newspaper of the National and Agrarian

TABLE 1

RESULTS OF THE 1920 PARLIAMENTARY ELECTIONS
IN SLOVAKIA

Party	No. of votes	Proportion in %
Czechoslovak Social Democrats	510,341	38.051
Czechoslovak People's (in Slovakia)	235,389	17.550
Czechoslovak National Socialist	29,564	2.204
Slovak National and Agrarian	242,045	18.047
Hungarian Small Farmers	26,520	1.977
Hungarian National	4,214	0.341
Hungarian-German Christian Socialist	139,355	10.390
Hungarian-German Socialist Democrats	108,546	8.093
Jewish Parties	45,217	3.347
Total	1,341,191	100.000%

SOURCES: L. Liptak et al., *Politicke strany na Slovensku 1860–1989* (Political parties in Slovakia, 1860–1989) (Bratislava: Archa, 1991); *Slovensko v politickom systeme ceskoslovenska. Materialy z vedeckeho sympozia Casta 11.-13.11. 1991* (Slovakia in the political system of Czechoslovakia. Materials from a scientific symposium held on November 11–13, 1991) (Bratislava: 1992); Frantisek Vnuk, "Slovakia in Pre-Munich Czecho-Slovakia (1918–38)," in Joseph M. Kirschbaum, ed., *Slovakia in the 19th and 20th Centuries* (Toronto: Slovak World Congress, 1973), p. 103.

Party, *Slovensky dennik* (Slovak Daily), on April 22, 1920, declared: "The Social Democrats should not delude themselves into assuming that their voters are red. They are not red at all. All they want is bread, clothing, salt, kerosene, good shoes, better wages. The Social Democratic agitators promised them these things, now we shall see how they fulfill their promises."[23] This critique by the Social Democrats' closest challenger was not too far off the mark. In order to avoid a preelection split, the Social Democratic Party leadership in Prague forbade an open debate between the party's reformist right wing and its Marxist (Bolshevik) left wing, and the artificially unified party conducted an intensive preelection campaign built on the slogan "Support the impoverished Slovaks," which captured the minds of the materially deprived and politically illiterate voters. In this regard, the most successful campaign was conducted by the party's left wing. This wing, on January 16, 1921, at Lubochna reconstituted itself as the Slovak Communist Party and on May 15, 1921, at Prague merged into the newly constituted Communist Party of Czechoslovakia.

As a result of the loss of the elections to the Social Democrats, in

March 1921, the progovernment national agrarian coalition of Hodza, Srobar, and Dula split into two separate wings: one national, under Dr. E. Stodola,[24] who formed the Slovak National Party, and one agrarian, under Dr. Milan Hodza, who joined the Czech Agrarians in the all-national Agrarian Party (founded in 1899). In November of that same year, Andrej Hlinka, head of the Slovak People's Party, severed the coalition ties of April 1920 with Dr. Jan Sramek's Czechoslovak People's Party and proclaimed its independence.

On May 25, 1920, as a pro forma gesture, President Masaryk announced the formation of the second Czechoslovak government, headed by Premier Vlastimil Tusar, leader of the Social Democratic Party. While the National Assembly remained almost the same in party representation, the new, so-called "red-green" coalition had a prevailing majority, even though the ministries of the interior, finance, and agriculture were retained by the nonsocialist parties. From Slovakia there were: Ivan Derer as Minister Plenipotentiary for Slovakia (MPS), Ivan Markovic as minister of defense, and Vavro Srobar as minister of health and physical education. Prior to the second general election in 1925, Ivan Derer, Martin Micura, and J. Kallay held the position of MP for Slovakia. The ministry for unification and public administration and law was led by Vavro Srobar, Vojtech Fajnor, Ivan Derer, and Ivan Markovic; Markovic also served as minister of national defense. Srobar was also minister of education and national enlightenment, and Dr. Milan Hodza served as minister of agriculture.

Not only did Slovak politicians gain representation in both the legislative and executive branches of the new Czechoslovak government, but Slovak society changed considerably. For the first time Slovaks became full-fledged citizens of the state. The swift abolition of the privileges held by the aristocracy swept away the superior position of Magyar birthright in the nobility as well as in the Magyarized gentry. The new republic also enabled the Slovaks to develop their organizational needs in open public forums. With the adherence to the general electoral voting rights of 1918, broad Slovak masses became not simply objects but subjects of daily political life. The relatively radical land reform, though it adversely affected the aristocracy and the large landowners, considerably helped the small farmers and landless peasants. Similarly, the laws pertaining to better working conditions and laws affecting the economic and social conditions of the working class, initiated by the socialist coalition parties, had a strong impact on the changing mode of life of Slovak society.

Above all, however, the introduction of mandatory school attendance and teaching in the native language brought rapid improvement in the literacy and knowledge of the Slovak population, which served as a precursor to the modernization process of Slovak society.

Without doubt, the greatest single democratic attribute of Slovakia's advancement during the First Republic was education. According to Brackett Lewis (quoting official Hungarian statistics of 1914), there were 214,267 Slovak children attending Magyar elementary schools and only 42,186 attending Slovak elementary schools, and Slovakia had only 365 Slovak schools and 539 Slovak teachers; on October 28, 1918, when the Czechoslovak Republic was officially declared, Slovakia had 429 Slovak primary schools taught by Slovak teachers and no colleges or universities.[25] By 1933–34 that situation had changed considerably. Slovakia had 12,469 children enrolled in 151 preschool institutions (maternal school, nurseries, and crèches), with 190 teachers and 142 assistants; institutions teaching in Magyar, German, and Polish totaled less than 30 percent of the 151. The same year, Slovakia had 560,244 boys and girls enrolled in 4,160 elementary schools with 10,489 teachers; about 65 percent of those institutions taught in the Slovak language. In 1934, Slovakia had 55,146 boys and girls enrolled in 167 civic schools (*mestianske skoly*), which had a four-year curriculum for the age group from eleven to fifteen, with 1,375 teachers, 90 percent of whom used Slovak as the instruction language.[26]

Statistics for 1933–34 show that there were 205 "Czechoslovak" secondary schools of general education (*gymnasia, realne gymnasia*, reformed *realne gymnasia*, and *realne skoly*) with 88,562 students using Czech and Slovak instructional languages throughout Czechoslovakia, but there is no breakdown of the "Czechoslovak" data.[27] Lewis's reference in 1936 to forty such schools in Slovakia may be an exaggeration; he also shows eighty German, eight Magyar, one Polish, and four Carpatho-Russian (Ruthenian) secondary schools with a total of 33,400 students.[28] In 1932–33, there were thirty-seven Slovak technical schools with 14,748 students and 337 Slovak teachers and 251 Slovak trade continuation schools with 10,497 students and 1,242 Slovak teachers.[29]

Before 1918, Slovakia had no commercial schools with Slovak instruction, but in 1933 there were eighty-three commercial academies, forty-five two-year commercial schools, and sixty-six commercial continuation schools with Slovak as the language of instruction.[30] The same year, there were 1,031 agricultural schools in Czechoslovakia, of which

753 schools with a student population of 13,928 were taught by 4,247 teachers using "Czechoslovak" as the language of instruction.[31] Just how many of these schools were Slovak and how many Czech is a matter of conjecture.

It is much easier to identify instructions of university rank. In 1932–33, there were twenty-seven institutions of higher learning in Czechoslovakia. Of these, three were Slovak institutions (Comenius University, the Government Pedagogical Academy, and the Academy of Music and Dramatic Arts, all in Bratislava), eighteen Czech, five German, and one Ukrainian university. The three Slovak institutions of higher learning had 2,728 students taught by 174 professors and 143 assistants.[32]

In addition to the vastly expanded formal educational system in Slovakia, a law passed in February 1919 called for the establishment of educational committees in every community. The committees were to set up libraries and offer courses and lectures for adults under the supervision of the ministry of education. One result of this two-pronged educational effort, formal for children and informal for adults, was the lowering of the illiteracy rate in the country. In Slovakia, illiteracy dropped from 14 percent in 1921 to 6 percent in 1930. In 1910, Slovakia had an illiteracy rate of 39 percent.[33]

As the data just presented suggest, after decades of being at the mercy of Magyarization and assimilation policies of the feudal Kingdom of Hungary, the creation of Czecho-Slovakia offered new favorable conditions for the development of the Slovak language and culture as well as for the aspirations of a much improved standard of living. The Czechoslovak Republic introduced a general democratization process and, within its framework, assumptions for the constitutionalization of the Slovak nation. Paradoxically, during the "Slovakization" process of Slovakia, a denial of Slovak legitimacy, on the one hand, was compensated with extensive support for democratization, on the other. Participants in this process were thousands of Czech Slovakophiles, teachers, experts, and others—mostly state employees with qualifications that Slovaks lacked.

As mentioned previously, during the first years after the revolution and especially during the breakaway time from Hungary, Czech assistance to Slovakia was indispensable and necessary. This was fully acknowledged and supported by bona fide Slovak nationally oriented circles. At the same time, however, a group of about 120,000 Czechs in Slovakia acquired key positions in the state administration, the military, security and the police, the judiciary, the railroad, the postal service, and the school system. The results of the Czech assistance to Slovakia were most evident in the growth of Slovak education—available to a large population within the network of the elementary and secondary school system and in educating young Slovaks in the spirit of Masarykian democracy. Courses in the humanities, medicine, and the natural sciences were taught mostly by Czech professors at Comenius University in Bratislava, but until 1938 Slovaks were obliged to attend schools in Bohemia or Moravia for technical and military studies. By the second half of the 1920s, the first generation of the Slovak intelligentsia, taught under the auspices of the idea of a unitary Czechoslovak state and equipped with the knowledge of administrative skills and techniques, was eagerly awaiting the opportunity to fill jobs commensurate with qualifications in public, economic, and political areas. However, these positions were already taken, if not permanently, at least for the distant future. The situation became even more unrewarding when it became evident that the generous enthusiasm of the original volunteers coming to Slovakia from the Czech Lands was gradually replaced by purely pecuniary motivations. Furthermore, there were all-state political parties that guaranteed positions in state offices (or at least employment as janitors and custodians of state property) to their potential Czech voters in Slovakia. Frequently, decisions concerning the neglect or violation of civil rights and national respect of citizens aroused a response of irrational anti-Czech feelings on the Slovak side and a feeling of ingratitude and injustice on the Czech side. As a result, persistent misunderstandings caused enough pent-up emotions gradually to produce a "time bomb" effect in the hands of the antidemocratic political powers to seek the liquidation of Czecho-Slovak democracy.

THE ECONOMIC POSITION OF SLOVAKIA AND THE GREAT DEPRESSION

Postwar economic disintegration occurred as a result of planned dismantlement of industrial production on Slovak territory during the last phase of World War I. Before the Hungarian Red Army left Slovakia in July 1919, they made certain that most of the food reserves and agricultural products were depleted; they moved abroad most of the industrial enterprises belonging to Magyar owners, and they destroyed several railroad lines and bridges. The unfavorable economic conditions continued to last after the war because of the pending international agreements that would have guaranteed more stable relations between Czechoslovakia and its neighbors. The licensing of enterprises with foreign capital in Slovakia also moved with intentional slowness, such that only three out of fifty-one enterprises in Czechoslovakia made their headquarters in Slovakia by the end of 1924; and even in these, the most significant positions were controlled by Czech investments.

In the postwar recession, Slovak capital investments were minimal. During this time the large-scale dismantling of industry from Slovakia was justified as a need for modernization and rationalization of work. In twenty years in Slovakia 184 new industrial enterprises were created, with 7,003 jobs, but 167 enterprises and 13,386 jobs were eliminated.[34] Behind the argument that ineffective and unprofitable production had to be discontinued and outmoded enterprises dismantled and liquidated stood first of all the hard-fought struggle for competition between the strong Czech banks and industrial complexes. The perception from Prague of Slovakia as an "agricultural preserve" contributed to the neglect of industrial development in the area. As a result, several factories and mines were forced to close down and rampant unemployment triggered a surge of emigration to countries seeking cheap labor.[35] At the end of January 1927 unemployed workers and farmers from around Plesivec, supported by numerous political parties from the left to the right, took to the streets to protest the dismantling and moving of two factories to Hungary. The following month similar protests were organized by unemployed workers and farmers in eighteen cities to protest the plundering of Slovakia and the intentional destruction of industry in Slovakia.

After the revolution in Czecho-Slovakia a land reform was instituted that affected 1,407,400 hectares of land in Slovakia, of which 507,200 hectares were agricultural land formerly owned by foreign aristocracy and large landowners.[36] In contrast to the Czech part of the republic, the reform in Slovakia was slow—it lasted until 1929—and incomplete; a large portion of land was returned, after considerable litigation, to the original owners, and the rest remained undivided land. This land also included what became known as the "leftover estates," some of which then became a tool for political corruption, especially among the representatives of the Agrarian Party, and thus the subject of numerous scandals. In Bohemia and Moravia most of the landowners had medium-sized farms, but in Slovakia the majority of the landowners held small farms. About one-half of the confiscated agricultural land (247,600 hectares) was sold by the government to small recipients, averaging about 1.55 hectare allotments. The undivided large estates employed a large percentage of farmworkers and landless peasants.

Slovakia had about 37 percent of all the agricultural land in the republic, of which 32 to 33 percent was arable. Toward the end of the republic, however, only 23 percent of the land was used for coarse agricultural production and only 13 percent for market production. The lack of effectiveness of Slovak agriculture was attributable to the small size of the farms. These farms, of less than one hectare, accounted for 22.6 percent of all agricultural enterprises, yet totaled only 62,693 hectares, 1.3 percent of the land in Slovakia.[37]

During the agricultural crisis in 1929, it became evident that Slovakia lagged behind Czech Lands not only in industrial but also in agricultural development—this in spite of the fact that when the Czecho-Slovak state was created, the eastern part of the republic, Slovakia, was designated as an agrarian area. According to this argument, Slovakia was supposed to have become a counterweight to the industrial area of Bohemia and Moravia and in that way to guarantee the economic counterbalance of the two nations. In reality, however, Slovakia—from the point of view of the managers of Czech capital—had become not only agrarian but also a reserve for raw materials. The persistent differences in the degree of economic development between the two areas of the republic were due to lack of knowledge about conditions in Slovakia, bureaucratic indifference in Prague, the application of competitive and partisan political interests, preferences given to many other problems, and the limitation of state and private funds. For the decision makers it took, relatively speaking, a long time not just to recognize the differences between the two areas of development but to appreciate what those differences meant in terms of social, cultural, and economic inequality.[38]

Czechoslovakia did not immediately feel the effects of the great depression that began in the autumn of 1929. The Czechoslovak economy was heavily dependent on exports of both consumer goods and raw materials, and through tariff laws and other preventative measures, major industrial countries were able to postpone the approaching world recession until 1930. But their actions contributed to a rapid rise in unemployment, starvation, and emigration in countries such as Czechoslovakia. Capital investment, collectivized electrification, and the introduction of the automobile contributed greatly to a new economy that made the economic crisis in the metal, electric, and chemical industries relatively mild compared to other sectors of the economy; favorable conditions also prevailed in the financial field. By the end of 1930, however, there was a general economic downturn. The social fallout, manifested throughout the world from 1930 to 1933, was especially heavy in Slovakia and Carpatho-Russia.

Prior to the depression, demonstrations organized by the Communist and Social Democratic Parties for wage demands, strikes against unemployment, actions of solidarity, and so on very often ended in skirmishes with the police, sometimes resulting in casualties and collective litigation against the demonstrators for unlawful provocation. Less frequently workers reached a compromise with employers, and in some cases such actions ended in favor of the workers. Official records show 258 strikes in 1928 and 223 strikes in 1929. As the economic crisis deepened, strikes declined. In 1930, there were 149, and from 1931 to 1935 it was practically impossible to organize a strike. In Slovakia, the greatest movements were strikes of agricultural workers in the west, strikes of forest and construction workers in the central region, and strikes of lumber mill and mine workers in the east. The central government and the progovernment organizations reacted to the discontented strikers with the usual political rhetoric but offered no solutions. It is interesting to note that during these difficult years, for the first and last time in the existence of the Czechoslovak Republic, the seat of the minister of the interior was occupied by a Slovak representative of the Agrarian Party, Juraj Slavik (1929–1932), a man who was politically and morally responsible for a series of unpopular repressive acts. Incidents of shooting into the masses at Kosuty in May 1931, and later in Polomka, Telgart, and other cities, resulted in a harsh response from liberal democrats at home and abroad.

The coalition government in Prague tried new approaches to find solutions to the old problems in Slovakia. Starting in 1927, at Bratislava, conferences were held about economic issues in Slovakia with participants from the Slovak industry, business and trade, various government ministries, and Slovak regional offices. Their sponsor was Dr. Milan Hodza, minister of agriculture. Recommendations for solving the troublesome economic situation in Slovakia were identified as the construction of railroads, new rail tariffs (which were 30 to 35 percent higher than in the Czech Lands), equalization of the income tax (which was 10 percent in Slovakia and only 3 percent in the Czech Lands), publication of state statistics and the fulfillment of state commitments for delivery quotas, availability of state loans at a low interest rate, greater share in private and state investments, greater participation of Slovak industry and trade in autonomous associations and committees, and, finally, regard for equity in taxation of business enterprises. According to Public Law no. 76/1927, Slovak branches of business in the Czech Lands were taxed twice—at the headquarters in Slovakia and at the branch in Bohemia-Moravia. This policy, the critics claimed, had lowered the potential for social benefits in health, educational, and cultural activities.

By custom, economic issues were regularly debated at the representative Land offices, where members of the coalition and the opposition could agree on solutions to regional problems. The purpose of the recommendations made at Bratislava was to reach equal rules and regulations applicable to industrial and trade activities throughout the republic as a first step toward eliminating underdevelopment in Slovakia. According to Slovak economists, when the two economically uneven territories were united, it was incumbent upon the founders of the republic to pursue a prudent policy, in the interests of the unitary state, which would, first of all, support the development of the weaker partner so that the entire country could benefit. Slovak economists like Imrich Karvas and Pavol Zatko warned that it would be impossible to achieve unification of two unequally developed territories on the basis of free competition. They pointed to the fact that Slovak industrial participation in the postwar economic expansion was minuscule and that the state economic policy after the revolution left Slovak industry completely on its own, without any support from Prague.[39]

But for all the conferences, solutions to the Slovak economic problems were not sought in earnest until the great depression was well under way. In January 1931, the Economic Institute for Slovakia and Carpatho-Russia (NARCS) was established. The aim of NARCS was to take care of the general economic and social development in the eastern part of the republic. Its task was to establish cooperative work with the already existing economic institutions, like the Central Association of Slovak Industry, chambers of commerce and trade associations, the Agricultural Board, and the Committee for Economic Issues in Slovakia—all of which became members of NARCS along with the representatives of the Slovak Land and its political parties (the Agrarian,

Hlinka's Slovak People's Party, the Social Democratic Party, and the People's Party). Kornel Stodola became chairman of NARCS and Imrich Karvas general secretary. The initiative for the creation of NARCS came directly from Milan Hodza, who in January 1930 returned to the political arena equipped with a well thought out concept of Slovak regionalism emphasizing economic development.

In the 1930s, demands for the industrialization of Slovakia were looked at more seriously. In their party platform for the 1935 elections, the Social Democrats emphasized the need to solve the problems of underdevelopment and poverty through industrialization and social reform. This was, in effect, also their attempt to overcome the narrow or simplistic perception of the all-state "Czechoslovakistic" parties. This program, like others calling for broad political and administrative decentralization, saw in the Slovak issue not a controversial but only a regional problem. With Milan Hodza becoming the new premier in November 1935, central government focus on Slovakia's real needs, as well as the prospects for implementating solutions to problems, became quite realistic. The representatives of NARCS prepared a list of Slovak demands in the areas of transportation, agriculture, industry, commerce, health, and education as well as self-government, and in April 1937, they submitted that list to President Benes for consideration. Repeatedly, the document referred to the need for equalization of the Slovaks with the Czechs for the sake of strengthening unity in the republic.

What actually changed the politics of economic development in Slovakia was the military-strategic aspect of future security of Czechoslovakia. The first steps in this direction were taken because of the worsening of the foreign policy situation for Czechoslovakia after Adolf Hitler established himself as Führer of the German Reich. Slovakia occupied a significant strategic position in the military defense of the state, as had already been recognized in Czechoslavakia's mutual security agreement with France signed in 1924; it was implicit also in a treaty signed in 1935 with the Soviet Union, following which Prague began to construct new highways and railroads from the west to the east. Entrepreneurs who moved inland from the areas neighboring Germany were given privileges by the state. As a result, several new enterprises were created in Slovakia for military-strategic production—arsenals in Dubnica and Povazska Bystrica, refineries in Dubova, chemical plants in Novaky and Handlova, branches of the Bata shoe factory in Batovany and Svit, and so on. New hydroplanes built on the river Vah created ten thousand jobs for unskilled labor. But this economic revival of the mid- and late 1930s failed to reach the precrisis conditions. In reality, the new economic boom in Slovakia was looked upon as a compensation for the losses from previous years. It can be argued that in this period a modern infrastructure was erected that after World War II (abused though it was) served as a foundation for future industrialization of Slovakia.

STATE CENTRALISM AND THE DEMAND FOR SLOVAK AUTONOMY

The so-called Men of the Revolution left the decision of Czecho-Slovak relations in their combined state to freely and democratically elected representatives. In contrast to the centrist concept of a unitary state, an autonomist movement began to take shape in Slovakia as early as 1919. The followers of the autonomist camp were politicos who closely identified with the Pittsburgh Agreement signed on May 30, 1918. They demanded full political legislative, administrative, and judicial autonomy for Slovakia within the state boundaries of Czechoslovakia. At the beginning of the movement there were perhaps certain differences among them about when Slovakia should acquire the autonomous status. The dedicated autonomists were both Slovak national parties— the Slovak People's Party (known from 1925 on as Hlinka's Slovak People's Party or HSLS) and the Slovak National Party (SNS). With the exception of the years 1927–1929, both were known as opposition (to the central government) parties. To the end of the republic in 1938 they demanded Slovak autonomy within the framework of the Czecho-Slovak Republic; nevertheless, these demands were of the specific needs for Slovakia (economic, social, cultural) as well as the need for state organs with all-Slovak participation for solving problems in Slovakia.

The so-called centralist parties, the Slovak Agrarians (since 1922, part of the Czechoslovak Agrarian Party), the Social Democrats, the National Socialists, and the Slovak wing of the Czechoslovak People's Party, rejected demands for political autonomy by pointing out that it would represent a step toward dualism and a threat to the territorial integrity of the state. The concept of limited administrative autonomy was accepted by Milan Hodza, the Slovak Agrarian leader, who tried to cooperate with the autonomists, as well as by other Slovak politicians, like Ivan Derer, who were staunch followers of the unitary state system. Such autonomy occurred first in the form of the association of Slovak *zupy* (administrative areas) and its organs, and later, after the installation of the Land administrative system in Slovakia, in the form of a Land Diet.

At the beginning of the 1920s the decline of the office of the MPS signaled a deepening asymmetry between Slovakia and the historic lands. In 1921, discontented factions of the pro-autonomist political parties, in open defiance of the idea of a unitary Czechoslovak state system (especially with regard to the framing of the Constitution of 1920), published their first proposals for legislation regarding Slovak autonomy. The authors of the proposals were F. Juriga, L. Labay, V. Tuka (members of the Slovak People's Party), and E. Stodola, (chairman of the Slovak National Party).[40] Juriga sought to commence Slovak autonomy as early as 1925; Stodola demanded legal guarantees for Slovakia to acquire political equality gradually, over a period of about ten years. Both proposals represented an opening for a possible compromise solution. Vojtech Tuka's proposal for a confederation uniting two independent states was realistically unacceptable because it would have meant that Slovakia would break away from Czechoslovakia.[41] On January 25, 1922, representatives of the Slovak People's Party submitted in the National Assembly their first official legislative proposal about Slovak autonomy, which fully respected the unitary system of government in an indivisible Czechoslovak state.[42] The parliament never took up the matter for discussion.

The second parliamentary elections, in 1925, gave the autonomist camp in Slovakia a convincing victory. The Slovak People's Party's 34 percent of the total vote was more than twice as great as the percentage for the two major Czechoslovak parties combined (see Table 2). Consequently, during the second postelection period (1925–1929), there were drastic changes in the political landscape of the Czechoslovak Parliament in Prague. In 1926, German activist parties joined the coalition, and on January 15, 1927, Hlinka's Slovak People's Party became a participant in the Czechoslovak government. A major reason for this belated decision on the part of Hlinka's Slovak People's Party was played behind the scenes by the Slovak minister, Milan Hodza, and by the leader of the Agrarian Party and then premier, Antonin Svehla, who made a commitment to initiate a reform of public administration and the establishment of the Land system in Slovakia—a move that the au-

TABLE 2

RESULTS OF THE 1925 PARLIAMENTARY ELECTIONS
IN SLOVAKIA

Party	No. of votes	Proportion in %
Hlinka's Slovak People's	489,111	34.309
Czechoslovak Agrarian	248,034	17.398
Czechoslovak Communist	198,111	13.896
Hungarian National (+ 3 German parties)	109,635	7.670
Hungarian Regional Christian-Socialist	98,337	6.897
Czechoslovak Social Democrats	60,635	4.253
Jewish	38,442	2.696
Czechoslovak National Socialist and Carpatho-Russian Labor	36,909	2.589
Slovak National	33,435	2.485
Czechoslovak National Democratic	24,954	1.750
Czechoslovak People's (Catholic)	18,036	1.265
Western Slovakia's Christian-Socialist	17,285	1.212
Czechoslovak Industrial-Trade	11,576	0.812
Other parties with less than 10,000 votes	41,095	2.768
Total	1,425,595	100.000%

SOURCES: L. Liptak et al., *Politicke strany na Slovensku 1860–1989* (Political parties in Slovakia, 1860–1989) (Bratislava: Archa, 1991); *Slovensko v politickom systeme Ceskoslovenska* (Slovakia in the political system of Czechoslovakia) (Bratislava: 1992).

tonomist parties took to be a step toward Slovak autonomy. Their expectations proved to be an exaggeration: Hlinka's party received two minor posts in the new government—the ministry of unification (Dr. Marko Gazik) and the ministry of health (Dr. Jozef Tiso), which the autonomist leadership considered mere tokenism. And the budgetary allocation of the Land system revealed that the change was more a formality than a genuine step toward self-rule in Slovakia.

On July 1, 1928, Public Law no. 125 (also known as the organization law of political administration) went into effect, according to which Czechoslovakia was divided into four Lands: Czech, Moravian-Silesian, Slovak, and Carpatho-Russian. With the establishment of the Land system in Slovakia, most of the agenda, but not the competence, previously handled by the MPS and the *zupy* were transferred to the various Land organs. Although the purpose of the land system was to permit greater local participation in the decision-making process, the final decision-making power was vested in the central government in Prague. One-third of the Slovak Land Office's members were named by the central government upon the recommendation of the president of the Land Office, who was responsible to the minister of the interior. The first president of the Slovak Land Office was Jan Drobny, a member of the HSLS, which satisfied one of the requirements of the HSLS to join the central government in Prague. His nominated deputy was a member of the Agrarian Party, Jozef Orszagh.[43] The first Land and district elections were held on December 2, 1928 (see Table 3). Although these elections were basically different from the parliamentary elections, the nominated members in combination with the Agrarians secured a narrow majority over the HSLS.

During the participation in the coalition government in Prague, Hlinka's Slovak People's Party could also claim credit for the passage of a congruous law (No. 122/1926) that was part of the negotiated conditions before joining the central government. HSLS reciprocated by supporting the Agrarian proposal for a law pertaining to placing duties on agricultural products. The presence of HSLS in the coalition government also contributed to the speedy agreement between the Vatican and Czechoslovakia—a modus vivendi that took effect in February 1928.

TABLE 3

RESULTS OF THE DECEMBER 2, 1928, LAND
ELECTIONS AND ITS REPRESENTATION

Party	No. of votes	Elec. rep.	Nom. rep.	Total rep.
Hlinka's Slovak People's	325,830	9	6	15
Slovak National	31,706	1	—	1
Czechoslovak People's (Micura)	43,717	1	1	2
Czechoslovak National Democratic	26,429	1	1	2
Agrarian	271,295	8	8	16
Regional Christian-Socialist	140,435	3	—	3
Hungarian National and Spis-German	104,011	3	—	3
Czechoslovak Social Democratic	96,916	3	1	4
Czechoslovak Communist	190,775	5	—	5
Czechoslovak National Socialist	36,076	1	1	2
Jewish	45,254	1	—	1
Total	1,312,444	36	18	54

SOURCES: The daily press and the *Krajinsky vestnik pre Slovensko 1929* (Land journal for Slovakia, 1929).

But HSLS's participation in the government did not fully satisfy the expectations of the moderate wing of the party and soon strengthened the position of the opposition to coalition politics. The next polarization, which prompted the members of the HSLS to leave the government, occurred during the so-called Tuka affair.

At the beginning of 1928, the Slovak People's Party daily, *Slovak*, published an article written by Professor Vojtech Tuka entitled "Ten Years After the Martin Declaration."[44] In this theoretical essay dealing with the philosophical state of affairs of the Slovaks in Czechoslovakia, Tuka predicted that Slovakia would acquire self-rule the following October, and if it did not, there would ensue "lawless conditions" on Slovak territory that could make all Czechoslovak laws there null and void. This prediction was based on a "secret clause" supposedly contained in the 1918 Declaration of Turciansky Sv. Martin. The Slovak leaders of the all-state parties in Slovakia (M. Ivanka and I. Derer) condemned the article as provocation against the Czechoslovak Constitution and initiated an inquiry into Tuka's previous antistate activities. Shortly after, Tuka was accused of committing treason and conspiracy against the republic in 1923 and 1924. In November 1928 (Tuka's predictions not having been fulfilled), the Czechoslovak parliament stripped Tuka of parliamentary immunity, and within a matter of days he was indicted on criminal charges. The trial against Tuka turned out to be the greatest political trial of the First Republic. Based on the charges brought in the indictment (the relevant documents about Tuka's activity in the Hungarian irredentist movement were not discovered until 1955), in October 1929 Vojtech Tuka was sentenced to fifteen years in prison for conspiracy to commit treason against the state. However, the opponents of Slovak autonomy were less interested in punishment of Tuka than they were in discrediting HSLS and possibly Hlinka himself, who continued to trust Tuka, supporting the accused without any reservation. During Tuka's prolonged trial, serious divisions surfaced within the party. In early 1929, Tuka's leading critics were expelled from HSLS, including F. Juriga, F. Tomanek, and J. Kubis. Other casualties included Marko Gazik, who was replaced as minister of unification by Andrej Hlinka's devotee L. Labay. On October 8, 1929, after Tuka's sentence was pronounced, the disappointed members of HSLS immediately abandoned the coalition in Prague. As is apparent in Table 4, the Tuka affair had a definite effect on the parliamentary elections held that December, in

TABLE 4

RESULTS OF THE 1929 PARLIAMENTARY ELECTIONS
IN SLOVAKIA

Party	No. of votes	Proportion %
Hlinka's Slovak People's	403,683	28.260
Czechoslovak Agrarian	278,979	19.530
Hungarian Regional Christian-Socialist	226,917	15.890
Czechoslovak Communist	156,242	10.660
Czechoslovak Social Democrats	135,506	9.488
Czechoslovak National Democratic	53,745	3.763
Czechoslovak National Socialist	43,968	3.078
Czechoslovak People's (Catholic)	36,548	2.559
Bloc of Polish and Jewish parties	33,679	2.358
Czechoslovak Industrial-Commercial	30,134	2.110
German Voting Association	13,704	0.959
Hungarian Regional Small-Farmers, Indust. and Workers	6,901	0.483
Juriga's Slovak People's	5,395	0.377
German Socialist Democratic and Workers	4,824	0.337
League Against Restr. List of Candidates	1,810	0.126
Total	1,432,035	100.000%

SOURCES: L. Liptak et al., *Politicke strany na Slovensku 1860–1989* (Political parties in Slovakia, 1860–1989); *Slovensko v politickom systeme Ceskoslovenska* (Slovakia in the political system of Czechoslovakia) (Bratislava: 1992).

which the HSLS, though it remained the strongest political organization in Slovakia, lost many votes to the centralist parties.

The election results convinced the party leadership that their "gentlemen's agreement" tactics with the coalition partners had been disastrous for gaining voters' confidence; HSLS, though it did not abandon the demand for legislative autonomy, put it on hold. Meanwhile, autonomists kept pressuring the Czechoslovak National Assembly and the central government in Prague to comply with certain already established rules for Slovakia. For example, the minister for Slovakia was supposed to have been a minister with certain parliamentary authority exempt from central control. This "minimal program," as the leaders referred to it, closely resembled the one advocated by Kornel Stodola (chairman of NARCS) and was clearly within the perception of Hodza's plan calling for the expansion of administrative authority in Slovakia.

Neither the acquired legal subjectivity of the Slovak Land nor the Land representation could eliminate the persistent demand for territorial autonomy and a Slovak Diet. The new situation that developed at the beginning of the 1930s, culminating in the most serious economic crisis of the century, only strengthened this demand because of the acute need for speedy and effective economic and social solutions in the area. On May 8, 1930, HSLS submitted in parliament a new proposal for Slovak autonomy, which the senate again shelved.[45] The proposal sought to amend one paragraph in the Constitution of 1920 so as to extend to Slovakia the same autonomy accorded to Carpatho-Russia.

Dissatisfaction with administrative reform in Slovakia was also rife in the Slovak National Party, which in early 1932 published a party program under the title "What Does Slovakia Demand?"[46] That autumn, the leaders of the autonomist parties—Andrej Hlinka (a Catholic priest) and Martin Razus (a Lutheran minister)—proclaimed a mutual strategy for both parties in the struggle for Slovak autonomy.[47] In the first half of the 1930s, the movement for Slovak autonomy was moving on an ascending path. Hlinka's Slovak People's Party, again in opposition, combined pressure tactics and expressions of discontent to air its demands for remedies to economic, social, and cultural needs. For example, HSLS opposed the new handbook of Slovak grammar and syntax, which contained many Czech words, idioms, and rules and was designed to bridge the Czech language and its Slovak "dialect." It was prepared by Matica Slovenska, and its pro-Czech employees were purged at its May 1932 general meeting. In August 1933 the party organized antigovernment demonstrations during the 1,100-year commemoration of the consecration of the Pribina church at Nitra. In disputes concerning the advanced demands, the argument of national interest was frequently used as defense. The autonomists focused on opposing the closing of industrial production in Slovakia, condemning auctions and the confiscation of properties, and working against the brutal intervention by the police and the military against strikers and demonstrators. The verbal radicalism of HSLS against government policy equaled only the stereotypical oratory of the parliamentary representatives of the Czechoslovak Communist Party.

As Nazism in Germany was gaining in power, and in Czechoslovakia the political conditions were worsening, tension between the coalition government and its opposition—from both the German minority party and HSLS—gradually increased. It can be argued that several of HSLS's demands had the appearance of blackmail because with the increased pressure in the Czech-German border disputes, the central government in Prague had to be keenly aware that the survival of the republic depended on Slovak loyalty. Prague also knew that in the presidential elections in 1934, the Slovak autonomists did not vote for T. G. Masaryk. In 1927, HSLS also cast its blank ballots, and in 1935 (after Masaryk resigned), party members supported Eduard Benes's candidacy for president only after pressure from the Vatican.

The last parliamentary and Land elections in pre-Munich Czechoslovakia were held in May 1935 (Table 5). In the spirit of the previous agreements, HSLS and SNS entered the elections together as an Autonomist bloc (joined by the Polish and Ukrainian autonomists), which in Slovakia became the indisputable victor. But since the Czechoslovak coalition retained its majority, the composition of the coalition governments changed very little up to the Munich crisis in September 1938. In these governments Slovakia was represented by Milan Hodza as premier from November 1935 and Ivan Derer as minister of justice.

After the elections, the HSLS leadership resumed its activities. On

TABLE 5

RESULTS OF THE 1935 PARLIAMENTARY ELECTIONS IN SLOVAKIA

Party	No. of votes	Proportion %
Autonomist bloc (HSLS, SNS, Auton)	489,641	30.121
Agrarian Association, Polish People's	286,739	17.639
Regional Christian-Socialist and Hungarian National	230,713	14.912
Czechoslovak Communist	210,785	12.967
Czechoslovak Social Democrats	184,389	11.343
Czechoslovak National Socialist	51,930	3.194
Czechoslovak Industrial-Commercial	41,996	2.583
Czechoslovak People's (Catholic)	37,489	2.306
National Community of Fascists	32,609	2.006
Sudete German (after merger with Carpatho-German	27,558	1.695
National Unity (Csl. National Democratic and National League)	25,490	1.568
Others	6,210	0.333
Total	1,625,549	100.000%

SOURCES: L. Liptak et al., *Politicke strany na Slovensku 1860–1989* (Political parties in Slovakia, 1860–1989); *Slovensko v politickom system Ceskoslovenska* (Slovakia in the political system of Czechoslovakia) (Bratislava: 1992).

May 31, 1935, Dr. Jozef Tiso (a Catholic priest) submitted to the head of the government, Jan Malypetr (an Agrarian), a memorandum with thirty-two demands.[48] This was the most conciliatory step so far taken by the HSLS leaders, for the memorandum did not include the usual direct demand for Slovak autonomy but only a revised version of the laws about public administration in Slovakia, namely, the expansion of the authority of the Land organs. Negotiations concerning the memorandum bogged down in the early stages and were not resumed again until November 1935, when Hodza replaced Malypetr as premier. The HSLS leaders had high hopes for their cause when Hodza became premier and therefore concentrated on four basic demands: (1) constitutional recognition of legal personality of the Slovak nation, (2) a parliamentary assembly for Slovakia within the context of the Pittsburgh Agreement, (3) revision of the language law, and (4) a ministry for Slovakia. Hodza declined to accept these demands, and consequently HSLS participation in the government was again postponed until 1938.

The aim of Hodza's government was to strengthen Czechoslovakia's internal stability by following a prudent foreign policy that would not endanger its sovereignty and would provide security and defense capability for its people. Concerning the organization of public administration in Slovakia, Hodza promised to expand the authority of self-ruling organs, but only within the framework of the existing Land system of government. For this, Hodza had the full cooperation and support of the coalition parties from Slovakia.

5 The Munich Crisis and the Disintegration of Czechoslovakia (1938–1939)

From its beginning, Czechoslovakia struggled with minority problems that it was unable to resolve. Indeed, the very composition of the minorities, resulting from the acquisition of minority-occupied territories added to Czechoslovakia at the expense of the defeated countries in World War I, was the main reason for the creation and artificial maintenance of a fictional Czechoslovak nation. Against a minority of 3.3 million Germans and almost 700,000 Magyars, the new state mustered a ten million majority with a statistically proclaimed "Czechoslovak" nationality, of which the Slovaks *unofficially* constituted 2.3 million. The percentage of representation of the Czechoslovak nation was even more unbalanced in regard to other nationalities in the state. Table 6 lists the composition of nationalities in Czechoslovakia according to the official 1930 census.

According to the census, contiguous Czech land represented 52,371 square kilometers, with 7,471,053 people, and the contiguous Slovak territory had 37,132 square kilometers, with 2,640,448 people, less than two-thirds of the total territory (64.99 percent). Furthermore, from the very beginning the crucial political representation of the two strongest

The sections "The Role of the Third Reich in Slovak National Development" and "March 14, 1939—Establishment of the Slovak Republic" are based on the Slovak text by Dusan Kovac.

TABLE 6

CZECHOSLOVAK CENSUS, 1930

National origin	Number	% of total
Czechoslovak	9,688,943	66.92
German	3,231,718	22.32
Magyar	692,121	4.78
Ruthenian	549,043	3.79
Jewish	186,474	1.29
Polish	81,741	0.56
Miscellaneous	49,465	0.34
Total	14,479,505	100.00%

SOURCES: "Scitanie ludu v CSR 20 dna 1.12. 1930" (Census of people in Czechoslovakia taken on January 12, 1930), *I. Ceskoslovenska statistika* (Ist Czechoslovak statistics), vol. 98 (Prague, 1934). See also, A. Bohac, "Narodnosti v Ceskoslovenske republice. Statistika a soucasny stav" (Nationalities in the Czechoslovak Republic. Statistics and current status), in *Idea Ceskoslovenskeho statu* (Idea of the Czechoslovak state) (Prague, 1938), p. 59 ff.

minorities acted against the territorial integrity of Czechoslovakia. The loyal, prorepublican minority parties had a relatively negligible influence on their constituency even during the time of their participation in the government. During 1918 and 1919, with the support of the Allied Powers, the Czech military and other state security organs successfully prevented the Germans and Magyars from breaking away some of the border territories. From 1920 to 1923 the territorial dispute with Poland over the Teschen area was also solved, at least temporarily. But the minority problem persisted, even though it did not constitute any immediate danger for the republic, since for the time being the Versailles and Trianon treaties kept the weakened neighboring states from rendering meaningful support to the domestic irredentist movements. A much more serious problem for the Czechoslovak leaders during the first decade of the republic was the Magyar minority, whose demands for the readjustment of the Slovak-Hungarian borders reached a climax in 1927 and 1928 and resulted in the signing of an agreement on the border status in which issues of navigation and transportation on the Danube River were resolved.[1]

On the other side of the coin, Czechoslovak democracy tried to achieve peace among nationalities by institutionalizing proportional representation of minorities in state and local governments on all levels and by making adjustments through legislative enactments of appropriate laws. The Czechoslovak Constitution postulated equality of all state citizens as far as civil and political rights were concerned; it provided for access to public service, offices, and ranks; for performance of business and occupation; and for the use of the mother language in private contacts, religious matters, the press, and open public meetings. The basic document followed the principles established by the international treaty protecting minorities stipulated in the Treaty of St. Germain of September 10, 1919. Any attempt to denationalize a person was prohibited by law. Public Law no. 122/1920, the so-called language law, gave priority to the "Czechoslovak language" in two equal wordings (Czech and Slovak) as the "official state language of the republic" and the right of minorities to express themselves in their own (second) language before the courts and all public offices in townships where at least 20 percent of the citizens spoke the same language. This law legalized the national character of the Czechoslovak Republic, although the state in reality had a nationality character, and in practice the above-mentioned principles were up against numerous obstacles. In the central offices the principle of proportional representation and equal access of citizens to public service and offices were not observed. The minority issue was complicated by the advent of the economic crisis in the early 1930s. The worsening of the economic and social conditions of the population in minority (border) areas, more so than in the inland of Czechoslovakia, provided space for nationalistic and social demagoguery as well as anti-Czechoslovak propaganda among the minority movements and parties of the left and right.

CLIMAX OF THE MINORITY PROBLEM AND THE MUNICH PACT

The increasing militancy of Nazi Germany posed a real threat to Czechoslovakia, not only for strategic reasons but because of its large German minority.[2] Elections in the Czech border land in 1935 favored Henlein's Sudeten German Party (SdP), joined that same year by the Carpatho-German Party (KdP) under the leadership of Franz Karmasin. Matters were further worsened at about the same time by the Hungarian political parties, which traditionally held their positions within the Slovak spectrum but now intensified their own propaganda activities against the state. Suddenly, all opposition minority parties called for political autonomy.

Confronted with a barrage of accusations and innuendo, the Czechoslovak government struggled to find new solutions to the old problem of minorities. On February 18, 1937, the Hodza government issued a set of *New Directives Concerning Minority Politics in Czechoslovakia* in which it committed itself to finding concrete solutions for the economic, social, cultural, and language obstacles faced by minorities, and it simultaneously adopted a resolution about the expansion of authority of the president of the Land Office in Slovakia.[3] Both moves signaled the government's *volte-face*.

In the midst of these troubling times, on September 14, 1937, the first president of the republic, Thomas Garigue Masaryk, died. In Slovakia, as elsewhere in the country, throngs of people gathered to mourn the loss of the revered statesman and to demonstrate a united support of Czechoslovak democracy. Even the communists, following the popular front tactics of the Comintern, joined the prorepublic democratic forces in anticipation of winning over the working class from all other parties. At about the same time the camp of political opponents of the Czechoslovak Republic became quite active. The Carpatho-German Party was by now openly a tool of Hitler's and Henlein's political engine even as it enjoyed legitimacy accorded to it by the democratic regime of Czechoslovakia. The KdP clearly had the backing of the majority of the German population in Slovakia and isolated any activist German political organizations that failed to cooperate. In October 1937, Konrad Henlein named Franz Karmasin his deputy for Slovakia, and that December, in Berlin, the KdP and the Hungarian United Party, headed by Count M. Eszterhazy and I. Jaross, struck an agreement to cooperate in a joint program with Hlinka's Slovak People's Party (HSLS) seeking autonomy. The KdP and the Hungarian United Party of course perceived autonomy to mean the return of the Czechoslovak territory occupied by minorities to the "motherland" states; HSLS meant to use the support rendered by the nationalistic parties to strengthen its political pressure for autonomy on the central government. Although in ideological terms there were similarities among these opposition parties—and in HSLS the appearance of more and more radical and antidemocratic elements— there is no clear evidence of systematic and direct collaboration toward destruction of the republic. Though the leaders of HSLS exerted pressure on Prague, concomitant with their criticism they made public and official pronouncements that their party supported the Czechoslovak Republic. The exploitation of the "German card" arguments during the presentation of the Slovak national demands turned out to be a typical political strategy of HSLS during the last two years of existence of pre-Munich Czechoslovakia. The slogan "*V novom roku do utoku!*" (Onward to Attack in the New Year!) was a typical expression for the radical wing of the party for welcoming in the New Year (1938).

By then it was evident that the leading problem facing the republic was the minority issue, especially in regard to the Sudete Germans. In March 1938, Premier Hodza announced his government's intention to prepare a statute for nationalities to codify the nationality rights into one law. The work on this project was carried out in secret because of the threats to the country by Nazi Germany and the pressures of separatist movements at both ends of the republic. Officially, only the basic principles of the statute were made public.

The next month, Henlein's Sudeten German Party published what it called its "Karlsbad Program" demanding territorial autonomy for the Sudete Germans. In spite of opposition from the political left, the government entered into negotiations with the representatives of SdP. In harmony with Hitler's plans to liquidate the Czechoslovak Republic, and based on his personal directives, Henlein's demands were constantly changing. As soon as the government agreed to certain demands, new ones were put on the table. Finally, the Czechoslovak representatives made it clear that the government was willing to defend its territory militarily with the aid of its allies in the event of an attack. This determination was confirmed on May 21, 1938, when, alerted by German troop movements on the western border, the Czechoslovak government ordered a partial mobilization of its army. In Slovakia the mobilization was carried out in an orderly fashion.

In the critical situation in May and June of 1938, Czechoslovakia held its local elections. In Slovakia 2,831 (or 81.32 percent) cities and towns were eligible to elect their representatives, although only 1,452 (or 51.3 percent) exercised that privilege. These were the last democratic elections held in prewar Czechoslovakia. The chief competitors in these elections were the voting group of the Slovak Unity for Czechoslovak Democracy and the Republic (Agrarians, Social Democrats, National Socialists, Industrial-Commerce Party, Micura's Czechoslovak, People's Party, National Unity, and, surprisingly enough, also the Slovak National Party) and the HSLS, which presented the voters with a new, radical program for Slovak autonomy. Also participating in the elections were the two mutually supporting minority parties of KdP and the Hungarian United Party, as well as the Czechoslovak Communist Party, which took an independent stance. Because of the sensitive minority issue, the government forbade the publication of elections results. This permitted the partisan press to freely interpret the partial outcome of the elections in their local papers. From information revealed by the ministry of the interior to the members of the government, it appears that the majority of the votes were cast for the Czechoslovak camp, represented by the Slovak Unity (see Table 7).

During the elections on June 3, the leadership of the HSLS approved a third proposal to be enacted into law granting Slovakia its autonomy, which was confirmed by the party's extraordinary meeting.[4] An ailing Andrej Hlinka announced the proposal on June 5, 1938, at Bratislava during the celebration of the twentieth anniversary of the signing of the Pittsburgh Agreement. It was here that the idea of the militant Hlinka Guard was born. The next day, in the same city, a mass anti-HSLS demonstration calling for Czecho-Slovak unity, also known as "Agrarian Day," was held, with representatives of the government participating. The purpose of the demonstration was to underscore the fact that HSLS was not the sole organization speaking for Slovakia. Two months later, on August 16, Father Andrej Hlinka, a feeble and sick old man, died.

TABLE 7
RESULTS OF LOCAL ELECTIONS HELD IN SLOVAKIA
IN 1938

Party	Proportion %
Slovak Unity	43.93
HSLS	26.93
Hungarian United	17.59
Carpatho-German	3.30
Czechoslovak Communist	7.40
Others	0.85
Total	100.00%

SOURCE: *Archiv Narodniho muzea v Praze, F. I. Derer, karton 11, i.j. 542* (Museum of National Archives in Prague, F. I. Derer, carton 11, i.j. 542).

Three days later, HSLS put forward a proposal as "the leaders' political testament."

In the meantime, the government was preparing a statute for nationalities and was also working on a new language law and administrative reform. All three new laws were supposed to represent a counterweight to the SdP's Karlsbad Program, as well as to the demands of HSLS for Slovak autonomy. The anticipated government proposal revived the idea of the Land Diet with certain lawmaking authority. The proposed laws were negotiated among legal experts, Premier Hodza and President Benes, the ministers of different political parties, the coalition of six, and opposition leaders of the Henlein, Hungarian Unity, and HSLS parties. This complex political process was suddenly interrupted on August 3, 1938, by the "intermediary" mission of Lord Walter Runciman of Great Britain, which so strengthened the negotiating position of Konrad Henlein that the leadership of the SdP categorically rejected the "nationality statute," thereby effectively voiding the government proposal (dated July 19, 1938). Instead of pursuing its reform program, the Czechoslovak government succumbed to the pressures and officially accepted Henlein's demands. On September 12, after an aborted attempt by Henlein to create a putsch, the negotiations with SdP ended for good.

Suddenly, the Sudete German issue had become an international problem. At the meetings between Adolf Hitler and Neville Chamberlain at Berchtesgarden and Bad Godesberg and after mutual consultations, the British and French appeasers decided to give in to Hitler's demand for the annexation of the German areas in the Czech border territory on the basis of self-determination. On September 22 the Hodza government resigned and the new government of General Jan Syrovy declared a general mobilization, confirming the determination of the people to defend the republic. But in this crisis the defense alliance built with France in the 1920s and the Soviet Union in the mid-1930s, to come to the aid of Czechoslovakia in the event of an outside attack, failed to materialize. (In fact, it took France and Great Britain almost one year to declare war on Nazi Germany, and Stalin, on August 20, first concluded a trade pact and two days later a nonaggression pact with Hitler.) On September 29, 1938, the German issue in Czechoslovakia was decided in Munich by representatives of Nazi Germany and Fascist Italy on one side and the appeasing governments of Great Britain and France on the other. General Syrovy's government accepted the dictate of the European major powers, recalled the mobilized military units, and gave up Sudetenland to Nazi Germany without a struggle.

After the collapse of the negotiations with the SdP, talks continued between Hodza and Benes (representing the government) and Tiso and Sokol (representing HSLS). In these negotiations Benes committed himself to approving a Slovak parliament with broad competence, a new language law, and the resolution of several personnel issues. Prague's priority at this time was to stabilize the Czech-German issue, but HSLS had lost confidence in the preservation of a state that was in such close proximity to Hitler's Germany. Pressured by its radical wing, HSLS no longer wanted to agree with the central government on any solution other than the one it had proposed on June 4 about Slovak autonomy—in reality a federation of the Czechoslovak state.

The events led to Hodza's resignation and replacement by General Syrovy. Three Slovaks were given ministerial posts in the new bureaucracy: Vojtech Fajnor as minister of justice and Matus Cernak and Imrich Karvas as ministers without portfolio. Prior to Hodza's resignation, the leaders of the HSLS had already decided to negotiate with no one but the president himself. In toto, Benes's proposal of September 22, 1938, was very forthcoming but, after the Munich Pact, only a pro forma exercise in futility.

The negotiations between the procentralist coalition (minus the Social Democrats) and the representatives of HSLS reached a climax when on October 6, 1938, at Zilina, Slovak autonomy was announced.[5] One day prior to this announcement, President Benes submitted his resignation and left the country to resume his political activities in exile. On October 6 the Syrovy government declared full autonomy for Slovakia and named Jozef Tiso premier.

Within the framework of the Munich Pact, on November 2, 1938, the Vienna Arbitration (Germany and Italy serving as arbiters) decided to return to Hungary the (Hungarian) minority-occupied territory of southern Slovakia and to Poland about half of Carpatho-Ruthenia as well as part of the Teschen area. As a result, Czechoslovakia lost 19,430 square kilometers (779 townships, including Kosice, to Hungary, seven townships to Poland, and Petrzalka and Devin to Germany) and 859,885 inhabitants.

Immediately after the declaration of Slovak autonomy, procentralist parties ceased to exist, including the antagonist Communist Party, which went underground. With the exception of the Social Democrats and, at first, the Slovak Nationalist Party, most political parties were absorbed by HSLS-*Strany slovenskej narodenj jednoty* (HSLS-Parties of Slovak National Unity) or its abbreviation, HSLS-SSNJ. On November 17, 1938, many of the representatives of the former political parties joined the HSLS-SSNJ club; on November 22 the government of autonomous Slovakia prohibited the functioning of the Social Democratic and Jewish Parties; and on November 25 the Slovak Nationalist Party was discontinued and one month later was absorbed by HSLS-SSNJ. Representatives of former political parties, connected with centralist politics of Czechoslovak governments (Hodza, Derer, Ivanka, and others), either left the country or dropped out of political circulation.

On November 19, 1938, the centralist parliament in Prague enacted constitutional law no. 299, regarding autonomy for the Slovak Land.[6] With this act in parliament, the original name of the state, Czecho-Slovak Republic, was officially signed and sealed. On the same day, the Czecho-Slovak parliament also approved autonomy for Ruthenia (or Carpatho-Russia), which was renamed Carpatho-Ukraine. Both laws were enacted without discussion. Only the communist deputies voted against the two measures. On December 18 elections into the first parliament of the Slovak Land were held. Only one list of candidates was available to the voters—members of the HSLS-SSNJ (sixteen out of seventy representatives elected belonged to other parties, including minority parties).

THE ROLE OF THE THIRD REICH IN SLOVAK NATIONAL DEVELOPMENT

Before the German-Czech crisis, under the code name Fall Grün (Green Case), Nazi Germany's goal was to annex Bohemia and Moravia and to give Slovakia to Hungary or Poland in return for their participation in a war against Czechoslovakia. However, Hungary's hesitation turned Hitler against the wavering position of Budapest, and he refused to give Hungary more territory than what was prescribed by the Vienna arbitration. After the conquest of Czechoslovakia, Hitler had plans to provoke a war against Poland and retake territories Germany lost in World War I. The annexation of Bohemia and Moravia to the German Reich was not a simple matter. Because the signers of the Munich agreement had guaranteed the integrity and security of the remainder of the Czechoslovak territory, any forceful annexation of Bohemia and Moravia into the German Reich—willingly or unwillingly—had to be interpreted by the Western Powers as a *casus belli*, if only to save public opinion in Great Britain and France. That is when Hitler began to see the value in Slovakia. According to Hitler's scenario, if the Slovaks declared state independence, then Czechoslovakia would cease to exist and the guarantees given at Munich would lose their validity under the principle of international law known as *rebus sic stantibus*. Under those conditions, Hitler calculated, it would be possible to occupy Bohemia and Moravia without a military conflict. Thus, for a few months Slovakia became the focal point of Hitler's European politics and the tool for achieving his original goal.

It is worth noting that during the trial of Jozef Tiso before the Slovak National Court (December 2, 1945–April 15, 1947), Tiso testified that he did not know that Hitler needed Slovakia for his political-military objectives and was unaware that the independent Slovak state supposedly contributed to Hitler's justification for destroying Czechoslovakia. If Tiso's declarations were truthful, it can be argued that HSLS representatives were poorly informed in foreign affairs because Tiso was one of the most knowledgeable politicians among them.

The Slovak followers of HSLS were supposed to have become an important conduit between Hitler's Nazi ideology and the Slovak people at large. Several leaders of HSLS had very close ties with the highest-ranking Nazi functionaries, who promised them support and "protection." The main broker between the Slovak politicians and the Nazis was the Olomouc-born leader of the Carpatho-German party, Franz Karmasin. Also influential in this respect was the Austrian Nazi leader Arthur Seyss-Inquart.[7]

In October 1938, General Hermann Göring received the deputy premier of the contemporary Slovak government, Ferdinand Durcansky, who sought state independence for Slovakia. Durcansky went to Berlin as a private citizen, without the knowledge of his government or the Slovak Land Diet. In the presence of Seyss-Inquart, Karmasin, and Alexander Mach, Durcansky declared that Slovakia wanted state independence and at the same time desired military, political, and economic aid from Germany. Durcansky and Mach willfully and voluntarily stated that it would be possible to declare state independence at the first session of the Slovak Land Diet because the majority of its members were in favor of an independent Slovak state, which of course was only a conjecture. Durcansky further promised that Germany would have great influence on the guidance of the Slovak state and that the German minority would have one minister (meaning, obviously, Karmasin). On February 12, 1939, Hitler, in the presence of Karmasin and the German foreign minister, Joachim von Ribbentrop, received Vojtech Tuka, who addressed Hitler as "mein Führer" and pretended to speak in the name of the Slovak nation, although he had no such authorization or mandate from anyone. Tuka told Hitler that "the Slovak nation will be glad to fight under the Führer's leadership for the preservation of European civilization."[8] Notes made of the reception made it clear that Tuka argued that Slovak coexistence with the Czechs had become impossible from both a moral and a political point of view. The Slovaks were part of the Czech state only because they were under the impression that the present government was a transitional one, but he and his colleagues were determined to submit to the call of the Slovak public and realize the independence of Slovakia. The fate of Slovakia depended on the Führer. Tuka, in his own words, stated, "I am placing the fate of my nation in your care." In short, some members of HSLS were willing and able to declare Slovak independence right then and there. Jozef Tiso and Karol Sidor, the most powerful authorities in the HSLS camp, hesitated.

The domestic political crisis in Czechoslovakia reached its climax in March 1939. During the March 4–6 meeting of the HSLS leadership group, the radical wing of the party was forced to accept a policy decision according to which the final goal of HSLS politics must be the creation of the independent Slovak state. Since this decision failed to mention the immediate declaration of an independent Slovakia, it can be surmised that the declarations by Tuka, Durcansky, and Mach in Berlin were not based on a mandate and therefore amounted to nothing more than arbitrary pronouncements by these radical members of HSLS.

In Berlin the Nazis began to show some nervousness when they learned that HSLS was dragging its feet. Hitler believed that he would be successful in annexing Bohemia and Moravia into his Reich within one year to the day of the Austrian *Anschluss*. Hence the D-day for Hitler was March 1939.

Relations between Slovakia and Prague in post-Munich Czechoslovakia were still quite strained, not so much because of a well-defined competition but rather because of the internal politics of the two nations and, of course, the European crisis in general. Hitler took advantage of this situation and saw to it that in Prague the Czech politicians had "enough information" about the Slovaks' goal of independence. As expected, the Prague government reacted to these rumors with military force. On March 10, 1939, the Prague government deposed Jozef Tiso as premier of Slovakia for allegedly working in the direction of separation, with the support of the Fascist Hlinka Guards. Tiso appealed to Hitler. In Slovakia martial law was followed by military dictatorship. The Czechoslovak army arrested hundreds of people. Then on March 11 Karol Sidor was named the new premier of the Slovak government. Tiso left for his parish at Banovce and Bebravou. Military action by Prague had played out exactly the way Hitler envisioned it and thus it fulfilled his expectations for victory.

Tension in Slovakia continued to swell. Several leaders of HSLS, especially the radicals, escaped into neighboring Austria. The Hlinka Guard and armed units of the German minority, *Freiwillige Schützstaffel*, were preparing for confrontation with the Czechoslovak army. During this turmoil Berlin sent its negotiators to convince Tiso and Sidor that the time had come to declare Slovak state independence.

MARCH 14, 1939— ESTABLISHMENT OF THE SLOVAK REPUBLIC

Since the deposed premier of the Slovak Land, Jozef Tiso, and the newly appointed premier, Karol Sidor, failed to satisfy Berlin's wishes concerning the immediate declaration of state independence, Hitler took a drastic step and invited Tiso to Berlin. Here Hitler bluntly informed Tiso that if Slovakia did not declare its independence, he would "leave Slovakia to its fate," which Tiso interpreted to mean either annexation to Hungary or dividing Slovakia among the three neighbors—Germany, Poland, and Hungary. The visit was well orchestrated to achieve Hitler's goal. Tiso met first with von Ribbentrop, and then, after he had been sufficiently persuaded, he was given an audience with Hitler, who reiterated von Ribbentrop's promises. Tiso gained only one concession: From Berlin he asked President Emil Hacha to convene the Slovak Diet on March 14, 1939.

During the parliamentary session, Tiso informed the representatives about his discussions with von Ribbentrop and Hitler. The Slovak Diet,

Mach noted in his memoirs, received the news with no surprise but in a somewhat gloomy atmosphere.[9] Representative Peter Zatko described the situation as follows:

> A large segment of representatives I did not know, nor did I know the thinking of a great majority in the Slovak Diet, I was surprised [to see] how many of them, after Tiso's report, were puzzled, hopeless, how many of them were asking themselves the question: what to do, how to answer. I did not have the impression that it is a gathering which welcomed Hitler's announcement. The president of the Diet, Martin Sokol, appeared to be a supporter of CSR [the Czechoslovak Republic] because he told me: I will have to declare such an independence. I will be glad if by doing so I don't drop off.[10]

Representative Pavol Carnogursky's recollections of the time are similar.[11] From this subdued reaction, Slovaks developed a theory that the Slovak state was actually one of the "lesser evils"—the worst evil being the inclusion of all of Slovakia into Hungary.

The president of the Slovak Land Diet prepared the law for the Slovak state. The first paragraph stated: "The Slovak Land is hereby declared to be an independent and sovereign Slovak state. The Diet of the Slovak Land is hereby transformed into a lawmaking legislature of the Slovak state."[12] The Slovak Land Diet enacted the law and then named the new government with Jozef Tiso at its head. With this final act, on March 14, 1939, the Slovak Republic was officially established as the new sovereign entity of Slovakia.[13]

Hitler first summoned President Hacha and Foreign Minister Chvalkovsky to Berlin and convinced them to place the fate of the Czech people in his hands. Then on March 15 he transformed Bohemia and Moravia into a German protectorate, which was promptly occupied by German forces—the Czechs offering no resistance. The following day, Tiso put Slovakia under German protection but without military occupation. After twenty years of existence, Czechoslovakia was erased from the map of Europe.

Hitler had achieved his plan, and he used the declaration of the Slovak Republic on March 14, 1939, as an excuse to assert himself in the destablilized central European region. Before 1939, problems affecting Czecho-Slovak relations, though serious, were not pushing the Slovaks toward an independent state; HSLS advocated a policy of autonomy, not independence. The idea of an independent sovereign Slovak state was conceptualized only after the Czechoslovak Republic, under pressure from Adolf Hitler, began to disintegrate. Even then, at the beginning of 1939, only a few young radical members of the Hlinka party advocated complete independence.

6 Slovakia During World War II (1939–1945)

Slovakia entered the era of sovereign statehood with resignation, not exultation. The majority of the population, who perceived Nazi Germany as the aggressor and the main instigator of the European crisis, did not believe that under Hitler's protection they could live as they liked—or could, indeed, preserve their newly won sovereignty. When the German army moved into Moravia, on March 15, 1939, it did not stop at the Slovak border; on the same day, it crossed over into Slovakia and occupied the territory all the way to the Vah River. After difficult negotiations, the Slovak government finally succeeded in saving the western borders of the state, for the price of a German military zone along the Moravian-Slovak border. Another problem developed in Slovak-Hungarian relations. In accordance with the Vienna Arbitration of November 1938, Slovakia had lost its southern territory to Hungary. Then on March 15, 1939, in a simultaneous action with Germany's move into Moravia, Hungary occupied Carpatho-Ukraine (Ruthenia) and annexed it after heavy fighting with the inhabitants, who had driven out the Czechs and, under Augustin Voloshin, had enjoyed independence for one day. During the occupation of Carpatho-Ukrainian territory, Hungarian troops crossed over into Slovakia. A military conflict

---

The sections "Slovak Collaboration with Nazi Germany" and "The Holocaust of the Slovak Jews" are based on the Slovak text by Dusan Kovac.

ensued, which resulted in a loss of Slovak territory with about 40,000 inhabitants in the east near the Carpatho-Ukrainian border.

On this considerably diminished territory, the Slovak Republic—one of the smallest countries in Europe—was recognized both de facto and de jure by twenty-seven states, including all the major powers except the United States.[1] In Bratislava some states had embassies, others only consulates, but the Slovak Republic's international position soon lost its luster.[2] In response to Slovak participation in the war against Poland (September 1939) on the side of Nazi Germany, Great Britain and France withdrew their diplomatic representatives.[3] Because of the German-Soviet nonagression pact, Slovakia had relatively friendly relations with the Soviet Union, especially in the economic and cultural realm,[4] but after the Nazi attack on the USSR on June 22, 1941, the Slovak Republic was internationally isolated, and its foreign relations dwindled to states under the control of or influenced by Hitler's Germany and a few neutral countries.

SLOVAK COLLABORATION WITH NAZI GERMANY

The formal sovereignty of the Slovak state was for all practical purposes only a façade. In reality everything that happened in the Slovak Republic was under the strict control of Nazi Germany. Immediately after the March 16 decision placing Slovakia under German protection, the Slovak Republic had to sign with Nazi Germany a "defense treaty" (March 23, 1939), according to which Germany committed itself to uphold the integrity of the Slovak territory in exchange for the subordination of Slovak military and foreign policy to German interests. Through this agreement, Germany also acquired a decisive role in the Slovak economy.[5]

Collaboration with Hitler's Germany was no doubt, in the Slovak political leaders' minds, the lesser of two evils, the greater evil being occupation and the carving up of Slovakia among Germany, Hungary, and Poland. From a long-term point of view, however, the policy of collaboration was futile. In his ideological statements, Hitler made no secret of his contempt for the Slavic nations. While the war was going on, however, he needed peace in the hinterland. He knew that Slovakia's fictitious sovereignty, administered by indigenous quislings, would guarantee him such peace. Therefore, he used Slovakia to demonstrate how a nation could live and prosper under protection of the Reich—looking ahead to military victory, which would of course end Slovak sovereignty. For the Slovaks a military defeat would mean that the Slovak collaboration with Hitler was equally futile.

Nonetheless, the leaders of HSLS, however gloomily they had arrived at independence, were not satisfied with a simple rationalization that the existence of the Slovak state must be perceived only as a choice of one of the "lesser evils." They attempted to create a new state ideology based on the glorious idea that the Slovak Republic was the culmination of a "one thousand-year-old struggle among the Slovaks to achieve their own statehood," and they began to mass-produce historical myths reaching back in history to Prince Pribina and Svatopluk, whom they called the first Slovak king. But the fabrication of such a false national ideology could not cover one serious weakness—the fact of collaboration with Hitler. Most citizens of Slovakia considered national socialism and Hitler a social evil, yet they were being told by their highest-ranking Slovak representatives that Hitler and the German Reich were the Slovaks' best friends and defenders. Many Slovaks did not accept this propaganda, and the notion that collaboration was the lesser evil proved an uncomfortable position that had consequences at the end of the war.

Serious problems soon developed in Slovakia's domestic politics. The Slovak Republic was a state with an unambiguous totalitarian political system. For the Slovak people, who for nearly two decades had experienced democratic development, the new state was, in terms of human rights, definitely a step backward. During the state's entire existence, Slovak citizens had no opportunity to express their political preferences at the ballot box. Although the Slovak Constitution stated that the parliament must be elected every five years, it never occurred to the ruling HSLS to legitimize this constitutional stipulation with the parliamentary elections in the independent state; the body elected in 1938 as the Slovak Land Diet continued to function as the parliament of the sovereign Slovak state. When the Slovak state was created, the Land Diet authorized the government "in the transition period" to do everything it deemed necessary to maintain law and order and to secure the interests of the state. This "transition period" lasted from 1938 until 1945. In 1943, the parliament's mandate was extended until the year 1946. Elections had no meaning anyway: Slovakia developed a one-party system, monopolized by the HSLS. Outside HSLS, the only legal parties that had legitimacy were those of the German and Hungarian minorities. The Deutsche Partei (German Party), which relied on Germany's protection, had extraordinary privileges and made every effort to interfere in Slovakia's internal politics. According to the Slovak Constitution, Hlinka's Slovak People's Party was the state party, and it occupied and controlled all the significant institutions and organizations. Nothing could take place in the state without its knowledge. Since without membership in HSLS it was difficult to fathom any sort of government career, all state employees tried hard to become members of the party. HSLS membership swelled from 50,000 in 1938 to 300,000 in 1943.

Tiso and his cohorts had no choice but to abandon the original ideological concept of HSLS as a nationalistic state based on a class differentiation—clearly, such a concept was in basic disagreement with the national socialist system. But though the radical wing of HSLS, headed by Vojtech Tuka and Alexander Mach, strived to impose the concept of Slovak national socialism along the Nazi German model, they were never quite successful because Hitler lost interest in pursuing that goal. Socialism had less impact on domestic policy than on foreign policy. Thus the Slovak Republic political system, though totalitarian in principle, was perhaps less oppressive and less regimented than its counterpart in Nazi Germany.

The people of Slovakia soon learned that their independence and sovereignty were only an illusion. Germany interfered in all its affairs, especially the makeup of the Slovak government. All important posts were assigned to people approved by Berlin. Shortly after the establishment of the Slovak Republic, for example, Karol Sidor—next to Tiso the most important personality in HSLS and Hlinka's first choice as a successor—had to accept political retirement as punishment for his stubborn refusal to declare Slovak state independence. Furthermore, Sidor was an outspoken Polandophile and hardly acceptable as Hitler prepared to attack Poland from Slovakia. Sidor was moved to a less important post as Slovak ambassador to the Vatican.

Increasingly, Tiso's government was hardly more than a puppet government. Although in the first phase of the war the foreign minister, Ferdinand Durcansky, worked to set Slovakia free of German dependence, in July 1940 Hitler sent for Tiso to "persuade" him to make certain personnel changes in his government—namely, to get rid of Durcansky and replace him with Vojtech Tuka, the radical national socialist. This was followed by sending Nazi "advisers" to Bratislava to occupy key positions in all the Slovak ministries and public offices and make certain that Slovakia would not be inclined to stray. Shortly thereafter, the Slovak Republic entered into a pact against the Comintern and thus became a member of the Berlin-Rome-Tokyo axis.[6]

Between 1939 and 1945, to the extent that Slovakia still had a political life, the two major factions of HSLS vied for power. The ideology of Jozef Tiso and his moderate wing was based on conservative ideas of state empires and authoritative states with certain Christian characteristics.[7] Tuka and Mach, at the head of the other faction of radical Fascists, openly advocated German national socialism and endeavored to make Slovakia its "great model." Tuka's argument was that Slovakia could demand protection from Germany only by proving itself worthy of such protection. In January 1941, on Tuka's initiative, the fourteen points of Slovak national socialism were published and disseminated in the country. Behind the struggle for power between the two wings of HSLS, there were several clashes among politicos with high personal ambitions. Tiso and his group had certain support in the parliament as well as among the people at large. The radical group was completely isolated, supported mainly by the paramilitary units of the Hlinka Guard under the command of Alexander Mach, and even they were not absolutely dependable in a struggle against Tiso.[8] Both groups counted on Hitler's support, and the radical wing, which Hitler undoubtedly favored, was assigned key positions in the government. But Hitler's main goal in Slovakia was to maintain peace so that he would not have to deploy any of his troops there. Hitler was satisfied with the easily persuaded Tiso and his group at the helm of the state, and he never endorsed Tuka and Mach's plan to remove Tiso at an opportune time with the assistance of the Nazi German leader in Slovakia, Franz Karmasin. Tiso remained in power until the end of the war, but he had to make several concessions to Hitler in order to save his position. In the end, it was only Nazi Germany that had something to gain from this struggle, a fact Hitler knew from the very beginning.

By disregarding the collaboration aspect with Nazi Germany as well as the undemocratic attributes of the regime, it is possible to argue that in a large portion of the Slovak society, Slovak statehood found a positive response. It was evident that in many respects the conditions in the Slovak state, at least during the first few years of its existence, were more favorable than those in the surrounding states, including Nazi Germany. Slovakia had a high rate of employment, in part because of war-stimulated industrial expansion and the opportunity for many Slovaks to work in Germany for higher wages. Every year about 40,000 Slovak citizens left to work in Germany. For Slovaks who were not of draft age and those who did not mind the presence of German soldiers, German advisers (*Beraters*), and the fact of collaboration, life in their "micro-world" was quite satisfactory. Many Slovaks who before 1939 were ineligible for jobs in the state bureaucracy, schools, science, armed services, and so on now had an opportunity for speedy advancement. Although the state administration was under undiscernable Nazi German control, it was in Slovak hands. Eligibility of many Slovaks was also made possible through the expulsion, shortly after March 1939, of almost 20,000 Czech state employees who had come to Slovakia after 1918. Even greater opportunities for Slovak job eligibility were created through the exclusion of the Jewish population from the Slovak economy.

For a time Slovakia enjoyed the results of a war-booming economy. To satisfy demand, several new enterprises were created, and older ones expanded their production. A new infrastructure was built with a network of new roads and rail lines, which created new jobs for many Slovaks. The economy did, on the whole, improve the standard of living, though in some areas the economy was stagnant, and starvation existed in some regions. Worst off were people in the mining regions. The biggest strike in Slovakia during the entire war period was in Handlova in October 1940, where both Slovak and minority German miners walked out, much to the embarrassment of the leaders of the Deutsche Partei, who always maintained that they had "their people" under control. Not all members of the German minority, it seemed, were sympathetic to the Nazis.

In spite of the loss of a large portion of the most fertile land to Hungary, the sale of agricultural products had increased both in volume and in prices that favored the producer. Under such conditions basic commodities were plentiful, and the Slovak currency was stable and highly valued. Cultural development, too, flourished. Construction was completed at the University of Bratislava and the Technical University, and a new University of Economics was created in the same city. In 1942, the Slovak Academy of Arts and Sciences was established. A new generation of Slovak artists and scientists, well prepared under the

Czechoslovak system of education, added new impetus to the advancement of sciences and art in Slovakia. All this was fully exploited by the leaders of HSLS, who portrayed the Slovak Republic as an island of peace and prosperity. Yet all this praise could not alter the truth, especially the fact that Slovakia was becoming further subordinated to Nazi Germany.

The Slovak army joined Germany in war operations. For its part in the invasion of Poland, Slovakia regained the territory occupied by Poland shortly after the Munich dictate and also, as a bonus, several townships that had been added to Poland after 1918. After the Nazi attack on the Soviet Union in June 1941, the Slovak Republic almost immediately declared war on the USSR and sent two divisions to assist the German army. In 1942, the rapidly deployed Slovak military fought its way to the Caucasus. The puppet regime in Bratislava glorified Slovak participation in the war, but in reality, the fighting morale of the Slovak soldier was not very high. To some extent it resembled the morale of Slovak soldiers in World War I, when there were desertions to the side of the Soviet Red Army. By early 1944, the rapid division ceased to be campaign-ready and withdrew into Transylvania. The second, so-called security division was later moved to Italy as an auxiliary building unit.

The war permeated not only the Slovak economy but the daily life of every citizen. Slovakia produced weapons in munitions factories at Dubnica and Povazska Bystrica. As the main consumer, Nazi Germany determined what would and what would not be produced, but as the war went on Germany gradually lost the capability and willingness to pay for its purchases. Not only did the German debt slow the Slovak economy, but Slovak industry was increasingly exploited by German firms, which became involved both in production and in capital investment. One firm, Herman Göring Werke, besides controlling large industrial enterprises, especially munitions plants, acquired large sections of forest land all over Slovakia.

As early as 1943, the Slovak economy began to show certain signs of a looming crisis, inevitably affecting also the standard of living. Suddenly there were problems with basic supplies, corruption was on an increase, and the black market began to flourish, with unusually high prices. Only the more affluent could afford to buy certain goods such as clothing, shoes, and coffee. In proportion to the increase in economic difficulties, discontent among the population also increased. The "showcase window" suddenly lost its luster. The fact that the situation was even worse in the neighboring countries, including Nazi Germany, did not ameliorate conditions in Slovakia.

THE HOLOCAUST OF THE SLOVAK JEWS

The origin of the Jews in Slovakia dates back to the time when the Habsburgs ascended to the Hungarian throne in 1437. With the arrival of German colonists into central Slovakia and the development of mining industries, interregional commerce and finance flourished in the region. Jews who migrated into the area from the surrounding regions were instrumental in enriching the nobility as a result of their commercial skills, for which they were rewarded the same civil rights as the other citizens in the kingdom. Although during the Counter-Reformation period Jews retained freedom of worship, they lost some of the civil rights, which were later restored under Leopold II's aristocratic nationalism. In consequence, the aspiration of many Jews in the Hungarian kingdom was to serve the magnates and gentry in their feudal setting. Since to earn one's living by manual labor was against true feudal customs, many Jews became highly educated and thus represented a large segment of the Hungarian intelligentsia and bourgeoisie.

After World War I, in Slovakia, as in Hungary, many Jews still kept the stigma of an "outcast race," derived from the Middle Ages. However, what might have been the situation centuries ago certainly was not the case during the time of the Czechoslovak Republic. Until the dismemberment of the republic in 1939, Jews on Slovak territory, whether they spoke Slovak, Hungarian, German, or Yiddish, were loyal supporters of the country's democracy and its national integrity. Many of their sons and daughters distinguished themselves in contributing to the progress and well-being of Slovak society in every sphere of endeavor. While many Jews born and educated before the Great War were adhering to traditional religious practices, practically all young Jews were linguistically assimilated to Slovak and had a liberal attitude toward religion. Nonetheless, in spite of their loyalty and the numerous contributions made by Jews in Slovakia, as early as January 23, 1939, the leaders of Hlinka's Slovak People's Party were determined to nullify those achievements by fiat.

Slovak totalitarian dictatorship was most revealing in the actions of the regime toward the small (less than 2 percent) Jewish population.[9] Anti-Semitism in Slovakia was, from the very outset, a part of HSLS ideology. Anti-Semitic measures were introduced in Slovakia under the autonomous Slovak government, but when Slovakia became a satellite of Nazi Germany, pressures from Berlin were exerted with the request to "solve" the Jewish issue in Slovakia according to the Nazi model. Although the pressure was clearly there, the Holocaust of Slovak Jews cannot be attributed solely to Nazi German influence. Many of the anti-Semitic attacks in Slovakia by Alexander Mach and President Jozef Tiso were no different from the anti-Semitic actions carried out by the National Socialists in Germany. The Slovak Jews gradually found themselves outside the protective laws afforded to citizens in civilized societies.[10]

Anti-Jewish measures commenced as if preplanned with the establishment of the Slovak Republic on March 14, 1939. Jews were restricted from holding certain jobs. They were expelled from state employment and prohibited from functioning as teachers, officers of the armed services, and so on. Next came the seizure of properties. The Jews lost ownership of industrial enterprises, businesses, and their personal property. This process was ideologically referred to as *arizacia* (Aryanizing), which meant that all properties held by the Jews had to be transferred into the hands of Caucasians of non-Jewish descent. It was an ideal opportunity for many members of HSLS—especially its functionaries—and the members of the Hlinka Guard to satisfy their parasitic appetite by becoming the number one Aryanizers. Since the Nazi German minority also wanted a share of the booty, the competition for it prompted Franz Karmasin to lodge an official complaint that his followers were deprived the privileged position of becoming Aryanizers.

Governmental decrees of the Slovak puppet regime also prevented Jews from performing the so-called free professional services in which the Jewish share was relatively high, especially among doctors and lawyers. At the same time drastic measures were introduced to prohibit the Jewish population from acquiring a higher education. Only the basic schools in isolation from the Aryans were available to Jewish students.

What followed next, as in Warsaw, was complete isolation of the Jewish population. Non-Jews were prohibited from contact with Jews and vice versa; Jews were not allowed to visit public places like movie houses, theaters, coffee houses, and swimming pools, nor could they travel freely. Many Slovak city parks and town squares posted signs that read: "Entrance for Jews, Gypsies, and dogs is forbidden!" As in Germany and elsewhere, Jews were forced to wear on their clothes an embroidered Star of David. Everything moved toward complete isolation of the Jewish population—the ghettos multiplied, and work camps prepared for them.

On September 9, 1941, the Slovak government enacted a set of anti-Semitic laws, the so-called *Codex Judaicus* or Jewish Code, which was prepared on the basis of the Nazi Nuremberg Laws. Some members of HSLS first attempted to place the anti-Semitic laws on a confessional (social) basis, but without success, and the Slovak anti-Semitic laws became racial in substance. Against such a conceptualization, objections were also heard from the Vatican. For example, Cardinal Maglione sent to Karol Sidor, the Slovak ambassador in the Vatican, a note in which he pointed out: "The Holy See received the news with great disappointment that also in Slovakia, namely in a country where almost the entire population professes to follow the best Catholic tradition, on September 9, this year, the publicized 'governmental edict' established a 'racial legislation' containing different provisions openly contradicting Catholic principles."[11] The Vatican protested not only against the racial legislation but also the fact that many of the Jews subjected to those laws were Catholic converts: "Neither can the Holy See remain indifferent to the painful situation of so many of its sons of Jewish origin who suffer as a result of these and other exploiting measures of the cited order. They are deprived of many rights, isolated from the rest of the citizens, and in contrast to these citizens will find themselves in an unequal moral, social, and economic position so that many of them will be forced to take a heroic stance in order to remain loyal members of the Church—and it is possible that many of them will also be in peril."[12] In characteristic fashion the Slovak government completely ignored this note of complaint from the Vatican.

The culminating measure of the Slovak anti-Semitic policy was the deportation of Slovak Jews to Nazi death camps. According to authoritative sources and studies by Ivan Kamenec, about 57,000 Slovak Jews perished; about 30,000 Jews survived the tragedy of genocide.[13] In order to legitimize the actions of the puppet Slovak regime, on May 15, 1942, the Slovak parliament enacted a law that sanctioned the deportation of Jews (post facto), revoking their citizenship and confiscating their property. Only two categories of Jews were exempt from this law: those who before 1939 became members of Christian religions and those who before September 1941 married a non-Jewish partner. Such marriages were later forbidden. Jews who received a pardon from President Tiso were also saved. According to Frantisek Kuruc, none of the priests who were members of the parliament voted against this measure.

Willingly or not, the Slovak government accepted Berlin's offer to deport the Jews from Slovakia and make them "work in the eastern territories." The forced deportation of about 60,000 Jews from Slovakia to starvation camps took place between March and October 1942. For every deported Jew, the Slovak government had to pay Germany 500 marks to cover "settlement costs." The Vatican continued to lodge protests. On March 14, 1942, the state secretary of the Vatican, Msgr. Tardini, dispatched a note to Ambassador Sidor in which he stated: "According to the news received by the State Secretariat, all members of the Jewish race, regardless of religion, age, or sex, are in immediate danger of being expelled from the Slovak Republic. These individuals (about 80,000) are supposed to be deported—separately men, women and children—to Halic and the outskirts of Lublin. The State Secretariat would like to believe that this news is unfounded because it does not consider it possible that in a country that desires to be guided by Catholic principles such regrettable measures with such grave results for many families could be taking place."[14]

The Vatican repeated its protests against racial laws and deportation.[15] The Holy See found it extremely troublesome that something like this was taking place in a country headed by a Catholic priest. Cardinal Maglione addressed this issue in an open letter sent to the Vatican chargé d'affaires in Bratislava, Msgr. J. Burzio: "The Holy See received the sad news about the measures of the Slovak government against the non-Aryans with deep regret. It is even more grave that this law, according to your report, was enacted in the presence of several priests who are members of the parliament."[16] In the margin of the response to the British government, which had also lodged a protest, Vatican State Secretary Msgr. Tardini, added: "It is a tragedy that the president of Slovakia is a priest. Everybody knows that the Holy See cannot stop Hitler, but who will understand that it cannot bridle him?"[17]

The Vatican found Tiso's anti-Semitic speeches very disturbing, especially because he tried to defend these inhumane acts with religious arguments. In one of Tiso's declarations, he made reference to God's commandment that people are supposed to love themselves. According to Tiso, this selfishness dictates that people must get rid of everything harmful to them. The Slovaks were harmed by the Jews, he said, and therefore following God's commandment, they must get rid of the Jews. This kind of speedy demagoguery was too much for the Vatican, and it continually reminded Tiso's puppet government that God's main commandment is to *love thy neighbor.*

Soon it became public knowledge that the Jews were being deported not to work camps but to starvation camps. And in October 1942, following a decision of the Reich Security Office, the deportation transports came to a halt; but it was too late. Almost 45,000 Jews from Slovakia had already become victims of the Holocaust. Additional deportation by Nazi Germany from Slovakia occurred in the autumn of 1944. At that time, another 13,000 Jews were deported to death camps and many Jews were killed by SS units during the anti-uprising terror in 1944.

The Jewish Holocaust in Slovakia is one of the most tragic chapters in Slovak history, and the responsibility for it lies directly with the Slovak puppet government. Many members of the Hlinka Guard took an active part in this inhumane and criminal act, and numerous Slovaks enriched themselves during the "Aryanizing" process of Jewish property. With the exception of the extreme fanatics organized in the behemoth of the totalitarian dictatorship, more enlightened Slovak citizens received the anti-Jewish measures with embarrassment and resistance. When news about the mass murder of Jews from Slovakia in Nazi concentration camps became known, the authority of the Slovak government diminished in the eyes of some, and a polarization of society set in. By early 1944, Slovak society was clearly divided into those who supported and those who opposed the Slovak puppet regime of Nazi Germany; and the latter group was growing in numbers and determination.

UNDERGROUND RESISTANCE AND THE SLOVAK NATIONAL UPRISING

The first organized resistance against the HSLS-installed regime was started by the communists shortly after Nazi Germany launched its attack on the Soviet Union in June 1941. Until then many former members of the outlawed Communist Party had either joined the

HSLS or had become Nazi sympathizers after the signing of the Nazi-Soviet Pact in 1939. After June 1941, however, Slovak communists changed their loyalty again and spearheaded project "Soviet Slovakia," which sought the annexation of Slovakia to the Soviet Union.

Another group engaged in organized resistance against the Slovak puppet state came from groups headed by former politicians who represented parties absorbed by HSLS after the establishment of the Slovak Republic. This group was known as the Citizens Bloc. All participants in this bloc, including Social Democrats, were noncommunists, many of them Evangelical (Lutheran) church leaders who were dissatisfied with the political clericalism and the privileged position of the Catholic Church in the pro-Nazi Slovak state. The Citizens Bloc also included groups that sought the renewal of Czecho-Slovakia, though perhaps in a different form from the pre-Munich system, and it leaned toward collaboration with the Czechoslovak government in exile (London).

The Slovak government, assisted by a huge police network, monitored all suspicious characters and movements. As early as June 1939, for example, the secret service discovered a resistance organization known as the Revolutionary Youth of Slovakia, which consisted primarily of young students and some workers. Most of the leading functionaries of the former political parties, especially the illegal Communist Party, were gradually imprisoned; others opposing HSLS were placed under surveillance. During the early years of the war there were no favorable conditions in Slovak society to enable expansion of the resistance.[18] The thrust of the resistance lay mostly abroad.

Slovak refugees in Poland created a military unit that later formed a large segment of the Czechoslovak army corps, which eventually fought under General Ludvik Svoboda on the side of the Soviet Red Army. Slovaks also fought in defense of France. Slovak General Rudolf Viest (1890–1945) was commander of the First Czechoslovak Division in France. Slovaks fought as members of the Royal British Air Force. A Slovak by the name of Jozef Gabcik (1912–1942) was a member of the assassination team flown in from Britain in May 1942 that killed Reinhard Heydrich, head of the Reich Security Office in Prague.[19] The Slovaks fought also in partisan (guerrilla) units in the Ukraine, Belaruss, Italy, and France. The total number of Slovaks who fought against Hitler's coalition was almost as large as the number of mobilized Slovak soldiers who fought on the side of Nazi Germany.

The active military resistance also had a political organization under the leadership of the former president of Czechoslovakia, Eduard Benes, who along with Milan Hodza, Stefan Osusky, and other political exiles in London attempted to set up a government in exile similar to the one organized in London by T. G. Masaryk during World War I. Benes was instrumental in gaining recognition for this government from the states engaged in war with Hitler. Although both Hodza and Osusky were committed to renewal of the Czecho-Slovak Republic, they differed with Benes on the form such a renewal would take.[20] Benes wanted Czechoslovakia to be renewed in its pre-Munich form, as a unitary state. Hodza and Osusky demanded a greater right to self-rule, or, as they outlined in a memorandum they prepared in collaboration with Vladimir Clementis (1902–1952), a Slovak communist in London, a federated government. Serious dispute and discord followed. Hodza briefly held a position in Benes's exile government, but both he and Osusky soon parted company with Benes. Hodza devoted the next several months to his study, which he published in 1942 in London under the title *Federation in Central Europe*. It was Hodza's political epitaph; shortly after that he emigrated to the United States where he died in 1944. After the fall of Paris in 1940, Stefan Osusky, as Czechoslovak ambassador, lost his pouvoir and support in London.

The events of the war supported Benes's personal ambitions. After Winston Churchill was named prime minister, Benes's last political barrier was removed, because this meant the end of Neville Chamberlain's Munich politics. Under Churchill, the British government officially recognized Benes's government in exile, and after June 1941, so did the Soviets. With Benes's rising political credibility abroad, his conceptualization of a unitary Czechoslovak state was for all practical purposes unchallenged.

Three main events contributed to making the resistance in Slovakia operational: (1) Slovakia's entrance into war against the USSR, which met with resistance among the Slovaks, (2) the brutal anti-Jewish measures of the Slovak government, and (3) the reversal of the tide of war after the battle of Stalingrad. Concomitant with that was Benes's growing reputation. As news of Benes's government in exile reached Slovakia, the leaders of the domestic resistance accepted the basic concept of an anti-Hitler coalition, which also meant the renewal of Czecho-Slovakia. The communists, in the meantime, gave up plans for a Soviet Slovakia after Moscow recognized Benes's provisional government. Most of those who joined the resistance movement did not accept Benes's plans for a renewal of centralism and unitarism; however, they demanded for Slovakia a broad system of self-rule based on the principle that Slovak vernacular signified *rovny s rovnym* (equal with equal).

At the end of 1943, the representatives of the Citizens Bloc and the communists signed what was then known as the Christmas Agreement, and together they formed a central organ for the resistance called *Slovenska narodna rada* (SNR, Slovak National Council, SNC).[21] The Citizens Bloc was represented in SNR by Jozef Lettrich (1905–1968), Jan Ursiny (1896–1972), and Matej Josko (1907–1969); the communists were Karol Smidke (1897–1952), Gustav Husak (1913–1991), and Ladislav Novomesky.[22] Later on, the SNR acquired new members.[23] The most important point of the Christmas Agreement was the preparation of the armed uprising and the overthrow of HSLS dictatorship.

In 1944, the development of the war in relation to Slovakia clearly pointed toward two alternatives: (1) the Soviet Red Army might reach the Carpathian passes and enter Slovakia and the Danube basin before German troops could occupy the area; or (2) the German army, not trusting the Slovak military units (two divisions, under German command), might invade Slovakia in order to occupy vital communications and to fortify and defend the Carpathian passes. After a thorough examination of all possibilities and circumstances, the military leaders and members of SNR decided that whichever of these two eventualities should occur, the underground Czecho-Slovak army and the entire population would begin a general armed insurrection with the aim of driving the Nazis from Czecho-Slovakia.

The military and political plans of the leaders of the underground (including the communists) were submitted to the Czechoslovak government in exile, with whom the military and political leaders were always in contact, and through London to the Allied Command. On August 4, 1944, in order to establish direct contact with the Soviet High Command, Lt. Col. Mikulas Ferjencik and Karol Smidke were flown to the Soviet side of the front with detailed plans for the uprising. Beginning in early July, attempts had been made by SNR to send their emissaries to meet with the representative of the Soviet government, General Georgi K. Zhukov, at Vinica, but because of behind-the-scene intrigues plotted by the communist leader, Gustav Husak, and Capt. Jan Stanek, head of the intelligence division of the Ministry of National Defense in Bratislava, against the noncommunist members of SNR, the originally scheduled flight to meet with General Zhukov never materialized. In Moscow, instead of receiving assistance and cooperation, the two emissaries were confined in isolation.

President Benes, General Sergej Ingr, and others in the exile government in London suspected a possible attempt by General Ferdinand Catlos, Slovakia's minister of national defense, to negotiate a truce with the Soviet High Command and without Tiso's knowledge.[24] On August 9, based on the information received from the commander of the Slovak underground military headquarters (SVV), Lt. Col. Jan Golian, about Catlos's plan to send his own airplane with personal emissaries to establish contact with the Red Army, instructions from Benes regarding "emissaries from Slovakia" were sent to Brig. Gen. Heliodor Pika, head of the Czechoslovak military mission in the USSR. According to these instructions, "all delegates from Slovakia must accept the political and military command of the government in exile and any attempt to negotiate either by Catlos or others from the quisling circles of the Slovak government must be rejected."[25] From the point of view of the government in London, the so-called Catlos plan was doomed to failure. General Pika communicated the gist of the note to the Soviet High Command, but received no response. On August 18, in anticipation that his offer to the Soviet High Command for "joint maneuvers" in the Carpathian passes would be accepted, General Catlos asked the German Military High Command to return the two Slovak divisions stationed in Romania and Italy immediately to Slovakia to secure the rail transportation network between Mincola and the High Tatras. The Germans denied the request (August 26): the two Slovak divisions would remain where they were, and when the front moved closer, the passes at Lupkov and Dukla would be defended by German units. As to the future disposition of the Slovak units under General August Malar, that would be decided by the command of Northern Ukraine.[26]

Meanwhile, preparations in Slovakia were begun with speed and efficiency. Some members of the Slovak insurrection movement held very important posts in the Slovak Ministry of National Defense and were therefore able to fulfill orders given by SNR.[27] While the underground Czecho-Slovak army was making preparations, a great concentration of guerrilla forces was assembling under Soviet command in the eastern, central, and northern parts of Slovakia. From the end of July to September, twenty-four partisan groups with 404 men were flown into Slovakia from the Ukraine under the auspices of the Soviet Central Command of the partisan movement.[28] Since these guerrilla units were better known to the Slovak communist leaders than to the noncommunist members of SNR or the underground Slovak military command in Banska Bystrica, their operations were coordinated in Kiev and not in London. As early as August 13, without informing SNR or SVV, guerrilla units commanded by Soviet officers started blowing up road and railway bridges, blocking tunnels, raiding military objectives, attacking police organs, and threatening adherents of the Tiso regime.

The noncommunists in SNR viewed all this with grave anxiety because these guerrilla actions threatened the strategy for a well-planned military and national uprising. Perhaps the gravest consequence of the hasty guerrilla actions was the loss of the two battle-worthy Slovak divisions, which on August 3 were placed under the German command of Northern Ukraine and were held accountable for the lack of security in the Saris-Zemplin war zone.[29] These two Slovak divisions (numbering about 38,000 soldiers) played a key role in the military planning developed by SVV and approved by SNR and London to enable a swift penetration of the Red Army through the Carpathian passes into Slovakia and the Danube basin. These plans failed to materialize because two days after the official outbreak of the armed uprising, August 29, the German troops began to disarm both divisions.[30] Most members of the divisions were taken prisoner, several were taken to concentration camps, a few managed to join the partisans in eastern Slovakia, and a small segment fought its way through into resistance territory.[31] When Slovak officers made contact with the Soviet commanders of partisan units, they soon learned that the Slovak soldiers were more or less a burden to their operations and therefore urged them to move on toward central Slovakia, which soon became the temporary safety zone for the Slovak National Uprising. The Ukrainian General Staff of Partisan Movement (USPH) in Kiev had no interest in the Slovak military units in eastern Slovakia and hence did not support their operations.[32]

On August 28, the Tiso government accepted Nazi Germany's offer of military intervention and approved the immediate deployment of German troops to restore order on Slovak territory. Based on the Slovak-German agreement of 1939, the German units were to assist the Slovak army and other security units and were to be subordinated to the commander of the Slovak army, who was empowered to determine the duration of their presence. In a radio message the next day, General Catlos informed the Slovak population about the arrival of German troops and asked Slovak soldiers and civilians not to oppose this move. Shortly

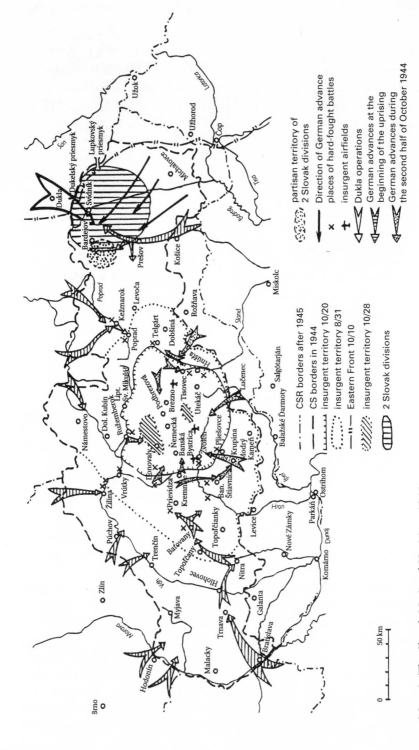

Map 6. The Slovak National Uprising, 1944

after that, Lt. Col. Jan Golian, commander of SVV in Banska Bystrica, announced the encrypted message: "The watchword 'Begin the Evacuation'—is valid starting today at 20:00 hours." That evening the first clashes began with a vengeance between the units of the Czechoslovak resistance forces and the advancing German troops. The long-awaited Slovak National Uprising (SNU or SNP) had officially begun. The next day Free Slovak Radio began broadcasting patriotic programs to encourage the freedom fighters in their struggle against the foreign enemy. Within a few hours SNR held its first meeting on free territory and issued a declaration pledging to seek a "new Czechoslovak Republic" to be built on the principle of national equality of Czechs and Slovaks. In this first official document, the leaders of the resistance movement referred to Czechoslovakia without a hyphen. They also pledged to join the "Allied nations, who through their struggle and immense sacrifices, are securing a free and democratic life for the nations of the whole world—including our small nation."[33]

During the first few days of the SNP the First Czechoslovak Army in Slovakia numbered about 18,000 soldiers and officers. After the first mobilization on September 5, its numbers grew to 47,000. The Tiso government had at its disposition only about 8,500 soldiers and officers from garrisons in western Slovakia. The military units of the First Army were organized in one air and six tactical groups covering a territory of about 1,700,000 people. After a second mobilization of the reserves, up to the age of forty, on September 26, the First Army had about 60,000 men in addition to about 6,000 to 8,000 partisans operating separately under the coordination of the USPH in Kiev.[34] The partisans were first headed by the Slovak communist leader, Karol Smidke, who along with Mikulas Ferjencik had just returned from Moscow, and later by the Soviet Colonel Alexej N. Asmolov, who received his orders from Kiev, not Banska Bystrica.

General Rudolf Viest flew from London through Moscow to Banska Bystrica and on October 7 took over the command of the resistance military operations in Slovakia. He found very little cooperation between the First Czechoslovak Army and the partisan organizations. It was a mirror image of the political conditions existing in the SNR. As the highest political organ of the Slovak resistance, the SNR combined groups with two main political orientations: the Citizens Bloc, represented by the Democratic Party, and the communists, represented by the Slovak Communist Party and the Social Democratic Party. Its plenum (the lawmaking body of SNR) and the newly created Board of Commissioners (eleven executive offices of SNR) were under the joint chairmanship of Vavro Srobar for the Citizens-Democratic Bloc and Karol Smidke for the Slovak Communist Party. (In order to avoid any complications with the internationally recognized Czechoslovak government in exile or the international community in general, the sections of the executive branch of SNR were called commissions rather than ministries.) The Slovak National Council acknowledged from the very beginning that it considered the government in London the sole Czecho-Slovak representative abroad, but it also implied that the Czechoslovak government in exile was not competent to insert itself in Slovakia's internal matters. When the government in exile sent a delegation headed by Frantisek Nemec to Banska Bystrica with authorization from President Benes to take charge of the government in resistance territory, the SNR only permitted the members of the delegation to become advisers and not decision makers.[35] In London, however, the exile government took credit for the resistance in Slovakia, leading Western statesmen and the media to assume that the political and military significance of the uprising was Benes's accomplishment and that in Slovakia it was the Czechs who revolted and were fighting for their freedom. Even President Franklin D. Roosevelt referred to "our Czechoslovak comrades-in-arms who are today so bravely contributing to the liberation of their homeland," with no mention of the Slovaks or Slovakia.[36]

Since the First Czechoslovak Army in Slovakia was poorly equipped, with light armor and only one Czechoslovak air squadron (flown in from the USSR), the need for war matériel, medicine, and food by the end of September was desperate. On October 7, 1944, SNR sent to London a three-member delegation (Jan Ursiny for the Citizens Bloc, Lt. Col. Mirko Vesel for SVV, and Ladislav Novomesky for the Slovak Communist Party) via Bari on an American B-17 to seek the necessary aid and resolve some of the misunderstanding between London and Banska Bystrica. Both the Slovak delegation and Benes and his government representatives stood firm on their positions; in the end the Slovaks lost on all issues, including the offer of U.S. aid, because Benes would not disappoint Moscow. As far as coordination of military aid to the First Army in resistance territory was concerned, the line of command was through General Ingr in London to Brigadier General Pika in Moscow and then to Lieutenant Colonel Golian or, after October 7, to General Viest in Banska Bystrica. Based on the Czechoslovak-Soviet agreement of December 12, 1943, the Soviet Union was obliged to provide the Slovak resistance movement with enough light armor for about 50,000 soldiers, to engage the Soviet air force in strategic bombing of the enemy, and to provide Red Army units for any needed tactical support during the uprising.[37]

The main German drive began on the eve of August 29, led by the 178th Armored Sapper Division Tatra, through the Vah Valley in the direction of Zilina (the main railroad center). Fierce fighting ensued near the mountain pass of Strecno, with a stubborn but ill-organized rebel defense, assisted by a brave French partisan unit. The German attack was mounted with the support of tanks and overwhelming air superiority. As a result, the Tatra division penetrated as far as Vrutky. From there it turned south into the Turiec Valley. At about the same time, the German reinforcement battalion Schaeffer was fighting its way from Poland through Kezmarok in the direction of Ruzomberok, where it met severe resistance from Czechoslovak military units stationed in Liptovsky Sv. Mikulas and Ruzomberok. From the west, about 75 kilometers from Bratislava, the reinforced armored regiment Schill moved up the river Nitra toward Topolcany, and a German attack group, supported by two battalions of riflemen, came from the southwest, engaging the resistance military units from Topolcany. From eastern Slovakia, which was in the operation zone of the Northern Ukraine army group, a force composed of units of the First Armored Army of the 357th Infantry Division advanced against the insurgence. The total estimated strength of the Nazi German military machine thrust against the insurgents during the first phase of the campaign numbered about four divisions. During the month of September 1944, not only was the first German onslaught repulsed but in some areas the insurgent forces counterattacked.[38] The soldiers and officers of the First Czechoslovak Army in Slovakia fought with valor and great sacrifices to defend their territory from Nazi German occupation. The German military command was equally determined to put an end to the resistance and restore the rear of the German eastern front to "normalcy" and free the double-track strategic Bratislava-Zilina and Zilina-Kosice railway line. The struggle for the railway junction of Zilina lasted almost two weeks, and the line to Kosice was still not open.

In the meantime, on September 4, the Czechoslovak government in exile appealed to the Soviet government, based on the December 16, 1943, agreement, to obtain military support for the insurgents and instructed Zdenek Fierlinger, Czechoslovak ambassador to Moscow (who had been present during the Benes-Stalin negotiations in December 1943), to do so without any delay. But that help took more than two weeks and a personal letter from Klement Gottwald, the Czech communist leader in London, to the Soviet foreign minister, V. M. Molotov, asking the Soviet government to transfer the Second Czechoslovak Airborne Brigade from the Russian front to the Tri Duby (Three Oaks) aerodrome near Banska Bystrica.[39] It took the Soviet air force six weeks to fly in 2,800 men. Not all were troops; some were Soviet guerrilla officers, and there were also some Czech and Slovak communist agitators and politicians who had been spending the war in exile in Moscow. Among the arrivals were the former Czech communist deputies Rudolf Slansky and Jan Sverma and the new commanding officer of USPH, Soviet Colonel Asmolov.[40] Slansky, who became Asmolov's deputy, "was very successful in establishing contact with the Czech Lands where he sent experienced comrades with political instructions and material for party organization."[41]

According to Slovak military historian Jozef Jablonicky, in early October there was an opportunity, when General Viest took command of SVV, "to achieve a smooth and successful unified command of all armed forces on resistance territory—the army and the partisans. Soviet Marshal Ivan Konev issued an order according to which all partisan units on resistance territory were supposed to be subordinated to General Viest." However, the representatives of the Communist Party did not agree with this strategically sound orientation: "Jan Sverma, Rudolf Slansky, and Karol Smidke, on October 10, 1944, in a radiogram to Moscow gave assurances that: 'The partisan movement is under the influence of KSS [Communist Party of Slovakia], on the other hand, Viest and the rest of the Slovak officers are using their full power against our influence.' Therefore the authors of the radiogram had no interest in making Viest a recognized decision-making authority also for the partisans."[42] It would appear that Soviet political strategy superseded the military one, even at the cost of human lives. By mid-October General Viest and his staff knew that the German army was preparing for a new offensive against the resistance forces in Slovakia; Viest also knew that his forces were not prepared to repel such an attack. On October 17 he informed General Ingr about the situation: "1,600 new recruits and still more to come have no weapons. Temporarily they received only 150 rifles for training. In addition to the new recruits, there are about 5,000 reservists who also lack weapons. For these reasons, we cannot relieve the units which spent too much time on the battlefield."[43]

The shortage of arms and equipment was also closely monitored by U. S. Navy Lt. James Holt Green, who on September 19, with five other American military personnel, had landed at Tri Duby aerodrome in one of the three B-17s carrying weapons, ammunition, and medical supplies for the resistance forces. All six were members of the Organization of Strategic Services (OSS). They were later joined by another nine, who in toto formed the U. S. Military Mission attached to the First Czechoslovak Army in Slovakia. The other two missions were from Great Britain and the Soviet Union and were headed by Maj. John Sehmer and Maj. Ivan Ivanovic Skripka, respectively. On October 7, when six B-17s delivered about fourteen tons of arms and equipment to Tri Duby, Lieutenant Green sent to Bari (his headquarters) intelligence reports about German targets, documents, Slovak newspapers, and a description of the conditions in the resistance territory. Among other things, he pointed out that SVV "estimated to hold the resistance territory for about five weeks. Furthermore, that General Viest and President Benes convincingly promised that outside aid would arrive in sufficient number and quantity. . . . The Russians have delivered very little material; however, the airplanes brought many Russian partisans in civilian clothes."[44] Referring to his previous messages sent to Bari, Lieutenant Green again emphasized that the resistance fighters had an absolute shortage of heavy armaments: "I consider it a tragedy that no aid had arrived for two reasons. From the point of view of the resistance movement and the Slovak population as well as from the point of view of American military interests."[45] The U.S. air force made a second delivery of urgently needed supplies, but the aid was sent under very sensitive political conditions. President Benes, in his negotiations with President Roosevelt in May 1943, had made no attempt to seek U.S. military aid for future resistance operations in either Slovakia or in Bohemia and Moravia. Therefore, when on September 22, 1944, the Czechoslovak minister of foreign affairs, Jan Masaryk, officially sought American assistance, it was too late, because in December 1943, Benes had already agreed with Stalin to have all future military aid and operations implemented through Moscow.

On October 18–19, 1944, German units under SS General Hermann Hoefle, the supreme commander of the German armed forces in Slovakia, began their final onslaught against the resistance forces from all directions. The decisive factor of the German success was the Eighteenth

SS Division Horst Wessel, which opened the German offensive with heavy armor advancing from Hungary. In the northern sector, German forces were substantially strengthened with the arrival of the SS Brigade Dirlewanger, which, after the crushing of the Warsaw uprising, was moved to Slovakia. The Muslim SS Regiment with the 708th and 271st Divisions were stationed in western Slovakia, and the Fourteenth Division Galizien was in place in the area of Zilina and Ruzomberok. Units of the armed group Henrici were in the vicinity of Poprad, and the group Wittenmayer was in the Kralova Lehota area. In comparison with the limited possibilities of the insurgents, all these German reinforcements, together with the units already engaged, represented a military strength of about seven divisions.[46] The insurgents had no chance against the concentrated German offensive.

On October 22, General Viest reported to General Ingr in London about the deteriorating conditions in resistance territory. Viest made it clear that it would be practically impossible to hold the corridor along the Hron Valley between Brezno-Banska Bystrica and Zvolen, where he had most of his troops. He suggested that the next best alternative was to continue the fighting in the mountains. The next day, the last flights from Tri Duby to Soviet territory evacuated the wounded and family members of leading resistance leaders, among them Vavro Srobar and Jan Pull. With their departure, the air bridge between resistance territory and the Soviet Union ceased to exist. On October 24, Ingr sent new instructions to Viest "to hold in central Slovakia a secure area under the control of resistance forces until the arrival of the Red Army."[47] These instructions proved to be unrealistic, for on October 26 the German units occupied Zvolen, and that same day the political and military leaders of SNP left Banska Bystrica and retreated into the mountain range around Donovaly. Around noon came a telephone call from the German commander in Zvolen to the office of the general staff, asking for the commander-in-chief of the resistance forces. The Germans were seeking unconditional surrender. When the operations chief asked General Viest for a reply, he ordered the operations chief to hang up the phone, which he did. Thus the offer to surrender was never accepted.[48]

In the afternoon of October 27 resistance units began their retreat from Banska Bystrica. Among the last to leave the city were the members of the Second Czecho-Slovak Airborne Brigade. Later that evening the German troops of the armored regiment Schill took Banska Bystrica without a fight, and the headquarters of the resistance became an occupied city. As the retreating soldiers and civilians headed toward the mountains near Donovaly and other nearby villages, they moved into a valley exposed to German dive-bombers.[49] Military units rapidly disintegrated and chaos set in. The same day General Viest issued a special operation order to transform the army into partisan units and apply hit-and-run tactics. Viest designated five groups and areas of operation for partisan warfare. This was his last order, and many commanders either did not receive it or chose not to follow the directive.

The retreat from Bystrica lasted almost one week, with a temporary command post established by Viest for two days at Donovaly. On October 28 Generals Viest and Golian (who had been promoted to general on September 5, 1944) left Donovaly with a group of officers from the general staff and headed east toward the Lower Tatra Mountains with the objective of reaching the area of Polany, where awaiting them was a cache of weapons and food as well as huts in remote areas. The long continuous mountain hike in rain, wind, and snow was very arduous. Viest—almost sixty years old—developed leg pains and the fatigue associated with them. On November 2, Viest's advance guard near Sv. Ondrej (Hronov) ran into a German unit. During the fighting that ensued, the Germans captured several soldiers and officers of the Viest-Golian group. Both generals and the rump of their group of soldiers and officers made it to a small village on the other side of the Hron Valley, Pohronsky Bukovec, where that night they found haven in the homes of reliable local citizens. The generals and their loyal comrades-in-arms finally had the opportunity to change clothes and get a good rest after more than a week in the mountains. Their rest was short-lived. The next day, in the early hours of November 3, the Germans arrived and captured the two generals. Viest and Golian were taken to Germany as prisoners of war and eventually executed.[50]

The same fate awaited Lt. James Holt Green, Maj. John Sehmer, and most of the members of the U.S. and British military missions. In the early morning of December 26, 1944, the special German punitive unit Edelweiss (about 250 soldiers) surrounded the log cabin that served as the American quarters and began shooting into the building. When the shooting ended, fourteen members of the U.S. and British military missions, some wounded, were ordered out and led away toward the town of Polomka. The rest of the German unit continued to search toward the peak of the mountain, where it encountered a partisan unit and engaged it in fighting for about three hours. Only six of the Americans involved in the mission survived.

Units of *Einsatzgruppe* (H SIPO) (Substitute Unit) and *Sicherheits Dienst* (Security Services, SD) soon moved into the area. Their main function was the pacification of the territory occupied by the Nazis. Units of the security service and the police, in cooperation with the Hlinka Guard (HG), the combat-ready units of the HG (POHG), and the *Heimatschutz* (Home Defense), used terror and reprisals against the civilian population, racial minorities, and participants of the uprising. Information on the results of the brutality and loss of lives and property during the uprising varies, depending on the sources: statistical reports presented by the Tiso government, documents retrieved from Nazi Germany after the war, and the reports collated by the Museum and Archives of SNP after February 1948. It would, however, be no exaggeration to claim that in dozens of mass graves more than four thousand bodies were exhumed, almost one hundred villages were burned, and an additional thousand people were herded into freight trains and taken to prisoner-of-war and concentration camps in the German Reich.[51]

It is important to point out that not all resistance fighters were blameless of committing similar inhuman acts of brutality and murder. The lawless execution of exponents of the Tiso regime in Brezno nad Hronom, the removal and execution of German minorities in the villages around Horna Nitra and elsewhere, the shooting of innocent victims on the bridge at Hajniky, and the mass graves in Sklabina, Sklene, and other places in resistance territory exemplified the personal and unruly behavior and savagery of some members of the partisan units. In several instances where laws were breached and crimes committed by uniformed members of the army, they were court-martialed and executed the very same day; but not all the criminals were exposed to a trial and justice. The most notorious case occurred just before the uprising officially began, when the entire German military mission was shot in the courtyard of the Slovak garrison in Turciansky Sv. Martin. The mission, which was in transit to Romania, was persuaded to spend the night in the garrison because of the presumed danger from partisans. The next morning, August 28, 1944, the German military mission with all their families were executed, in direct contradiction to the order from the commander of the illegal resistance army, Lt. Col. Jan Golian, who requested that the prisoners be sent to Banska Bystrica. The resistance officer, 2d Lt. Cyril Kuchta, ignored Golian's and (commander of the garrison) Colonel Perka's orders and instead followed the order of the partisan commander, 2d Lt. P. Velicka, who was under the command of USPH. In the garrison's courtyard, Kuchta commandeered a unit of submachine gunners and ordered the shooting of Germans.[52] This act of brutality—radically opposed to the rules of the Geneva Convention dealing with prisoners of war—soon provoked a series of reprisals from the equally bloodthirsty Nazi side. Their victims included innocent civilians as well as regular army recruits and officers. On the Slovak side, renegades and, in some instances, deserters were very often pathological criminals parading under the banner of "resistance fighters." For them, the lives of civilian population had practically no value. The innocent often became the victims in this revolutionary game of struggle.

After the Czechoslovak army and partisan command left Donovaly, USPH and Col. Alexej N. Asmolov, the commander in Slovakia, became the new "leader" of the resistance in Slovakia. The activities of more than forty partisan units (bands, groups, detachments, and brigades) were coordinated by the General Staff of the Partisan Movement in Czechoslovakia (HSPO), which operated from the end of October 1944 to February 19, 1945, out of the mountains of the Lower Tatras. HSPO received orders from USPH in Kiev. It had about 8,000 partisans of various backgrounds, many of them former members of the military, including about thirty different nationalities (former prisoners of war). Organized by military commanders of the rump two divisions disarmed by the Germans before they could join the planned operations from Banska Bystrica, some early partisan units included Krivan and Sergej and their detachments: Janosik, Sloboda, Hurban, Stefanik, Zula, and others. Among the better-known partisan units of nonmilitary personnel were Yegorov, Chapayev, Shukayev, Zingor, Secansky, Kvetinsky, and Nalepka. These partisan units operated in the rear of the German eastern front, where they blew up highway bridges, railroad tracks, telephone lines, and ammunition depots; attacked small outposts and sentries; placed field mines in strategic locations; and gathered information about enemy troop movements. Although because of their diversionary tactics the partisans were less effective than the army in tying down the enemy, they did create a feeling of insecurity among the enemy that was effective enough to weaken the enemy's will to fight. Since Moscow had never been interested in sharing victory in battle with anyone— especially the Slovaks who fought against them—the command in Kiev was instructed to support the partisan form of warfare, enabling the communists to lay the foundation for the postwar political developments. For this and other reasons, the Slovak National Uprising cannot be considered a total military success. The planned linkage between the Slovak units and the Red Army units never materialized, and there was no rapid forward movement of the eastern front through Slovakia in the direction of Vienna.

AFTER
WORLD WAR II

PART THREE

7 The Slovak Question in Postwar Czechoslovakia

The struggle for Slovak autonomy in a liberated Czechoslovakia started on August 29, 1944, with the outbreak of the Slovak National Uprising (SNP). Spearheaded by the Slovak National Council (SNR), the main objective of the uprising was to remove the fascist regime and restore a democratic Czechoslovakia. As a result of the fierce fighting by former members of the Slovak army and partisans, a fairly large territory in central Slovakia was liberated until the end of October 1944, when the uprising was pushed into the mountains, where it continued as partisan warfare.

The Soviet government had been asked to provide military assistance to the resistance forces in liberated Slovakia—once in early August by the SNR delegation flown to Vinica and Moscow and again on September 4 by the Czechoslovak government in London and through Zdenek Fierlinger, its ambassador in Moscow. On the basis of the December 12, 1943, agreement between the USSR and Czechoslovakia, the Soviet leadership agreed to supply the resistance forces with certain military aid and at the same time prepare plans for a Carpatho-Dukla operation. According to these plans, the 38th Army of General K. S. Moskalenko of the First Ukrainian Front and the First Czechoslovak Army Corps were supposed to have penetrated through the Carpathians to the Slovak area between Presov and Stara Lubovna.[1]

The Carpatho-Dukla operation began on September 8 but failed to make any headway against a strong German defense. There were two more attempts to break through the German lines, one on September 21, when the first Czechoslovak village (Kalinov) was liberated, the other on October 6, when the First Czechoslovak Army Corps came close to Dukla Pass and consequently liberated the village of Vysny Komarnik. But from the point of view of the Czechoslovak resistance, the Carpatho-Dukla operation was a failure because the main objectives were not met. After the First Czechoslovak Army in Slovakia was pushed into the mountains, the Carpatho-Dukla operation ended. About 20,000 Soviet and 5,000 Czechoslovak soldiers were killed in battle during the operation. Before the end of the year, the Germans had to abandon their highly fortified natural defense line because the Red Army penetration through the southern plains of Hungary and the northern plains of Poland threatened to encircle the German army. Only minor battles were fought in November and December 1944, when cities such as Snina, Humenne, Michalovce, Svidnik, and Trebisov and some 500,000 inhabitants were liberated.

The next battles were part of the winter offensive undertaken by the First, Second, and Fourth Ukrainian Fronts of the Red Army, who brought liberation to Kosice and Presov in eastern Slovakia in mid-January 1945. A few weeks later Poprad and Brezno nad Hronom were also liberated. A major movement of armies took place during the spring offensive in March 1945, when practically all of central Slovakia was liberated, followed in early April by the liberation of Trnava, Zilina, Ruzomberok, and Turciansky Sv. Martin. During the liberation of Bratislava, April 4, the most significant role was played by the Seventh Army Guard, led by Lt. Gen. S. M. Sumilov, which was part of the Second Ukrainian Front under Marshal R. J. Malinovsky.

After ferocious, though unsuccessful, fighting in the Carpathian Mountains, the First Czechoslovak Army Corps, under General Ludvik Svoboda, was again ordered into battle during the January offensive near Levoca and Kezmarok. For weeks the unit fought a heavy battle to liberate Liptovsky Sv. Mikulas.

A complicated situation developed in Moravia as the war drew to a close. On April 26 the armies of the Second Ukrainian Front entered Ostrava, extending the German-Soviet battlefield in a line from Brno to Vyskov to Zilina to Ostrava. One week earlier the Third U.S. Army, under General George S. Patton, crossed the western borders of Czechoslovakia and held the line from Karlove Vary to Plzen to Ceske Budejovice, which was supposedly agreed upon between General Dwight Eisenhower and the Soviet Military High Command. Although any further advance into the predetermined Soviet sphere of operations could not occur without Soviet consent, according to Prime Minister Winston S. Churchill, "there was no agreement to prevent General Eisenhower, Supreme Commander of the Allied Armies, from occupying Prague if it were militarily feasible."[2]

Because the situation in the center of Bohemia was not secure, General Eisenhower on May 4 sent a personal message to the chief of the Soviet General Staff, General Antonov, about U.S. readiness to advance to the Elbe and Moldau rivers in Prague. The Soviet General Staff was much opposed to the suggestion on the grounds that such a move could lead to chaos among the armed forces. The Soviets, bent on political gain, were determined not to lose the opportunity to be the sole liberators of Prague.[3]

On the morning of May 5, when the news broke that Hitler had committed suicide and Germany was on the verge of capitulation, an uprising against the German garrisons took place in Prague. The uprising, led by the Czech National Council, an underground political organization established at the end of April 1945, was set off by the raising of the Czechoslovak flag. German signs were torn down, and passing German soldiers were shot at from roofs and windows. The Germans were disarmed, and about two thousand barricades were built in four days. The Czechs were joined in their fight by units led by renegade General Vlasov, consisting of former Soviet prisoners of war who had fought on the German side for a couple of years but now turned against their master to break through the German lines so that they could surrender to the Americans as prisoners of war.[4] About 300 of them were killed in the fighting.

The Prague Uprising ended at noon on May 8, 1945, a day thereafter celebrated in the Czech Republic as Liberation Day. The representatives of the Czech National Council and the German command in Prague signed a protocol mediated by the International Red Cross, according to which the Germans were to cease fighting immediately and be guaranteed free passage without arms in a westerly direction.

Early in the morning of May 9, Soviet tank units of the First Ukrainian Front arrived in Prague from the direction of Dresden to render assistance to the Czech defenders of the city, but German troops had already signed the protocol and moved out of the city. Radio appeals for help from the resistance fighters in Prague went unanswered for several days because the U.S. troops closest to Prague were not permitted to give the needed assistance.

Two basic documents defined the transition of the liberated territory from Soviet military operations to Czechoslovak civilian rule: the Czechoslovak-Soviet agreements of March 1939 and May 1944. The same agreements also defined the war booty claimed by the Soviet Union as well as the financial and food supply commitments from Czechoslovakia to the Red Army. As early as May 3, 1945, the premier of the provisional government of Czechoslovakia informed the government about mutual complaints by both citizens and Soviet officers about all kinds of violations.⁵ From the day liberation began, the commanders in Slovakia engaged in mass requisitioning of livestock and occupied sugar and flour mills, breweries and distilleries, food storage areas, and warehouses. Similar violations also took place in Bohemia and Moravia. According to the agreements, food supplies to the Red Army were supposed to have been requisitioned only by the central offices of the Czechoslovak government, but according to the ministers of trade (Ivan Pietor) and supply (Vaclav Majer), "the food supply that we deliver to the Russians, they are sending from our territory to Austria."⁶ When the United Nations Relief and Rehabilitation Administration (UNRRA) learned about the transfer of livestock from Czechoslovakia, it was determined to stop the meat supply to Czechoslovakia paid for by UNRRA. But because of successful intervention by Prague, the supplies continued. The stationing of the Red Army units in Czechoslovakia cost the government 950 million koruny per month, or a total of seven billion koruny up to the end of 1945. In addition, the official value of the so-called war booty (which had to be redefined in another agreement in September 1945) transferred to the Soviet Union was another three billion koruny, which according to experts represented only a fraction of the real value.

The saddest chapter in the liberation of Czechoslovakia was the fate of Czechoslovak citizens who were arrested by Red Army security police and sent to concentration camps in the Soviet Union. According to deputy foreign minister Vladimir Clementis, immediately after the war his office handed to Soviet ambassador Valerian Zorin a list of 5,300 persons who were deported from Slovakia, but as late as 1947 neither he nor the members of parliament representing the Slovak Democratic Party could get an answer from the Soviets. In 1956, political prisoners returning from Soviet concentration camps revealed that they had seen thousands of prisoners from Czechoslovakia.[7]

Months before the liberation of Czechoslovakia began, the Benes government in exile had already been making preparations for the creation of the future state. On January 22, 1945, President Benes engaged in thorough and systematic discussions with the Czech and Slovak communists. A few days later he initiated similar discussions with the representatives of the noncommunist political parties residing in London. His objective was to create an acceptable new government on the liberated territory. At that time it was understood that the Czechoslovak government in exile would resign before the president's departure from London and that it would be authorized to do the work abroad until the new government was named. The assumption was that the government would consist of representatives of political parties in the National Front, that is, the Communist Party, the socialist parties, the People's Party, including the agrarians (but not the old Agrarian party), and delegates from the Slovak National Council (SNR).[8]

It was generally understood that the new government would be a people's democracy erected on the structure of national committees in public administration, determined to take drastic measures in the economic life of the nation, cleanse the nation of Nazi and Fascist elements, and build a Czechoslovak army on a new foundation. The foreign policy of the new state was to be based on the spirit and text of the Czechoslovak-Soviet Agreement of December 1943, and SNR was informed that immediately upon the arrival on liberated territory, a new government would be announced that would include representatives of the council.[9]

Negotiations concerning the new Czechoslovak government took place in Moscow from March 22 to 29, 1945. Even though preparatory work had been done in London on different issues awaiting the future government, the politicians in exile did not bring any specific proposals, and when Benes and the political party delegates met with the Czech communist leader, Klement Gottwald (who in the meantime had moved to Moscow), it was decided that the first item on the agenda would be one proposed by the Communist Party of Czechoslovakia (CPC) with the proviso that the proposal would first be negotiated between the CPC and representatives of the Socialist bloc (the National Socialists and Social Democrats) and the People's Party—that is, with all political entities except the SNR. The SNR was supposed to discuss the proposed government program independently and then meet with the rest of the delegates in regard to chapter 6 of the proposal—relations between the Czechs and Slovaks and the composition of the government; SNR delegates were absent from many of the negotiations. The CPC proposal outlined a government based on a broad national front, consisting of representatives of all social segments and political orientations engaged in the liberation struggle. Its aim was to bring the government into close cooperation with the USSR and other allies and thus enable it within a short time to hold general elections for the National Assembly, which would then draft a new constitution.

The overarching guideline of Czechoslovak foreign policy was assumed to have been a tight alliance with "the victorious Slavic superpower of the East," that is, the USSR; the Czechoslovak-Soviet Agreement of December 1943, which embodied mutual assistance, friendship, and postwar cooperation, was to be the clearest determinant of the future foreign policy of the Czechoslovak state. One of the major tasks of the government was to be the expansion of the Slavic line of foreign policy—the establishment of friendly relations with close Slavic nations.[10]

As far as the treatment of the German and Hungarian minorities was concerned, the principle of collective guilt was applied. The Germans and Hungarians were threatened with loss of their Czechoslovak citizenship unless they had been active antifascists, had fought for the preservation of pre-Munich Czechoslovakia, or had been persecuted for these acts during the war. Another important task of the government was to be the indictment and punishment of all war criminals, traitors, and collaborators. Toward that end, local national committees were supposed to create special people's courts in cities and towns, with a National Court for the prosecution of especially important war criminals. From the economic point of view, the primary objective of the government was, according to the proposal, to put all enterprises quickly in full operation and "to place the entire financial and credit system under general state control."[11]

The proposed program of the new Czechoslovak government was negotiated by Klement Gottwald, Vaclav Kopecky, Rudolf Slansky, Vaclav Nosek, and Bohumil Lastovicka for the Communist Party of Czechoslovakia; Zdenek Fierlinger, Bohumil Lausman, Vaclav Majer, and Vaclav Pacak for the Social Democrats; Jaroslav Stransky, Josef David, Frantisek Uhlir, and Prokop Drtina for the National Socialists; and Msgr. Jan Sramek and Frantisek Hala for the People's Party. The original proposal submitted by the CPC was approved without any substantive changes, and the discussion of the sixteen individual headings passed without any serious conflicts. The reasons for the approval were numerous: the improved credibility of CPC because of the success of the USSR in the struggle against fascism, the location (Moscow) for negotiations and the subdued atmosphere of the negotiations, the cleverly applied tactics of the communists during the discussions, the influence of the (unsuccessful) results of the Slovak National Uprising, and, above all, the recognition that there was a need for substantial political, economic, and social changes in the new state.

The only problem area was that of Czecho-Slovak relations, presented in the sixth heading of the proposed program. The SNR delegation—J. Gustav Husak, Laco Novomesky, and Jozef Soltesz for the Communist Party of Slovakia and Vavro Srobar, Jan Ursiny, and Jan Styk for the Democratic Party—was bound in its negotiations by a document enacted on March 2, 1945, that dealt with the legitimacy of the state.[12] The SNR insisted that the future state be built on the foundation of equality between the Czech and Slovak nations. In the SNR's perception this meant the adoption of a federal system of government, although the term "federal" was not explicitly used. Granting that the SNR delegation—because of the strong influence of CPC—yielded on the point of federalism, it persisted on the recognition of legitimacy of the Slovak nation, which was also to have been reflected in the development of the common state.[13]

The representatives of the Czech National Socialist Party strongly criticized the wording of this section of the proposal. The old spirit of Czechoslovakism among the London group of émigrés was very much alive, and they absolutely opposed the SNR's resolution. The common state of the Czechs and Slovaks was to be constructed within the same framework as that under the First Republic. Jaroslav Stransky, the leading representative of the National Socialists, proposed that the new Czechoslovak government would be cognizant of the desire of the Slovaks to live in a common state with the Czechs as a legitimate nation, but this proposal did nothing more than postpone the solution to a later date, sometime after the liberation. That the SNR was to be a legitimate, but temporary, revolutionary entity of state power on Slovak territory became evident in the discussions that followed, in which the situation in Slovakia was treated as simply an "unavoidable revolutionary interlude."[14] Finally, though a compromise was reached that resulted in keeping the text in heading VI intact, the issue of the specific political role to be played by the Slovak nation in the new common state still remained unclarified. The noncommunist Czech political parties made future collaboration with the Slovak noncommunist parties much more difficult because they failed to understand the meaning of political power behind the Slovak issue.

The negotiations in Moscow also decided the composition of the new government. Of the twenty-five positions in the government, nine were given to the Slovaks: two deputy premiers, four ministers, and three state secretaries. The CPC gained the most important positions—for example, the ministries of the interior, agriculture, and information, which were significant to planning future strategy and acquiring a monopoly of power.

The Slovak and Czech delegates left Moscow for Kosice on March 31, 1945, and on April 4, at Kosice, President Benes named the first government of the National Front.[15] When the members of the government met in Kosice, they stood face to face with new realities—the newly named government could not intervene in Slovak matters because these were exclusively handled by Slovak institutions. This situation did not improve even after the April 1945 agreement about the sharing of lawmaking powers between Prague and Bratislava, according to which SNR transferred all lawmaking authority in all-state matters—foreign policy, defense, and foreign trade—to the president of the republic; all other matters remained in the power of the Slovak administrative organs independent of Prague.

Complications soon developed in the area of sharing of power between the Czechs and Slovaks, which to a great extent was also a reflection of the concept of "guided democracy" on which the new political system was erected. If President Benes was one of the key architects of this new political design, as historians and political analysts contend,[16] then it is not surprising that Benes and Stalin saw eye to eye on many issues, including the position of Slovaks in the future Czechoslovak Republic:

> On the question of the Slovaks. . . . It is important to keep the Slovaks at home firmly in hand. Because of their small number, no separation must be permitted, it would be a tremendous stupidity. . . . There was a reference to the issue of language. President Benes, answering Stalin's question about the difference between Czech and Slovak, says that there are disagreements about it but that he is of the opinion that Slo-

vak, from a scientific point of view, is the same as Czech; however, he himself always has been and still is very liberal on the issue of language, also nationality, and especially as far as the decentralization of administration of the entire republic is concerned. Stalin emphasizes that Slovakia must not think of becoming independent. It belongs to Czechoslovakia.[17]

Benes's commitment to Stalin and the Soviet Union was unmistakable in 1943 after his return to London from Moscow. He made that clear to the British ambassador to Czechoslovakia, Sir Philip Nichols, on March 23, 1944, when he said: "The British government, the Foreign Office should now be aware that after my trip to Russia [negotiations with J. V. Stalin], we have all of our international problems solved—and I won't argue over this anymore with anyone. The Soviets will certainly support us in everything."[18] Benes had already declared his stance to General Charles de Gaulle (Algiers, January 4, 1944): "The alliance with Russia is a categorical imperative, especially since the Red Army will occupy Poland, Hungary, and a large portion of Germany, that is, states that have demands against Czechoslovak territory."[19] Benes was convinced that he and his country could become a "bridge between the East and the West." As "bridge builder" he was among the first statesmen to advocate the "convergence theory." He believed that the postwar trend in the Soviet Union would be toward democratization of the political process combined with some aspects of free enterprise and that the West would move to a welfare state and social democracy. His commitments in his negotiations with Stalin in December 1943 probably reflected his beliefs and prognosis of postwar developments, in which he expected to play a major role.

"GUIDED DEMOCRACY"

The program prepared and submitted by the CPC and approved by the other Czech political parties and SNR became not only the foundation of the recovery plan for the common Czechoslovak state but also the foundation for a new political system known as "people's democracy." For all practical purposes the "democracy" was guided or engineered by political leaders, not by the constituency. The key institution representing the arch of the political party structure in postwar Czechoslovakia was the National Front.

Certain events in the early stages of the development of this system were to have important effects on the creation of a democratic civil society in the country. The representatives of the six political parties—all participants at the March 1945 Moscow meeting—prohibited the renewal of fascist and other political parties responsible for the Munich decisions; political parties could only be created and legitimized after they had pledged to uphold the principles of the government program. In other words, for their own reasons, the representatives of the six political parties that constituted the National Front prevented the legitimate creation of any government opposition.

Not all the reasons were selfish. Noncommunist politicians were under the illusion that the communists had changed their attitude and no longer desired to rule the entire society. At the same time, however, the communists anticipated that the National Front would become an effective device to serve their communist political interests, as a guarantor of a sound investment in the development of state recovery and the maintenance of people's democracy. But there was also at this time a prevailing opinion that cooperation between the Soviet Union and the Western powers would continue, and many politicians, including Benes, because of experiences dating back to the Munich crisis and the Great Depression of the 1930s, articulated leftist ideas and values. The noncommunist political parties and the CPC were ready to collaborate on joint projects designed to rebuild Czechoslovakia as a nation-state of Czechs and Slovaks; they also had common goals in regard to citizens of German and Hungarian nationality. At the same time, the noncommunist politicians were counting on the institution of free, democratic elections, which they were quite sure the communists in Czechoslovakia could never win. This kind of thinking lay behind their illusion that only through cooperation within the National Front would they be able to keep the communists bound to a democratic platform and democratic rules of procedure.

With the fulfillment and realization of the Kosice government program in postwar Czechoslovakia, several major changes were noticeable in power politics as well as in social and economic areas. The new structure of the Czechoslovak economy and its method of operation were not very clearly formulated. The assumption was that citizens who collaborated with fascism would lose their property by placing it under state control until such time as the lawmaking organs would decide their status. Yet the program did not mention state confiscation or nationalization of properties, shrouded as it would be in the complex issue of the credit and finance system as well as the management of key industrial enterprises, natural resources, and energy. Individual nationalization decrees prepared at the Ministry of Industry (headed by the Social Democrat Bohumil Lausman) grew in number day by day and, against government opposition, were duly signed by Benes on October 24, 1945, shortly before the opening of the first session of the Provisional National Assembly, thus preventing any discussion of the issue. Benes justified his ploy in the name of avoiding a political crisis.[20]

This act of arbitrary decision marked the beginning of a nationalized economy and the end of free enterprise in postwar Czechoslovakia. It was in full accord with Benes's concept of socializing democracy—a state opposed to economic liberalism and having the power to maintain exclusive control over the economy. In no other industrialized nation of Europe did postwar nationalization go as far. Entire industrial sectors were nationalized: all the mines, the energy and power industry, the steel and weapons industry, the cement and wood products industry, the banking and finance sector, and so on. In other sectors, the criterion for nationalization was the number of workers. All industrial enterprises with a workforce of more than sixty had to be nationalized—in all, 3,040 industrial enterprises. After signing the nationalization decrees, Benes declared that the entire world was closely watching Czechoslovakia's socialization process, which must succeed so that the socialization principle would not be compromised. Because Czechoslovakia was politically and socially mature, it was, according to Benes, in the forefront of the socialization movement.[21] Nationalization was meant "to build a new economy and social order."[22]

The sweeping nationalization of industry changed Czechoslovak society at its very foundation. The power of financial capital, and with it most of the so-called "bourgeois class," was liquidated or replaced by the nationalized sector of the economy. Economic power shifted into the hands of the National Front, where the strongest positions were held by the CPC and the Social Democrats. And with the shift of economic power, the power of the parliament was also diminished. Since most important decisions were made in the National Front, the government no longer felt any responsibility toward the parliament; decisions of the National Front were made by consensus, and discussions in parliament were nothing more than window dressing.

Interest groups, especially the labor unions, played an important role in this new system of "guided democracy." Spearheaded by the CPC before the liberation, all political parties agreed to the merger of labor unions into one, called *Revolucne odborove hnuti* (Revolutionary Trade Union Movement) or ROH. This made labor such a strong political power that the government could not ignore it when it came to key issues. Under communist leadership, ROH and its executive committee—*Ustredni rada odboru* (URO)—controlled over two million workers who were eager to implement the new economic and social order of the country.

Perhaps the most drastic change in postwar Czechoslovakia under the National Front government was the treatment of nationalities, particularly Germans and Hungarians. The gist of the nationality policy was reformulated by the Czechoslovak government in exile in London and was an outgrowth of Benes's politics of revenge and a desire to rebuild Czechoslovakia as a nation of Czechs and Slovaks. This could only be achieved through the displacement of all Germans and Hungarians from the new state.[23] Benes's most valuable ally on this issue was the Soviet Union. By 1943, Stalin had concluded that national minorities in Central Europe were a source of disorder, and he thought that their transfer was the best solution.[24] Although after his meeting with Stalin, Benes received tentative approval from the United States and Great Britain for the transfer of Czechoslovak Germans, by early 1945, when Benes asked the British government to support a law intended to strip all Czechoslovak Germans of their citizenship, he was rebuffed.

The revived Czech nation apparently was possessed by a blind hatred for anything "German." Inspired by the program announced after liberation by President Benes and the provisional government as well as by members of the liberating armies, radical Czech nationalism opened up the floodgates for a freewheeling persecution of "all" Germans suspected of collaboration with Hitler's Germany. The memories of the shameful experiences from the late 1930s and the hard times during the occupation, combined with the appeal for socialization and the renaissance of Slavic brotherhood under the aegis of the victorious great ally, the Soviet Union, made the Czechs and Slovaks enthusiastic for a national state without "non-Slavic" minorities.

During the first weeks and months after the liberation of Bohemia and Moravia, old German settlers, prisoners of war, and German army defectors from the eastern front were subjected to various forms of persecution. For all practical purposes, Czechoslovak citizens of German nationality were eliminated from normal life and became objects of all types of civil, legal, political, social, and cultural sanctions. During the summer of 1945, widespread forced migration of the German minority took place. Germans were driven out of the country in what became known as the "wild transfer," or they were pushed from the border areas into the heartland, where they were used as forced labor. There were few restraints on how far discriminatory measures could go: civilians, the military, members of the national security guard, the militia, the revolutionary guard, and partisans all took part, and local authorities either could not, or would not, prevent such acts. As a result, there were many instances of groundless violent crimes committed against innocent people.[25]

One of the worst cases of abuse of civil rights and democratic principles of justice occurred on July 31, 1945, at Usti and Labem, an industrial town on the Elbe River a few miles from Saxony. In the afternoon of that day, there was an explosion in a cable factory that had been used by the German army as an ammunitions warehouse. The explosion was blamed, without any positive proof, on the "werewolves" (German guerrillas) and their local German collaborators. According to official reports, about twenty-eight people were killed, among them Czechoslovak citizens of German nationality, and thirty-nine seriously wounded, including ten Germans. Less than half an hour after the explosion, Czech civilians and men in uniform attacked unarmed Germans in the streets and in their homes. At about the same time the bridge across the Elbe, where German workers were expected to pass on their way home from Schicht enterprises, was secured by armed civilians and uniformed Czech soldiers and officers. Around 4:30 P.M. the homebound Germans were attacked, brutally beaten, and thrown into the river. Many victims were women and children. Those who had managed to stay alive in the river became targets for their attackers. Czech soldiers, along with their commanding officers, mowed down the victims with machine guns. Appeals of the chairman of the local national committee, J. Vondra, to stop the shooting were ignored. The "hunt for Germans" continued throughout the afternoon and evening. Between 2,000 and 3,000 people became victims, and 1,000 bodies were fished out of the Elbe near Pirn in Saxony.

While this massacre was taking place, Stalin, Churchill, and Truman, the Big Three, were discussing the collective transfer of the German minorities at Potsdam. Government officials in Prague blamed the incident on the "werewolves" and their local collaborators, and they tried to convince the major powers that the incident was the result of unbearable conditions in the border area. In their view, coexistence with the German minority was impossible and the group's expulsion was critical. Two days later, in Article XIII of the final report of the Potsdam Conference, the Big Three agreed to an orderly and humane transfer of German minorities from Czechoslovakia. There were claims that the July 31 explosion was caused by negligence of Czech watchmen because all Germans had left the warehouse forty minutes before the explosion. There is also evidence that on the day of the explosion many new arrivals in the city came fully armed and that prior to the explosion a number of Germans were warned by Czech friends that they would be attacked. It was also claimed that the security chief at the plant had a doctor's appointment that afternoon and that immediately after the explosion the military commander was heard to exclaim: "Now we will get revenge on the Germans!"[26]

Widespread anti-German hysteria and the lawlessness in liberated Czechoslovakia were also evident in Prerov on June 18, 1945, where a military transport train (no. 2059) bound from Prague to Slovakia with Slovak units of the demobilizing First Czechoslovak Army Corps had halted alongside a transport from Sluknov and Rumburk carrying Slovak civilians, many of German ancestry from Dobsina and vicinity, some of whom had been voluntarily evacuated, others forcibly, from Slovakia in early December 1944 by the retreating German army. These citizens—some with spouses of Hungarian and Slovak nationality—had been used by the Nazi war machine as forced labor and were now returning home to the land of their ancestors. If they had been culpable of Nazi collaboration, would they have been eager to go home in Slovakia, or would they have sought refuge in Germany? Both transports were awaiting clearance to proceed on their way.

That morning, Lt. Karol Pazur (a security officer of the Fourth Division) had demanded that the District National Committee (DNC) in Prerov issue warrants for the apprehension of "Germans and collaborators." According to the security chief of the Prerov DNC, Vladimir Vincena, "after I refused to comply with his [Pazur's] request, he looked for another victim."[27] The other "victims" were Sgt. Bedrich Smetana, Lt. Maj. Eugen Surovcik, and others aboard the military train. After consulting with other officers, Pazur and Smetana requested twenty submachine gunners from Lt. Maj. Surovcik, transport commander of the

Seventeenth Army Regiment.[28] They then forced 265 people from the transport carrying the civilians to leave everything behind and march to a place called Svedske Sance (Swedish Trenches) near Horne Mostenice. In the meantime, Lieutenant Pazur forced the local national committee at Lovesice to provide him with men and equipment to dig a large pit. Seventy-one men, 120 women, and 74 children were machine-gunned in groups of ten, in their underwear, facing the freshly dug pit. The shooting lasted from ten in the evening of June 18 until five the next morning—forty days after the war had ended. The victims' possessions (money, jewelry, savings books, etc.) were taken by the soldiers, and their documents were burned nearby. The clothes of the victims were taken into the village. The men who tossed the victims into the pit were then themselves killed and buried with the other victims.[29]

Although these monstrous crimes were investigated by local authorities in Prerov on the following day (part of the investigation included two Soviet officers of the military headquarters in Prerov), it took two years before the military procurator in Bratislava began an official investigation of Lieutenant Pazur and Lieutenant Major Surovcik, the main culprits. Sergeant (now 1st Lt.) Smetana was by then in jail for a murder committed in July 1945; he was interrogated but not charged for the crimes of murdering 265 civilians in Prerov. Surovcik's criminal investigation was dismissed on July 16, 1948, for lack of evidence. On June 4, 1948, 2d Lt. Karol Pazur was placed under arrest in Bratislava and in January 1949 was sentenced by the High Military Court to seven and a half years in prison. The following June 29, the Highest Military Court in Prague increased the sentence to twenty years, but on February 28, 1951, by presidential decree, the sentence was reduced to ten years, and a year later Pazur was given amnesty. It was revealed during the investigations that Pazur had a criminal character; hereditary symptoms of mental deficiency (on his father's side); a dubious background, including voluntary departure to seek work in Germany (which he had avoided in his homeland); membership in a German representative soccer organization; and membership in the HSLS and Hlinka Guard. In 1932, his brother Julius was convicted as a spy for Hungary; during the Slovak Republic he became a zealous member of the Hlinka Guard and then volunteered in the Nazi SS. In 1949 Julius was in a Trencin prison. Their sister, Etel, was known for befriending German officers during the occupation and was suspected of spying for Nazi Germany.

During the investigation and trial of Pazur, several officers of the

Fifth Division of the general staff, including the notorious criminal Bedrich Reicin, intervened on his behalf.[30] In 1969, seventeen years after his release, Pazur led one of several delegations of the former members of the First Czechoslovak Army Corps to Susice during the twenty-fifth anniversary of the Slovak National Uprising. There, according to his military prosecutor in 1948, Col. A. Rasla, Pazur was welcomed and hugged by General Frantisek Sadek as a former hero, and "when Pazur approached me . . . he shook my hand and said, 'I forgive you—then such were the times!' "[31] It could not have been characterized better even by a civilized, innocent bystander.

The times the criminal referred to were the long-awaited peace when, as stated in the July 16, 1948, indictment, Pazur had an opportunity to hand over the entire case of the suspected treason and collaboration to the proper authorities. "He could have done so because it was long after the end of the war and on our territory the people's courts were already in operation."[32] Instead, the prosecutor argued, "What is at stake here is only a moral inferiority which the accused is trying to disguise with patriotism. . . . Thus, with this act the accused damaged not only the good name of the Army, but also our entire nation."[33] The ultimate tragedy at Prerov, Usti nad Labem, and many other places was the drastic abandonment by many Czech and Slovak "patriots" of the goals of the war and liberation. If the teachings of T. G. Masaryk, the founder of Czechoslovak democracy, had been remembered, these and other crimes could have been prevented because we would have been reminded of his warning: "Very often hatred, for example, toward another nation, is considered love toward one's own nation. It is greater, however, not to have that hatred but to love positively."[34] Because of not remembering, Czechoslovak morals were lowered to the same level as those of the Nazis in Lidice. Democracy and its judicial system had no chance.

When the Big Three approved the transfer of German minorities from Czechoslovakia on August 2, 1945, at the Potsdam Conference and the government in Prague finally put an end to the "wild transfer" techniques, conditions arose for organizing an orderly transfer under international supervision. Preparations for this exodus lasted until January 1946, with new institutions responsible for the transfer logistics as well as the organization of concentration centers for the Czechoslovak Germans. Every day from January until October 1946, four to six transports of German deportees left for U.S.- or Soviet-occupied zones of

Germany. Each deported German could carry only 50 kilograms of personal belongings—no valuables. The rest of it was confiscated and became state property. In this manner, the Czechoslovak government deported 2,251,000 Germans, of whom 1,464,000 were transferred to the American zone and 814,000 to the Soviet zone of occupied Germany. Citizens' rights were restored to 55,017 Czechoslovak Germans.[35]

In general, it can be argued that the Czechoslovak government was successful in deporting practically all Czechoslovak Germans from its territory in spite of the economic difficulties the deportation created and the regrets, opposition, and direct criticism the government encountered from responsible Western sources.[36] Nevertheless, the signing of the German-Czech Declaration of Reconciliation in April 1997 confirms the old adage that what has been done cannot be undone. What remained to be said about the tragedy during the war and the peace in Czechoslovakia was eloquently expressed by President Roman Herzog of the German Federal Republic on April 29, 1997, before a special joint session of the Czech Republic's two houses of parliament: "We Germans want to ask forgiveness and we want to forgive."[37]

Somewhat different was the outcome of the transfer of the Czechoslovak Magyars. Even though the intentions of President Benes and his friends in the leadership circles toward the Hungarian minority were analogous to those of the Czechoslovak Germans, he was unsuccessful in his attempt to secure approval for a similar deportation from the United States and Great Britain, and he could not even count on the unambiguous support of the Soviet Union. The situation was further complicated by the fact that after liberation, power on Slovak territory, whose southern regions were inhabited by the Hungarian minority, was transferred to the Slovak National Council, not the government in Prague.

Based on the Kosice Agreement, and supported by presidential decrees nos. 33, 71, and 88 of 1945, all Czechoslovak Magyars except those who were anti-Nazi and anti-Fascist were automatically deprived of Czechoslovak citizenship and subject to deportation or forced labor. Those affected by these decrees were men from age sixteen to fifty and women from age eighteen to forty-five. The Resettlement Office, established by presidential decree no. 27 of 1945, was in charge of "resettling" the Magyars from Slovak territory.

The experiences in Slovakia did not resemble the wild transfer committed on Czech territory. Nevertheless, during May and June 1945, about 30,000 Magyars—most of whom came to Slovakia after the 1939 occupation—were either forced out or left the country voluntarily. In the meantime, the Slovak Resettlement Office (SRO) arranged for organized deportation of Magyars within Czechoslovakia. Since the Magyars had lost their citizenship, the SRO could decide arbitrarily where to resettle them. By November 15, 1945, 12,000 Magyars were resettled in Czech territory, mostly in areas experiencing a shortage of labor.[38] There were three official waves of deportation of the Magyars from Slovakia to Bohemia, including the former border area of Sudeten territory where the shortage of labor, especially on farms, was considerable. More than 60,000 Magyars were deported to Bohemia and Moravia from Slovakia.

While the deportation of Magyars into Bohemia and Moravia was going on and plans for mass deportation of Magyars into Hungary neared their implementation date, the government in Budapest entered into bilateral negotiations with Prague about an exchange of Slovak minorities in Hungary for Hungarian minorities in Czechoslovakia. On February 27, 1946, the Czechoslovak Hungarian Agreement on Exchange of Population was signed in Budapest. According to this agreement, the same number of Magyars from Czechoslovakia could be resettled as the number of Slovaks in Hungary would voluntarily resettle in Czechoslovakia. There were 95,421 Slovaks (out of 477,000) who volunteered for resettlement.[39] But this agreement did not resolve the issue of transferring the Magyars from Czechoslovakia. One big hurdle was the limited value of movable property that the Magyars were permitted to take with them. The Czechoslovak delegation insisted on unilateral deportation if the Hungarian government refused to accept its offer. The threat from Prague became even more acute when the 1946 Paris Peace Conference refused to honor the Czechoslovak request for unilateral deportation of Magyars. This refusal was also supported by the Soviet Union. Because of this diplomatic setback, Czechoslovakia continued to persecute the Hungarian minority as well as resettle Magyars into the former Sudeten territory in Bohemia.[40]

After it became clear that Prague could not count on international support for ridding the country of Magyars, a solution was invented: "Re-Slovakization." According to this concept, Magyars who themselves or their ancestors were Slovaks and became "victims of Magyarization" could apply for Czechoslovak citizenship. A list of about 140,000 Magyars was submitted to Budapest by the deadline of August 29, 1946. The official exchange of minorities between Czechoslovakia and Hungary commenced on April 12, 1947, but was later discontinued because of disagreements between the negotiating parties and changes in political systems in Czechoslovakia and Hungary.

In February 1948 changes of Czechoslovakia's political system resulted in changes in policy toward the Hungarian minority. After consultations among the ruling communist parties, the Czechoslovak leaders of CPC, headed by Klement Gottwald, declared that discrimination against nationalities must be replaced by discrimination against the bourgeois class. Consequently, on July 8, 1948, at the meeting of the Central Committee of CPC, Vladimir Clementis submitted the adjusted policy proposal toward the Hungarian minority. It called for the extension of citizenship rights, abrogation of any minority status, prevention of any political organization, and creation of parallel schools of all grades for Hungarian children.[41] Two weeks later, after the representatives of the two governments met, Viliam Siroky announced that the CPC had found the solution for the Hungarian issue in restoring citizens' rights and state citizenship to the Hungarian population.

THE GOTTWALD COALITION GOVERNMENT

Of the six political parties in postwar Czechoslovakia, two were communist—the Communist Party of Czechoslovakia (CPC) and the Communist Party of Slovakia (CPS). Of the four noncommunist parties, one was the strongest Slovak party, the Democratic Party (DP), and another was the strongest noncommunist Czech party, the National Socialist Party (NSP), with about half a million members. The two weakest parties were the People's Party (PP), with about 350,000 members, and the Social Democratic Party (SDP), with about 300,000 members. The latter, hoping to arrange a merger with the communists, established very close relations with the CPC; indeed, two of its leaders, Zdenek Fierlinger and Evzen Erban, were fellow travelers taking orders from the communist leaders. Gottwald and Slansky knew exactly what was going on in other parties of the National Front through reports on the activities of their "competitors" from a well-established network of reliable undercover agents and spies. Since there could be no opposition party as such in the National Front, the only opposition to National Front policies was voiced in parliament by noncommunist members and in the democratic press, especially *Dnesek* (This Day), *Kriticky mesicnik* (Critical Monthly), and *Nova generacia* (New Generation). In contrast, the communists relied heavily on the unions, whose leadership consisted of communists and fellow travelers to get their points across.

The first postwar parliamentary elections in Czechoslovakia were held on May 26, 1946. The elections conformed to the strictest pattern of those of a parliamentary democracy: they were free, secret, direct, and proportional. The communists were the clear winners, with 38 percent of the votes (40 percent in the Czech Lands, 30 percent in Slovakia). The other parties trailed; the National Socialists won 18 percent, the People's Party 16 percent, the Social Democrats 13 percent, and the Slovak Democratic Party 14 percent. But in Slovakia the SDP represented 62 percent of the votes cast, so that they with the communists formed a substantial left-wing majority bloc. The communists received unusually strong support from the farmers because by then a large number of them were recipients of land expropriated from the German minority. There were also many opportunities and careerists who supported the communists because it was assumed that the communists, backed by the mighty Soviet Union, were the party of the future.[42]

The results of the vote in Slovakia were particularly interesting. In Slovakia the CPS received only half as many votes as the DP, and the Slovak National Council (SNC) and its Board of Commissioners (BC) were mandated to reorganize on a basis of two-to-one in favor of the Democrats, instead of fifty-fifty as it had been up to this time. This unexpected upset created a crisis situation for the communists in Slovakia, and their strategists quickly began to search for ways to prevent DP from utilizing the great victory in the rearrangement of power in Slovak ruling institutions. Finally, they came up with the proposal to offer DP entry into the government under certain conditions, which if refused would result in the party's expulsion from the National Front and dissolution. At the same time the position of the central government in Slovakia would be strengthened. Some of the arguments (threats) advanced by CPC at that time were very reminiscent of the pre-Munich arrangements between President Benes and the separatist leaders of HSLS, especially when the possibility of disbanding SNR was mentioned. The result of this crisis resolution was the Third Prague Agreement between the Czechoslovak government and SNR.[43] It was an agreement of two unequal subjects linked to a faint resemblance of a federal type of system and a departure from the spirit of the Kosice governmental program expressed in the motto "Equal with equal." The agreement revealed new centralistic tendencies in the decision-making process as well as the renewal of an asymmetric model of a unitary state, which established a new direction for Slovakia in the state structure—a direction determined by the central authority of the state.

In spite of the Democrats' overwhelming victory, communist Gustav Husak remained the chairman of the Slovak Board of Commissioners. The Third Prague Agreement made certain that confusion between the administrative powers of the Board of Commissioners—and the Czechoslovak government in Prague—would be eliminated in favor of the central government. Before the elections, three points of view prevailed in the country: the Slovak nationalist, the Czech nationalist, and the Czechoslovak communist. Slovak nationalists perceived the powers of the Board of Commissioners to be sovereign in all Slovak matters except foreign policy, defense, and treasury; Czech nationalists viewed Czechoslovakia as a unitary state, with the Slovaks as a separate but equal nation. Benes and other noncommunist leaders opposed the loose federal union the Slovaks sought and proposed instead the creation of three autonomous and equal "Land" governments—one for each of the territories under a central government. The communists opposed the Land system and recommended instead that Slovakia should function as a constituent governmental entity with executive authority but subordinated in all political matters to the central government in Prague. It is important to point out that until the 1946 elections, the communists had favored Slovak autonomy, but after their defeat in Slovakia they endorsed the leading role of the central government in Prague. In the final discussions of the Slovak issue, the communists were supported by the National Socialists against the Democrats, which helped to resolve the crisis situation in Slovakia following the May 1946 elections.[44]

As soon as the election results were complete, President Benes invited the leader of CPC to help form the second government of the National Front. On July 2, 1946, the Gottwald government became a reality. It included nine communists, three Social Democrats, and four seats for each of the remaining noncommunist parties as well as two nonpartisans positions, which were held by Jan Masaryk as foreign minister and Ludvik Svoboda as minister of national defense. In Gottwald's government the same communists held the same key positions, which included the ministries of the interior, finance, and information. The Democrats were admitted into the Gottwald government with the proviso that the DP follow the democratic policies of a unitary state of Czechoslovakia.

On July 11, the new Constituent Assembly approved the governmental program. One of the first tasks of the building program of the Gottwald government was to draw up and enact the constitution of the postwar republic, which would reflect the principles of the Moscow negotiations and the Kosice and Prague agreements. They did not, however, succeed in producing such a document before the communist takeover in February 1948. In the economic area the government set a goal to prepare a two-year plan for the recovery of the national economy, which was also to include a program of industrialization in Slovakia.

Within a few weeks the law concerning the two-year economic plan was drafted, and on October 25, 1946, it was approved by the newly constituted parliament. The main goals of the plan were, by the end of 1948, to reach a 110 percent level of total industrial output compared to 1937 values and, as far as Slovakia was concerned, to make its economic level more equal to that of Czech areas. Section IV of the law made specific investment designations for Slovakia. The economic plan was prepared in such a clever way that all political interests could find some appeal in its total design. To begin with, the government and all CPC made a commitment that no further nationalization would be necessary and that all sectors of the national economy, from the point of view of the ownership of the means of production, would be considered equal and could expect appropriate support from the government. As far as CPC was concerned, however, these promises and commitments were nothing more than a tactical ploy.

The building program was committed to extensive investments in industrialization in Slovakia. This had on the whole a very favorable response from the Slovaks because it represented the first serious effort in contemporary Czechoslovakia to deal with this issue. The two-year plan did not, however, mention the role of SNR and the Board of Commissioners, or the nature of the role of Slovak central institutions in the realization, management, and supervision of the economic plan; the authority for decision making, as suited the communists, was exclusively in the purview of the central government in Prague. The communists counted on the emphasis on the economic problem to overshadow all other issues, above all the political role of the Slovak nation in the state structure. The gradual trend was toward the creation of a centralist form of economic management, which, of course, included Slovakia on the same planning board.

Another portentous aspect of the Gottwald government was the calculated effort to monopolize the power of the state security system. Since liberation, the communists controlled the Ministry of the Interior as well as the security chiefs of both the Land national committees and the district committees in Bohemia and Moravia. Until the May 1946 elections, the commissioner of the interior in Slovakia was a communist, after which a nonparty general, Mikulas Ferjencik, took over; most of the security chiefs of the national committees also were communists. In all instances, the primary objective of the communists was to concentrate on the most valuable sector of the bureaucratic organization, namely, the one that dealt with intelligence; these were state security, intelligence units of the armed services, the Land departments of security, and the seventh division of the Commission of the Interior. In these departments the committee heads and most of the staff were communists, along with some who had taken part in the resistance, especially partisans, and had close ties with Soviet security organs.

"Undesirables" in the security organization were easily gotten rid of. For example, one of the military intelligence officers from the London exile group, General Bartik, was "associated" with a former agent of the Nazi intelligence service, Vondracek; Bartik, a Social Democrat, was replaced by a communist, Pokorny—who after K. A. Frank's execution entered into the protocol an interpolation fabricated to compromise the resistance activity of Vladimir Krajina, the general secretary of the National Socialist Party. After Pokorny accomplished all the "dirty work," he was in turn replaced by a fellow-traveler, the unaffiliated General Janda. By then, however, the communists were in total control of political intelligence in the country's security system; Janda's task was simply to maintain the status quo. Meanwhile, the communists built a reliable network of informers in all political parties; they infiltrated the offices of all leading political leaders and occupied the so-called security positions of all ministries with their own people. Even the office of the president was not exempt.

A similar network of communist control was established in the military. Immediately after the war, with the direct involvement of Lev Zakharovich Mekhlis (the Soviet general of the NKVD), a counterintelligence system was organized in the Czechoslovak armed services. Its immediate task was to cleanse its own ranks of "unreliable" officers.[45]

Military counterintelligence went far beyond its designated authority; it became involved in surveillance not only of military personnel but also of certain politicians against whom it organized surreptitious actions. Under Major (later General) Bedrich Reicin, a member of the CPC since 1929, military counterintelligence became the fifth division of the general staff, working in close collaboration with Soviet intelligence organs. The noncommunist political parties, suspicious of communist machinations, demanded that all political intelligence in the country be coordinated and managed by one central agency under the supervision of the government executive—in other words, accessible to all party leaders—but after the communists won the election, their promise to consider such a proposal and act on it favorably evaporated. The only central intelligence operation was the section of the Central Committee of the CPC, headed by comrade Svab, who was subordinated to Rudolf Slansky.

As far as postwar foreign policy was concerned, the primary guideline for Czechoslovakia was to maintain close and friendly relations with the USSR, its leading ally in every respect. This principle was advanced not only by the communists but also by noncommunist party leaders, who thought it was unavoidable because of the possibility of a future threat from Germany. Just how much influence the Soviet Union had on instigating fear in the minds of the policymakers and the shaping of foreign policy is evident from several cases involving the decision-making process. As early as June 29, 1945, Czechoslovakia had to sign an agreement officially ceding Carpatho-Ukraine (occupied by the Red Army since early 1945) to the Soviet Union. In spite of strong objections from Czechs and Slovaks who were not informed about Benes's promise to Stalin in December 1943 that "it is necessary in all cultural matters to make Carpatho-Russia conform to the rest of the Ukraine,"[46] Stalin expressed satisfaction with that interpretation and never permitted Czechoslovakia to establish administrative power on that territory. Similarly, in the case of the Czechoslovak claim to recover the territory of Teschen lost to Poland, the Soviet Union backed out of a promise to support Prague in regaining the prewar boundaries, although it already had the support of Great Britain for Teschen under Czechoslovak administration.[47]

Another example of unilateral Soviet influence on Czechoslovakia in the postwar period was the signing of a secret treaty on mines in October 1945 between the premier and five vice premiers of Czechoslovakia and Valerian A. Zorin, the Soviet ambassador at Prague. The only other Czech officials who knew about the treaty were Jan Masaryk, the foreign minister, and Hubert Ripka, the foreign trade minister. The treaty gave the Soviets absolute control over uranium production from the Bohemian mines of Jachymov (Joachimstal). After the treaty was signed, the entire area was closed off so that only Russian personnel, mining specialists, intelligence officers, and East German research workers could enter. Those mines later became infamous for their use in holding political prisoners, thousands of whom perished there. The press was forbidden to mention the Jachymov mines. In January 1946, when Foreign Minister Masaryk made reference in his speech at the United Nation's opening session that Czechoslovak uranium would never be used for the manufacture of atomic weapons but would instead be used to cure and heal people, the Soviet ambassador made an angry call to the Czechoslovak Ministry of Foreign Affairs. A few minutes later Premier Zdenek Fierlinger and Vice Premier Klement Gottwald cabled Masaryk with orders to never again attempt to state any important part of Czechoslovak policy, particularly regarding uranium, without first getting specific approval from the government in Prague. In his reply, Masaryk protested against the harsh tone of the dispatch and at the same time assured both his government and the Soviet ambassador that his reference to Czechoslovak uranium was a figurative matter and did not mean a departure from the terms of the secret uranium treaty. He also reminded his critics that his speech about the future peaceful use of Czechoslovak uranium had been applauded by the Soviet delegates present.[48]

Perhaps the most convincing case of Soviet influence was the government's policy decision of how to deal with the prevention of starvation in 1947, when Czechoslovakia was afflicted by a catastrophic drought. Relief was offered in the form of the Marshall Plan. On July 4, 1947, the Czechoslovak government unanimously accepted the joint British-French invitation to join the preparatory conference of the Marshall Plan in Paris. Five days later, a delegation consisting of Gottwald, Masaryk, and Drtina (replacing Ripka, who was ill) was on its way to Moscow to confer on the question of the suggested Franco-Czechoslovak alliance, which had run into difficulties on a comprehensive economic agreement. No one knows what passed at the first meeting between Stalin and Gottwald. But at the second meeting, between Stalin and the entire Czechoslovak delegation, Stalin made it abundantly clear that the Marshall Plan was an anti-Soviet scheme that was incompatible with the

Soviet-Czechoslovak Agreement of 1943.[49] Before returning to Prague, the Czechoslovak delegation signed a five-year economic agreement with the Soviet Union. Under Stalin's persuasion, the Czechoslovak government, including the noncommunists, convinced that Czechoslovakia's close alliance with the Soviet Union must be maintained, withdrew from any further participation in the Marshall Plan negotiations. As postwar developments in Czechoslovakia continued to move Czechoslovakia further and further into the Soviet orbit, the noncommunist politicians seemed not to realize what was happening.

8 The Communist Dictatorship

From July 1947 to February 1948, the leadership of the Communist Party of Czechoslovakia (CPC) was determined to seize the monopoly of power in postwar Czechoslovakia. This decision was influenced not only by the May 1946 election results, particularly in Slovakia, but also by the international communist movement. In September 1947 the Communist Information Bureau (Cominform) was established in Warsaw. The Cominform included the nine communist parties making up the Soviet bloc, plus France, which enabled Moscow to intervene in political as well as economic affairs of the bloc countries. At that time, the Cominform was very critical of the peaceful parliamentary method of acquiring the monopoly of power in the state.[1]

In the fall of 1947, the CPC began making thorough preparations for the decisive political battle with its enemy, studying and analyzing the various means for the takeover of political rule in the state. Five alternative plans were developed, each of them outlining detailed scenarios of parliamentary and nonparliamentary forms of struggle. Thus when the main political crisis occurred in February 1948, the CPC already had an advantage over the noncommunist political parties.

The last two sections of this chapter, "The Soviet Model of Government" and "The Slovak Question Reexamined," are based on the Slovak text by Dusan Kovac.

The main problem faced by the noncommunist politicians was their inability to make a thorough political analysis of the regime taking hold in Czechoslovakia and the strategies the CPC might use. The noncommunists were still following the path of old traditional methods of parliamentarism, which had less and less meaning in Czechoslovakia. The situation of the noncommunist politicians was further complicated by the regime's guided democracy. Because the National Front made it very difficult to create an atmosphere of a smoothly functioning united bloc of democratic powers, the CPC could always point to the obvious weaknesses in the government as a pretext for making accusations against those who tried "to destroy the National Front" and, after they were ousted, to ask for their replacement with "new" members who would be loyal to the government of Klement Gottwald.

The domination of the Ministry of the Interior and the control of its security organs by the communists since liberation were another encumbrance imposed on the noncommunist and democratic forces by the 1943 Moscow Agreements. A formidable force in the final showdown between the communists and noncommunists during this crisis period was organized labor. With a membership of over two million members, labor organizations were controlled from the top by communist leaders, who could depend on their support on a moment's notice. Although the head of the Czechoslovak army, General Ludvik Svoboda, was a nonpartisan, President Benes was not known to be a politician who would use the power of the military to enforce his policy. As a politician who claimed to be above partisan politics, President Benes was in reality a tragic personality.[2] After leaving the country and going into exile in 1938, his prime objective was to realize a policy that would nullify the embarrassment suffered at Munich. This policy, as it developed, was one of close friendship with and dependency on the Soviet Union, the establishment of a limited democracy or people's democracy, and ultimately the victory of communism in Czechoslovakia.

There are several interpretations of the events starting in September 1947 that led to the revolutionary situation in February 1948.[3] On October 6, 1947, the Slovak commissioner of internal affairs, General Mikulas Ferjencik, announced the discovery of a cache of weapons and secret radio transmitters belonging to some fascist elements in Slovakia who were in contact with the former foreign minister, quisling Ferdinand Durcansky. Prominent members of the Democratic Party (DP) were implicated. On October 30, the vice premier for the Democratic

Party, Jan Ursiny, was forced to resign, and his secretary, Otto Obuch, was arrested. Two general secretaries of the Democratic Party, Milos Bugar and Jan Kempny, were also arrested after they willingly surrendered their rights to parliamentary immunity. On the same day, URO, the executive committee of the trade union movement (ROH), held its meeting at Bratislava and demanded the resignation of the entire Board of Commissioners—which would include several Democratic Party leaders. The chairman of the board, Gustav Husak, a communist, complied with the URO demand and immediately submitted the resignation of the board. That same day the Slovak National Front held a meeting at Bratislava that was attended not only by the representatives of the political parties—as prescribed by the rules—but by representatives of URO, agricultural organizations, and the Association of Slovak Partisans, all communist auxilliary organizations. The meeting failed to resolve the issue, and it was referred to the National Front. Gottwald called the meeting of the National Front, with representatives of URO and agricultural organizations, for November 4. When the representatives of the noncommunist parties refused to attend the meeting with communist auxilliary organizations present, Gottwald rescheduled the meeting for November 17–18, without the auxilliaries. Even so, the communists got most of what they were after. In Slovakia the DP was forced to give up control of three commissions. After the elections of 1946, DP had nine commissioners and CPS five; they shared the chairmanship of the board. General Mikulas Ferjencik, Benes's confidant and a nonpartisan, headed the commission of the interior. After the reorganization in November 1947, Ferjencik remained commissioner of the interior, but the department of state security was transferred from his supervision to the communist Vaclav Nosek, who was the minister of the interior in Prague. The three new commissioners were Pavol Blaho, representing the newly created (after May 1946) Slovak Freedom Party (FP); Jan Becko, representing the renewed Slovak Social Democratic Party (SSDP); and another Slovak Social Democrat, Dr. Buza, who was compromised during the war and therefore easily manipulated by the communists.

Like the "conspiracy" in Slovakia instigated by agent provocateurs to disrupt and weaken the power of the DP, in Bohemia the so-called spy affair in Most was designed to compromise the National Socialists (NSP). In September 1947, former 1st Lt. Pravomil Reichl was arrested in Most for treason and espionage. In the spring of 1947, Reichl had been approached by agent provocateur Vladimir Podivin and Ministry of the Interior agents Mueller and Oravan, who represented themselves as agents of the U.S. foreign service. These agents convinced Reichl that the communists were planning a revolt and that the Americans were willing to supply weapons for defense against the communists. As a result, Reichl illegally visited the American zone in West Germany. When he returned to Czechoslovakia in the autumn, he was arrested with a host of accomplices, including a Captain Kraka, and held in a military prison for interrogation. In the presence of a Soviet major and other members of Soviet security organs, the accused were forced to admit that they acted upon instructions from Petr Zenkl, vice premier for the NSP; Prokop Drtina, minister of justice for NSP; and Vladimir Krajina, member of parliament and general secretary of NSP. The first official news about the Most affair was released simultaneously by the Ministry of the Interior and the Ministry of National Defense on November 17, 1947.

Between Czechoslovakia's rejection of the Marshall Plan in July 1947 and the two major incidents in November, there were also some minor incidents initiated by the communists as part of their strategy to flush out the enemy and prepare for the final battle. On September 10, 1947, the communists made an attempt to assassinate three Czech members of the government who were considered the most responsible for blocking the communist-proposed "tax on millionaires," which was to pay for the losses of the farmers in the severe drought of the preceding summer. The three targets were Petr Zenkl, the vice premier; Prokop Drtina, the minister of justice; and Jan Masaryk, the foreign minister. Packages containing bombs were prepared in a Moravian town, Krcman, but were discovered and defused before they found their targets. Investigations by the Ministry of Justice showed that the plot was planned by the branch of the CPC in Olomouc and that a communist member of parliament, Jura Sosnar, and Gottwald's son-in-law, Alexej Cepicka, were involved. The security organs, controlled by Vaclav Nosek, refused action against the suspects and kept the unsolved case under investigation. The communists were fully aware that once they won the elections (scheduled for the spring of 1948), or the monopoly of power in the state before the elections, court proceedings for any of their crimes would become meaningless. They desperately concentrated on victory.

Still another incident, in December 1947, involved the status of state employees. By the end of 1947, the bloated bureaucracy had about 120,000 more employees than were actually needed. The communists started a campaign against older, experienced civil servants, accusing them of having collaborated with the Protectorate government and the Tiso regime, and they refused to support any pay increases until the older civil servants had been replaced by younger ones. When the issue was tabled in the National Front, the head of URO, Antonin Zapotocky, threatened a national meeting of labor union delegates to vote on further nationalization and adjustments in state employment. Meanwhile, the communist minister of the interior, Vaclav Nosek, proceeded to pack the security departments of his ministry with loyal members of the CPC.

In early January 1948, the communists conducted a secret public opinion survey, according to which the projected outcome of the late spring 1948 elections would have meant a 10 percent loss of communist votes. Thus on January 20, 1948, the Presidium of the Central Committee of the CPC decided to seize power in Czechoslovakia by the end of February. The CPC then set about mobilizing its auxiliary mass organizations and placing them on alert. On February 15, the minister of agriculture, Julius Duris, called for a national congress of farm commissions (unions) to be held on February 25—three days after the URO meeting previously scheduled by Antonin Zapotocky. On the same day, *Rude pravo*, the main organ of the CPC, carried an article announcing a national celebration of the Red Army to last from February 22 to March 29, 1948, in conjunction with the Czechoslovak Soviet Friendship Association on the opening day. Thus, while the communists were making preparations for the usurpation of power through their auxilliary mass organizations under the pretext of celebrating the Red Army and Czechoslovak-Soviet friendship, a governmental crisis was brewing in the parliament.

THE FEBRUARY 1948 COUP D'ETAT

The issue around which the crisis revolved was control of the national security organs. At a cabinet meeting on February 13, Minister of Justice Prokop Drtina delivered a lengthy and thorough indictment against the minister of the interior for the systematic and gradual staffing of the most important positions in the security organizations with communists whose names were submitted to him by the special division for security matters at CPC. According to Drtina, during that week alone, the commander of the national security corps in Bohemia, Colonel Dybal, had removed eight district police chiefs—including Dr. Mainer from Plzen, who uncovered the evidence that the legendary communist hero Julius Fucik was a Gestapo informer—and replaced them with loyal communists. The majority noncommunist ministers immediately voted to instruct the absent minister of the interior, Vaclav Nosek, to revoke Dybal's decision—this was the first time the communists had been outvoted in Gottwald's government. But Premier Gottwald refused the noncommunist ministers the right to deal with this issue because "it was an internal matter" of the Ministry of the Interior and the minister was not present to defend himself. On the same day members of the Presidium of the Central Committee (CC) of the CPC met and instructed Gottwald to contact the member of the Politburo of the Central Committee of the Communist Party of the Soviet Union, Yudin, who was in charge of Czechoslovak affairs. The general secretary of the CPC, Rudolf Slansky, was to inform Pexa-Voda, representative of CPC attached to the secretariat of the Cominform, of the situation; Slansky was also told that after consultations with the Cominform, CPC should be placed on permanent readiness. Thereafter, the Presidium of the Central Committee of the CPC met twice daily.

On February 17, the cabinet members of the Gottwald government met again, and again Vaclav Nosek was absent, claiming to be ill. In fact, he was deeply involved at the CPC secretariat in monitoring the crisis situation. The minister of information, Vaclav Kopecky, who represented Nosek, claimed that he was not adequately informed about matters. When the noncommunist ministers finally announced that they would not participate in the government until their decision of February 13 was carried out, Gottwald promised that Nosek would give a full report at the next cabinet meeting on February 20. While the cabinet meeting was still going on, Gottwald informed President Benes of the governmental crisis. He told Benes that the noncommunist ministers were sabotaging the government operation and that they wanted to eliminate communists from the government. In reply, according to Jaromir Smutny (Benes's chancellor), Benes tried to reassure Gottwald that he knew nothing about such attempts and that he insisted on his position that all parties making up the National Front must be in the government and therefore would not allow any party to be expelled. Apparently Benes also told Gottwald that he disagreed with his stance not to allow the government as a whole to interfere in the affairs of individual ministries. He asked Gottwald to be patient and to accept the principle of parliamentary democracy, according to which the minority must respect the wishes of the majority. After Gottwald left the president's office, Benes apparently was informed through his political secretary, Petr Zenkl, about Gottwald's complaints and his reply.

After the cabinet meeting, which ended at four o'clock in the afternoon, the ministers of NSP, PP, and DP met in the office of Vice Premier Jan Sramek. As they vented their anger, minister Hubert Ripka proposed that they resign. Sramek evidently agreed and noted that he could not see any other way out. That evening, Ripka supposedly informed minister Vaclav Majer (a rightist Social Democrat) that the ministers of NSP, PP, and DP were prepared to submit their resignations unless Dybala's measure was revoked.

The vehicles of political pressure were now moving on a collision course. The communists were making plans for the next wave of nationalization and were confident of having the support of the Social Democrats, not to mention the labor unions, which were prepared to exert more pressure on the noncommunists in the government on February 22. On February 19, in this highly tense situation, Valerian A. Zorin, deputy foreign minister of the USSR, arrived in Prague—unannounced—presumably to assure Gottwald of military assistance from the Soviet government if that proved necessary. Shortly after Zorin's arrival, the U.S. ambassador to Czechoslovakia, Laurance A. Steinhardt, returned to Prague after brief consultations in Washington, D.C. He expressed moral and diplomatic support for the noncommunists. While Steinhardt came only with a briefcase, Zorin brought with him five generals who were housed in Zdenek Fierlinger's villa.

On the same day, after a meeting with members of the government, Zenkl, Prochazka, Hala, Kocvara, Ripka, and Stransky, minister Drtina met with President Benes in his office to discuss the deteriorating government situation. According to A. J. Jandacek, Drtina left the president convinced that "Benes knew what the issue was and that he will judiciously defend the democratic rights."[4] About the same time SDP representatives Bohumil Lausman, Blazej Vilim, and Frantisek Tymes pleaded with Klement Gottwald (in the presence of Vaclav Kopecky and Rudolf Slansky) to repeal the February 13 decision. Gottwald refused. Instead, he offered the Social Democrats two-fifths of all seats in a new government they would create together if the Social Democrats would agree. The SDP representatives rejected the offer, at which time Gottwald reportedly threatened them with destruction. This event, according to Jaromir Smutny, was significant because it persuaded Benes of how far the communists had already advanced in their preparation against the opposition.[5] After this encounter with the communists, Lausman and Vilim met with the president and told him that they had decided not to participate in the government decision-making process until Nosek yielded to the February 13 decision. According to Smutny, the Social Democrats never suggested the issue of resignations and Benes never raised it with them.[6] That evening the leadership of the SDP decided to continue to adhere to the February 13 decision, though the Fierlinger wing of the party succeeded in adding a proviso that by doing so the Social Democrats did not intend to disrupt national unity. This decision was then communicated by Blazej Vilim to Gottwald, who could tell from the content of the message that the party was split and looking for a way out. The same evening, Prokop Drtina visited Bohumil Lausman, chairman of the SDP, at his residence. In the presence of Frantisek Tymes, Drtina hinted to Lausman that the ministers of NSP would submit their resignations.[7] Lausman and Tymes then informed Drtina about the party's decision earlier that day. Lausman also informed the two nonpartisan ministers, Masaryk and Svoboda, about the SDP decision.

Gottwald's cabinet was scheduled to hear from Minister of the Interior Nosek on the morning of February 20 about his implementation of the February 13 decision regarding the Dybal measure, but when Zenkl, Hala, and Kocvara shortly before the meeting asked Gottwald whether or not the Dybal case would indeed be discussed, Gottwald declined to answer and asked the members of the cabinet to convene at three o'clock, when the minister of the interior and the minister of national defense would make a very important announcement about the Most affair. Apparently, in reply to this refusal, the ministers of NSP, PP, and DP decided to submit their resignations at once. Msgr. Sramek wanted to make certain that the Social Democrats would submit their resignations also, which would force Gottwald to step down and negotiate with the political parties to form a new government. But when the secretary of PP, Adolf Klimek, met with SDP head Bohumil Lausman, Lausman accused Klimek of confronting him with a fait accompli and declined to promise SDP's support. Apparently Sramek thought it was too late to retreat and saw in the option of resignation, which he believed the president would decline to accept, a lesser evil than elections under police terror.

That afternoon, the general secretary of NSP, Vladimir Krajina, attempted to deliver the written resignation to President Benes but was told that Benes was in a meeting with Gottwald. Fedor Hodza, general secretary of the Slovak DP, was also refused permission to see Benes; Jaromir Smutny, the president's chancellor, told Hodza that legal experts were studying the constitutional aspect of the government crisis, and he further informed Hodza that the president would not accept the resignations and would not name a new government because such a government would not consist of legitimate representatives of democratic parties. That evening, Frantisek Hala, minister of PP, did manage to see Benes and submitted to him the written resignations of all ministers of his party. According to Hubert Ripka, Ivo Duchacek, and Adolf Klimek, Benes firmly declared that he would not accept the resignations.[8]

Later that same evening the executive board of SDP met again, and minister Vaclav Majer proposed that SDP members of the Gottwald government join the other twelve democratic ministers in submitting their resignations. The proposal was rejected, and a new resolution was passed in which the main thesis held that since no party had withdrawn, the National Front was in full force and government business must continue; the ministers who submitted their resignations had acted in haste, but Gottwald must be reprimanded for failing to implement the government's decisions. The SDP leaders reiterated their support for the governmental program and demanded that the cleansing of the state security corps be carried out. For Gottwald, of course, it was not news because he had already learned from Fierlinger that SDP would not join the other twelve noncommunist members in submitting their resignations. Indeed, several hours before the SDP meeting, Gottwald was already negotiating for the new candidates who would fill the gap in his government. That same evening, according to Bohumil Lausman, members of the parliament for NSP and PP, Dr. Alois Neumann and Josef Plojhar, were introduced to Gottwald as candidates for the potentially vacated ministerial positions. Also that evening Dr. A. Sevcik of the Slovak DP supposedly offered his services.[9]

The CC-CPC presidium, which was of course fully aware of the various maneuverings, now decided to mobilize and arm all workers and place them in strategic locations throughout the country. Communist workers quickly seized the radio stations and other media and communication systems and made preparations to establish revolutionary action committees in factories and offices the following day. In the name of the working people, labor organizations issued hundreds of telegrams and resolutions supporting Gottwald's revolutionary government. At the same time the CC-CPC presidium announced that in resigning, the representatives of the three political parties had placed themselves outside the National Front, outside the platform of the governmental program, and were therefore counterrevolutionaries.[10] The SDP proposal to resolve the crisis in the National Front was rejected by the communists as a viable option. Instead, that evening, the leaders of the CPC demanded that President Benes accept the resignations and made it clear that they would not negotiate with them. Since only twelve out of twenty-six ministers had submitted their resignations, Gottwald was now in a good position to exert his pressure on Benes to achieve his goal.

On the morning of February 21, 1948, Bohumil Lausman, Frantisek Tymes, and Blazej Vilim reported to President Benes the decision of the SDP executive board. Apparently Benes told the representatives of SDP that if it was a mistake, he would have to accept the resignations and make certain that the new government was a government of political parties.[11] When asked about a list of members of the new government selected only by the communists, Benes is reported to have replied that if Gottwald brought such a list, Benes would submit it to the party leaders for their approval.[12] The position of SDP seems to have had a great deal to do with Benes's assurances to Gottwald and Nosek a short time later that he would follow the constitutionally prescribed rules and procedures. Gottwald presented Benes with a resolution adopted at the meeting in the Old City Square in which the president was urged to accept the resignations of the ministers and not to pursue further negotiations, at which Benes asked Gottwald what would happen if he did not accept the resignations. Both Lausman and Jandacek have said that Gottwald, in the name of the people, threatened Benes if he refused.[13] Benes then assured Gottwald that he would not appoint a new government without CPC representation or one in which Gottwald would not be premier; he made the same assurances to delegates of workers from Prague, Plzen, and Kladno.

On that day in Slovakia the communist chairman of the Board of Commissioners, Gustav Husak, demanded that all commissioners of the Slovak DP submit their resignations as a response of solidarity with the resigned ministers of their party; Husak then named his own directors to oversee the operation of those offices—in some instances there was a duality of power for at least one day.[14] Persons who were undesirable or under suspicion were simply denied entry into the government buildings by the police, which de facto "resolved" the crisis.

On February 22, early in the morning at the National Theater in Prague, the long-planned festive meeting of the founding of the Czecho-slovak-Soviet Friendship Society got under way. In the presence of Soviet Deputy Foreign Minister Valerian Zorin and Red Army General D. D. Lelyushenko, Premier Gottwald made a promise that no one in Czecho-slovakia would ever be subjected to anti-Soviet slurs and trickery. One hour later, in the Industrial Palace at Prague, Gottwald greeted the 8,000 delegates of URO with a diatribe against the resigned ministers, whom he labeled agents of domestic and foreign reactionaries who must not return to the government. The delegates passed several resolutions call-ing for further nationalization of enterprises (with more than fifty em-ployees) and new land reforms.

President Benes listened to the radio coverage of these meetings at the presidential castle in Lany; what he heard prompted him to return immediately to Prague. Bohumil Lausman, who saw Benes later that day, has said that Benes told him he was afraid of a possible civil war and killings and that he could not ignore the possibility of Soviet inter-vention and in the interest of peace would probably accept the resigna-tions of the twelve ministers the next day.[15]

Around noon on February 23, President Benes received Premier Got-twald and Minister of the Interior Vaclav Nosek, who presented the president with documents, apparently found during a search of the sec-retariat's office of NSP, that allegedly made the party culpable of involvement in the preparation of an armed uprising. According to Ripka's account of the meeting, Benes insisted that Gottwald adhere to parliamentary custom and deal with the three parties whose ministers submitted their resignations; Gottwald rejected the idea and, with slan-derous language, attacked the resigning ministers, especially Petr Zenkl.[16] Ripka's account further says that Gottwald told the president that he would submit a list of candidates whose names were mostly drawn from the members of parliament, an offer that Benes refused, saying that it was his duty to deal only with legitimate representatives of political parties.

Gottwald and his party now clearly had the upper hand. That eve-ning, at the first meeting of the Central Action Committee of the (Re-newed) National Front (CACNF), representatives of all political parties and nonpartisan civic organizations participated in a well-scripted program endorsing Gottwald's platform. Present at the meeting were Generals Svoboda, Bocek, and Klapalek. General Svoboda announced that the army would always be on the side of the people and that those who brought strife and did not want to cooperate with others would have to be removed. He did not mention the president, whom he had seen earlier that day and to whom he had promised that the army was fully behind him and remained the guardian of democracy and constitutionalism.[17] The delegates elected Antonin Zapotocky chairman of CACNF and Alexej Cepicka its general secretary. The National Front created by the agreement of the six political parties participating in the Moscow negotiations in March 1945 had now ceased to exist.

On February 24, President Benes spoke with the representatives of the Slovak DP: Chairman of the Board of Commissioners Jozef Lettrich, Vice Premier Stefan Kocvara, Minister of Transportation Ivan Pietor, Minister of Unification Mikulas Franek, and State Secretary of the Ministry of National Defense Jan Lichner. After explaining to Benes the reasons the ministers of DP had submitted their resignation, Lettrich—who was head of DP—posed the question whether or not the president would yield to communist pressures and accept the resignations submitted by the noncommunist ministers. It was quite evident by now that Gottwald and the others would not resign. Lettrich concluded his report by reassuring the president that though he could always count on the support of the Democratic Party, the party would like to know the president's position in this situation.

Benes restated his previous position, telling the Slovak delegation that he did not and would not accept the resignations and that he would name a new government only after all interested political parties agreed. He also said that if Gottwald would not deal with the noncommunist party representatives, then he himself would speak with them. Benes emphasized the point that just as he could not seat a government without the communists and Gottwald as premier, neither could he establish a government without the participation and representation of other political parties. He agreed with Lettrich and his fellow delegates that Minister of the Interior Vaclav Nosek had an obligation to carry out the cabinet, and he assured the delegation that he would not change his opinion and would continue to uphold his position in the crisis. When Kocvara, Pietor, Franek, and Lichner asked what the president would do if Gottwald still refused to yield, Benes replied that he would address the nation and tell the citizenry that his efforts had not led to a resolution. And what would he do after that? Although Benes reportedly told the Slovak delegation that chaos and a situation similar to the post-Munich era might follow, Lettrich is said to have characterized Benes after the meeting as one who was saving his own neck and not the situation.[18] Benes's discussion with the Slovak DP delegation was his last with representatives of democratic political parties.

That evening the communists stepped up their terror. Action committees were fully established in all plants, enterprises, and offices, including the office of the president. All anticommunists were let go and replaced by communists. All newspapers and journals were put under the control of the Ministry of the Interior, as were all broadcasting stations. Orders for arrest were issued against politicians such as Jan Ursiny and editors such as Pavel Tigrid. Gottwald challenged SDP minister Vaclav Majer to resign. Majer refused, pointing to his party's resolution of the previous day, according to which SDP decided not to join the resignation of the twelve ministers. Later that evening, Bohumil Lausman agreed with Zdenek Fierlinger that SDP would be led by the action committee with Fierlinger at its helm. In a formal letter the action committee recalled Vaclav Majer from his position as minister of food, and in a letter Lausman informed Majer that he was expelled from the party. At last, Gottwald had a free hand to reorganize his government with his own followers.

On February 25, 1948, before noon, President Benes received Premier Gottwald and Minister Nosek, who insisted that he sign the authorization of the new government list. Benes was still wavering in his decision to accept the resignation of the twelve ministers, so Gottwald gave him an ultimatum to sign it by 4:00 P.M.; the "people" would wait no longer. At 1:00 P.M., Prague radio announced that the president approved the formation of the new government, but according to Benes's personal physician, Dr. Oskar Klinger, Benes was refusing to sign the new government list as late as 3:30 P.M.[19] Then, after talking with his spouse, Hana, President Benes signed the list shortly before 4:00 P.M.

President Benes received the new government on February 27. All the key posts were held by communists, left-wing members of SDP (like Fierlinger, Lausman, and Jankovcova) were represented, and the other parties each had a "representative" chosen not by themselves but by the communists. They included Alois Neumann and Emanuel Slechta for NSP, Josef Plojhar and Alois Petr for PP, and Jan Sevcik for the Slovak DP. At President Benes's request, Gottwald supposedly assigned Vavro

Srobar a ministerial post. Zdenek Nejedly returned as minister of education, and the communist trade union leader Antonin Zapotocky became a vice premier. The procommunist minister of defense, Ludvik Svoboda, continued in the new government, as did Jan Masaryk (a nonpartisan) in the position of foreign minister. Eleven days later, on March 10, 1948, Masaryk's body was found in a courtyard of the foreign ministry. The communists called it suicide, but an investigation during the Dubcek era of the Prague Spring indicated (without hard evidence) that the incident was political murder.

While Gottwald was driven in his limousine from Hradcany Castle to Wenceslaus Square with the signed list of new government members of the government in his briefcase, university students in Prague (the only organized opposition) demonstrated in front of the castle, shouting out the name of T. G. Masaryk, freedom, and democracy and pledging their support and willingness to make sacrifices if necessary. A delegation of students headed by Antonin Navratil was received by the president's chancellor, Jaromir Smutny. Soon the police dispersed the student crowd, but not before a policeman shot and seriously wounded one student. More than one hundred demonstrating students were jailed and interrogated. President Benes succumbed to Gottwald's constraining force, to the terror of the communist street tactics, and to the fear of potential bloodshed and chaos. There was no violent struggle—threats and fear did the job. It was a peaceful and well-managed revolution.[20] The noncommunist majority in the government seemed mostly surprised and unprepared. The same can be said for President Benes, whom Churchill called "a master of administration and diplomacy" who failed because he did "not take violent decisions at the supreme moment": "He was too experienced a diplomatist," Churchill wrote, "too astute a year-to-year politician to realise the moment and to stake all on victory or death."[21] To this writer the February 1948 events (and those preceding it) are a reminder of what can happen when the democratic process produces undemocratic results. It happened twice in Czechoslovakia.

In 1950, Ferdinand Peroutka, in an article entitled "Was Dr. Eduard Benes Guilty?" claimed that Benes was not solely responsible for the 1948 events, that other politicians, too, who returned to Czechoslovakia in 1945 from London via Moscow bore responsibility for the policy decisions that caused the collapse of democracy in 1948. However, Peroutka attributes the communist success in February 1948 primarily to the "situation" in which a small country—Czechoslovakia—had to face a giant—the USSR.[22] The crux of the matter is that after the 1938 Munich debacle, Benes sought protection and support for his small country not from the West but from the East. Benes and his government were reminded of that in 1944, during the Slovak National Uprising. When U.S. Ambassador to Prague Laurence A. Steinhardt told Petr Zenkl that Czechoslovakia could count only on U.S. moral support, he must have been clearly aware of treaty obligations and the rules of international law.[23] Furthermore, in his secret dispatch no. 309, of April 30, 1948, addressed to George C. Marshall, U.S. secretary of state, Ambassador Steinhardt made it quite clear that, though Czechoslovakia had avoided the postwar political situation that developed in Poland, "it was only a matter of time, [that] the crisis in Czechoslovakia would develop."[24] Today, when archival documents can be scrutinized, the answers to Peroutka's question and similar ones become much clearer. The evidence suggests that the commitments to build a Soviet-style "people's democracy" in Czechoslovakia and a foreign policy closely tied to the Soviet Union were made by Benes in December 1943 and endorsed by all political party leaders in March 1945 at the Moscow Conference.[25] After that, the planted seed began to sprout and grow. To blame the communist takeover in 1948 on the smallness of the country or the international situation at Tehran and Yalta—as some writers do—is an oversimplification. By then the die was cast. Benes's mind about future Czechoslovak-Soviet relations was made up long before late November 1943, when the Tehran Conference was held, or the Yalta Conference in 1945. In retrospect, it should be self-evident that small nations seeking protection and guarantees for the freedom and well-being of their people do not enter into alliances and friendship agreements with dictatorships.

THE SOVIET MODEL OF GOVERNMENT

The communists lost no time in establishing totalitarian rule in the country.[26] They purged universitites (where about 20,000 students and hundreds of professors were expelled), the press, civil service, the arts and cultural organizations, and even sports clubs. Under Vice Premier Zapotocky, the CACNF named new chairpersons for the purged noncommunist parties—all of them loyal to the communists. On March 10, 1948, CACNF submitted to the parliament its new (radical) governmental program. It was unanimously approved by 230 members; 59 members failed to attend, and 11 members left the session before voting began. Within six weeks (April 10) the membership in parliament shrank from 300 to 155—almost half of the members having been jailed or expelled or forced to resign under duress; some went into hiding and eventually left the country and went into exile. When the last session of parliament was held on May 9, 1948, 244 old and new members approved the new people's democratic constitution. Instead of signing the document, President Benes resigned. On the same day, the purged parliament was dissolved and new elections were held, on a joint list, with no opposition candidates. In Bohemia and Moravia the results were 90 percent for the list, and in Slovakia, 86 percent. On June 14, the new parliament then elected Klement Gottwald as president, and Antonin Zapotocky became the premier. One month earlier, Fierlinger and Gottwald announced the fusion of the rump SDP with the communists, which was actually carried out on June 27. By September 6, 1948, when Benes died, Czechoslovakia was tightly controlled by the communists.

In Slovakia, as in the Czech Lands, all state organs were now in the hands of the communists. The chairman of the Slovak National Council (SNC) was Karol Smidke. All "undesirable" members of SNC were expelled. The Slovak DP, renamed the Revival Party (RP), became an appendage of the Slovak National Front (NF), firmly in the hands of the communists, just like the Freedom Party (FP). The communist machinery moved with equal speed to take over the entire economy. All enterprises with more than fifty employees and all wholesale businesses that had not already been nationalized were now put under state control.

According to the original communist plan, the agricultural issue was also supposed to have been solved in a "revolutionary" manner. The largest permitted size of privately owned agricultural land was fifty hectares; the rest of the land was supposed to have been distributed among small farmers and landless farmworkers. But it soon became evident that land redistribution was nothing more than a "revolutionary slogan" to win over the farmers to communism. Although shortly after February 1948 the Zapotocky government still issued certificates of ownership to new owners of land, by early 1949 the communist regime had begun to convert Slovak villages into cooperative farms. Officially, the creation of cooperatives was voluntary, but in reality collectivization was carried out under duress and with brutal force. After November 1948, those who opposed collectivization were sent into forced labor camps, sanctioned by law for "the class enemies and the enemies of the people's democratic order." Children of "class enemies," including farmers who failed to fulfill the compulsory quotas of agricultural production, had no access to schools of higher education and were expelled from jobs.

The results of this forceful process were drastic changes in the social structure of Slovak society. Private enterprises ceased to exist. All small businesses, including offices of private doctors and attorneys, were nationalized. In a relatively short time practically all citizens became state employees. In a similar manner the collective farmers became state employees of a peculiar type because for all practical purposes they lost further claim to "their own" land and as a result lost interest *in* the land.

The communists were successful in imposing their power and influence on all levels of government and society. As soon as the revolutionary (crisis) situation developed in Prague, the communists organized action committees made up of communists and fellow-travelers. The action committees were quickly established throughout the country and became the main vehicle for carrying out widespread "cleansing" in all institutions.[27] And the Communist Party members quickly became a new social elite. Their only qualification was a Communist Party ID card.[28]

The legitimization of the elite and the replacement of the leadership on all levels of society could not have been achieved so quickly without an atmosphere of threat and fear. In April, less than two months after the communist takeover, the first political inquisition was started in Slovakia against the members of the former Democratic Party. Its chairman, Jan Ursiny, and most of the other party functionaries were condemned to long-term imprisonment. Several trials were a fabrication of the security organs, brought to a desirable conclusion through the manipulation of the new judiciary.[29]

The thorn in the eyes of the communists was the church, and in Slovakia, above all, the Catholic Church. In 1949, all religious organizations were placed under state supervision, then, in 1950, the communists introduced new security measures, which were used one night to liquidate all monasteries. Most of the monks ended up in work camps. Later on the convents were also abolished. The followers of the Catholic faith were supposed to have been daunted by trials of Bishops Jan Vojtassak and Michal Buzalka. And the trial of Bishop Pavol Gojdic was the culmination point of the destruction of the Greek Orthodox Church in Slovakia.

The communist regime also intimidated the intelligentsia through widespread process of "verification," which resulted in sending many people to "production" camps for reeducation. They were replaced by reliable communists, in many instances people with only a few weeks' preparation and no formal education. Many intellectuals fled the country. The communist regime made every effort to prevent the escape of about 60,000 citizens, who then became political refugees in various states of Western Europe, mostly in West Germany. Attempts to cross the border into Austria or Germany became a life-risking undertaking. The borders with noncommunist countries became an "iron curtain." The public in Slovakia was subjected to a one-sided communist propaganda; all foreign news broadcasts from the West were jammed, and no newspapers from capitalist countries were available to its citizens. The new communist society had to be built in complete isolation.

In a relatively short time, the regime liquidated all "germs" of civil society. "Bourgeois" associations were either eliminated or were transformed into a unified state system of organizations directed by the Communist Party and its ideology. Any attempts at civic initiatives were nipped in the bud. The citizen was to become an obedient executor of the will of a single political party, and all "activity" was limited to the execution of different orders and resolutions and listening to speeches favorable to the regime at organized gatherings.

In the early 1950s, the criminal machinery of the system, which in a relatively short time destroyed all "enemy forces" in the country, turned on its own. In November 1952, secretary-general of the CPC Rudolf Slansky, former foreign minister Vlado Clementis, and twelve others were publicly tried for treason, sabotage, and espionage. They were all found guilty and hanged.[30] Before 1953, during the twilight of the Stalinist dictatorship, trumped-up charges and so-called trials led to death sentences for 233 citizens; 178 people were subsequently executed. Of course, these figures do not include the thousands of victims who perished or were permanently crippled in uranium mines at Jachymov and in work camps or those who were liquidated without trial by security organs.

The natural response to the cruel and open communist dictatorship in the society was alienation and resistance. As early as 1949, an illegal radio transmitter, "White Legion," began to broadcast appeals for peaceful resistance. The movement was soon discovered by the security organs, and sixty people were brought to trial; three of the accused were sentenced to death and executed. In the Catholic Church, an underground organization was formed among some younger believers in the church doctrine. But conditions for any organized civil disobedience were very unfavorable because the communist dictatorship held the entire society under strict control. Long before the February coup state security (StB) had established a thorough network of agents and collaborators whose task was to report any sign of organized resistance. In the atmosphere of the Cold War, when the population was exposed to fears of a possible third world war, hopes of assistance from abroad were also vanishing. Thanks to Czech and Slovak émigrés, the population was receiving, via clandestine receivers, Western news from the Voice of America and Radio Free Europe, but listeners were in constant jeopardy.

While the communist regime engaged in terrorism against its people, it also made attempts to win over segments of society, especially young people. The communist leadership considered this task a "struggle" to be waged as a compulsory assignment by all auxiliary organizations of the party, especially art and cultural associations. A pseudoromantic pathos was invented to produce the expected results. The communists also found that it was possible to win over the youth through various building projects, for example, the "Youth Railway Track," and, of course, through a battery of slogans about building a classless and just society by creating a new socialist person. But the inability of the communist regime to compete with Western European countries in the economic area and the increased terror in society soon dampened the success of communist propaganda.

After Stalin's and Gottwald's deaths in 1953, the communist regime mellowed somewhat. By then, however, society was completely terrified, its spirit broken, and its will dehumanized. Signs of public opposition to the Stalinist model of political system were not noticeable until the struggle for power ensued in Moscow and its spillover affected its satellite states. In all the satellite states the new generation of communists had shown a certain dissatisfaction with the Stalinist methods of operation. This dissatisfaction burst out in the June 1953 revolt in the Democratic Republic of Germany, in the October 1956 revolts in Hungary and Poland, and in public disclosure of Stalin's crimes at the Twentieth Congress of the Communist Party of the Soviet Union (CPSU). Also by then, a reform movement within the Communist Party had made itself known in Slovakia.

THE SLOVAK QUESTION
REEXAMINED

After the coup in 1948, the communist regime strengthened the central powers of the state. Any efforts to increase the authority of the Slovak political institutions were considered dangerous and were resolutely repudiated. The gist of political centralism was the fact that the CPS, which now ruled Slovakia, was fully subordinated to the CPC. In documents, the official reference for this relationship was the "organizational amalgamation of CPC with CPS."[31] This move was thoroughly and decisively planned immediately after the communist coup, and on September 28, 1948, the administrative merger issue was endorsed by CC-CPS. Although the name—Communist Party of Slovakia (CPS)—and its organs remained the same, in reality they became a cog in the central apparatus of CPC, without any kind of autonomy.

In April 1954, a trial of "bourgeois nationalists" was held in Slovakia, with Gustav Husak, Ladislav Novomesky, and several other leading communists among the accused. This trial had an anti-Slovak connotation. Among other things, it was also an attempt to get even with the generation of the Slovak National Uprising that advocated a federal model of state system for Czechoslovakia. The trial also became a measure to prevent any new attempt to raise the Slovak issue. Incidentally, Husak and Novomesky were found guilty and sentenced to prison for life and ten years, respectively, on charges of Slovak separatism.

Several communists in party and state leadership were clearly aware that the Slovak issue could become intense at any time. They also knew that the issue could not be permanently solved by terror. A plan was developed simultaneously to solve the problem through industrialization of Slovakia. Since, according to some Marxist theorists, the Slovak issue was only a problem of Slovak development falling behind that of Bohemia and Moravia, it followed that if Slovakia could succeed in catching up economically with the Czech Lands, the pesky Sovak problem would be solved.

The politics of economic equalization failed to make the Slovak issue disappear. On the contrary, industrialization, modernization, and with it the noticeable growth of the Slovak intelligentsia cast the Slovak issue in a new light. During the first major crisis in the Communist bloc, in 1956, when Hungarian students staged a counterrevolution, the CPC, afraid of similar unrest in Slovakia, symbolically, but not intact, expanded some of the authority of the Slovak legislature, SNR; the naming and recalling of the commissioners was moved into the competence of SNR, but all basic issues were still decided by the leadership of CPC. As soon as the Soviet tanks suppressed the revolt in Hungary, the CPC quickly came up with anti-Slovak measures, for which the centralist bureaucrat, secretary-general of CPC and from 1957 president of the republic, Antonin Novotny, was quite famous. The new Constitution of 1960, in a strictly voluntaristic fashion, pronounced Czechoslovakia to be a socialist state and officially renamed the state the Czechoslovak Socialist Republic.[32] The new constitution practically eliminated the last remnants of Slovak self-governing organs and introduced a rigid system of unitarism. It abolished the Board of Commissioners, and with it the last vestiges of administrative rule of the Slovak political organs. In all these measures the CPC dismissed the dissatisfaction with the communist dictatorship in Slovakia as no more than a nationality phobia. The problem was not as simple as it first appeared: in addition to studying potential political and economic reforms, a segment of Slovak reformed communists began to examine the organization of the state administration because in Slovakia dissatisfaction with centralism could not be completely eliminated even by terror.

The notion that the Slovak issue would automatically be solved once the economic development of Slovakia was brought up to the level of Bohemia and Moravia was no longer just a plan on the drawing board. Concrete steps were being undertaken to industrialize Slovakia. Large industrial complexes were built, especially in the eastern part of Slovakia. But industrialization, combined with urbanization, had contradictory results. Though expanded industry created many new jobs, it increased the problems connected with the growth of industrial cities, a drastic change for most Slovaks. Whereas in 1947 almost half of the population was working in agriculture, by the end of the 1980s only 13 percent of the population did that kind of work, while during the same period employment in industry increased fourfold—from 200,000 to 800,000. The large number of foundries and aluminum, chemical, and cement factories, few if any of which were concerned about pollution, had ultimately disastrous effects on the government. Moreover, because several huge enterprises did not produce final products, their effectiveness within the framework of the entire economy was limited. Even so, this process also had a positive feature. There is no doubt that it greatly enhanced Slovak modernization by transforming the economy from an agrarian society to an industrial one.

After the first shock of collectivization, agriculture stabilized. The state-funded grants to cooperative farms gave agriculture in the 1960s a new dynamic. Many farmers and their families became employed in industry, which resulted in a considerable increase in the standard of living in the countryside. The villages also changed in appearance. Electrification, sanitation, and the creation of an infrastructure were followed by new housing projects to accommodate the collective farm workers. At the end of the communist period the village population had the highest standard of living in Slovak society.

The communist rulers tried to isolate the country from the rest of the world for other than ideological reasons. From the end of the 1950s it was evident that the Soviet bloc states were falling behind the Western European states. The communists were keenly interested in further development of the country, but because of the strong centralist system in which every trifling matter had to be decided at the highest level of decision making, further development was impossible in Slovakia.[33] Compared with before the war, Slovak citizens were economically better off: the quality of living had improved, a new communication system had been built, there was no unemployment, the citizens had certain social achievements, and their educational level had risen. In general, one can argue that modernization was progressing in spite of communist centralism. But compared with the Western European countries, the rise in the standard of living and the modernization process was much slower, and very often it came at the expense of the quality of life and the environment.[34] By the early 1960s it became obvious that the chief cause of the failure of the economy was the maze of centralized planning.[35]

Even the CPC had to realize that the only way to deal with the economic problem was the old way. The Twelfth Congress of CPC, held at the end of 1962, determined on a new drive to improve the economy, and in 1963 it launched a seven-year plan for economic development. It was an official admission that the previous five-year plan was a failure. Events in 1963 confirmed this because the year proved to be quite the opposite of the start of an economic breakthrough. The seven-year plan was withdrawn, to be followed thereafter by vague annual plans that no one took seriously. In January 1965, for example, CC-CPC issued a document entitled "About the Main Directions of the Improvement of the Planned Management of the National Economy and About the Work of the Party." Every statement in it was vague and theoretical. And in May 1966, when the Thirteenth Congress of CPC again set up its main goal to "improve the system of planned management of the economy" and called for the preparation of the five-year plan for 1966–1970, it was abundantly clear that it was no more than another futile attempt to solve the "quadra angles of a circle." The economy and the entire society were in a deep crisis.[36]

9 Slovak Participation in the Prague Spring

Dissatisfaction with the economy was not the only sign of crisis in the Czechoslovak state as the decade of the 1950s drew to a close. The willfulness of the new political elite and the suppression of freedom of expression and the press were increasingly an irritant. Year by year, dissatisfaction with the communist dictatorship widened and intensified. If the communists had been at first successful in misleading the general public and winning over a large segment of the population, including the intelligentsia, with the idea of building a new social order, the political trials in the 1950s, the atmosphere of constant terror, and the omnipotence of the new ruling elite opened the eyes of many citizens. More and more, too, Czechoslovak citizens felt isolated from the rest of the world. Although opportunities for travel were very restricted, information from the West still trickled through via foreign broadcasts, especially Radio Free Europe and the Voice of America, and also from persons who for one reason or another were permitted to travel beyond the Iron Curtain. Czechoslovak citizens still heard a little about what was going on and how people were living in countries that were not under Soviet control.

The ruling elite could no longer hide the fact that the country's economy was stagnant; clearly, the dynamic development of West European

---

This chapter is based on the Slovak text by Dusan Kovak.

and American economies could not be matched and outpaced (as N. S. Khrushchev had prophesied) by the ossified, centralized, bureaucratized system of communist countries. The integrative measures in Western Europe served as an additional impetus for economic development, but the attempt to integrate the East European economies in a centralized system under Moscow's control would not have the same effect. Thus at the beginning of the 1960s it was already clear that the gap between the East and the West was widening, the economy in the Eastern countries was lagging, and the standard of living was deteriorating. Even though Czechoslovakia and the German Democratic Republic were the most advanced states in the Communist bloc, they visibly trailed behind Western Europe. Both regions—Eastern and Western Europe—had been an integral part of the advanced industrial world before the war; the contrast between the two economies was now a direct demonstration of the inability of the centralist model of the communist economy.

The inability to express opinions freely, censorship of the press, and the abolition of civic and church organizations, especially to a traditionally religious citizenry, were increasingly odious. Especially in Slovakia, the regime's policy to instill atheism was met with open resistance.

The most important events leading to the Prague Spring of 1968 actually took place in 1967. A prominent role in these events was played by the Fourth Congress of the Czechoslovak Writers' Union, held on June 27–29, 1967.[1] At this meeting the writers collectively asserted themselves as the representatives of the discontented elements of society and as spokespersons of the basic demands of Czechoslovak citizens. The Writers' Union congress thus became the rallying point for protesting against the policies of the Communist Party. The writers called for a return to the culturally civilized European sphere; they demanded the abolition of censorship and pushed for openness as well as acceptance of the European context of Czech and Slovak culture. In various reports and discussion papers by Milan Kundera, Pavel Kohout, Ivan Klima, Ludvik Vaculik, Vaclav Havel, and others, the writers demanded openness in the cultural area and in society as a whole, as well as removal of persistent dogmatism. The delegation of communist officials who were in attendance watched the proceedings with great apprehension. Then, when a letter by Alexander Solzhenitsyn, the persecuted Russian writer, was read to the audience, the entire delegation, headed by ideologue Jiri Hendrych, walked out of the meeting in protest. After the congress ended, all those who demanded democratization of the society, renewal of civil rights, and the end of censorship were subjected to strong criticism. Heavy pressures from party and state organs prevented the most outspoken critics of the regime from being elected to leading positions in the writers' organization, and the resolution calling for the abolition of censorship was rejected. Instead, reprisals against the critics of the regime followed immediately. When the proceedings of the meeting were published, however, support from the general public was overwhelming. Thus the congress became a significant catalyst for the developments in the months that followed.

In Slovakia, general discontentment with the communist regime intensified because of the state's centralization policy, which dismantled Slovak self-ruling organs. President of the Republic Antonin Novotny created a storm of opposition when on Slovak soil he made anti-Slovak pronouncements.[2] He became the embodiment not only of the centralistic bureaucratic system but also of the anti-Slovak element in Czech society.

Novotny went to Turciansky Sv. Martin in August 1967 to take part in the centennial celebration of the founding of the Slovak secondary school. His behavior both before and during the festivities seemed to the Slovaks purposely insulting. He refused to include Slovak leaders in his entourage—Alexander Dubcek, who at that time was the first secretary of the CC-CPS, remained in Bratislava in protest. The program included the placing of a wreath at the National Cemetery in Martin, where many notable representatives of the Slovak past are buried. Thousands of people waited for Novotny's arrival at the cemetery, but instead he visited an agricultural cooperative. Because of a threatened assassination attempt, he did not show up at the hotel where he was booked for the night. When his entourage drove through Mosovce, the birthplace of Jan Kollar, instead of stopping, as the villagers had expected, to place a bouquet of flowers at Kollar's monument, the motorcade rushed Novotny through the village. At the Matica Slovenska (Slovak Heritage Foundation), which he referred to as a nationalistic organization—a direct slur on Matica's interest in the Slovaks abroad—Novotny refused to sign the guest book and left the institution with threats to the organization's activities. Then when about half of the invited guests indicated their displeasure by failing to show up for the banquet, Novotny left in a hurry and his wife ostentatiously returned all gifts she had received.

The discord could no longer be denied, and the Slovaks obviously felt insulted at this provocation.[3]

Criticism of Novotny was not confined to the Slovaks. At the September 1967 session of the CC-CCP, Notovny was openly criticized for violations of the principles of collective leadership and subjectivism. There was even sharper criticism at the October meeting of the CC-CPC. Alexander Dubcek gave a speech in which he stressed shortcomings within the party organization and the alienation of the party from society. Novotny, in rebuttal, accused segments of CPS leadership of bourgeois nationalism—led by Alexander Dubcek. The accusation did not sit well with the Czech communists, and the CPS leadership reprimanded Novotny, whereupon Novotny appealed to the Communist Party of the Soviet Union. Leonid Brezhnev, the CPSU secretary-general, went to Prague in early December to evaluate the situation and, to everyone's surprise, declined to intervene in what he called an internal matter.

Novotny had no intention of capitulating, and when criticism against him kept growing, he made an attempt to solve the problem through military action. Novotny had substantial support among high-ranking military officers and in the security organs, as well as among many loyal communists in the party apparatus. With their help, he prepared a plan for military intervention, including a list of enemies—politicians, military leaders, writers, artists, scientists—numbering more than one thousand. The CC-CPC leaders judged unreliable were to be placed under the supervision of the state security, the StB. The contemplated military intervention was planned for sometime after Christmas 1967. It did not materialize. Novotny failed to receive the green light from Moscow and had to abandon any type of armed intervention. By the time of the next meeting of the CC-CPC, which was summoned into session immediately after the New Year's holiday in 1968, Novotny had lost his majority support.

At the end of 1967, people openly began to oppose Novotny. In the entire country, but especially in Slovakia, the press expressed dissatisfaction, particularly the Slovak weekly *Kulturny zivot* (Cultural Life). In December, students in Bratislava moved in a procession through the streets carrying pictures of Novotny marked with prison bars over his face. The police did not interfere. It was clear that the drama was just beginning.

ALEXANDER DUBCEK
AND "SOCIALISM WITH A
HUMAN FACE"

The abortive attempts to reform the economy had convinced many rank-and-file communists, especially economists and leading intellectuals, whose influence was important for the future development of the country, that cosmetic changes were inadequate and that the entire system must be overhauled.[4] The key to every decision was, of course, in the hands of the Communist Party; and in the second half of the 1960s, these reform-minded communists occupied the top positions and were increasingly influencing policy decisions. At the CC-CPC meetings of January 3–5, 1968, reform-minded communists argued against conservative party bureaucrats. It was no coincidence that at the helm of the critics against Antonin Novotny stood a Slovak, Alexander Dubcek (1921–1992), the first secretary of CPS at Bratislava.[5] Dubcek rebuked Novotny not only for his basic political mistakes but also for his tactless behavior toward the Slovaks. Novotny was then relieved of his function as secretary of the CC-CPC, to be replaced by Alexander Dubcek, the first Slovak given the highest post in CPC. This marked the beginning of what is known as the Prague Spring.

Gradually, changes occurred in the leading positions of the party and the government as well as the parliament. By the end of February this process accelerated the scandal about the defection to the West (Italy) of so-called "clover" General Jan Sejna, one of Novotny's loyal collaborators, following the disclosure that he had pilfered state property—by selling clover seeds for his own profit. It was a prime example of the corruption existing at the highest levels. As a close friend of Novotny's son, Jan Sejna had had a miraculous career. Without higher education or experience he had become a general, a high party functionary, and the leading party secretary at the Ministry of Defense. Sejna eventually was brought to the United States for interrogation, which shocked the leaders of the Warsaw Pact because it was discovered that Sejna took with him many top-secret military documents.[6] This scandal brought down Novotny, who resigned on March 22, 1968. One week later, General Ludvik Svoboda, former commander of the First Czechoslovak Army Corps in the USSR and minister of national defense during the

February 1948 coup, was elected president of the Czechoslovak Socialist Republic. It should be noted that during the early 1950s, Svoboda had been a victim of Stalinist politics and was demoted from minister of defense to accountant on a cooperative farm. There were also changes in the government. The old dogmatic communist Jozef Lenart was replaced by Oldrich Cernik, who favored more radical economic reforms. Another communist favoring reforms, Josef Smrkovsky, became chairman of the National Assembly.

Changes also occurred in the leadership of CPS. As first secretary of CC-CPS, Alexander Dubcek (who in January became first secretary of the CC-CPC) was replaced by the conservative communist apparatchik Vasil Bilak, but since the presidium of the CC-CPS elected several new members who belonged to the proreform group, Bilak's power was considerably curtailed.

The motto of the Prague Spring was "Socialism with a human face." The leaders of CPC made a commitment to reform the socialist system. Press censorship was liberalized, and citizens were given more freedom to travel abroad. Projected economic reforms, prepared by the Czech economist Ota Sik and colleagues including the Slovak economist Eugen Leobl, were laid out to introduce certain elements of the market economy.[7]

All these reforms were heartily opposed by the conservative communists, for personal as well as ideological reasons. The outcome of the struggle between the communists seeking reforms and those opposing it was the CPC Action Program, which was adopted on April 5, 1968. The original plan of the reform-minded communists was to present the members of the party and the general public with a concise, simple, and intelligible program. Though the Action Program did in many ways resemble earlier so-called reform programs, it contained measures that, to the communist world, were revolutionary: a program of basic democraticratization of the internal operation of CPC, a demand for equality between CPC and all the other political parties and civic organizations, guarantees of basic civil liberties, democratization of economic management, and the encouragement of private enterprise in service jobs. It also included a demand for an active policy with Western Europe and a demand for the realization of a federal system based on symmetrical arrangements between the Czechs and the Slovaks. All in all, the program was too ambitious and too cumbersome and in many ways dated by Czechoslovak developments. The Action Program that the CPC adopted a month and a half later was, however, much worse because the original proposal was shelved by the reactionaries headed by Vasil Bilak and replaced by a new one devoid of all basic reforms.

The main issue dividing the antireform and proreform communists was the date for calling the extraordinary Fourteenth Congress of the CPC. The proreformists were eager to hold the meeting as soon as possible, hoping that the new CC-CPC, which would be elected at the congress, would give additional support to the needed economic reforms. The conservatives sought a delay, citing the "time required for preparation." In the meantime, a meeting of district and area secretaries of CPC was held in Prague. The secretaries received ample support from the conservative *apparatchiks* who urged them to move in their direction. They were told that it was also the desire of Moscow to go slowly on reforms, and this was confirmed by Alexei Kosygin, the Soviet premier, who was in Karlove Vary at the end of May, supposedly for health reasons. The date for the congress was finally set for September 9, 1968.

The attempt to hold a special congress of the CC-CPS proved equally difficult. The Slovak conservatives wanted a date later than the CPC congress; the reformists wanted it before, arguing that if the CPS congress were held after the CPC congress, the Slovak communists would be morally obliged to accept the decisions of the CPC congress. The reformist arguments prevailed, and the congress of the CC-CPS was set for August 26.

In a relaxed atmosphere the grass roots society began to show new life without any encouragement from the Communist Party. People yearning for freedom began openly to display enthusiasm toward the rapid changes. In February 1968 the Czech journal *Literarne listy* (Literary Papers), which had closed down after the 1967 Congress of the Writers' Union, reappeared and became a major source of ideas for reforms. It was a sign that censorship had lost its significance. In June censorship was officially abolished.[8] Immediately after that a public declaration called "2000 Words" was printed in the Czech press.[9] This declaration, written by Czech writer Ludovik Vaculik, represented a reaction of the intellectual circles to the reform process, which under the pressure of conservative communists appeared to have lost its momentum. It was also an appeal to the general public to join and participate in the democratic process. The demands for democratization as expressed in the declaration went far beyond the plans for the reform-minded communists, and the CC-CPC immediately attacked the piece as a protest against CPC. The CC-CPS was even more critical, describing the declaration as "agitation against the republic" because it took a position against the monopoly of power of the Communist Party.

Nonetheless, the reenergized and reactivated society—but short of a civil society—inspired the creation of many new civic organizations that were completely outside the control of the communists. Such organizations included the Club of Active Nonpartisans (KAN) and the organization with an anticommunist orientation called Klub 231, a club of former political prisoners who had been sentenced to prison because they violated paragraph 231 of the "subversion law against the republic."[10] In May, a similar organization, Slovak Organization for the Protection of Human Rights, was founded by Emil Vydra. Several groups had even greater ambitions, proposing reforms that went well beyond the horizon of officially sanctioned socialism. The situation in 1968 did not, of course, permit open disclosure of these ambitions, but the overwhelming majority of the citizens supported the social movement led by Alexander Dubcek and the proreform communists. It is paradoxical that this was the first time in the history of Czechoslovakia that the Communist Party received spontaneous and undoubtedly majority support from the citizenry.

This growing movement toward reform had hardly gone unnoticed in Moscow and other socialist countries. As early as March 23, 1968, the leaders of the Soviet bloc, meeting in Dresden, expressed concern over the developments in Czechoslovakia. Brezhnev "invited" the Czechoslovak communists to Moscow, where on May 4 the Kremlin leaders issued an official warning—indeed, a reprimand—about the threat of growing counterrevolution in Czechoslovakia.[11] On May 8, after the Czechoslovak delegation had departed, representatives of the five other states of the Warsaw Treaty Organization (WTO) arrived in Moscow (absent Romania, which refused to take part in this or any future meetings against Czechoslovakia).[12] The most serious charges were lodged by communists from the German Democratic Republic, who criticized the reforms in Czechoslovakia for not being part of any "analytical" conceptualization of the CPSU. Independence from Moscow made them dangerous.

It had already been decided to hold WTO military exercises on Czechoslovak territory that June. After the official ending of the maneuvers, some units remained in Czechoslovakia until the beginning of August, causing widespread agitation among the general public. It was now abundantly clear that the future of Czechoslovak reforms rested entirely with Moscow. Dark clouds began to gather over the socialism with a human face.

On July 15, the CC-CPC was handed a letter signed by the five WTO countries (Bulgaria, East Germany, Hungary, Poland, and the USSR), accusing the leaders of the party and state in Czechoslovakia of negligence for not opposing the antisocialist and counterrevolutionary forces in the country. Both the CC-CPC and the CC-CPS rejected the letter as an interference in Czechoslovak domestic affairs, and its publication caused an uproar among the general public. At the end of July and the beginning of August, at Cierna and Tisou, on the border of Czechoslovakia and the USSR, Communist Party delegations of the two countries met to negotiate their differences. The CPC delegation, headed by Alexander Dubcek, resolutely rejected the accusations that Czechoslovakia was turning away from socialism. It was the same when the leaders of the Warsaw Pact countries met at Bratislava on August 3. There, however, Brezhnev succeeded in inserting into the preamble of the Bratislava Declaration a statement—obviously overlooked by Dubcek and his delegation—that the defense of socialist achievements was a matter for the entire Warsaw Pact.[13] This statement, soon known as the Brezhnev Doctrine, that the laws of international socialism were above the national laws of any member of the socialist community, was intended to justify intervention by other members of the WTO to restore socialism in countries where those laws had been violated. In the euphoric atmosphere of newly acquired freedom, these warning signals were, it seems, completely ignored by the communist delegation from Czechoslovakia. Dubcek and other communists considered military intervention into Czechoslovakia inconceivable, especially since they had made a commitment at Cierna that Czechoslovakia would never abandon socialism or the Warsaw Pact. On August 16, the Politburo of the CC-CPSU decided to invade Czechoslovakia. The following day, the Hungarian Communist Party chief, Janos Kadar, met with Dubcek and warned him about the danger of military invasion, which was approved on August 18 by the five representatives of the Warsaw Pact at their Moscow meeting.

THE CZECHO-SLOVAK FEDERATION

One of the chief achievements of the Prague Spring was the idea of creating a Czecho-Slovak federation.[14] It was thought that a federal system would remedy past mistakes and eliminate old grievances. Early in March 1968, at Smolenice, Slovak and Czech historians and political scientists met in conference to discuss changing the unitary Czechoslovak state into a federal system, and on March 14, the Slovak National Council drafted a constitutional law that would give the council full legislative powers on the territory of Slovakia. The draft law also envisaged the creation of a council of ministers of Slovakia, with Bratislava as the capital of the federated state. After some hesitation, on April 10, the demand for federalism was also endorsed by the CC-CPS. Five days prior to the CC-CPS demand for a new federal arrangement in the state, the CC-CPC had included the demand for a future symmetrical (federative) regulation between the Czechs and the Slovaks in its Action Program, and the program of the new government of Oldrich Cernik similarly called for a change of Czechoslovakia from a unitary to a federal system of government. These decisions and declarations signified a minor but official break with the harsh centralist system.

A public opinion poll on the subject of federalism taken at this time showed 60 percent of the respondents in favor of federation without any reservation and 26 percent favoring it with certain reservations; in Bohemia and Moravia the results were 52 percent and 31 percent, respectively. Those opposed were only 10 percent of citizens in Bohemia and Moravia and none in Slovakia. But behind these numbers there were some problems. For example, partial support for federation was expressed by the citizens who followed the slogan "First democratization, then federalization!" This slogan had many supporters among the Czech and Slovak communist functionaries, who seemed to think that separating democratization from federalization would at least postpone the act of federalization, if not stop it altogether. In response to this scheme, three Slovak writers—Ladislav Novomesky, Miroslav Valek, and Vojtech Mihalik—issued a statement in the journal *Cultural Life:*

> We are convinced that the thesis, first democratization, then federalization, which is now so popular and whose echo can be found even in *Cultural Life*, is mistaken because these two issues can neither be separated from each other nor prioritized one over the other, while we are of the opinion that the vital interests of the Slovak nation—that is, the realization of complete legitimacy and sovereignty of this nation— gives us the right to accentuate in this situation the idea of federation. Without it, without the culmination of the national revolution, there cannot be a real democracy, at least not a democracy that would serve the interests of the Slovak nation.[15]

Finally, the government took concrete action by approving a special commission for the preparation of a constitutional law concerning the federal arrangement of the Czechoslovak Socialist Republic, headed by Gustav Husak. The commission prepared such a law, which was eventually approved by parliament on October 27, 1968. The approved law mentioned that the two nations, Czech and Slovak, after fifty years of common state living together, decided to build their relationship "on a new and more just foundation." At the same time the law also expressed the view that "the voluntary federal state arrangement is not only a satisfactory expression of the right to self-determination and equal rights but also the best guarantee for our full internal national development as well as for the protection of our national legitimacy and sovereignty."[16]

The Czecho-Slovak federation had thus become a reality, but by the end of October 1968, the Prague Spring was only a memory. The country had been occupied by the armed forces of the WTO. In such a situation, of course, there could be no real democratic federation.[17] The federalism in Czecho-Slovakia satisfied neither the Czechs nor the Slovaks. From the Czech point of view, the new federal arrangement was subject to all kinds of interpretations and characterizations. Some Czech followers of centralism, for example, invented a rationalization that the Slovaks were given federalism with the assistance of Russian bayonets. In Slovakia, too, many were unhappy because federalism turned out to be only a formality—real self-rule in Slovakia did not exist. The federal state organs did not possess decision-making powers. Everything was decided at the highest level of the party organization, and the most important issues concerning the country had to be deferred to Moscow.[18] Since the CPC was not affected by federalism, state federalism amounted to nothing more than a disfunctioning paper institution. Such a federation, combined with a gradual intensification of communist dictatorship and terror, was unable to create the conditions necessary for at least an open airing of the still-clouded issues existing in Czech-Slovak relations. Because of the hardened communist dictatorship, the situation created by federalism after 1968 contributed to a worsening of Czech-Slovak relations. Just as the slogan "First democratization, then federalization" was false, so was its meaning in reverse. Federalization without democratization was only a fiction. That it was so became evident on the night of August 20, 1968, when the aspirations of both democratization and federalization were ruined by an early decision of the Warsaw Pact countries (made on August 18, 1968).

SOVIET MILITARY INTERVENTION AND THE RESTORATION OF THE CENTRIST-BUREAUCRATIC SYSTEM

Neither the Soviet leaders nor the party chiefs of the other Warsaw Pact countries were impressed by the citizens of Czechoslovakia or other countries who cheered for socialism with a human face. They saw in the Czechoslovak reform movement a dangerous development that could threaten their own positions. The party bosses in Moscow were very unhappy to see that the initiative for reforms originated outside the cradle of Soviet communism. As a result, several Soviet communist leaders who were inclined to support limited economic reform rejected the movement in Czechoslovakia.

The dogmatists in the Communist bloc decided to suppress the reform movement in Czechoslovakia with brutal military force. At 11:00 P.M. on August 20, 1968, military units of the Warsaw Pact countries entered Czechoslovakia.[19] The strategic operation was huge according to Central European standards: twenty-seven divisions, 500,000 soldiers, 800 airplanes, 6,300 tanks, and 2,000 artillery units. It was the largest military action in Europe since the end of World War II. Alexander Dubcek and the rest of the CPC leadership favoring reforms were taken in handcuffs, first to the Ukraine and then to Moscow. Czechoslovakia was occupied by the armies of the Warsaw Pact. Since the creation of the communist defense organization in May 1955, this was the largest military action ever taken—not against the "enemy" but against one of their own members.

During the night of August 21 the presidium of the CC-CPC issued a declaration that the military action of the Warsaw Pact countries against the Czechoslovak Socialist Republic was taking place without the knowledge of the president of the republic or any of the state or party organs. "The Presidium of the CC-CPC," the declaration said, "appeals to all citizens of our republic to maintain peace and to refrain from forceful resistance against the advancing armies. For this reason our army, security forces, or people's militia received no orders to defend the country. The Presidium of the CC-CPC considers this act of invasion to be not only a contradiction of the principles guiding the relations between socialist countries but a denial of all basic norms of international law."[20]

All major governing institutions—the parliament, the executive cabinet, and the CC-CPC—were called into session. Without the knowledge of the occupation forces, an extraordinary Fourteenth Congress of the Communist Party of Czechoslovakia was held at Prague-Vysocany. It very strongly condemned the military occupation of the country.[21]

During the occupation the Czechoslovak army was confined to the barracks, while on the streets there were strong demonstrations. On August 23 a one-hour general strike was held throughout the entire republic as a protest against the occupiers. At several places the soldiers of the Warsaw Pact used weapons against the unarmed civilian demonstrators. Several people were killed and many were wounded.

Finally, the leaders of the CPC and government, who were held under surveillance in Moscow, were forced to sign an "agreement" about consolidation. A delegation led by President Ludvik Svoboda sought the release of Alexander Dubcek and the other Czechoslovak political leaders. Instead, the delegation succumbed to Soviet intimidation. The Moscow negotiations, which were attended by the interned leaders of the party, government, and parliament—A. Dubcek, O. Cernik, and J. Smrkovsky—were in reality Soviet dictates.[22] In the final protocol signed on August 26, the Czechoslovak representatives had to agree with the invalidation of the Fourteenth Congress of CPC, make a commitment to take steps toward "normalizing" the country, and promise to remove from functions those people marked as "counterrevolutionaries" by the Soviet. The leading functionaries, including Dubcek, temporarily remained in their old positions, but the protocol placed certain restrictions on them as well as on the mass media. At the same time the Czechoslovak communists had to guarantee that they would retain in their positions and functions all communists who before August 1968 and after the military intervention fought against the "counterrevolutionaries." In return, the Moscow leaders made only a formal gesture that the military units on Czechoslovak soil would not interfere in internal matters and that they would leave the country as soon as the danger threatening socialism disappeared.

One of those in the Czechoslovak delegation at the Moscow "negotiations" was Gustav Husak. He made a favorable impression on the Soviet leaders and later became Leonid S. Brezhnev's favorite son. Immediately after his return from Moscow, Husak became involved in the proceedings of the extraordinary meeting of the CPS at Bratislava. There Husak was elected first secretary of the CC-CPS. The proceedings and results of this meeting were characteristic of that time. The congress started out with revolutionary fervor and established a linkage with the conclusions of the extraordinary Fourteenth Party Congress held in Prague-Vysocany. Husak made great efforts to reverse those conclusions, using demagogic arguments about the "Slovak issue"—less than 10 percent of Slovak communist delegates were present at the Prague meeting, he declared. Husak succeeded in distancing the Slovak congress not only from the Fourteenth Congress but also from the old, conservative communists. Their main representatives, headed by Vasil Bilak, were not even elected to the new central committee.[23] Only Husak was able to strengthen his new position.

Ten days after the invasion, on August 31, 1968, the CC-CPC approved the Moscow Protocol, and its measures were immediately introduced into the postreform socialist system. On September 13 the National Assembly passed a law affecting mass communication. On October 16 an agreement was signed in regard to the "temporary stationing" of Soviet troops in Czechoslovakia; no date for withdrawal was specified. Two days later a law was passed by the National Assembly regarding the temporary stationing of Soviet troops. While Dubcek nominally remained first secretary of the CC-CPC, the positions of the antireform communist functionaries grew stronger so that the proreform communists had to abandon one reform after another. In a militarily occupied and Moscow-controlled country, there was no longer room for reforms, even though the population still believed and hoped that future reforms were possible.

Among the former supporters of the reforms a strong group of so-called "realists" emerged, who, for the price of retaining their old positions, had succumbed to Moscow dictates. The bloc of proreform communists was split, and the most outspoken followers of the reforms were gradually pushed into isolation. This trend also gave a new orientation to the session of the CC-CPC held in Prague November 14–17, 1968. Two important organizational measures were adopted at that meeting. An executive committee of the presidium of the CC-CPC was created, which resulted in moving the decision-making powers of the large presidium to the small, antireform executive committee. On this new and powerful eight-member decision-making body, only two proreform communist leaders, Dubcek and Smrkovsky, were retained. With regard to state federalism, a politburo of the CC-CPC was created for managing party affairs in Bohemia and Moravia. It was headed by the "realist"

Lubomir Strougal. Since the CC-CPS was already under the management of another realist, Gustav Husak, the positions of Dubcek and other reform-oriented communist leaders had been considerably curtailed. It was only a matter of time before the "cleansing" of the party and state would commence.[24]

10 The Period of "Normalization" Under Gustav Husak's Leadership

The failure of the reform movement in Czechoslovakia was additional proof that reforms under communism were only an illusion; the communist system could not be reformed. Dogmatists and apparatchiks in Moscow and their local lackeys in Czechoslovakia moved systematically toward "normalization." In April 1969, Dubcek was removed from the position of first secretary of the CC-CPC and replaced by Gustav Husak. Husak had been one of the leading communists during the Slovak National Uprising in 1944, later an active participant in the communist revolution, and also a condemned-for-life prisoner in 1954 for his "bourgeois nationalist" sins. When Husak came into power he already had visibility and support from a segment of the population. Many proreform communists who looked upon Husak as their man were hoping that he would succeed in saving at least a certain portion of the Czechoslovak reforms, but the merciless reality of collaboration with the Soviet power soon removed all remaining illusions about reforms. Gustav Husak, who beginning in 1975 functioned as president of the republic, became a symbol of "normalization" and the most hated person in the state.

This chapter is based on the Slovak text by Dusan Kovac.

PURGES AND RETRIBUTIONS
IN THE PARTY, GOVERNMENT, AND
THE ARTS

In the history of Czechoslovakia the term "normalization" is applied to the period from 1969 to the middle of the 1980s—normalization being the slogan under which the communist dogmatists began to solidify their power and gradually the country on tracks that they considered "normal," away from the reforms and back to the rigid dogmatism of the 1950s.[1]

"Normalization" was gradual. It began immediately after the invasion of Czechoslovakia by Warsaw Pact forces and after the signing of the Moscow Protocol. By the end of 1968, it was clear that reforms in Czechoslovakia were no longer feasible. In protest against the antireform trend, a young Czech student, Jan Palach, committed suicide by self-immolation on January 16, 1969, in Wenceslaus Square in Prague. His tragic act could not reverse the trend, but it created agony within the society. At Comenius University in Bratislava, nineteen students went on a hunger strike from January 20 to 25, the day Palach was buried. Still, the "normalizers" continued their work without interruption. Equally unsuccessful was defiance by the unions. From March 4 to 7, 1969, the Seventh All-Union Congress was held in Prague. The proceedings of the congress were held in the reform spirit of 1968, and the adopted resolutions and new charter and statutes reflected it. A few days later, during the session of the CC-CPS at Bratislava, Gustav Husak, who was desperately trying to retain Brezhnev's favor, vehemently attacked the proreform journalists and other politicians. In early April the presidium of the CC-CPC adopted certain measures for the control of advertising. On April 13 at the airport in Mukacevo, Ukraine, Husak met with Leonid Brezhnev and received the final blessings before the planned session of the CC-CPC. The meeting was a clear signal of the big push toward "normalization" that followed. Gustav Husak became the leading secretary of the CC-CPC. Alexander Dubcek was given the post of president of the federal National Assembly but lasted in that position only until October, when he and Smrkovsky were removed from the parliament. For a short time Dubcek was ambassador to Turkey, but the "normalizers" pushed him out of that position as well, and for the next few years, until his retirement, Dubcek worked as a technician in forestry.

Shortly after Husak's rise to power the party machine headed by the antireformists had already begun to undo any vestiges of the Prague Spring. The hard-line communists who during the reforms had been excluded or felt threatened now began to gather around Gustav Husak. They were soon joined by other hard-liners, most of whom were incompetent people who in the atmosphere of reforms and competition among the intellectual elite had had little chance of acquiring more important positions. Now they had their opportunity. They were by and large opponents of Husak, who in 1968–1969 was considered a reform supporter. Now Husak had to embrace them as his own and in many instances conform to their ideas. Husak himself kept his position only because he was able at the right time to shift his political orientation toward the antireform policies.[2]

In order to gain the support of the federalists, Husak tried to present federalization as his work; as a former member of the revolutionary Slovak National Council, he had certain legitimate rights to such a claim. However, federalism as just a formality soon provoked Czech and Slovak populations against Husak. Of course, federalism, which presupposed a democratic regime with a transparent system of politics, could hardly function under a communist dictatorship that limited decision making to a small circle of CPC leadership. Therefore, it was logical that as early as 1970 a constitutional law was passed that weakened the powers of the national institutions and strengthened centralism. In this regard, federalism became a victim of "normalization."

All achievements of democratization in 1968 were gradually quashed. Although officially censorship remained abolished, the party organs found ways to manipulate and control the mass media. Such control was the first and most important task of both the "normalizers" and the Moscow party leaders. Somewhat surprisingly perhaps, willing collaborators among the journalists quickly appeared. On May 17, 1969, more than one hundred Czech and Slovak journalists published an announcement, "Into Our Own Ranks," criticizing "antisocialist" tendencies in the press since January 1968. Shortly after that the presidium of the Union of Slovak Newspaper Reporters published a statement pledging full support of the existing political line of the CPC. The few reform-leaning journals, such as *Reflex*, published by university students, and *Literarny zivot* (Literary Life), were closed down. Finally, on July 2, 1969, the principle of partisanship in journalism was revived at the all-state meeting of communist journalists in Prague. Afraid of losing their license to operate, many newspapers and journals, abandoning their critical and proreformist positions, began to "normalize" themselves.

Trips abroad, especially to Western Europe and other democratic countries, were curtailed. Communist activists (also known as the "healthy seed") began to organize purges. All communists had to go through verification. They were asked to agree with the "international assistance" in August 1968. Those communists who took part in the reforms were expelled—which meant also loss of employment, not only in the party organization but in leading enterprises, schools, scientific institutions, the military, and state administration. Hundreds of thousands of people lost their jobs as a result of "verification," and they were assigned to new inferior and poorly paid jobs.

The highest party organs began to rescind most of their resolutions, starting on September 9, 1969, with CC-CPS and CC-CPC actions. At the November 1969 all-state conference of communist functionaries of the national committees, a key decision was reached to "cleanse" the national committees of "opportunists." Similar action was taken in other organizations and institutions of the country. On November 20, 1969, the Central Audit and Control Commission of the CPS decided that the leading Slovak intellectuals and employees in the media would have to submit to party screening.

At the beginning of 1970, the CC-CPC decided to "exchange membership ID cards." This process, combined with reeducation, became the main tactic of the normalizers against all proreform communists. In Slovakia 53,000 communists, half of whom were members of the intelligentsia, were expelled from the ranks of CPS, which then issued instructions for a "reeducation" program of nonparty members employed in universities, research institutes, the army, state administration, the mass media, cultural institutions, and art associations. This reeducation process in turn cost thousands of members of the intelligentsia their jobs and membership in their respective organizations. The whole cleansing process was carried out efficiently but rather quietly: there were no political monster-trials as in the 1950s, nor did even the most notorious opponents of "normalization" receive "exemplary punishment." Nevertheless, the "cleansing" affected many qualified people and caused large-scale paralysis for the entire country.

The "cleansing" process was applied differently in the two parts of the country. In Bohemia and Moravia, but especially in Prague, leading scientists and university professors were removed from their posts and assigned manual labor; in Slovakia the cleansing was more subtle and less humiliating. Though the accused were forced to leave their positions, the new jobs assigned to them were in museums, libraries, and similar places where the work and atmosphere were not so demeaning as factory work, for example. But in Slovakia, as in the Czech Lands, the victims had to sign a pledge not to engage in research, writing, or politics. Many Czechoslovak citizens took advantage of the political turmoil and escaped to the West.

Their new ideology turned out to be a simplified catechism of Marxism-Leninism. In December 1970, the CC-CPC issued a document entitled "Lessons Learned During the Period of Crisis by the Party and Society." All workers in leadership positions, teachers, scientists, and cultural workers had to submit their approval of this document, and anyone who refused to do so was immediately dismissed. The basic thesis of the "Lessons"—the "manifesto of neo-Stalinism"—was rejection of the reforms and the return to state centralism and a rigid planned economy.

ECONOMIC AND TECHNOLOGICAL STAGNATION WITH A TOLERABLE STANDARD OF LIVING

It was to be expected that the leading party functionaries who returned to power after August 1968 made every effort to remain in power. At the same time they were trying to exalt the centralist model of management over the entire society. The National Front (NF) was revived, once again subjecting all political parties and civic organizations to Communist Party rule. Proof of this was the 1971 election of Gustav Husak as chairman of NF.

The CC-CPC designated May 1969 for holding its Fourteenth Party Congress (the Fourteenth Congress of the CPC held during the August 1968 invasion had been declared null and void by the Moscow Protocol). At the new Fourteenth Party Congress, those elected into the CC-CPC and all other functions were exclusively old-line communists (dogmatists) and "normalizers." Except for a few changes, the functions allotted to these members lasted throughout the next two decades, until the fall of the communist regime in November 1989. The Communist

Party also staged new parliamentary elections, with a single list of candidates approved by antireform party hacks. In Slovakia, 99.9 percent of the vote went to the candidates-normalizers of the NF (though only 99.8 percent of qualified voters participated in the elections). Although the elections were held in an atmosphere of intimidation, the results were obvious proof that the elections were officially manipulated to satisfy communist demands.

The agricultural cooperatives held their all-state meeting in April 1972. The labor unions met in June 1972, at which time they annulled all resolutions that were not in compliance with the normalization policy. From then on, the labor unions were an obedient auxiliary organization of the Communist Party, willingly carrying out all party decisions. In September, all youth organizations were merged into one Socialist Union of Youth.

The communists always regarded culture and science as the greatest potential threats to their power, but there were enough cooperative artists and scientists to help the CC-CPC in its effort to keep the dissidents in line. A document entitled "For the New Creative Deeds of Socialist Art" and sessions of the highest party organs dedicated to the issues in science aimed to transform the arts and sciences into obedient servants of the party. In addition, the communist normalizers considered the role of ideological vigilance over the society a significant prerequisite for the permanent strengthening of their own positions and for the prevention of a return to reforms.

For the economy, the consequences of political developments were enormous. Continued retrogression in the development of the world economy and the growing isolation from the world marketplace gave no encouragement or hope for basic improvement of the Czecho-Slovak economy.[3] From the middle of 1973 on, prices of raw materials on the world market showed a steep increase. At that time Czechoslovakia was purchasing about one-third of its raw materials abroad at world market prices, but whereas the economically advanced countries were gradually able to equalize their balance of payments, in Czechoslovakia, where power had shifted back to the old, incompetent cadres and the ossified methods of planning, production declined sharply and a deep economic crisis developed. Party leaders resorted to the panacea of five-year plans, with their unreal and voluntaristic goals. Czechoslovakia began to distance itself economically from the advanced industrial countries even more, and soon it fell to the level of a Third World nation.

The government was forced to restrict its purchases of food and agricultural products from abroad. Though the October 1975 sessions of the CC-CPC and CC-CPS issued a plan for self-sufficiency in basic food products, the plan was not realized. Agricultural production barely met the minimum levels, primarily because of the overuse of fertilizers, which, of course, harmed the environment and human health. The huge state support of agriculture ruined the entire economy.

Mining and the machine tool industries were the next to suffer. State financial support kept these sectors of the economy afloat as well, even though their products were far from competitive on the world market. In spite of all the optimistic plans and communist slogans, the standard of living in Czechoslovakia declined. In a dramatic situation, economists and politicians decided to employ all means and resources to keep the economy and social situation at least on an acceptable level but at the price of giving up on development plans regardless of what that meant for future generations. The economy and the state budget moved completely in tandem; communist dreams about the future had been changed into tenacious efforts to muddle through from one year to the next.

In Slovakia, the end of the reforms meant a return to old, extreme forms of economic management. Industrialization continued, huge factories were being built, and the supply was growing, and though the demand on the world market was low, there was still a market for some products in the Eastern bloc. The technology used in production was old and inferior, and products often continued to accumulate in overstocked warehouses, but employment was always at 100 percent, thanks largely to the USSR. The Soviet Union was not only the largest client for Czechoslovak goods but also the largest supplier of raw materials, particularly to Slovakia, which of all the Eastern bloc countries was the most heavily dependent on raw materials. The large industrial enterprises in Slovakia—chemical, copper, aluminum, and energy—though they kept employment high, had a devastating impact on the natural environment. All major rivers were polluted; foul air caused forests to die and made hundreds ill. Throughout the area, the general state of health was on the decline. Large armament plants were also a liability for Slovakia. They were directly dependent on the existence and needs of the Warsaw Pact. The ruling communist leaders were able to compensate for the stagnation, especially in Slovakia, by considerably reducing the inventories and by making no investments in technology and modernization. Everything that was produced was also consumed. Even with such sacrifices the standard of living failed to rise in Czechoslovakia.

THE SLOVAK UNDERGROUND
OPPOSITION MOVEMENT

As soon as "normalization" became a reality, the reaction from the disenchanted people in the country led to an increase in underground activities against the communist regime. Their immediate sources of inspiration were the ideas raised at the Helsinki Conference of 1975. After the signing of the Final Act of the Conference on Security and Cooperation in Europe (CSCE) on August 1, 1975, the opposition forces in Czechoslovakia decided to exploit this favorable situation. By signing the Final Act, Czechoslovakia committed itself to upholding human rights.[4] After the Czechoslovak parliament ratified the Helsinki Final Act, the document became part of the Czechoslovak legal system. But, as the criticism at the Belgrade review conference of the CSCE in 1977 documented, the Czechoslovak party and state organs failed to satisfy the demands set by the Helsinki Accords in the areas of human rights, religious freedom, and living conditions. It was therefore no coincidence when the opposition forces in Czechoslovakia began to organize themselves on the basis of human and religious rights and on environmental concerns.[5]

In defense of human rights, on New Years Day 1977, an informal underground association was formed in Bohemia. Its declaration, called Charter 77, referring to the freedoms mentioned in the documents signed at Helsinki, noted: "The rights and freedoms that these Accords guarantee are important values of civilization sought after in history by many progressive people and whose legalization can significantly enhance the humane development of our society. Therefore, we welcome the joining of the government of the Czechoslovak Socialist Republic in the Helsinki Accords. Their publication, however, again urgently reminds us of how many basic civil rights in our country so far— unfortunately—exist only on paper."[6] Then followed a long list of violations by Czechoslovakia: violation of the freedom of expression, denial of citizens the right of freedom from fear, violation of the right to education, denial of the freedom to disseminate information, suppression of the freedom of religion, nonexistence of free and independent institutions protecting the citizens, violation of the freedom of privacy through telephone tapping and mail censorship, denial of a citizen's right to peacefully leave the country, and existence of politically motivated criminal trials. In their declaration the signers, all 242 of them, supported the ideals of civil participation and civic responsibility: "The responsibility for upholding civil rights in the country falls, of course, into the realm first and foremost of political and state power. However, it is more than that. Every individual bears his/her responsibility for the general conditions, hence also for the fulfillment of agreements that bind to it not only the governments but also all the citizens."[7] From that time on Charter 77 expressed itself regularly on political and social issues—from upholding human rights to ecological issues. All told, during the entire period of Charter 77, about two thousand citizens signed various releases on different topics. Among the first spokespersons of the Charter 77 were philosopher Jan Patocka, historian and political scientist Jiri Hajek, and the writer Vaclav Havel.[8] After that, Charter 77 spokespersons alternated from among the list of two thousand.

The normalizers reacted to Charter 77 with reprisals. The signers of the charter were placed under surveillance, often jailed, and exposed to organized denunciation and condemnation for aiding and abetting the "imperial powers." In April 1978, the signers of Charter 77 founded the "Committee for the Defense of the Falsely Accused" for the purpose of investigating and publishing (underground) cases affecting judicial and police persecution. During the ten years of its activities the committee cited almost 800 cases of unjust persecution. Making these facts more or less public alerted the world to the politically motivated persecutions and trials, and in many cases the exposure succeeded in reducing the meted-out punishment and even helped the release of certain prisoners, if only because the Czechoslovak government could not completely ignore the protests exerted by world public opinion.[9]

The thrust of the Charter 77 movement was mostly in Bohemia and Moravia, but in Slovakia there was also a group of signatories and supporters who, in collaboration with their Czech colleagues, made the dissident movement an all-out underground enterprise watched and persecuted by the state security (StB).[10] The core of the movement in Slovakia was a group of intellectuals headed by philosopher-publicist Milan Simecka (1930–1990). Another group in the underground movement responsible for organizing effective opposition to the regime was the ecologically sensitive organization of defenders of nature and the environment. And, after years of silence, Alexander Dubcek also joined the ranks of the dissidents. In 1976, when the German Democratic Republic (GDR) was preparing to hold a conference of European communist parties, Dubcek sent letters to the representatives of these parties, requesting that the conference examine the situation in Czechoslovakia and, specifically, state its intention to defend the proreform communists in Czechoslovakia who were being politically and socially persecuted by the regime. The conference failed to address Dubcek's plea; nevertheless, the publication of his letters again placed the situation in Czechoslovakia in sharp focus for the European public.[11]

The relatively small response to Charter 77 in Slovakia may be explained in part by the fact that the "normalization" process was less drastic and less severe on Slovak intellectuals than it was on intellectuals in the Czech Lands. In time, however, the disgruntled Slovak citizens were also organized into underground opposition groups against the regime for causes such as violations against human rights, environmental issues, and religious rights. The changes in the USSR and Mikhail S. Gorbachev's policies of perestroika and glasnost gave new impetus to these opposition movements.

Gorbachev's advancement to secretary-general of the CC-CPSU in March 1985 aroused hopes for the relaxation of tension in the entire Soviet bloc, but the liberalization movement sanctioned by Moscow was slowest in the two most developed countries of the Soviet bloc, the GDR and Czechoslovakia. Fearing loss of the power they had held since the millitary occupation of 1968, the Czecho-Slovak communists rejected all reforms. The once-favored slogan "Soviet Union—Our Example" acquired a bitter taste. Suddenly the ruling power of the party and state felt threatened by Soviet policies, while the underground opposition in Czechoslovakia felt vindicated.

In this new situation several civic groups became invigorated. Under the influence of Gorbachev's policies, and the support they had received in the foreign press, the proreform communists, headed by Dubcek, also became more active. In Slovakia a strong opposition movement against the regime developed among the church-going population, especially the Roman Catholics, who for too long had had to endure the systematic suppression of religious freedom and the unceasing controls imposed by the state and the StB. By that time an underground church existed in Slovakia, serviced by former priests and religious dignitaries who had been denied the practice of their profession since the 1950s. A central figure in this movement was Bishop Jan Chryzostom Korec (b. 1924). In addition, Slovak intelligentsia with a Christian orientation organized under the leadership of a young lawyer, Jan Carnogursky.[12]

The decisive moment for active opposition toward the regime was Gorbachev's disclosure in April 1987 that the Soviet Union and its new leaders promised not to interfere in the domestic affairs of Soviet bloc countries. Although the new Soviet leaders did not go so far as to publicly condemn the 1968 military invasion of Czechoslovakia, Gorbachev let it be known that he had no intention of intervening on behalf of existing communist leaders. The underground opponents knew that the power of the communist regime depended on Soviet tanks and that, without them, the handful of communists in the leadership positions were nothing more than a small flock of lost sheep. Czechoslovakia had a large contingency of armed forces, members of the security organs, and supporters of the regime, but the opposition was confident that it could handle the situation.

A significant turning point occurred in 1988. On March 25, the Catholic Church in Bratislava organized a peaceful candlelight demonstration. The communist government tried to frighten the demonstrators, but when that failed, the police forcefully dispersed the peaceful demonstrators. Later, students entered the scene. Although for them the events of 1968 were nothing more than a childhood memory, they were keenly aware of the rigidity of the communist regime and the lack of freedom they themselves experienced. Students in Bratislava and other Slovak cities organized demonstrations in commemoration of three major events: the seventieth anniversary of the creation of Czechoslovakia, the twentieth anniversary of the occupation of Czechoslovakia, and the twentieth anniversary of the immolation of Jan Palach.

Manifestations in the cultural field also gained momentum. Critical articles appeared in newspapers and magazines. In conjunction with the commemoration of the creation of Czechoslovakia, articles were written about T. G. Masaryk, M. R. Stefanik, democracy, and the right to freedom. On November 16, 1989, on the eve of international student day, students in Bratislava organized a mass demonstration against the government. Another, stormier demonstration occurred in Prague one day later. By that time the ruling power was so indifferent to public demands that it merely registered and filed complaints against the growing numbers of dissidents.

FROM ONE-PARTY DICTATORSHIP TO POLITICAL PLURALISM

PART FOUR

11 The Crumbling Wall of Socialism and the Velvet Revolution

After experimentation with socialist reforms in Czechoslovakia during the Prague Spring, it became clear to most Czechs and Slovaks that any tinkering with socialism without the approval of Moscow was a perilous endeavor. Hence, after 1968, though tinkering with, adjustment to, and reform of socialism continued successfully in Hungary, less so in Poland, and only barely in Bulgaria—always endorsed by Kremlin leaders—in Czechoslovakia the trend was backward, not forward.

THE COLLAPSE OF COMMUNIST RULE

Unlike Poland and Hungary, where communist power gradually lost its legitimacy before it collapsed, the Communist Party and government in Czechoslovakia continued to exercise full control without needing to seek compromise solutions to economic, political, or social problems. The party dictatorship that reemerged during "normalization" lasted until mid-November 1989. Then, after the collapse of communism in East Germany and Bulgaria, Czechoslovak leaders opted for a peaceful transition. They invited dissident leaders to Hradcany Castle, where they negotiated the transfer of power with them. Hence, the process of transition in Czechoslovakia—better known as the Velvet

Revolution—was swift, compressed into a three-week period. It began with a student march on November 17, 1989, and ended on December 10, when a coalition government dominated by noncommunists took power.[1]

The prelude to the Velvet Revolution included several events that built tension in the country, but no crises. For example, the Husak regime was criticized for years by intellectuals, although not as openly or frequently as the regimes in Poland and Hungary. Although the economy in Czechoslovakia was declining, it did not face the crisis experienced in Poland or Hungary. Popular dissatisfaction in Czechoslovakia existed, but it was subdued. The demonstrations in Prague and Bratislava were few and much smaller than those in Warsaw, Gdansk, Cracow, and Budapest. The reason is obvious: legitimacy in Czechoslovakia, as in the German Democratic Republic, Bulgaria, and Romania, was weak because the party ruled by sheer power and intimidation rather than by dialogue and consent.

The citizens in Czechoslovakia did protest against the totalitarian regime from time to time: at the twentieth anniversary of the Soviet occupation in August 1988, the seventieth anniversary of the creation of the Czechoslovak state in October 1988, the fortieth anniversary of Human Rights Day in December 1988, and the twentieth anniversary of the self-immolation of Jan Palach in January 1989. In the spring of 1989 the members of the opposition launched a successful petition drive for the release of Vaclav Havel, who had been arrested and jailed while attending a memorial for Jan Palach. Havel and other prominent cultural figures then launched the June "Just a Few Sentences" petition, which called for democratization in Czechoslovakia, and in five months' time, it had over 30,000 signatures. In August there were demonstrations on the twenty-first anniversary of the invasion of Czechoslovakia and in October, on the seventy-first anniversary of the founding of an independent Czechoslovakia. The totalitarian rulers allowed only a silent gathering of Human Rights Day supporters because it attracted international attention. During the embryonic state of the demonstrations the regime did not hesitate to use repressive measures against protestors. The security police and in some instances even the people's militia were dispatched. Many demonstrators were retained, interrogated, indicted, and either sentenced to prison or banished to remote areas to perform physical labor. Any citizens who verbally expressed support or agreement with the opposition or signed petitions were persecuted. But neither persecution nor threats of job loss could stop the destruction of the decaying system.

The brutal use of force against the citizens and the outlook for more severe political reprisals turned more and more members of the society against the regime. The alienation of society also had repercussions in the party and government. Concerned about the future success of the Communist Party, critics in the CPC and CPS raised questions about the neglected reforms. At the same time, several members of the StB and the people's militia grew apathetic toward the establishment's orders to take forceful action against their peacefully demonstrating fellow citizens.

In late October and early November 1989, the strained situation in the country reached a culmination point when a flood of East German refugees poured into Czechoslovakia with the intention of making their way into West Germany. To Czechoslovak society, this was an obvious sign of the imminent collapse of the neighboring totalitarian regime. When the Czechoslovak government yielded to pressures by Western governments and international humanitarian organizations to allow the refugees to exit into West Germany, citizens in Czechoslovakia associated this action with freedom. This hope was strengthened when, on November 12, 1989, Pope John Paul II declared the blessed Anezka Premyslovna to be a saint. In a few days the pent-up emotions of the Czechoslovak people exploded. The events commemorating the International Student Day on November 17, 1989, became the fuse that ignited the revolutionary fervor that within a few weeks' time toppled the communist dictatorship.

On November 15, 1989, the communist regime of Milos Jakes and Gustav Husak approved, and the Prague municipal authorities administered, a permit for a demonstration initially planned by independent groups in commemoration of Jan Opletal, a Czech student killed by the Nazis in 1939. Since the event, in an unusual twist, was to be cosponsored by the official Socialist Youth Union headed by Vasil Mohorita, a member of the CC-CPC secretariat, the authorities could hardly disapprove it. Thus on Friday, November 17, 1989, a peaceful assembly of citizens gathered at Albertov Square in Prague to commemorate the fiftieth anniversary of the closing down of Czech universities by Nazi occupation forces. The attendees, most of them students, shouted slogans against the present totalitarian regime and called for the renewal of democracy. The demonstration proceeded in a peaceful manner, and toward evening the demonstrators began their march toward downtown. The march was apparently led by a state security agent named Ruzicka (alias Zifcak), who had infiltrated the independent students' groups. He eventually deviated from the prescribed route, leading the demonstrators directly into a cordon of waiting policemen in Narodni trida (National Street), where they were attacked by the police and anti-terrorist units. During the chaos that followed the assault, agent Zifcak himself pretended to have been killed. Another StB agent, Drahomira Drazska, then infiltrated the dissident community and allegedly spread the news about the death of the fictitious student "Martin Smid." By the time it became known that there were, after all, no casualties, the public was in a frenzy. People in Prague were running into the streets demanding the resignation of the representatives of the totalitarian regime and the return to democracy.

The demonstrations continued the next day, with crowds increasing. Manifestations and labor strikes engulfed the entire country. On November 19, at the Theater Club in Prague, a gathering of dissident students joined by artists announced the formation of the Civic Forum (CF) with Vaclav Havel as its leader. Its declaration let it be known that it was able and willing to negotiate with government leaders about the situation in the country and express the public's demands. It also called for the resignation of those communist leaders who joined in the occupation of Czechoslovakia in 1968 and those responsible for the brutality against the students two days before. The final point of the declaration called for the immediate release of all political prisoners. The following day in Bratislava, representatives of cultural and scientific organizations, disturbed by the violence used against the students in Prague, formed their own Public Against Violence (PAV). In the meantime, 100,000 to 150,000 citizens gathered in Wenceslas Square in Prague, demanding fundamental political reforms and condemning the police for their brutality against the students at Narodni trida. The striking students in Prague issued a condemnation of the internal political conditions and appealed to the workers of the country to hold a general strike on November 27.

As a sign of solidarity with their colleagues in Prague, students in Slovakia joined in the strike on all Slovak universities, reiterated the demand for the immediate investigation of the brutalities committed at Narodni trida, and declared their support for a general strike on November 27. The dissidents were also joined by the revisionist communist movement *Obroda* (Rebirth). Why the sudden dissident movement in the CPC? Opportunism and timing favored such a movement. At the lower levels of the party and state organizations, party functionaries were faced with unpredictable situations. These loyal "soldiers" in the field, well disciplined to carry out orders from their superiors, now were up against angry crowds and unrelenting criticism from all sides. The confusing and contradictory directives coming from the vascillating center only added to the helplessness of the party apparatchiks, and their attitude of "wait and see" contributed to the rapidly collapsing management of the totalitarian regime. Political partners in the National Front were bolting from the CPC, and most of the party's media personnel were joining the opposition. A large segment of the rank-and-file members of the party also turned against the neoconservative leadership of the party. The pragmatic wing of the CPC took a cautious position because it realized that the only possible road to resolving the political crisis and satisfying the public would be through dialogue with the opposition.

The turning point came on November 21, two days after the Theater Club gathering, when Premier Ladislav Adamec met with Havel and other representatives of the Civic Forum and agreed that thereafter the most pressing issues would be resolved jointly after holding mutual consultations. The following day, the neoconservative members of the party leadership (among them Gustav Husak, Karel Hoffmann, Milos Jakes, Jan Fojtik, and Alois Indra), frantically searching for ways to stay in power, had several units of the people's militia brought into Prague. But they lost their nerve to issue orders for an open attack on 200,000 demonstrators in front of Melantrich (Publishing House) on Wenceslas Square, where Vaclav Havel addressed the crowd with an open invitation to all to join the Civic Forum. After some militia members let it be known that they were not interested in intervention, several militia units dissolved themselves and went home. When Miroslav Stepan, head of the CPC in Prague, was booed by the same workers that he wanted to agitate against the demonstrators, the neoconservative communist leaders knew they had lost all support at home, and abroad.

Also on November 22, at Adamec's request, the procurator general began to investigate the causes of violence against the students on November 17. The archbishop of Prague, Cardinal Francis Tomasek, issued an apostolic letter to the people of the country in which he declared that he could no longer be silent. On the same day in Bratislava large demonstrations initiated by the students and PAV broke out against the regime; the next day actor Milan Knazko and Alexander Dubcek spoke to 50,000 demonstrators about human rights, access to the media, and the need for social reform. In Prague, Milos Jakes, head of the CPC, condemned all opposition groups and held them responsible for disrupting the socialist system, but the neoconservatives realized they were fighting a losing cause; one day later Jakes resigned his position and another member of the party central committee, Karel Urbanek, was elected to take Jakes' place. With the resignation of Jakes other neoconservative leaders of CPC were also relieved of their positions. The public reacted to the news with great enthusiasm. Demonstrators all over Czechoslovakia demanded greater human and civil rights. At Wenceslas Square alone, almost 300,000 people showed up, and at the Square of Slovak National Uprising in Bratislava, about 500,000 demonstrators demanded reforms. The demonstrations continued the next day. Since November 26 was a Sunday, the crowds everywhere were increasing in numbers. The meeting between Adamec and Havel became public knowledge. At a special session of the CC-CPS that same day, five leaders of the neoconservative wing of the party—Ondrej Saling, Gejza Slapka, Elena Litvajova, Viliam Salgovic, and Stefan Rybar—were removed from their positions. Like the CPC, the CPS also planned to hold a special session of congress in January 1990.

Although the leadership of the labor unions had endorsed the demand for an investigation of the November 17 police action against the students, it had rejected the demand for a general strike called for November 27. Nevertheless, on that day from noon to two o'clock in the afternoon in all regions of Czechoslovakia, people stopped work in support of the dissidents' demands for civil initiatives and the restoration of democracy. The following day a second official meeting was held between the representatives of the Civic Forum and those of the federal government and the National Front. They agreed that on December 3 a new federal government would be constituted that would then submit to the Federal Assembly a proposal of changes in the constitution (no. 100/1960). In return, the representatives of the Civic Forum promised to ask the students and artists to end their strikes.

On November 29, 1989, the Federal Assembly repealed Articles 4, 6, and 16 of the constitution; Article 4 pertained to the CPC and its leading role in society, Article 6 to the role of the National Front representing the alliance of all social organizations and political parties under the leadership of the CPC, and Article 16 to make Marxism-Leninism the only acceptable ideology in politics, culture, and education. The Federal Assembly also established a parliamentary commission to investigate the events of November 17. With these changes in the constitution the forty-year monopoly of power of the CPC and CPS finally ended and a new era promising basic political changes toward building a pluralist democracy began.

On the same day *Rude Pravo* and *Pravda*—the main organs of the CPC and the CPS—published their enemy's *Programove zasady Obcianskeho fora* (Program Orientation of the Civic Forum) and Premier Adamec addressed the nation, blaming the leaders of his party (CPC) for twenty years of economic ruin and raising questions about the 1968 Warsaw Pact invasion. While Adamec was speaking on national television, Alois Indra resigned his position as president of the Federal Assembly, but Gustav Husak expressed his determination to continue as president of the republic.

At Bratislava (November 30), representatives of the government of the Slovak Socialist Republic and PAV negotiated the implementation of changes approved in the constitution, the lifting of state control over religious institutions, and the reevaluation of events in 1968. The chairman of the SNC, Viliam Salgovic, one of several Slovak communists who supported the 1968 occupation of the country, was stripped of his position. On the same day the SNC elected another member of the CPS, Rudolf Schuster. The SNC then issued a proclamation about the contemporary political situation in which it identified itself with the proclamation of the Federal Assembly the previous day and the changes in the constitution. It called for the creation of the commission to investigate the police brutality of November 17 and expressed its support for a law-abiding state built on socialist principles, political pluralism, and a sound economic system in which the Slovak Socialist Republic would play a decisive role. There was no mention of replacing the socialist planned economy with a market economy.[2]

On the last day of November 1989, the federal government instructed the minister of the interior to immediately remove the fortified barriers between the borders of Czechoslovakia and Austria. Thus began the meltdown of the iron curtain in Czechoslovakia. When Gustav Husak named a new government on December 3, 1989, with Ladislav Adamec again as premier, the Civic Forum and PAV issued a statement of dissatisfaction with the composition of the new Czechoslovak government. Of the twenty-one members of the new government, sixteen were communists, three were without political affiliation, and one each were from the Czechoslovak Socialist Party and the Czechoslovak People's Party. Since many of the new members were suspect because they were closely tied to the ruins of the totalitarian regime, the new Adamec government on the same day passed a resolution condemning the 1968 invasion of Czechoslovakia, and it also submitted a proposal to Moscow to begin negotiations regarding the departure of Soviet troops from Czecho-Slovak territory. These efforts failed to appease the critics, for the general public rightly interpreted the appointment of six-teen communist ministers as an attempt to circumvent any public involvement in the decision-making process. On the following day, in Moscow, representatives of the Warsaw Pact countries denounced the invasion of Czechoslovakia in 1968 by their armies as an act contrary to the rules of international law. The public was still not content, how-ever, and in Prague and Bratislava as well as other larger cities, hundreds of thousands of demonstrators expressed their disappointment in the composition of the new government. The boisterous demonstrations continued until December 7, when the Adamec government submitted its resignation.

Three days later, after consultations with his party and the leaders of the new political groups, President Gustav Husak named a new "federal government of national understanding," with the communist Marian Calfa as premier. Shortly after meeting with the new government, Husak resigned. The new Calfa government also had twenty-one members, but only ten represented the CPC. Two members were from the Czechoslo-vak Socialist Party, two from the Czechoslovak People's Party, and there were seven specialists nominated by both CF and PAV. On December 19, Premier Calfa presented to the two houses of the Federal Assembly the program of the government of national understanding, which con-sidered its main goals the preparation of free elections and the transfer to a market economy within a democratic society.

On December 6, two days after the reconstruction of the SNC, the government of the Slovak Socialist Republic under Pavol Hrivnak was dissolved, and on December 11 a new Slovak government headed by another communist, Milan Cic, was established. In the new seventeen-member Slovak government, two positions were not filled, six members were communists, and nine were without political affiliation. On the same day about 200,000 residents of Bratislava and its vicinity partici-pated in a march from Bratislava to Hamburg, a small town in Austria, opposite Devin Castle, to show their appreciation for being able to cross the borders that had been sealed for forty years under communist dictatorship.

In the meantime, the reconstructed Federal Assembly approved the newly appointed governments, and on December 28 Alexander Dubcek was elected as its chairman. After twenty-one years of persecution he resumed his political career. On the following day the Federal Assembly unaminously elected Vaclav Havel president of Czechoslovakia. Shortly after the election, President Havel promised to lead the country to free elections and democracy. Thus the first stage of the reform movement under the so-called Velvet Revolution in the Czechoslovak Socialist Republic had come to an end.

THE RETURN TO "CIVIL SOCIETY" AND POLITICAL PLURALISM

The second stage of the Velvet Revolution involved laying the foundation for democratic pluralism. Unlike Poland and Hungary, pluralism in Czechoslovakia did not come into play until the end of November 1989. At that time, however, the articulation of interests was not very clear or authoritative in either terms of democratic theory or constitutional law.

During the forty years of communist rule, the Czechoslovak regime destroyed the meaning of democratic ideas, values, institutions, social cohesion, and, above all, individualism and private ownership. Memories of the past were too insubstantial to count as a reason for establishing a new political party system, effective parliamentarism, or popular participation in the decision-making process. Two new generations under communism had produced a society with very different attitudes, moral values, and work habits from those the society had known before the communist takeover. From the day Vaclav Havel became president, democracy was perceived by the members of the Czecho-Slovak society not as a rational choice of people with equal influence but rather as a choice of a two-nation collectivity with emphasis on the two national rights articulated through civil society. In reality, postcommunist Czechoslovakia faced a Catch-22 situation. In 1989 the country had no civil society, and it therefore could not articulate individual preferences in a pluralistic fashion customary to democracies. It is fair to argue that

Czechoslovakia was transformed from above rather than from below. With the nationalistic bent overarching a variant of liberal democracy (a mix of socialist economy and the observance of human and political freedom), the hastily gathered decision makers set for themselves certain goals as a reaction to rather than a democratic requirement for the previous totalitarian communist system.

The first and most important requirement of the move toward a democratic system was to hold free and democratic elections in the country. The dates for the general elections were set for June 8 and 9, 1990, and on January 23, 1990, the Federal Assembly passed a law governing the registration of new political parties.[3] But before elections could be held, the country had to have a political system based on the separation of powers, the rule of law, a multiparty organization, and a sustainable economy. All that was a difficult and complex task, especially in view of the fact that communism was not treated as an alien ideology imposed by a foreign occupation force, like Nazism during World War II, and there were therefore no retributions, trials, or restitutions for crimes committed by the communists. On the contrary, most communists (with the exception of the most notorious figures at the highest level of party leadership) remained in privileged positions, especially in the smaller towns and villages. To complicate matters further, during the early stages of transformation, a gap developed between the remnants of the incompetant communist bureaucracy and the new, inexperienced dissident rulers. Reforms and modernization were slow and cumbersome, and attempts to emulate Western societies were frequently blocked by the still influential communist powers. The emerging values and interests of social groups were not only outmoded and lacking in dynamism by Western standards but were also to a great extent residues of the Soviet system that were out of alignment with social realities.

One of the misconceptions among the Czech and Slovak publics during the Velvet Revolution was the assumption that economic prosperity and well-being in postcommunist Czechoslovakia were simply a matter of replacing the procommunist regime with a pro-Western, noncommunist government. The task was much more complex than that. The transformation process to democracy after World War II had primarily concerned the form of government and the legal relationships between the state and society; in the postcommunist period an additional urgent task was to reform the collapsing economy. Whereas after the defeat of Nazism in 1945, capital remained in the hands of its owners and as a rule the owners remained in charge of their capital, after the collapse of communism in 1989, the problem was how to transfer the hitherto state-owned productive assets to other forms of property and, to this end, how to create an entirely new class of entrepreneurs and owners. Furthermore, there was a question of priorities: Could the country develop a democratic system without a free market economy?

Based on the experience of countries like Pinochet's Chile, some Czech economists wrongly believed that democracy in Czechoslovakia did not demand the emergence of a market but that the market required the development of a democracy. Hence they argued that the first requirement in the transformation process should be to institutionalize democracy and then deal with the basic economic transformation in the country.[4] A similar view was advanced by the intellectual proponents of the Prague Spring reforms. They believed in 1989 as they had in 1968 that the process of reforming the economy would, over the course of a few years, change to a democratic movement that would "sweep away the old leadership."[5] The assumption was that the combination of the hitherto planned economy with a limited market economy and the democratization of the decision-making process would not impede but rather reinforce each other. Such perceptions made privatization of production a slow and tedious process. Most citizens of postcommunist Czechoslovakia preferred government-subsidized housing, transportation, health care, and a centrally determined price system to the realities of a competitive market. That preference played an important role in the creation and alignment of the political party system in the country. In 1989 Czech and Slovak intellectuals with direct access to power were again responsible for the development of a new democratic system. Whether it was their association with the past communist regime, their belief system, or simply submission to the popular demand for a state-controlled price system and other major economic and financial institutions, many intellectuals in Czechoslovakia favored social security and welfarism, combined with a particular brand of liberal democracy.[6]

It can be argued that the goals established for the postcommunist democratic system of Czechoslovakia in 1989 were more similar to the 1968 Prague Spring reforms than either the pre-February 1948 or pre-Munich 1939 democratic tenets. To put it another way, when Alexander Dubcek was elected chairman of the Federal Assembly and Vaclav Havel was elected president of the republic, most policymakers looked upon the Velvet Revolution as a means to implement the Prague Spring reforms of twenty-one years earlier. Prognosticators at home and abroad were curious to know whether or not postcommunist Czechoslovakia would break away completely from the post–November 1989 idea of "socialist pluralism" and pursue a road toward a democracy along Western lines or try to revive the process of liberalization as it was programmed in 1968 under the label "The road to democratic socialism."[7]

In the case of Czechoslovakia the transformation process toward democracy fell into two periods. The first—liberalization—lasted from the end of December 1989 to June 8–9, 1990, when the first free elections were held after forty-four years; the second—democratization—began after the June 1990 parliamentary elections and continues today in both the Czech Republic and Slovakia.

The rapid disintegration of the Czechoslovak party-state in 1989 produced a power vacuum that was hastily permeated by highly fragmented alliances. More than forty political parties were founded between November 17, 1989, and the beginning of February 1990; eighteen parties were started in Slovakia alone. After four decades of communism, Czechoslovakia had no viable political and domestic society, which presupposes a whole range of voluntary associations and social movements in an active political community. It lacked a "political society" that would have made the "accommodation" between the state and domestic society possible, as happened in Poland and Hungary before and during the collapse of communism. As a result, the fragmented political forces were prone to radicalization around not only political and economic issues but also ethnic and religious identities.

Before the November 1989 crisis each part of the socialist "federal" state of Czechoslovakia showed a different dynamic. Under communist rule Slovakia became highly industrialized and urbanized with an upgraded infrastructure, educational system, and standard of living. In spite of human suffering and suppression of civil liberties and human rights, many Slovaks, especially the working class, considered "socialist modernization" a positive development. The Czechs, however, viewed the communist experience negatively, especially the period of normalization, which in the Czech Lands was more severe than in Slovakia and more despairing to the proreformists. Slovak society was less polarized than the Czech Lands. In Slovakia, where open civic dissent was limited to a small number of signatories of Charter 77, the thrust of dissent was religious, spearheaded by the Catholic Church, with primary emphasis on the freedom of religion and less concern about overall social decay. The dissident Slovak Catholics were responsible for the first mass candlelight demonstration in Bratislava in March 1988. Although there were small groups of dissidents composed of independent intellectuals, artists, and environmentalists who occasionally criticized issues closer to their professional interests, none of these groups articulated any awareness of a full-blown crisis until after November 17, 1989, and the events in Wenceslas Square in Prague. The mass transformation of political loyalties and the openness of antiregime demonstrations followed in Slovakia in a domino effect.[8]

On February 26, 1990, the Czechoslovak Socialist Republic and the Union of Soviet Socialist Republics in Moscow signed an agreement about the departure of Soviet troops from Czechoslovak territory by the end of June 1991. Shortly after that, dissident groups in Slovakia articulated their priorities: ecology, economic problems, nationality problems between the Czechs and Slovaks, and social security. By election time in June 1990, however, the leading issue in Slovakia was no longer ecology but the unfulfilled national aspirations, even though, after long and complicated negotiations, the Federal Assembly, on April 20, 1990, had renamed the country as the Czech and Slovak Federal Republic.

Until February 17, 1990, when the Christian Democratic Movement (CDM) was officially founded at Nitra, Public Against Violence (PAV) was the strongest political organization in Slovakia. The Slovak Communist Party then became the target of attacks from all political groups and movements, and its power and influence were tarnished. Probably because of CDMs appeal to Slovak national awareness based on Christian love and solidarity, the movement attracted many supporters and made it a strong competitor of PAV. The sudden rise in popularity and the potential for winning a majority in the June parliamentary elections motivated several leaders of smaller parties and groups, for example, the Democratic Party (DS) and the Freedom Party (FP), to join CDM in a coalition against CPS. Even so, PAV was still the most popular movement.[9]

As late as March 1, 1990, however, PAV was unable to unseat SNC's president, Rudolf Schuster (a communist). Instead, the communists were able to organize a strong demonstration in support of Schuster and against the new name of the state, the state emblem, the Slovak anthem, and PAV proposals for dealing with nationality problems. More important, among the communist demonstrators there were also members of the still active Stur (literary) Association, the Slovak National Party, and other groups and movements that had strong feelings about Slovak national interests. Since early 1990, the issues of nationalism and national minorities, especially the Hungarian minority, played a significant role in the Slovak political arena—issues PAV had either underestimated or neglected.[10]

The source of the nationalities issue was television coverage entitled "Dialogue About the Position of Nations and Nationalities in the Czechoslovak Socialist Republic," which aired January 3, 1990. In this novel and unscripted program, some participants spoke candidly about oppression of the Hungarian minority and about the apparent genocide of the Ukrainian national minority. The program elicited many written responses, some favorable and others critical of the Hungarian position. Most of the unfavorable responses were sent to Matica Slovenska (whose representatives appeared on the program) and to the editorial board of *Verejnost* (The Public), the official PAV daily. Since most of the responses dealt with the treatment of the Hungarian national minority, the problem of minorities was narrowed down to Slovak-Hungarian relations. Whereas Matica Slovenska took a more critical stance against the Magyars living in Slovakia, PAV and *Verejnost* were more conciliatory or perhaps indifferent. In its February 23, 1990, issue, *Verejnost* praised the unity of the two nations (Czech and Slovak) and various nationalities during three months of transformation.

A short while after that, the Independent Hungarian Initiative, the Cultural Association of Hungarian Working People in Czechoslovakia (*Csemadok*), and a group of activists headed by the former dissident Miklos Duray sought to strengthen their position in the postcommunist state, to achieve, it appeared, some kind of autonomy in southern Slovakia.[11] All of a sudden there were suggestions for building a Hungarian university in Komarno and for the establishment of a federal institute for minority issues, which, in an interview with *Verejnost* (no. 13/1990), was also supported by the Czech premier Petr Pithart. In response to the demand by the Hungarian national minority, Matica Slovenska began to organize branches all over southern Slovakia, followed by the Stur Association. In early March 1990, a new conscienceness of Slovak nationalism inspired the formation of new political movements and parties such as the Slovak National Party (SNP) and the Independent Slovak Party (ISP). After negotiations in Komarno, the Slovak-Hungarian issue died down, but Czech-Slovak relations heated up. The hyphenated name of the new state became an irritant to several Slovak nationalists in the Federal Assembly. On March 30 the criticism was primarily directed against President Vaclav Havel, CF, and PAV. During the short exchange, Slovak members of the parliament called for an independent Slovak state.[12] The "hyphenated meeting" in the Federal Assembly was condemned by both the PAV and CDM, and a few days later the Assembly revised the name to use a capital S. The wave of nationalism in Slovakia continued to pressure the leaders of PAV into admitting that relations between the two nations and their national minorities were an acute problem that required dialogue and peaceful resolutions.[13] The rise of nationalism and the revival of spiritual life were weakening PAV as they strengthened the positions of CDM, SNP, and ISP. The visit of Pope John Paul II added additional enthusiasm to the supporters of CDM, making the party a favorite to win the June 1990 parliamentary elections. In early May the Catholic Church openly endorsed CDM and urged its parishioners to support the party in the forthcoming elections.

Another political organization approaching the elections with great optimism was the Democratic Party (DP), which had been established in September 1944 but renamed by the communists in February 1948 as the Party of Slovak Renewal. On December 10, 1989, the name reverted again to Democratic Party. The speedy reorientation of the party and the declaration of continuity with the past was confirmed when party delegates elected Martin Kvetko chairman. Kvetko, former member of the pre-February 1948 Czechoslovak parliament and commissioner of the SNC for agriculture and food supply, had spent most of his life in exile working for Radio Free Europe, and under his leadership the party tried to build on the popularity of the 1946 elections, when DP received more than 60 percent of the eligible votes in Slovakia, juxtaposed against the realities of 1990. Because the greatest support of the party came from the intelligentsia, it was unlikely that DP could soon boost its membership and become a major political organization; also, though outwardly the party gave the impression that it was doing well, the leadership suffered from internal strife and lack of public appeal. Kvetko was respected as an elder statesman, but he was criticized for having been absent from Slovakia for more than forty years and out of touch with conditions there. Allegedly Kvetko disagreed with several of his colleagues on issues relating to national-democratic and social orientations as well as on the question of autonomy for district organizations.

The old Freedom Party (FP), on the other hand, was clear and decisive. It dated back to March 1946, an offshoot of the DP under leaders who disagreed with the DP program. The leaders of FP wanted to replace the federal system with a confederated system, which they believed could end the majority rule over the minority and the feeling of discrimination that went with it.[14]

Toward the end of April 1990, three parties—FP, the Independent Slovak Party (ISP), and the Slovak National Party (SNP)—entered into an agreement to form a Slovak National Bloc that would work out a unified strategy for the June parliamentary elections. But the leaders of the three parties failed to agree on what the strategy should be. Statements by the leaders of SNP before the mass media as well as the inability of the party to distance itself from political extremism at some of their meetings led to a rupture with the leaders of FP, who emphasized that advocacy of a confederate system of government should not be equated with the idea of an independent Slovak state.[15] The SNP profited from this experiment because of the wave of nationalism taking hold not only in Slovakia but also in the rest of Eastern Europe. The Czecho-Slovak issue and the problem of national minorities in the country served not only SNP but also the movement known as Coexistence, which was organized by members of national minorities under Miklos Duray. In a similar fashion the new wave of nationalism gave rise to the creation of the Hungarian Christian-Democratic Movement (HCDM).

As the wave of nationalism encouraged parties and movements to capitalize on the emotional issues of national aspiration and the protection of minority rights, the communists in Slovakia entered the preelection campaign as an "emerging modern leftist party interested in solving social problems in the spirit of national understanding, political toleration, and cooperation with other parties and movements."[16] The aim of CPS was to regain the lost sympathies of the general public by recasting its role to the time when the communists did not enjoy the monopoly of power. In line with this strategy, the CPS's May Day 1990 celebration in Bratislava was considerably toned down. However, in spite of some successful election campaign gatherings, for example, in Ziar nad Hronom and Martin, CPS's appeal for support from the new left in Slovakia fell on deaf ears.

According to various pollsters a month or so before the elections, in the Czech Republic, CF still had a dominant lead over many other parties, but in the Slovak Republic, PAV was losing ground; public opinion polls showed CDM ahead by 29.1 percent compared with PAV's 13.1 percent.[17] But PAV still had certain advantages over the challengers, mainly because its party platform, "Opportunity for Slovakia," appealed to more voters than the narrowly focused platforms of several other parties. Its approach to the state federal system, for example, considered the Czech and Slovak republics as two separate sovereign entities, with the sovereignty of the federal government being only a derivative or delegated establishment. The PAV platform made it clear that the two national republics must manage their own affairs while entrusting to the federal government the functions of foreign affairs, defense, and finance; its goals for the federal system were strong republics and competent republican governments and parliaments.[18]

Another plus for PAV in the preelection campaign was the appearance of some well-known former dissidents, including Alexander Dubcek, Jan Budaj, and Milan Knazko, and also such notables as Milan Cic, Frantisek Miklosko, Miroslav Kusy, Milan Simecka, Fedor Gal, and Vladimir Meciar. None of the other political parties or movements could claim as many sophisticated politicos as PAV. In addition, in mid-May the official PAV publication, *Verejnost*, became a daily, while other political parties were still scrounging around to get their information out to the voters. Another advantage for PAV was the support it received from its sister organization, CF, and from President Vaclav Havel as a "nonpartisan" supporter. Havel's appearance in Bratislava on June 4, 1990, less than a week before the elections, gave the party an enormous boost. It was determined to win, and toward that end its leaders mobilized all resources to confront their opponents and win over as many voters as possible.

THE JUNE 1990 PARLIAMENTARY ELECTIONS

Before January 23, 1990, when the Federal Assembly passed a law governing the registration of new political parties, the general public in Czechoslovakia, after four and a half decades of communist dictatorship, knew next to nothing about political parties. By the time of the elections the following June, there were sixty-six political parties and movements registered in Czechoslovakia. Twenty-three parties, movements, and coalitions were competing for seats in the two houses of the Federal Assembly, the House of the People, and the House of the Nations—sixteen in the Czech Republic, seven in the Slovak Republic. For four and a half decades voters had been accustomed to only two political preferences: the official list as presented by the regime and the illegal opposition movement representing a struggle for human rights and compliance with international laws and agreements. When the floodgates of political organizations were opened in January 1990 and democratization became equated with political pluralism, the political fever of organizing new political parties and movements became a fad rather than a responsible commitment to democratic statecraft. After all, politicians in Czechoslovakia were "free" to organize as many parties and movements as the diversity of interests would allow. All they needed were 1,000 signatures from the new party's supporters. But with much to choose from, on the eve of the 1990 elections, less than 3 percent of the population were members of political parties.

On February 27, 1990, the Federal Assembly, against Havel's wishes, passed a new electoral law establishing a system of proportional representation but permitting a limited selection of candidates.[19] According to this law, only registered political parties and movements could compete in the election, although registration alone did not guarantee a place on the ballot. A party was required either to prove that it had 10,000 card-holding members or present a petition signed by 10,000 supporters whose addresses and birth certificates could be verified. Sixty days before the elections, qualified parties and movements could submit to a regional electoral committee a list of party candidates who had to be at least twenty-one years of age. The law also allowed parties to run candidates who were members of other parties or had no affiliation. The election campaign was limited to forty days, ending two days before the election. Campaign costs were the responsibility of each political party, but parties receiving more than 2 percent of the total vote were entitled to 10 koruny (35 cents) from the state for each vote cast for their party. Every party eligible to run was given four hours of free broadcast time on television and radio. The approved lists of candidates were officially posted at the National Committees (NC) in each town or village (city or town halls) thirty days prior to the elections. Three days before the elections, eligible voters received copies of the same lists—separate party tickets with candidates' names listed in numerical order of party slates. The voters then cast one vote for the House of the People and one for the House of the Nations.

On April 19, 1990, the Federal Election Commission[20] announced that twenty-three political parties and movements met all prerequisites stipulated by the election law and could compete for Federal Assembly seats.[21]

The dominant themes of the campaign were the possibility of linking social justice with political and economic democracy, the confiscation of the Communist Party's assets and the party's future role, and relations between Czechs and Slovaks. The key issue in the Slovak Republic was autonomy. Although no major political party actually advocated a separate state, PAV and others, especially SNP, stated that they sought the right to "rule in their own house," leaving only defense and a part of foreign policy under the power of the federal government.[22] The diversity and depth of the election issues were so complex that voters found it difficult to distinguish among the many parties and candidates seeking their support.

Many politicos felt their main task was to defeat communist candidates. The only tension between the rival candidates occurred on May 16 and 17, when the leader of CDM and Federal Deputy Premier Jan Carnogursky accused President Havel of violating campaign ethics. On May 16, when Havel and Premier Marian Calfa visited Slovakia, television news coverage showed them surrounded by people displaying PAV badges; the following day in a nationally televised rally in Prague, Havel openly endorsed the candidates of CF currently in government. The Central Election Commission criticized the live television coverage and asked that all political parties and movements except CF and PAV be given an additional ten minutes of air time to compensate for the incident.[23]

A much more serious controversy was "Sachergate," which began in early April after Oldrich Hromadko, head of the CF security committee, and Ladislav Lis, chairman of the military and security committee of the Federal Assembly and a CF deputy in parliament—both former communists—criticized the minister of internal affairs, Richard Sacher, an official of the People's Party (PP), for retaining in their posts hundreds of secret police officials, including General Alojz Lorenc, the former (communist) deputy minister of internal affairs responsible for state security, and a direct liaison to Soviet KGB chairman Vladimir Kryuchkov. The two accusers were then joined by Deputy Interior Minister Jaroslav Prochazka, who alleged that Sacher planned to use the secret police to gather information on the "moods of the public." In retaliation, unidentified employees of the ministry furnished the media with documents compromising Hromadko and Lis. The human rights movement, Charter 77, defended Hromadko and Lis, stating that both had left CPC and had participated in dissident activities.[24] On May 8, CF and PP agreed that Hromadko would leave CF and Prochazka the ministry of interior, and that CF supporter Jan Ruml would be appointed the new deputy minister of interior with direct responsibility for the secret police.

But the trouble continued. Near the end of May, Sacher disclosed that 10,000 confidential secret police files were missing from the archives and that the only existing copies were in the hands of the Soviet KGB. This meant that falsification of documents and possible smear campaigns could not be ruled out. The chairman of the PP and vice chairman of the Federal Assembly, Josef Bartoncik, was accused of collaboration with the secret police as an agent under the communist regime. Bartoncik denied the charges and filed suit against the accusers, calling the charges "preposterous lies."[25] The accusations against him were, he said, part of a backlash against the formation of a strong Christian Democratic Union—a coalition of PP, CDM, and a number of small right-of-center parties and movements, including the Christian Democratic Party, the Association of Entrepreneurs, Masaryk's Democratic Movement, the Farmers Party, and several others. Immediately after the election on June 10, President Havel's adviser, Jiri Krizan, Deputy Minister of the Interior Jan Ruml, and Pavel Rychetsky, the general procurator of the Czech Republic, announced that Bartoncik had admitted to having served as confidant of StB until May 1971 and as agent no. 15301 (alias Hajek) from October 1971 until 1988. Bartoncik decided to withdraw immediately from all political activities.

To assure a strong showing in the June election, three former auxiliary parties or satellites in the National Front, namely, PP, SP, and DP, together with the Social Democrats, proposed to ban the CPC (and therefore also CPS). The official reason given was the lack of response by CPC to the demand that it relinquish the innumerable assets the party had accumulated in the years of its rule and to break completely with its totalitarian ideology and practices. Civic Forum leader Jan Urban criticized the demand as "immature" and expressed the hope for political means to neutralize CPC. On May 17 a rally in Wenceslas Square of about 50,000 people to commemorate the student march six months earlier that led to the country's Velvet Revolution turned into an anticommunist demonstration, with speakers demanding a ban on CPC and confiscation of its property.[26] Both CPC and, in Slovakia, CPS continued to campaign, with a new party emblem of two cherries rather than the traditional hammer and sickle. *Rude Pravo* (Red Justice), the CPC daily, was still a powerful force and probably the most widely read newspaper in the country. The party still had close to one million members, and as a reformed party it tried to appeal to voters worried about social problems.

The CPC-CPS had sufficient funds for the campaign but was intimidated by its past; the new parties were ambitious but poor. On May 14 the Central Election Commission in Prague decided to advance to the newly established parties and movements loans totaling 20 million koruny to cover election campaign costs. Political parties belonging to the former National Front were excluded from the offer. Even so, some parties and movements were better off financially than others.[27]

According to observers from the West, including the United States, Czechoslovakia's first free elections in forty-four years were orderly, and they conformed to the established rules of democratic procedures. The turnout of voters was higher than predicted: 96 percent of the electorate cast its ballots. Voters elected representatives to the Federal Assembly (national parliament of the Czech and Slovak Federal Republic national parliament) and the respective National Councils in the Czech and Slovak republics (the parliaments of the Czech and Slovak Republic). One hundred fifty seats were filled in each of the constituent houses of the Federal Assembly: the House of the People and the House of the Nations. In the latter, seventy-five representatives were elected from the Czech Republic and seventy-five from the Slovak Republic. Tables 8 and 9 show the representation of parties and movements in the two houses of the Federal Assembly.

As predicted by various public opinion polls, the winner in the Czech Republic by an absolute majority was CF, which secured sixty-eight seats in the House of the People and fifty seats in the House of the Nations. Contrary to the prognostication of the pollsters, in the Slovak Republic, CDM received only eleven seats in the House of the People and fourteen seats in the House of the Nations. The victor in Slovakia by a simple majority was PAV. The second strongest party in the Czech Republic and third in the Slovak Republic was the communist (CPC-CPS). In both republics the combined seats of representation gave the communists twenty-three seats in the House of the People and four seats

TABLE 8

DISTRIBUTION OF VOTES AND SEATS IN THE FEDERAL ASSEMBLY, HOUSE OF THE PEOPLE, JUNE 1990

Ballot no.	Political party or movement	% of votes received			No. of seats received		
		CR	SR	Total	CR	SR	Total
5	Public Against Violence (PAV)	—	32.54	32.54	—	19	19
7	Civic Forum (CF)	53.15	—	53.15	68	—	68
10	Communist Party of Czechoslovakia (CPC)	13.48	13.81	27.29	15	8	23
12	Coexistence Movement (CM)	0.08	8.58	8.66	—	5	5
16	Slovak National Party (SNP)	—	10.96	10.96	—	6	6
17	Christian Democratic Movement (CDM)	—	18.98	18.98	—	11	11
20	Association for Moravia and Silesia (AMS)	7.89	—	7.89	9	—	9
23	Christian Democratic Union (CDU)	8.69	—	8.69	9	—	9
(18)	Other parties and movements	16.71	15.13	31.84	0	0	0
	Totals	100.00	100.00	200.00	101	49	150

SOURCE: Frantisek Ciganek, *Kronika demokratickeho parlamentu 1989–1992* (Chronicle of Democratic Parliament, 1989–1992) (Prague: Cesty, 1992), pp. 86, 204.

TABLE 9

DISTRIBUTION OF VOTES AND SEATS IN THE FEDERAL ASSEMBLY, HOUSE OF THE NATIONS, JUNE 1990

Ballot no.	Political party or movement	% of votes received			No. of seats received		
		CR	SR	Total	CR	SR	Total
5	Public Against Violence (PAV)	—	37.28	37.28	—	33	33
7	Civic Forum (CF)	49.96	—	49.96	50	—	50
10	Communist Party of Czechoslovakia (CPC)	13.80	13.43	27.23	12	12	24
12	Coexistence Movement (CM)	—	8.49	8.49	—	7	7
16	Slovak National Party (SNP)	—	11.44	11.44	—	9	9
17	Christian Democratic Movement (CDM)	—	16.66	16.66	—	14	14
20	Association for Moravia and Silensia (AMS)	9.10	—	9.10	7	—	7
23	Christian Democratic Union (CDU)	8.75	—	8.75	6	—	6
(18)	Other parties and movements	18.39	12.70	31.09	0	0	0
	Totals	100.00	100.00	200.00	75	75	150

SOURCE: Frantisek Ciganek, *Kronika demokratickeho parlamentu 1989–1992* (Chronicle of Democratic Parliament, 1989–1992) (Prague: Cesty, 1992), pp. 87–88, 204.

in the House of the Nations—forty-seven out of 300 seats in the Federal Assembly (see Table 10). The two Catholic parties, CDM and CDU, combined ended up with only forty total parliamentary seats. To political leaders who campaigned to unseat the communists, the parliamentary election was both a surprise and a disappointment.

The electorate produced other surprises as well. Shortly before the election, opinion polls predicted that SNP had virtually no chance of being represented at the federal or national level. Yet SNP received six seats in the House of the People and nine seats in the House of the Nations; SNP may have gained quite a few votes from voters who had earlier planned to support CDM but changed their minds when they discovered CDM's platform was not nationalist enough. Still another surprise was the support for the Coexistence Movement, a coalition of representatives of ethnic minorities (mainly Hungarians), which received five seats in the House of the People and seven seats in the House of the Nations. Another group, the Hungarian Democratic Initiative, successfully ran on the PAV ticket. The Romanies (Gypsies) failed to gain 5 percent of the vote in Slovakia and were eliminated, with a host of other smaller parties and movements for the same reason. More surprising was the failure to gain representation by the Green Party, the Democratic Party, the Czechoslovak Socialist Party, and the Social Democratic

TABLE 10

COMBINED SEATS OF REPRESENTATION IN THE
FEDERAL ASSEMBLY, JUNE 1990

| | | Parliamentary seats | | |
Rank	Political party or movement	CR	SR	All seats
2	Public Against Violence (PAV)	—	52	52
1	Civic Forum (CF)	118	—	118
3	Communist Party of Czechoslovakia (CPC-CPS)	27	20	47
8	Coesistence Movement (CM)	—	12	12
7	Slovak National Party (SNP)	—	15	15
4	Christian Democratic Movement (CDM)	—	25	25
5	Association for Moravia and Silesia (AMS)	16	—	16
6	Christian Democratic Union (CDU)	15	—	15
	Totals	176	124	300

Party. None of these received enough support to be represented in any of the three parliaments. Out of twenty-three registered political parties and movements that entered the first Czecho-Slovak free parliamentary election in forty-four years, only eight received sufficient support to be represented in the three parliaments after June 9, 1990.

The overwhelming victory of the two major movements, CF and PAV, was a clear indication that trouble was looming. Because both movements lacked organizational cohesion, discipline, and a unified political philosophy, there were doubts that the umbrella organizations serving a variety of small political parties and civic groups with disparate philosophies could become the political mechanism needed for a smooth transformation to democracy. The main question was whether or not CF and PAV would transform themselves into serious political parties, and, if so, what the consequences would be to democratization.

On June 12, 1990, President Vaclav Havel announced that he would like Premier Marian Calfa, a Slovak member of PAV, to lead the new government. Havel made his announcement after meeting with leaders of CF and PAV.[28] Since Havel had made the choice of Calfa conditional upon his continuation in office—a day before the announcement Havel was reported as saying he would not seek a second term for himself unless the new government was to his liking—Calfa's critics were forced to give in to Havel's choice. The main objection to Calfa's continuation as premier was, of course, his communist past: he had been a member of the CPS-CPC since he was eighteen years old (in 1964) and had continued in various high posts until January 18, 1990, when he joined the Public Against Violence movement and then ran on its ticket in the June elections. On June 29 President Havel swore in the new Czecho-Slovak federal government and thereby formally completed the country's peaceful transition from communism to the initial stage of democratization.[29]

As Table 11 shows, of the sixteen members of the streamlined government, six were independent, five were members of CF, three were members of PAV, and two were members of CDM; ten were Czechs and six were Slovaks. The two major movements, CF and PAV, had the key ministries: the economy, legislation, foreign affairs, internal affairs, finance, foreign trade, and labor and social affairs. The number of deputy premiers was reduced from six to four, seven former ministries and offices were abolished, and three were renamed under two new ministries. In parallel with the Czechoslovak federal parliamentary elections on June 8–9, 1990, the Slovak parliament—the Slovak National Council—

TABLE 11

THE NEW FEDERAL GOVERNMENT, JUNE 1990

Position	Name	Party	Nationality
Premier	Marian Calfa	PAV	Slovak
Deputy Premiers			
Economic Reform	Vaclav Vales	Ind.	Czech
Legislation	Pavel Rychetsky	CF	Czech
Human Rights, Rel. & Cul.	Jozef Miklosko	CDM	Slovak
Foreign Affairs	Jiri Dienstbier	CF	Czech
Cabinet Ministers			
Defense	Miroslav Vacek	Ind.	Czech
Internal Affairs	Jan Langos	PAV	Slovak
Finance	Vaclav Klaus	CF	Czech
Foreign Trade	Slavomir Stracar	PAV	Slovak
Labor and Social Affairs	Petr Miller	CF	Czech
Transportation	Jiri Nezval	Ind.	Czech
Telecommunications	Theodor Petrik	CDM	Slovak
The Economy	Vladimir Dlouhy	CF	Czech
Strategic Planning	Pavel Hoffmann	Ind.	Slovak
The Environment	Josef Vavrousek	Ind.	Czech
People's Control	Kvetoslava Korinkova	Ind.	Czech

KEY: CF Civic Forum; CDM Christian Democratic Movement; Ind. Independent; PAV Public Against Violence.

held its separate elections. In 5,660 electoral districts with 3,622,000 eligible voters, 3,455,000, or 95.39 percent, cast their ballots to elect their representatives (see Table 12). Among the sixteen political parties movements, only seven qualified for representation.

On June 26, 1990, 147 out of 150 newly elected representatives (one-fifth of whom were members of the preceding council) were sworn in before the outgoing chairman of SNC, Rudolf Schuster, and by a secret ballot of 137 votes elected Frantisek Miklosko (PAV) their new chairman. Five vice chairpersons were also elected: Ivan Carnogursky (CDM), Jan Klepac (CDM), Laszlo Nagy (PAV-HII), Milan Zemko (PAV), and Olga Keltosova (DP). Unlike its counterpart, the Czech National Council, SNC suspended the principle of proportional representation, and, as a result, on June 29 M. Ftacnik (CPS) was elected a member of the SNC presidium, whereas A. Asvany (CM) failed to receive the votes required for representation in the presidium.[30] On the same day, in accordance with Article 129 of constitutional law no. 143/1968, con-

TABLE 12

RESULTS OF THE ELECTIONS INTO THE
SLOVAK NATIONAL COUNCIL, JUNE 1990

Political party or movement	% votes	No. of seats
Public Against Violence (PAV)	29.34	48[a]
Christian Democratic Movement (CDM)	19.20	31[a]
Slovak National Party (SNP)	13.94	22
Communist Party of Czechoslovakia (CPC-CPS)	13.34	22
Coexistence Movement (CM)	8.66	14
Democratic Party (DS)	4.39	7[a]
Green Party (GP)	3.48	6
Totals	92.35	150

[a]Represents the new coalition majority of 86 out of 150 deputies in the SNC.

cerning the Czechoslovak federation, the Slovak government of Milan Cic submitted its resignation and the new presidium of the SNC authorized Vladimir Meciar (PAV) with the organization of the new government of the Slovak Republic. He chose as his first deputy premier Jan Carnogursky (CDM). The new Slovak government was sworn in on June 27 before the new chairman of the SNC, Frantisek Miklosko, in the former Coronation Hall of Bratislava Castle.[31] The twenty-three-member cabinet of Premier Vladimir Meciar consisted of thirteen members of PAV, seven CDM members, and three members of the DP; PAV and CDM refused to enter into a coalition with SNP, CM, and GP, and they also refused to cooperate with the communists.

In compliance with President Havel's wishes, the Slovak and Czech governments each created a post of one minister without portfolio (Milan Knazko for Slovakia) whose only task was to ensure permanent cooperation between the republican government and the federal cabinet. In other words, the aim was to strengthen the national governments' ties with the federal government. Yet the program of the Meciar government of the Slovak Republic projected a different course for the near future.

The program that Vladimir Meciar presented to the Slovak National Council on July 2 called for "basic reevaluation" of relations between the Slovak and the Czech republics and with the Czecho-Slovak federal government—meaning, of course, reevaluation of the republic's right to self-determination. According to the new program, the federal and the national constitutions could complete the "common development" of both republics within the federal republic; the Czechs and the Slovaks would be "autonomous and equal subjects" in the European community of nations. Meciar emphasized the need to decentralize the federal state administration and to resolve the nationalities issue in Slovakia; the Slovak government would create a Council of State Information Policy, and Slovak radio and television would become independent public and national institutions.[32]

The new federal premier, Marian Calfa, presented his government's program to the Federal Assembly on July 3, following Meciar's orientation the previous day. The centerpiece of Calfa's program was the sensitive issue of the transition from a centrally planned to a market economy and in conjunction with it the promise to set in motion practical changes to stabilize the economy and control inflation and unemployment. Calfa's choice of Vaclav Klaus as his new finance minister instead of the more cautious Valtr Komarek (CF) indicated Calfa's determination to move rapidly and decisively. Klaus, Vaclav Vales (an independent and first vice chairperson), and Vladimir Dlouhy (CF) were all members of the previous government's successful economics team, which devised a five-stage process for transforming Czechoslovakia's economic system. First, monopolies suppressing competition were to be dismembered. Second, in order to force state enterprises to compete with one another and with the private sector, the government promised to tighten credit. Third, several state-owned companies were to be sold to private owners. Fourth, other enterprises were to be converted into joint-stock companies. Finally, large agricultural cooperatives were to be split into smaller enterprises. All these changes were predicated on the government's commitment that the markets would be free and sovereign, that control of the producers would cease, and that the government would no longer dictate resource allocation.[33]

Although the communists did not participate in the government coalitions at either the federal or the national levels, the so-called "war" waged against them during the June 1990 election campaign failed to make them disappear. With forty-seven seats in the Federal Assembly, the communists in the Slovak and Czech republics remained a political force to be reckoned with. The CPC and the CPS were viable organizations, able to adapt to new conditions and take advantage of new situations. For instance, long before the elections they bid goodbye to their most compromised functionaries and replaced them with new faces. After losing its monopoly in December 1989, CPC-CPS proclaimed itself as a new left-oriented movement championing the cause of the poor, the unemployed, retirees, and other socially deprived people. A few months after the elections, CPS was able to embrace a new identity, "the Party of the Democratic Left," and create an image of defender of socially weak groups. In the local elections in Slovakia in November 1990, the communists came in third after CDM and PAV, mainly by the use of skillful propaganda techniques that exploited the emotions of those who felt threatened by radical economic reform, unemployment, "Prague Castle" intrigues against the common people, and so on.[34] The communists were still not out of the picture.

12 The Breakup of the Czechoslovak Federation

In hindsight it can be argued that the lack of civic society enabled deposed communist leaders to apply the principle of *continuity* and exert their influence under the old "communist" constitution until the June 1990 elections. The post–November 1989 dissident politicians, heading more than forty newly organized political parties, movements, and coalitions, were united in their campaigns against the still influential Communist Party of Czechoslovakia. But after the establishment of the first parliamentary government, they were unable to agree either on a new democratic constitution or on several other issues, including Czecho-Slovak relations.

The parliamentary elections held on June 8 and 9, 1990, gave the coalition of Civic Forum/Public Against Violence a majority of 170 seats out of 300 in the Czecho-Slovak Federal Assembly. After the resounding victory, the coalition faced enormous hurdles to maintain cohesion and deliver all its promises. Controversies surrounding several legislative proposals within the parliament led to changes, splintering, and bolting of the coalition. On issues such as presidential powers, the coalition caused a rift between Czechs and Slovaks.

As predicted, ten months after the elections, the representation of political power in parliament had changed dramatically, owing mainly to the disintegration of the CF/PAV coalition as well as to the defection of some CF deputies to the Czechoslovak Social Democracy (CSD). The representation of six parties, movements, and coalitions after June 1990 was transformed into twelve major political parties and groups represented in the Federal Assembly as well as a plethora of splinter groups and independent deputies who had been elected on the CF ticket. On February 23, 1991, the congress of CF authorized the division of the forum into two political groups: a right-of-center party, known as the Civic Democratic Party (CDP), headed by finance minister Vaclav Klaus, and a political movement organized around the Liberal Club of CF, known as the Civic Movement (CM), headed by Pavel Rychetsky, deputy premier in charge of legislation. Both groups agreed to form a coalition that would remain in place at least until the next parliamentary elections in mid-1992. This division of CF, known as the Lany Agreement, was approved by the CF congress by a vote of 161 to 3, with three abstentions. Thereafter, politicians in the Czech and Slovak Federal Republic embarked on a ruthless course of self-centered struggle for power, which in a short time culminated in the breakup of the Czechoslovak federation.

ECONOMIC INEQUALITY

Public Against Violence reacted to the disintegration of CF by promising to cooperate with all the groups formerly associated with CF. However, the following month (March 1991) PAV itself split into two groups. This occurred when the Slovak premier, Vladimir Meciar, and his followers, after failing to convince the majority of the movement's leadership that of the five "pillars" of the program adopted by PAV in September 1990, Slovak national issues should receive the highest priority, broke off to form their own party, known as Public Against Violence—For a Democratic Slovakia (PAV-DS). Eight months earlier when the program was adopted, all "pillars" stood on equal footing, but the rising tide of nationalism in Slovakia convinced Meciar that now was the time to forge ahead against the reelected leader of the PAV movement, Fedor Gal, who defeated Meciar at the February 23 congress. The conflict between the Gal and Meciar groups culminated on March 5, when Meciar announced the formation of PAV-DS. Though Meciar promised to cooperate with the Gal group of PAV, it soon became clear that his intentions were quite the opposite. Meciar and his associates argued that the economic reforms proposed by the federal government and supported by the Gal leadership of PAV had not taken into account the fact that Slovakia was less industrialized than the Czech Republic. They also argued that privatization in Slovakia should proceed more slowly than in the Czech Republic and that the role of the Slovak government in managing the Slovak economy should be expanded rather than reduced as the federal reform program proposed. After arm twisting and unsolicited promises, some of the deputies in the Federal Assembly and the SNC declared their new loyalty to Meciar and the PAV-DS. A new parliamentary caucus representing PAV had been organized in the Federal Assembly on March 22. Of the fifty-eight deputies originally elected on PAVs ticket in June 1990, thirty-two joined the caucus. Alexander Dubcek and Milan Cic, the two most prominent members of PAV, declared their impartiality; about seventeen deputies did join the parliamentary caucus of PAV-DS.[1]

The struggle for power in PAV had already had a spillover effect when on March 7, five groups issued the so-called Declaration of the Sovereignty of Slovakia, which was also signed by a number of intellectuals. The declaration demanded that SNC declare Slovak laws to have precedence over those of the federation, and before it considered signing a treaty on a common state with the Czech Republic, Slovakia should become a fully independent state with its own army, currency, and foreign policy.[2] In support of the declaration, the chairman of the Slovak Heritage Foundation, Jozef Markus, and the leaders of SNP called for demonstrations. On March 10, the day before the demonstrations, Premier Meciar stated that the declaration's demands would not be approved by the Slovak parliament because they "were not shared by the majority of Slovak citizens."[3] Also on March 10 Meciar and Dubcek issued a joint statement asking Slovaks to remain calm and avoid extremist propaganda. Even so, thousands of people demonstrated on March 10 and 11 "in support of the declaration." President Havel called the situation in Slovakia appalling and condemned some of the signatories as representatives of the former centralist communist regime. On March 12 the leader of the new Party of the Democratic Left (PDL)— formerly CPS—responded to the criticism by defending the declaration as a "fact of life" that must be discussed seriously by the public and SNC.[4]

In the meantime, several nationalist groups called for demonstrations to be held on March 14, 1991, to commemorate the fifty-second anniversary of the establishment of the Slovak state. On that day, about

5,000 people gathered in Bratislava to celebrate the anniversary. When President Havel, on a one-day visit to Slovakia, appeared unexpectedly at the rally with his entourage, he was attacked by a mob of about 200 angry demonstrators shouting slogans like "Judas!" and "Czechs are greedy." Havel and his supporters escaped unscathed, but later that day, in a television address to the Slovak nation, Havel appealed to the people's democratic senses and asked them to remain within a federal Czecho-Slovak framework; but if the majority of Slovaks expressed their desire to live in an independent state in a democratic referendum, he promised to respect their decision.[5]

Earlier in 1991 political leaders of the two republics and the federation had held three rounds of talks about the form and contents of the new republic and federal constitutions. The stumbling block to a final agreement was CDM, which insisted that the country should become a confederation and that the two republics should conclude a state treaty before adopting a federal constitution. Finally, as a compromise, the parties agreed that the federal constitution should be preceded by a political declaration, not a treaty, stating the intentions to live in a common federal state.[6] A snag had just developed, on March 5, after Havel disclosed the contents of his draft of the federal constitution; according to Havel's thinking, the devolution of many powers to the republics had to be balanced by a strong federal state, and he therefore proposed that a unicameral 200-seat Federal Assembly replace the current bicameral one. He also suggested a thirty-member federal council composed of the republican parliaments with powers to delay the passage of laws approved by the Federal Assembly. The president's powers would also be increased to include the rights to declare a state of emergency, to dissolve the parliament, and to hold referendums.

All the Slovak parties, movements, and coalitions objected to Havel's proposal, but the greatest opposition came from CDM. The leaders of CDM felt that Havel's proposed constitution would weaken Slovakia—some deputies even called the proposal an insult to the Slovak nation—but the criticism was couched within their repeated challenge to the concept of economic reform, engineered and approved at the federal level in September 1990. In February 1991, arguing that the Scenario for Economic Reform approved in Prague failed to respect Slovakia's specific needs, CDM had published its own program demanding that the state play a greater role in the Slovak economy and that state subsidies be expanded beyond those proposed by the federal government.

Since September 1990, when the drastic economic reform by the federal government was promulgated, Slovak politicians had vehemently sought to obtain a regional economic reform specifically tailored for Slovakia.[7] The authors of the federal reform refused to yield on the issue, and the controversy continued for the rest of 1990 and throughout 1991. One of the features of the economic reform program was a severe reduction in the arms industry, which happened to be the primary industry in Slovakia. These two decisions sent a shock wave across Slovakia. The Slovaks had become accustomed to economic favoritism under the socialist plan of "equalization"; now it appeared that the redistribution of national income would no longer favor Slovakia, but rather the Czech Republic.[8] On January 8, 1991, at a press conference in Bratislava, Slovak premier Vladimir Meciar condemned the federal government's decision to convert the arms industry to peaceful production as "too costly a price to pay for a political gesture when the cost would be born by the Slovak people and not the federal government."[9] Not even the most powerful democratic and humanitarian countries with the most advanced economies, he declared, could afford to stop such production suddenly. The government of the Slovak Republic wanted a gradual rather than a speedy conversion of arms production, and the country would strive to respect all international agreements whereby the production of armaments would go hand in hand with the economy.

The problems facing Czecho-Slovak relations intensified with the effects of economic reforms launched at the beginning of 1991. In December 1990, only 5 percent of respondents polled in Slovakia (as opposed to 15 percent in the Czech Republic) said the economic reform program was "good" and that they would support it; 20 percent in Slovakia had no opinion. Eighty percent of the respondents in Slovakia (as opposed to 75 percent in the Czech Republic) thought economic reform would weaken the social "safety net."[10] Their opinions were prophetic. In January 1991, consumer and food prices in Czechoslovakia rose by 25.8 percent and 31.4 percent, respectively. In Slovakia the price of milk jumped from 2 koruny to an average of 6 koruny, butter from 10 to 21 koruny, and bread from 5 to 10 koruny.[11] As a countermeasure, in March 1991, the federal government agreed to a wage increase in order to prevent real wages from declining by more than 15 percent. Unemployment rose by 52.1 percent in January 1991, bringing the official rate to 1.5 percent, or a total of 119,500 unemployed. By election time 1992, the economic situation had worsened in both republics, but particularly in Slovakia. For example, during the first quarter of 1992 unemployment in Slovakia stood at 307,400, or about 12 percent of the Slovak labor force, whereas in the Czech Republic it was only 4 percent. The federal government had committed itself to a 25 percent cut in arms production by 1993, and in Slovakia, where the impact was most severe, the reduction was projected to affect at least 111 enterprises employing between 150,000 to 200,000 workers.[12] Both unemployment and consumer and food prices were on a steep rise while production output and real wages were steadily declining. Slovakia's output (in real GDP) declined from 220.9 billion koruny in 1989 to 171.2 billion koruny in 1992. With the collapse of the Council of Mutual Economic Assistance (in January 1991), the major markets for Slovak goods effectively disappeared, and because of the Scenario for Economic Reform, firms faced a new set of prices that often lacked the comparative advantage they used to have. The net impact was a deterioration of Slovakia's trade because import prices, especially of energy products, based on hard currency rose faster than export prices. Slovak industry was still heavily dependent on foreign raw materials (especially from the former Soviet Union), and the consequences were especially severe for industries that depended on such imports. Of course, strategists of political parties and movements took advantage of the prevailing economic conditions and freely publicized comparative tables, charts, and figures in the local press to show the differences between the Slovak and Czech as well as other nations' positions in different economic categories. For example, the two most frequently cited comparative figures of June 1992 (with January 1991 = 100%) showed industrial output for Slovakia 75 percent compared with 89 percent in the Czech Republic and unemployment 12 percent in Slovakia compared with 4 percent in the Czech Republic.

Since the orientations of the citizens in the Czech Republic were considerably different from those of the citizens in the Slovak Republic, the question that remained unanswered was: What kind of conceptualization and orientations prevailed among the citizens in the Slovak Republic on the issue of statehood before the June 1992 elections? Data from surveys and analysis of sociologists are quite revealing.[13] Twenty-one percent of the Slovaks questioned favored a unitary state with a parliament and constitution, 7 percent favored one federal government, 27 percent wanted a federation of two republics, 9 percent a federation of three republics (including Moravia and Silesia), 16 percent supported a confederation, 13 percent wanted an independent Slovak state, 3 percent preferred something else, and 4 percent had no opinion. A further breakdown of the responses revealed that at the beginning of 1992 there were three major orientations on statehood among Slovak adults. One group consisted of proponents of an independent Slovak state; a second group favored a joint state of Czechs and Slovaks, with some of the respondents leaning toward either a federal or unitary system of government. The third and most numerous group had ambiguous, uncertain, and confused perceptions: Some respondents indicated that they had no opinion on some questions asked; others combined wishful thinking with their own perception of reality. Some respondents in this group spoke of federation or a unitary state but also were in favor of an independent Slovak monetary system, a Slovak army, sovereignty of Slovak legislation, and so on. More than one-third in this group identified with an independent Slovak state.

THE 1992 ELECTIONS AND THE END OF THE CZECHOSLOVAK FEDERAL ASSEMBLY

Compared with the first postcommunist parliamentary elections of 1990, the political mood of the voters in the Slovak Republic was subdued, dejected, and uncertain before the second parliamentary elections of June 6, 1992. As the above-mentioned sociological surveys concluded, distrust in the new power elite in 1992 was much more intense in the Slovak than in the Czech Republic. The feeling of alienation in Slovakia was closely related to the general dissatisfaction with the post–November 1989 developments—frustration over the threat of reduced social benefits, distrust in privatization, fear of rising unemployment, conciliatory attitudes toward the communists, disappointment with the work of the new parliaments, weariness from lengthy negotiations over the framing of the new constitution, authoritarian nostalgia for law and order, and a certain anti-Western bias.[14]

The main issues in April 1992 were the cost of living and unemployment, followed by health care, indexing of income, crime, and pollution. Seventy-seven percent of the respondents from Slovakia agreed that the ties binding the Slovaks with the Czechs should not be broken. Although political parties and movements except the Slovak National Party (SNP) still supported the idea of a common state of Slovaks with the Czechs in some kind of political arrangement, more and more people in the Slovak Republic—62 percent compared with 43 percent in October 1990—had begun to think that the Slovaks had a losing relationship with the Czechs. In other words, in the period between the first and second parliamentary elections, the feeling of "injustice" among the Slovaks had increased significantly, inspiring their political leaders to appeal to voters' emotions in the forthcoming elections. One month before the 1992 parliamentary elections, PAV-DS, which had renamed itself the Movement for a Democratic Slovakia (MDS), was perceived in a public opinion survey as the political movement that would guarantee greater economic prosperity and better defend the interests of Slovakia. Most thought the movement had more capable politicians than any other party, movement, or coalition in the Slovak Republic. Next best in these categories was the Slovak National Party (SNP), then the Party of the Democratic Left (PDL) or the former CPS, followed by the Christian Democratic Movement (CDM), and finally the Civic Democratic Union (CDU), formerly Public Against Violence (PAV).[15]

Twenty-seven political parties, movements, and coalitions participated in the 1992 parliamentary elections. As Table 13 shows, twelve of these had proportional representation in the Slovak National Council

TABLE 13

COMPOSITION OF THE SLOVAK NATIONAL COUNCIL
BEFORE THE 1992 ELECTIONS

Rank	Political party or movement	No. of seats
1	Civic Democratic Union (CDU)	23
2	Party of the Democratic Left (PDL)	22
3	Christian Democratic Movement (CDM)	20
4	Movement for a Democratic Slovakia (MDS)	20
5	Slovak National Party (SNP)	17
6	Slovak Christian Democratic Movement (SCDM)	16
7	Hungarian Christian-Democratic Movement (HCDM)	8
8	Coexistence Movement (CM)	6
9	Hungarian Civic Party (HCP)	5
10	Democratic Party (DP)	5
11	Green Party (GP)	5
12	Independent Initiative (II)	3
	Total	150

SOURCE: *Volby 1992* (Elections 1992), p. 16.

(SNC) before the 1992 elections. Five political parties and movements led by the former PAV—now CDU—had over two-thirds of the representatives in the Slovak parliament. Thus any success of legislative politics was dependent on the cooperation of the coalition partners. According to Vladimir Meciar, in 1991 members of the ruling coalition had abandoned the government program; the most powerful political movement, the Civic Forum, split and thus relinquished its administrative responsibilities, which in turn divided Slovakia and deepened the distrust between the Czechs and Slovaks.[16] With these words the head of the victorious MDS justified the success of his political movement versus its chief rival the CDU, which had a very poor showing in the elections.

The results of the 1992 elections were shocking to both the CDU and the CDM. They were, however, extremely rewarding to MDS, formerly the weaker part of PAV, and the SNP (see Table 14). Similarly disappointing results were registered by the followers of the liberal-democratic strategy of the former Civic Forum (CF) in the Czech Republic, where the Czech electorate failed to support the Civic Movement (CM) and thus left it without parliamentary representation. The highest number of votes (29.7 percent) in the Czech Republic was carried by the CF-CDP (Christian Democratic Party) coalition. As a result of the June 1992 elections, the power in both republics and the Federal Assembly had shifted considerably.

In the Slovak Republic the election signified a new government created by a coalition of populist parties with national and social orientations and some authoritarian inclinations led by Vladimir Meciar's MDS. The first of the ten goals propagated by MDS during the final two weeks of the election campaign makes it clear that the political movement sought "through democratic and legitimate means to complete the development of Slovak emancipation: to declare the sovereignty of the Slovak Republic, to prepare a Slovak constitution, to strive for international legal recognition, to call for a referendum on sovereignty and a new arrangement of relations with the Czech Republic."[17] An even more provocative statement was contained in the platform of the SNP, which, incidentally, did not change its position on this issue, as did the MDS. It called for "the declaration of the Slovak Republic as an independent state and participation in the European Union under its own name."[18] In other words, political parties and movements made it abundantly clear that their proposals for solving the economic and social problems in Slovakia were closely tied to the political status of Slovak indepen-

TABLE 14

DISTRIBUTION OF VOTES IN THE SLOVAK NATIONAL
COUNCIL AND THE FEDERAL ASSEMBLY HOUSE OF
THE PEOPLE AND HOUSE OF THE NATIONS

Ballot no.	Political party, movement, or coalition	% of votes received in Slovakia		
		SNR	HP	HN
4	Assoc. for Moravia and Silesia (AMS)	0.12	0.15	0.15
6	Movement for Free Speech (MFS)	0.06	0.05	0.04
7	Movement for a Democratic Slovakia (MDS)	37.16	33.53	33.85
8	Party of the Democratic Left (PDL)	14.70	14.44	14.04
9	Party of Labor and Security (PLS)	0.96	1.02	1.02
11	Movement for Liberating Slovakia (MLS)	0.23	—	—
12	Freedom Party (FP)	0.30	—	—
13	Democrats '92 for One State	—	1.15	1.13
15	Coalition of CHM S Hung. Peoples Rty.	—	7.37	7.39
16	Slovak Christian Demo. Movement (SCDM)	3.05	3.45	3.24
18	Assoc. of Communists in Slovakia (ACS)	—	0.76	0.72
20	Coalition of CHM	7.42	—	—
21	Movement for Social Justice (NSJ)	0.11	0.25	0.06
23	Green Party (GP)	1.08	—	—
25	Christian Democratic Movement (CDM)	8.88	8.96	8.81
26	Civic Democratic Union (CDU)	4.03	3.96	4.04
28	Assoc. for the Republic (AR)	0.32	0.36	0.34
29	National Liberals (ML)	0.08	0.08	0.10
30	Green Party in Slovakia (GPS)	2.14	2.62	2.43
32	Civic Initiative of Romas (CIR)	0.59	0.53	0.55
34	Soc. Dem. Party of Slovakia (SDPS)	4.00	4.86	6.09
35	Communist Party of Slovakia '91 (CPS)	0.75	—	—
36	Coalition of Demo. Pty and CDP (DP-CDP)	3.31	3.95	3.66
37	Slovak National Party (SNP)	7.93	9.93	9.35
39	Slovak People's Party (SPP)	0.29	0.39	0.33
40	Hungarian Civic Party (HCP)	2.29	2.36	2.20
41	Independent Initiative (II)	—	0.43	0.36

SOURCE: *Narodna obroda* (National Review), June 9, 1992.

dence in authoritative decision making. The election results practically guaranteed the achievement of this requirement for the two political parties in the new Slovak parliament (SNC). Out of 150 seats in the SNC, almost half (74) were held by MDS and fifteen by the SNP. The second strongest party was the PDL, formerly CPS, with twenty-nine seats, followed by the CDM with eighteen seats, and the coalition of the

Hungarian Christian-Democratic Movement, Coexistence Movement, and the Hungarian People's Party with fourteen seats.

Since the concentration of power after the elections had shifted to the right in both republics, the two victorious powers—the CDP in the Czech Republic and the MDS in the Slovak Republic—began their negotiations about the succession to power. There were seven rounds of negotiations dealing with the future makeup of the federal government and the change in personnel of the federal administrative organs, economic problems, and the most sensitive issue—relations between the Czechs and Slovaks in the state system. On this last issue the two parties were far apart: CDP insisted on the federal system with one, single representation in the international community; MDS insisted on two separate representations, one for each republic. The negotiations were headed by Vladimir Meciar for MDS and Vaclav Klaus for CDP. In the fourth round, on June 19–20, 1992, at Bratislava, a political agreement was signed between the two negotiating parties as well as an agreement about the makeup of the federal government and its future program. The political agreement consisted of nine points, including agreement on the composition of the federal government and reducing the number of members from sixteen to ten and the number of ministries from twelve to five.

The third and most sensitive point of the agreement referred to the difference of opinions about the state system of Czechoslovakia. The negotiators accepted the existence of the Czech and Slovak Federal Republic, but they did not exclude the possibility of its termination, and during the fifth round of negotiations a month later (Bratislava, July 22–23), the negotiators reached agreement on the method of legitimately ending the federal system of the state: future negotiations concerning the abolition of the federal state would be shifted to the parliaments, specifically to specialists assigned to committees under the auspices of both the CNC and SNC. These committees would prepare a plan for the peaceful end of federalism, the legitimacy of which would then be guaranteed by parliamentary enactment. During the sixth round held in Brno on August 26, the negotiators developed specific rules concerning the final phase of the disintegration of federalism and the separation of the two states. The seventh and final round of negotiations between the delegations of CDP and MDS took place on October 6, at Jihlava. The parties then issued a communique stating that both parties respected their differing positions on the issues concerning the continued existence of the Czech and Slovak Federal Republic, that they favored a customs and currency union, and that they would sign a payment agreement as well as other agreements necessary for the future reciprocal relations. The negotiations also agreed on January 1, 1993, as the date for terminating the federal state.

It should be made clear that the Czechs were just as culpable as the Slovaks in the dissolution of the federal system. Since early 1990, most Czech politicians had been ill prepared to deal with the Slovaks as equal partners. Manifestations of this were, for example, the lack of confidence in sharing power between the federal and republic organs as well as the skepticism of Czech politicians toward making the federal system contingent upon a treaty agreement between the Czechs and Slovaks. As early as November 22, 1989, Vaclav Havel spoke publicly about the need for "authentic federalism" in the country, but because of his limited contacts with the Federal Assembly, Havel was unsuccessful in persuading the parliamentary deputies to adopt the constitution and thus preserve a common statehood.[19] Many Czech politicians were "tired of Slovak exploitation," and Czech perception of Slovakia had changed considerably by the spring of 1992. It was a common assumption that, at bottom, all Slovak politicians wanted "national emancipation"—which really meant the demise of the federal state. Shortly before the June 1992 elections, a large segment of the Czech political parties gravitating to the right of the center began to consider the demise of the federal state, and after the elections, when the victorious CDP and MDS began negotiations about the succession to power, any attempt to preserve the common state was viewed negatively, as being a leftist notion. Havel's resignation before the elections only reinforced the political helplessness of those, both Czech and Slovak, who were hoping to stop the process of disintegration.

Another flawed perception of the Slovaks by Czech politicians was their assumption that all Slovaks placed national values above civic values. After the 1990 elections, many Czechs looked upon Slovak society as one unified whole, that is, a community following national—bordering on nationalistic—values saturated with socialism. Writers like Ludvik Vaculik expressed the feelings of many Czechs who argued that the Czechs should not stand in Slovaks' way if they wished to separate. Not surprisingly, a popular slogan of "At si jdou" (Let Them Go!) developed in the Czech Republic among those who encouraged separation. After the 1992 elections the Czech press frequently used such headings

Map 7. East Central Europe, 2000

as "two civilizations," "artificially held together state," "Balkan-type divisions," "the infected leg" (to be separated from the healthy body), and so on. Coincidentally, during the 1992 elections the voters in the Czech Republic sought to elect strong political leaders—men like Vaclav Klaus, who let it be known that he favored either a smooth-functioning federation with the Slovaks or a civilized separation.

Most Slovak political leaders considered such an "imposed" federalism unacceptable, yet because they were not ready to abandon joint statehood, they began to promote an ambiguous notion of some sort of "confederation." But the often-used assertion that the Slovak voters who voted for Meciar must have known what to expect (namely, the demise of the federal republic) was equally applicable to the Czech voters. Klaus's CDP made the conditions about the prerequisites for a sound and stable statehood loud and clear, whereas Meciar's MDS was hesitant and misleading. Meciar's priorities seemed to be self-aggrandizement and the building of a power base for his party. Yet compared with the events in Yugoslavia, Western states looked upon the peaceful "divorce" in Czechoslovakia with admiration, recognizing the quest of the Slovaks for self-determination as justified.

THE SLOVAK CONSTITUTION

While the delegates of the victorious parties were still negotiating, on July 17, 1992, the deputies of the Slovak National Council approved a "Declaration of the SNC About the Sovereignty of the Slovak Republic." The declaration was supported by 113 votes, with 24 against, and 10 abstentions. The declaration was signed by Ivan Gasparovic, chairman of the SNC, and Premier Vladimir Meciar, the head of the MDS negotiating team. Before the negotiations were concluded, on September 1, 1992, the SNC had passed the new Constitution of the Slovak Republic, by a vote of 114 for, 16 against, and 4 abstentions. Two days later it was signed by the same two leaders in Knights Hall (now renamed Constitution Hall) of Bratislava Castle.[20] Recognizing that the Czech and Slovak Federal Republic was attempting to adopt a federal constitution, Article 7 of the Slovak constitution gives the state discretion to enter into a union with other states or to secede from such a union. Slovakia chose the latter course.

Like most contemporary constitutions in the world, the Slovak constitution proclaims adherence to the principles of a pluralistic democratic state governed by the rule of law with guarantees of civil and human rights to all its citizens. The individual citizen's rights are safeguarded by the rule and supremacy of law administered by an independent judiciary. Therefore, the state organs can act only in compliance with the laws of the land. The constitution attaches special emphasis to the role of the Slovak nation by referring in the preamble to its historical struggle for self-determination and national existence. Though Article 1 of the constitution states that the Slovak Republic is not bound by any ideology or religion, the document does not recognize the separation of state and church.

The constitution follows the parliamentary system first practiced in Czechoslovakia in 1918 after the disintegration of the Austro-Hungarian monarchy. Under this system the government or the executive branch is responsible to parliament, that is, the legislative branch represented by the Slovak National Council—the government is a reflection of the composition of the parliament. The SNC elects not only its own president but also the president of the Slovak Republic, who then becomes the head of the state. The president is elected for a five-year term by a three-fifths majority of all members by secret ballot. The president of the Slovak Republic can appoint or remove the premier as well as other members of the government. The members of the government are sworn in by the president of the Slovak Republic. Since the constitution does not expressly stipulate the responsibilities of the head of the state, the president is not obligated to recall a member of the government upon the advice of the premier. This gray area in the constitution became a matter of controversy in 1993, when the Constitutional Court of the Slovak Republic (case no. 206/1993) decided a case of disagreement between Premier Vladimir Meciar and President Michal Kovac regarding the interpretation of Article 102, paragraph (f), and Article 111 of the Constitution of the Slovak Republic. The issue before the court was whether or not the president had the right to recall Milan Knazko as minister of foreign affairs without the premier's recommendation to do so. According to the court's decision, the constitution cannot prevent the president from recalling a member of the government either without the recommendation or the knowledge of the premier. The latter has a recourse of threatening to resign, which would result in the fall of the entire government.[21]

A less serious problem also occurred in 1993, before the SNC could agree and elect Michal Kovac as the head of state, when the deputy premier and the foreign minister disagreed with the ruling PAV leadership on this issue. Although this deadlocked situation did not result in a paralysis of the government as a whole, it impeded the normal functioning of the foreign ministry.

Since the president of the Slovak Republic is designated by the constitution to be an integral part of the executive branch of the government, he or she is responsible to the parliament, which has the constitutional right to recall him or her for certain specified activities. The constitution makes it clear that the premier, vice premier, and ministers (not the president) are the supreme executive body in the state. Unlike some other modern democratic republics, in Slovakia the president does not have a dominant role either over the government or over the parliament. However, this conceptualization of the executive powers can and frequently does lead to misunderstanding between the president and the government—especially when there is a personality clash between the president and the premier, as was the case between Kovac and Meciar. Although the president, according to the constitution, is head of the Slovak Republic, in reality that office is more ceremonial than functional.

The president's powers are also weak because of the election process. Because the SNC, not the electorate, elects the president, the president cannot easily shrug off the influence of the political party or coalition that nominated and elected him or her to that office, nor can the president truly function as a statesman above party politics. In addition, the current method of presidential election can lead to partial or more severe paralysis of the government if the deputies in the parliament are unable to agree on a candidate. Even though Article 2 of the constitution stipulates that the power of the state is vested in the citizens, the citizens do not choose their candidates; they merely vote for political party slates. The elections determine the future makeup of the SNC, which then, through a lengthy and cumbersome process, elects the president and determines who shall govern in the state. The citizens are not the ultimate sovereign power even if the president disagrees with the SNC (parliament). It will be the political party leaders who ultimately pull the strings behind the scene in order to resolve the conflict, either by recalling the president or by dissolving the parliament. This restriction of the citizens' power is evident in spite of the legislative provision to permit the use of a referendum on a limited number of issues in the public interest. The referendum clause was added to the constitution before the 1992 elections and was intended to deal with the various proposals for resolving statehood in relation to Czecho-Slovak relations. Though negotiators agreed on the separation of the two states without calling for a referendum on the issue, Slovakia's ambition eventually to enter into the European Union could be decided by a referendum.

Most of the contradictions and weaknesses of the constitution are a result of the haste in which it was drafted, to meet the extraordinary situation that developed in the Czech and Slovak Federal Republic after the 1992 elections.[22] In addition to the weaknesses in the presidency already discussed, there are other oddities. Article 87, paragraph 4, requires the president to return a bill to the parliament if he is asked to do so by the government; in other words, in such situations the president becomes a messenger, not a decision maker, and the parliament, a testing ground for the government. Another peculiarity is contained in Article 82, paragraph 4, which states that during a recess or adjournment, the president of the SNC has the obligation to convene the parliament if he is asked to do so by the government. Article 84, paragraph 3, and Article 101, paragraph 3, stipulate that the president shall be elected by a three-fifths majority of all members in the parliament, but nowhere does the constitution explain how the president can be elected if parliament does not reach such a majority. Still another contradiction is between Article 35, paragraph 3, which establishes the right of citizens to work, and Article 35, paragraph 1, which guarantees the right of private enterprise; the right to work and full employment could be in conflict with employment policies of free enterprises and thus create a constitutional crisis. Similarly, Article 40 of the constitution states that through medical insurance, the citizens shall have the right to free health care; how free can it be "through medical insurance"?

Although the 1992 Constitution of the Slovak Republic contains many features that can be found in most of the contemporary democratic states, it is a document based on the concept that the highest organ of state power is the Slovak National Council, which is similar to the form of government established by the socialist constitution of 1960, with the exception that the present document has a specified division of powers among the three branches of government.[23]

EMERGENCE OF THE NEW STATE ORGANIZATION

At midnight on December 31, 1992, Slovaks celebrated not only the beginning of the New Year but the beginning of the new state. In the square of the Slovak national uprising in Bratislava, the state flag of the Slovak Republic was flown, a band played the Slovak national anthem, military salvos were fired, and politicians delivered patriotic speeches. It was a festive occasion. Nevertheless, the celebrations could not hide the fact that the majority of the Slovak population did not desire state independence. The ruling political elite denied by referendum Slovak citizens the opportunity to decide about the separation from the Czech Republic. In reality, more citizens in Slovakia were saddened by the end of the Czecho-Slovak federation than celebrated its demise.

On New Year's Day the celebration continued with a festive mass and a ceremonial session of the SNC, at which the deputies issued the Declaration on the Sovereignty of the Slovak Republic. According to the Declaration:

> The Slovak Republic as a sovereign, independent, and lawful state is one of the two successor states of the Czech and Slovak Federal Republic. The Slovak Republic expressed its principles of statehood by adopting its own constitution, notifying all parliaments and nations of the world and declaring its interest in membership in the European Union. By becoming the successor to all the rights and obligations derived from international treaties and agreements binding on the Czech and Slovak Federal Republic, the Slovak Republic declared its determination to adhere to the principles of a pluralist democracy, to respect and honor all human rights and basic civic freedoms. By adhering to the corresponding documents and commitments, the Slovak Republic is establishing basic guarantees of freedom, justice, and peace.[24]

The Declaration also alluded to the desire of the Slovak Republic to become a member of the United Nations and a contracting party to the Rome Convention on Human Rights and Freedoms. The SNC declared that the Slovak Republic would adhere to democratic and humanistic traditions and take a keen interest in establishing and maintaining diplomatic relations with all democratic countries in the world.

The festive declarations soon came up against hard realities. In contrast to the Czech Republic, where most institutions of the former federal system were preserved, in the Slovak Republic most of the state institutions had to be rebuilt from scratch—especially in the field of foreign policy, where an entirely new network of diplomatic corps had to be created, and in the military, where a new Slovak army had to be organized. The Slovak Republic is relatively small in size compared with other nation-states in Europe—49,030 square kilometers (or 18,925 square miles) and a population of 5,289,608. The population density is relatively low: 108 persons per square kilometer (or 279 per square mile).

As the successor state, the Slovak Republic assumed all legal and treaty obligations of the former federal republic. The citizen-elected Slovak National Council transformed itself into the parliament of a sovereign state and changed its name to the National Council of the Slovak Republic (NCSR). The government of the republic in the federal state became the government of the sovereign Slovak Republic. On the basis of the Constitution of the Slovak Republic, Michal Kovac (b. 1930) was elected president of the new Slovak Republic in February 1993. Within a short time the Slovak Republic established diplomatic relations with practically every country in the world. On January 19, 1993, by UN Security Council Resolution no. 800, the Slovak Republic became the 180th member of the United Nations.

On June 30, 1993, the Slovak Republic became an associate member of the European Union (EU). Its membership was not as smooth as anticipated because of opposition expressed by the delegate from Hungary, who was critical of Slovakia's treatment of ethnic minorities. However, the final vote by the members of the Council of Ministers enabled Slovakia to take advantage of the numerous economic and trade benefits offered by EU. On October 4, 1993, when the Slovak Republic signed the association agreement with the EU in Luxembourg, it automatically joined the free zone of trade with all other members and associate members. The association agreement was ratified by the European Parliament in Strassburg, the NCSR, and the fifteen-member EU parliament.

Although the division of the federal state was peaceful, it was neither smooth nor painless. Before the split, the negotiating teams agreed on a common tariff union and monetary system. The politicians were presumptuous in making promises to the citizens that the impact of the division would be unnoticeable. During the first few days the border between Slovakia and Moravia was only symbolic. Gradually, however, relations between the Czech and Slovak Republics acquired a formality similar to those between Slovakia and other neighboring countries. But the promises made before the breakup of the federal republic were ignored, and agreements were not honored. One month after the declaration of independence by both states, the agreement on monetary union was abrogated. On January 27, 1993, the premiers of both governments signed agreements about the monetary arrangement between the two new states, which culminated in the enactment of a law about currency separation, approved by the Slovak parliament on February 2, 1993. Immediately after that, all bank notes were exchanged for stamped ones, and from February 8 on, Slovakia had a new currency: the Slovak koruna (SK). At the same time new bank notes and coins were being prepared for circulation.

The new Slovak state was beset with difficulties from the very beginning. Its economy was in disorder, unemployment was high, and social conflicts were pervasive. The lack of a stable democratic system offered unlimited opportunities for many citizens to take advantage of the vague and confusing rules and inadequate legislation to maximize their personal ambitions and power. In early March 1993 when the representatives of the government and economic experts examined the state of the Slovak economy, they discovered that the breakup of the federation had caused serious problems in the area of price liberalization, the loosening of a tight fiscal policy, and high taxation, which placed a severe burden on the small- and middle-sized entrepreneurs responsible for the expansion of free enterprise in the country. Furthermore, Slovakia faced a lack of financial investments.

The most serious problem in the Slovak economy was the conversion of the arms industry to consumer production. In 1988 armament production represented 6.3 percent of the total industrial output in Slovakia; in 1989 it fell to 2.9 percent, and in 1992 to only 0.9 percent. Because the switch to consumer production required huge financial investments, which the Slovak Republic lacked, only 50 percent of planned conversion had occurred by 1990–1992.

Another serious problem for Slovakia as a result of the split between the two republics was the inability of many business enterprises to pay their taxes on time and to make mandatory deduction payments to National Insurance, which in turn affected the cash flow of health, education, and social institutions. Coincidentally, unemployment began to rise to new highs. By early April 1993, some 300,000 workers were out of jobs and more than 108,000 citizens were on welfare; in some areas, unemployment was as high as 20 percent, an alarming statistic. Inflation was equally alarming: in comparison with the year 1989, prices in Slovakia in June were 132.2 percent higher and the cost of living had increased an average of 11 percent. Gradually, the lopsided economic development was brought to a halt, and by 1995 the Slovak economy showed a mild increase in GDP. Compared with the United States and countries in the European Union, the Slovak standard of living was low, but it was tolerable.[25]

Perhaps the greatest void in the new status of the independent sovereign Slovak state was the core of a civic society with a tradition of constitutionalism. Although by January 1, 1993, Slovakia had a plurality of political parties, in practice party politics always favored the rights of the majority, with very limited or no recourse for the minority. The MDS—the majority party's leadership—became the key player in determining the policies of Slovakia immediately after coming to power. In the hierarchy of organized power, the former communists within MDS acquired all key government posts: premier, chairperson of the parliament, president of the republic, president of the constitutional court, minister of defense, minister of the interior, minister of foreign affairs, and procurator general. Similarly in the NCSR, three-fifths of the 150 members were former members of the CPS. These were not reformed communists who conscientiously left communism and vindicated themselves in dissent, but mostly individuals who were committed to collectivist ideas. With such a unique composition, the sovereign Slovak Republic distinguished itself from all the other postcommunist states.

The personnel policy of this "unique" new government often followed outmoded practices of purges in the state administration by replacing "disloyal" administrators with those loyal to the ruling MDS. Any critics of such practices, like the former head of PAV, Fedor Gal, were forced to leave the country—Gal left for Prague—or simply withdrew into a shell of political obscurity. Members of the media who criticized the regime were also intimidated by being branded as "anti-Slovak" or "unpatriotic." In the interest of "national unity," newspaper reporters were officially "reminded" to voluntarily engage in ethical "self-regulation"—the term used during the communist regime for "self-censorship." It is ironic that many of the reporters who refused to cooperate and continued to criticize Vladimir Meciar and his loyalists were the same reporters who before 1992 criticized Prague and its policies on economic reform and thus had a great deal to do with the victory of MDS and the subsequent demise of the federal system in Czechoslovakia. The media now criticized MDS for its failure to prepare adequately for the transformation process, for weaknesses in the tax and national insurance system, for the breakup of the monetary union with the Czech Republic and the resulting weakening of the Slovak currency, for the decline in trade, the insolvency of companies, strain in the state budget endangering the functioning of various sectors of the national economy, and so on.[26] The MDS, instead of responding to media criticism by allowing greater political diversity and generating increased grassroots participation, chose to unite the "umbrella organization" under its authoritarian leader, Vladimir Meciar, into a more disciplined party, which led to internal strife and the purge of the foreign minister, Milan Knazko, an anticommunist with pro-Western orientation and the only initiator of the November revolution in the MDS who supported Meciar in splitting PAV and establishing the MDS. After that, the former communists strengthened their position among the ruling elite. When Ludovit Cernak left the government in March 1993, the Slovak Republic ruled by a minority government of one party: the MDS.

The limitations of the one-party government became obvious during the first unsuccessful round of presidential elections in the NCSR, when Vladimir Meciar, nominating his own candidate, Roman Kovac, underestimated the need to bargain with other political parties, including his own MDS, and was successful only because the opposition parties could not agree on their candidate. The MDS's candidate was Michal Kovac—financier, former communist, Catholic with strong nationalistic feelings, and key player in the dismantling of the former federal system. As Chapters 13 and 14 reveal, the rivalry between President Kovac and Premier Meciar persisted in spite of the fact that they belonged to the same party. Although they disagreed on several key issues concerning the national interests of Slovakia, they were in full agreement on the breaking up of the Czechoslovak federation.

INDEPENDENT SLOVAKIA

PART FIVE

13 Going It Alone in a Democracy

Assuming that "democratizaton" does not automatically produce a sound and stable democracy is simply to imply that in contemporary Slovakia there is an ongoing process of trying to establish democratic institutions. This process began during the 1989 Velvet Revolution. One of the key players in that revolution, Vaclav Havel, called for an existential revolution—a new spirit of higher responsibility to arise "from below," to create plurality, diversity, self-organization, and independent self-constitution—which was to be based on new political structures developing alongside the old system and providing opportunities for participation that the communist system failed to offer.[1]

Unlike Poland and Hungary before the collapse of the communist regimes, Czechoslovakia had no coexisting or parallel structures in the spheres of culture, communications, trade unions, education, or even foreign contacts that could provide for a "parallel *polis*" that would allow citizens to become vested in "living within the truth" or light and thereby influencing and redeeming those "living within a lie" or darkness of the communist system. The parallel *polis* was introduced in post–November 1989 Czechoslovakia by former dissidents as a process to liberalize the country. In Havel's words, the polis "points beyond itself and only makes sense as an act of deepening one's responsibility to and for the whole, as a way of discovering the most appropriate focus of this responsibility, not as an escape from it."[2] The relevance of this concept, that is, the political form of citizen participation in politics, did not become applicable in Czechoslovakia until the roundtable discussions between dissident and communist leaders at Hradcany Castle during the Velvet Revolution. Even then, discussions of democratization in the postcommunist state were limited to a small group of dissidents residing primarily in Prague, with no participation from the people at the subnational level. It was here that the transformation—known as liberalization—to a form of governance was arranged with a set of mechanisms to ensure future civil liberties and to provide certain guarantees for elections by June 9, 1990. For many months after November 1989, large segments of Czechoslovak society had no effective means of influencing the decision-making process because political authority was still in the hands of a small group of new politicians who shared power with the old politicians. Until the first parliamentary elections in June 1990, Czechoslovakia experienced an accelerated process of liberalization (or a "parallel *polis*") that resulted in building the foundations of a democratic authority structure, namely, the establishment of a multiparty system. The initiative for democratization came from the Czech Lands, and in Slovakia the process developed with less enthusiasm; nevertheless, the emergence of political pluralism through the establishment of more than forty political parties, movements, and coalitions participating in three elections put an end to the hegemony of the communists as the ruling party.

As the June 1990 elections point out, competitive, free elections by themselves are an insufficient indicator of democracy. Some scholars argue that "democratic elections are nice, but democratic governance is crucial."[3] Democracy also requires the supremacy of the rule of law, civil liberties, equal treatment of minorities guaranteed by law, and a representative government with a rule-bound administrative organization accountable to the general public. Another essential requirement, especially applicable to the former communist states where private ownership was abolished, is the equitable distribution of economic resources. Concentration of economic wealth in the government can impede the competitive spirit of free enterprise, which depends on government noninterference and public confidence.

And in any democracy, the test of whether the constitution is worth the parchment it is written on depends on the conditions of its enforcement rather than on the stipulation to the letter of democratic rules and procedures. An example of what the constitution stipulates and what actually took place in Slovakia was the 1995 attempt to remove Michal Kovac from the office of president of the Slovak Republic. The instigators were the ruling majority leaders of the three coalition parties: the Movement for a Democratic Slovakia, the Slovak National Party, and the Association of Workers of Slovakia (AWS). Since they lacked the required three-fifths parliamentary majority to remove the president or change the constitution, they opted for other means to impede his power and influence. To begin with, the NCSR enacted new laws depriving the president from using any of his unspecified constitutional power and assigning such powers to other organs of the government. As a consequence, the president lost his power to name the director of the Slovak Information Service (SIS), which is also Slovakia's intelligence service. That power of naming and removing the director was suddenly administered "at the suggestion of the premier of the Slovak Republic."[4] By a similar act, in June 1995, the Slovak parliament shifted the right to name and remove the chief of the general staff of the Slovak army from the president (as the constitutionally designated commander-in-chief) to the government. In November 1995 the coalition majority amended legislation to limit the prerogative of the president to examine the petitions calling for a referendum.[5] In May 1995 the NCSR heard a report by the Special Control Organ (SCO) concerning the control of SIS, which was presented by a deputy of the MDS discrediting Kovac politically as the head of state. The report was followed by a vote of no confidence in the president, which did not carry. Then in September 1995, the government accused Kovac of "subverting the foundations of the constitutional system"[6] and requested his resignation. Although the constitution gives the president the right to "preside over the meetings and require reports from the government or from individual ministers," in October 1995, Premier Meciar accused Kovac of "illegal demands for 'reports of an intelligence nature' from government officials."[7] In order to embarrass the president further, the government asked the constitutional court to clarify relevant sections of the Constitution. When all these attempts failed, in October 1995 the ministry of culture began a petition drive for the removal of President Kovac. Signers of the anti-president "Statement by the Central Organs of the State Administration" were viewed by the coalition leaders as expressing loyalty to the government. At least two directors of the district offices who maintained loyalty to Kovac were removed from office in December 1995.

From 1995 to 1998 there were numerous examples of this kind of disregard for the supremacy of law and constitutional practices in Slovak politics. They caught the attention of both the opposition and members of the European Union, as well as decision makers in the United States who are keenly interested in the democratization of Eastern Europe and their inclusion into NATO and the EU. We shall deal with these issues in the last section of this and the early part of the next chapter.

SLOVAK NATIONALISM, HUMAN RIGHTS, AND THE QUESTION OF ETHNIC MINORITIES

Although Slovakia was undergoing a process of democratization, it cannot be said that its citizens were experiencing democracy. Close scrutiny of the Preamble to the Constitution of the Slovak Republic reveals that the drafters of this document placed greater emphasis on the principle of nation-state, which was a product of the evolution of European nationalism and could best be associated with the idea "every nation deserves its own state," than on the role of the individual in a democratic society. From this idea was derived the principle of national self-determination: "We, the Slovak nation, remembering the political and cultural heritage of our predecessors, the experience gained through centuries of struggle for our national existence, and statehood, mindful of the spiritual bequest of Cyril and Methodius, and the historical legacy of Great Moravia, recognizing the natural right of nations to self-determination, together with members of national minorities and ethnic groups living in the Slovak Republic. We, the citizens of the Slovak Republic, have, herewith and by our representatives, adopted this constitution."[8]

The basic document of the Slovak Repubic attempted to put an end to the age-old nationalistic quarreling between the Czechs and Slovaks. Since the Velvet Revolution, there had been no lack of polemics on numerous issues between the Czechs and Slovaks. As early as March 1990, during the "hyphen controversy" regarding the name "Czechoslovak" in the federal state system, the National Council for the Liberation of Slovakia called for a referendum and "the proclamation of an independent Slovak state."⁹ The controversy continued on such issues as Slovak separatism (criticized by the Czech writer Ludvik Vaculik) and Czech predominance (condemned by the prominent Slovak writer Vladimir Minac),[10] power sharing and the new form of constitutional coexistence between the Czechs and the Slovaks, privatization and the unfair impact of economic reforms on Slovakia, the contents of and the mode of adopting the new republican and federal constitutions, as well as other issues already discussed in the previous chapter.

Early evidence of Slovak nationalism manifested itself in four political trends. First, Slovakia's major organized political power, Public Against Violence and minor parties such as the Democrats and the Greens, defended Czechoslovakia's federal system while calling for more autonomy for both republics. The second major group, the Christian Democratic Movement, advocated establishment of a Czecho-Slovak confederation and allowing Slovakia to enter Europe "as a sovereign and equal entity."[11] The Slovak Freedom Party and the Movement for an Independent Slovakia went a step further and called for a sovereign, autonomous, and independent Slovak Republic but refused to be identified with the pro-Nazi Slovak state of 1939–1945. Finally, the SNP and the Independent Party of Slovaks became the greatest zealots of the establishment of a fully independent and sovereign Slovak state. Sovereignty was also strongly encouraged by the nationalistic Slovak press, which deluged its readers with the issue beginning in the spring of 1990.

In order to captivate Slovaks with the need for independence, the leaders of the SNP developed a two-pronged strategy. First, they described the history of Slovakia as an oppressed nation that first suffered under the Hungarians and then was used by the Czechs. Second, they depicted the Slovak nation as one of the oldest in Europe and one that existed long before the Czech nation. Thus the desire for renewal of the Slovak state was a natural development cherished by all patriots. The 1939–1945 Slovak state was explained as a positive in Slovak history, and allegations about its totalitarian character were dismissed as exaggerations by the enemies of the state. The SNP's message to the voters was loud and clear: help win the elections; make the Slovak Republic a sovereign state and the "true Slovaks" from abroad will offer us economic assistance.[12] In contrast to the Tiso era, the bulk of the followers of this latest form of nationalism were Slovaks without a politically defined religious orientation. Their claim to separatism—the desire to establish an independent and sovereign government and secede from the existing government—was based on cultural and social differences and closely tied to economic and political interests. Whereas in the pre-June 1990 election period their propaganda was directed primarily toward relations between Czechs and Slovaks, after the elections the focus shifted toward the exaggerated problems of coexistence between the Slovaks and Hungarians in southern Slovakia.

As domestic problems confronting the postcommunist transformation in the Czech Lands and Slovakia multiplied, so did the polemics on these issues. The period between the two parliamentary elections was too short to reach solutions that would have satisfied the goals of both nations within one common statehood. By April 1992, it was not only the SNP that embraced the neonationalist movement, but also active was the splinter MDS, which under Vladimir Meciar coalesced with the SNP after the 1992 elections to forge a monopoly of power in many ways antithetical to the democratic goals set for the postcommunist transformation of Slovakia. For example, when Meciar and his group met with Vaclav Klaus and his team to negotiate the future status of the federal republic, the die had already been cast in favor of Slovak nationalism as opposed to a democratic referendum. After the separation of the two republics and the emergence of the independent and sovereign Slovak Republic, Slovak nationalism acquired a new dimension. Having gained self-determination and independence, it became ethnocentric in a society that was, and had long been, heterogeneous. Of the 5,289,608 population—according to the 1991 census—there were 4,606,125 Slovaks (85.7 percent), 578,408 Magyars (10.8 percent), 65,216 Czechs (1.1 percent), and 38,979 Ruthenian-Ukrainians (0.7 percent); there were also a small number of Germans, Jews, Poles, and Croats, and (according to the Ministry of Labor and Social Affairs) 253,943 Romanies (Gypsies), although only 80,627 (or 1.7 percent) claimed Romany nationality in the census. In other words, almost 15 percent of the population was other than Slovak, and for some Slovaks this created a feeling of insecurity and xenophobia, especially toward the Magyars.

The xenophobia was not altogether an old animosity but was more recently aroused. In November 1989, leading representatives of the Hungarian minority involved in the dissident movement set up two major political organizations, the Forum of Hungarians in Czechoslovakia (FHC) and the Independent Hungarian Initiative (Hungarian initials: FMK). Though both agreed with the program of PAV, only the FMK joined the umbrella movement in early 1990. The FHC joined the Cultural Association of Hungarian Working People in Czechoslovakia (CSEMADOK), which since 1949 had been the sole Hungarian organization in Slovakia approved by the communist regime. For this reason, in 1989, FMK looked upon CSEMADOK as a "Stalinist relic" and wanted its role restricted to cultural affairs. While the FHC argued that nationality problems should be solved in conjunction with democratization, the FMK maintained that since minority rights could only be achieved in a democratic framework, support for democratization should take precedence over minority issues.[13]

Immediately after the Velvet Revolution, the Hungarian minority set up a number of independent organizations seeking to develop its cultural life and to express the interests of minority professions active in the cultural field. As soon as Czechoslovakia's electoral law was enacted in early 1990, leaders of the Hungarian minority committed to democracy considered the establishment of political parties an urgent matter. The new Slovak authorities responded with policies such as permitting the publication of the Hungarian independent daily, *A Nap* (The Day), under the aegis of PAV, and the expansion of the Hungarian language program on Slovak television from thirty to forty-five minutes a week, and the Czechoslovak Federation came out in favor of setting up a ministry for minority affairs in the federal government. President Havel told the reporters of the Hungarian socialist daily *Nepszabadsag* (People's Freedom) that a new federal constitution allowing such a ministry should be worked out as soon as possible.[14] Of course, the proposed constitution never materialized. In December 1989, the Slovak government, under the leadership of the communist leader Rudolf Schuster, appointed Sandor Varga, a member of the CSEMADOK's presidium, to the post of deputy premier in charge of nationality affairs. Varga then established a nationality council with powers to initiate legislation on minority questions and recommendations for appointments to various government posts.[15] The major initiative to ensure the ethnic minority rights came from Prague, not Bratislava, when on January 13, 1990, in Bratislava, foreign ministers Jiri Dienstbier and Gyula Horn agreed that the policies of both governments toward ethnic minorities should be "freed from all earlier ideological constraints" and that minorities were entitled to equal individual and collective rights.[16] Six days later a specific agreement for Hungarian-Czechoslovak cultural cooperation was reached at a meeting in Bratislava, and on January 26, President Havel on his visit to Budapest promised his support for setting up a Hungarian-language university in Slovakia.[17]

The early liberalization process appeared very promising for the ethnic Hungarian minority in Slovakia. Since 1989, the federal government in Prague had encouraged the Magyars to seek cooperation with Slovak democratic groups in order to improve their situation, but the newly established Hungarian organizations had only limited success. Not since the appointment of Sandor Varga as Slovakia's deputy premier in charge of nationality affairs had any Hungarian been appointed to a responsible post in the Slovak ministries of culture, education, or agriculture—offices directly involved in the management of interests affecting the lives of the Hungarian minority. Moreover, instead of the promised ministry of nationalities, the Czechoslovak Federal Assembly created a committee headed by deputy premier Jan Carnogursky, leader of CDM, to monitor the government's handling of ethnic minority rights. Carnogursky had been criticized in Slovakia's Hungarian-language press for publicly expressing anti-Hungarian views.[18] The counterpart of this committee in the Slovak parliament was given the task of monitoring the situation of ethnic minorities and advising the Slovak rather than the federal government on issues of concern. While welcoming the council and the committee, however, the spokesmen for the Hungarian minority expressed concern that as advisory bodies they could not remedy minority grievances, and they continued to call for the creation of a ministry of nationalities in the Czecho-Slovak federal government.[19]

The two most urgent Hungarian issues during the liberalization period were the alleged shortage of Hungarian schools and teachers and the open animosity toward the Magyars in Slovakia. After the Prague Spring, Hungarian-language training of teachers had been all but abolished, and there was an alarming shortage of Hungarian-language teachers. Hungarian deputies in the Federal Assembly, inspired by a grass-roots movement, launched a campaign calling for the creation of a Hungarian-language university in Komarno, on the Hungarian border. In April 1990, Hungarian deputies in the Slovak National Council proposed legislation to establish a Hungarian-language university, but the proposal was rejected with the explanation that such a university would not be acceptable to the Slovak public and would not meet the Czecho-Slovak educational system's standard. Instead, the minister of education, youth, and sports, Ladislav Kovac, had promised that a Hungarian teachers' training department would be added to the proposed new Slovak university in Nitra.[20]

As the Hungarian minority in Slovakia became more visible and vocal in their demands during the preelection liberalization period, many Slovak zealots became more agitated and defensive in their attitudes. Sporadic anti-Hungarian demonstrations took place in several mixed-population localities in southern Slovakia. In Bratislava, for example, when Jan Budaj, a leader in the PAV and of mixed Slovak-Hungarian background, was elected deputy speaker of the Slovak National Council, demonstrators gathered in front of the parliament building and demanded that ethnic Hungarians be expelled from Slovakia in order to create a "pure Slovak state."[21] Another demonstration, also in Bratislava shortly after the first one, had been organized in support of Slovakia's national sovereignty but turned into an anti-Hungarian rally. About 200 demonstrators chanted anti-Hungarian slogans such as "Magyars go to the other side of the Danube!" They also demanded the removal of Sandor Varga, Slovakia's deputy premier in charge of nationality affairs.

Alleged provocations, incitements, and public insults also occurred in the local Slovak press and public fora of organizations such as the SNP, the Slovak National Renewal, and the Stur Association. But when Pavol Mikula, member of the PAV presidium, was asked about nationality problems in Slovakia, he said, "There are no significant nationality issues": the Hungarian-language schools had been closed in Slovakia either because of "economic considerations" or because of the Magyars' "lack of interest."[22] Apparently Mikula, like many other Slovaks, interpreted the Hungarian demands as a threat of resurgent Hungarian chauvinism and in retaliation prompted Slovak activists to accuse the Magyars of depriving the Slovak minority living in the southern part of Slovakia of their rights.

Tensions worsened during the preparation of the "language law" in the autumn of 1990, when nationalist deputies in parliament tried to push through a draft prepared by Matica Slovenska that discriminated against the national minorities in Slovakia. According to this draft proposal, no other language beside Slovak could be used in official and public dealings—including even Czech, which until then had enjoyed the same status as Slovak in the federal republic. A second draft, presented by the Slovak National Council deputies representing the Hungarian coalition party Coexistence, played practically no role in the discussions because the competing draft was a third one, offered by the ruling coalition. This proposal suggested that in communities with an ethnic minority that constituted at least 20 percent of the population, the minority language would be acceptable in official business; unlike the first proposal, this third one did not impose any restrictions on the use of the Czech language in Slovakia. The law eventually approved in the Slovak National Council on October 25, 1990, by a vote of 82 to 51 with 10 abstentions, was an amended version of the coalition's draft.[23]

After the language law was adopted, Slovak university students boycotted classes, bus and tram operators staged a brief strike, and about eighty demonstrators went on a hunger strike. Peter Tatar, a PAV deputy and member of the SNC presidium, criticized the new measure as redundant because Czech and Slovak were already state languages and an administrative regulation would have been sufficient to guarantee the rights of the minorities.[24] As the first draft proposal indicated, however, the intent was not to guarantee but to curtail minority rights in Slovakia. When President Havel warned that certain activities might complicate Czecho-Slovakia's "return to Europe," radical Jozef Gallus (a commentator for the SNP's weekly *Slovensky Narod*) responded: "Europe will wait. There is no reason to be afraid of missing it. First we have to deal with domestic issues. The most precious one is the language law. Those who try to postpone it will pay dearly."[25]

Although Slovaks considered the new language law of 1990 a step backward, in May 1995, the Slovak Republic's Ministry of Culture announced the draft of a new act on the official state language. The next month Premier Meciar promised that representatives of the Hungarian coalition would have an opportunity to review the proposed bill, but no further meetings or discussions ever took place. Later, when the leaders of the Hungarian political parties complained, the government claimed that its promise had been fulfilled by discussing the bill in the Government Council for Ethnic Minorities, where the Hungarian parties were represented.[26] In late August the bill was submitted to parliamentary committees, where it was rejected. In the fall of 1995, representatives of the Hungarian coalition consulted with the representatives of the Council of Europe regarding the proposed bill. The government rejected the Council's comments and criticisms, but to show good face Vladimir Meciar met with his Hungarian counterpart, Gyula Horn, and held several bilateral talks regarding the official state language bill. In mid-November the Slovak parliament discussed the bill and after a few minor changes passed it with an overwhelming majority. The only parliametary deputies who voted against the bill were from the Hungarian coalition. Under the 1995 language law, which automatically annulled the official language act of 1990, the Slovak language was to be used in all spheres of life; though the new law did not deal with the use of minority languages as such, it clearly stipulated that periodical literature must be printed in Slovak. A year later, the 1995 law was amended to allow the use of minority languages in the press, but other provisions that allowed intrusion into the sphere of private matters, minority cultures, freedom of speech, and freedom of the media remained intact. The 1995 official state language law was in every respect another step backward in securing minority rights through legislation in Slovakia.[27]

In tandem with the proposed new language law, the government of Vladimir Meciar prepared a proposal for a new territorial and administrative management of the Slovak Republic. On October 17, 1995, the government announced its support for the creation of eight larger administrative units in which ethnic Hungarians were precluded from having either a majority or even a large representation. The Hungarian political parties immediately rejected the government proposal; by the end of the year, they were joined in a debate by all opposition parliamentary parties but were still unable to prepare a common proposal. The strongest criticism of the government proposal came from the parties of the Hungarian Christian Democratic Movement and Coexistence. They considered the proposal an attempt to centralize power and prevent the natural development of self-government. The Hungarian Civic Party (HCP) criticized the proposal as a complete departure from the original commitment to administrative reforms. On March 22, 1996, the National Council adopted the law on territorial and administrative division of the Slovak Republic based on the proposal originally submitted by the coalition's parliamentary majority. Almost all proposed amendments were rejected; the only major change permitted was the expansion of the regional districts from seventy-four to seventy-nine. In April 1996, President Michal Kovac returned the bill to parliament for further discussion, possibly on the advice of Max von der Stoel, Supreme Council of Europe High Commissioner, during his visit to Slovakia in January 1996. Von der Stoel objected to any gerrymandering attempt by the government that would have resulted in discriminatory practices. As soon as Premier Meciar succeeded in restoring the effectiveness of the coalition agreement, the National Council took up the bill and approved it on July 3, 1996, with no change.[28]

That the return of Meciar's coalition government after the 1994 parliamentary elections had intensified the conflict between the Slovak nationalists and the Hungarian minority at every level became evident when state grants for the development of minority culture were drastically cut and new regulations revoking the principle of self-rule were introduced. The government also announced that certificates of graduation and grade reports would be published only in Slovak, even in schools with a large number of minority students. The new 1996 language law made the situation even worse by failing to provide any protection and rights to use minority languages in Slovakia. Later in 1996 when the Meciar coalition government succeeded in pushing through its territorial and administrative law against considerable domestic and international criticism, the Hungarian minority in Slovakia was completely demoralized and helpless. The majority of Slovaks were elated. Even before the enactment of the two laws in 1996, 65 percent of Slovaks believed that the situation of the Hungarian minority was favorable—28 percent considered it privileged—while 75 percent of ethnic Hungarians considered their rights and possibilities for development limited and only 24 percent good; in spite of all the setbacks and handicaps imposed on ethnic minorities since 1994, "Slovaks basically did not change their view concerning the status of ethnic Hungarians. The opinion that ethnic Hungarians in Slovakia have favorable conditions for their progress was prevalent throughout the entire period of Meciar's government in power."[29]

Judging from various public opinion surveys taken in Slovakia between 1993 and 1996, it is safe to argue that although the ethnic Hungarians felt their rights were being methodically abridged under the authoritarian regime of Vladimir Meciar, the overwhelming majority of the Slovak population supported the confrontational policies of the Meciar cabinet.[30] The Hungarian answer for this attitudinal behavior could be found in demographic changes of the Magyar population in Slovakia for the past seven decades (from 1921, the first national census in Czechoslovakia, to 1991, the last census). Between the 1921 and 1991 census the Hungarian population in Slovakia decreased from 650,579 to 567,296 or 12.8 percent, although the total population of Slovakia increased from 3,000,870 to 5,274,335 or 75.8 percent. During the same period the Slovak population increased from 1,952,368 to 4,519,328 or 131.5 percent. According to the 1991 census, there was a 7–10 percent difference between the population that declared its nationality as Hungarian and those whose native language was Hungarian. Similar changes occurred during the re-Slovakization process when thousands of Magyars declared Slovak as their new nationality.

In areas where the Magyars were in the minority, their cultural and linguistics developments declined and the territory once dominated by Magyars was gradually transformed into mixed settlements with new conflictual conditions among that population. Though the Hungarian population was steadily declining, in 1991 Slovakia had 523 towns in which ethnic Hungarians numbered 10 percent or higher and 432 towns with a Hungarian majority. The average age difference between the Slovak and Hungarian population was also widening: the Magyars were getting older and the Slovaks younger. Most of the decline of the Hungarian population in Slovakia was due to the post–World War II large migration, when some Magyars fled the country, others were forcefully resettled into the former Sudeten territories in the Czech Lands, and still others were subjected to forced deportation into Hungary. But after the beginning of communist rule in 1948, many ethnic Hungarians also underwent real or fictitious change of national identity through assimilation, intermarriage, or self-denial. Not only is a growing portion of the Hungarian population in Slovakia living in mixed households, but the majority of children growing up in nationally hetergeneous families are, to the satisfaction of their parents, no longer claiming Hungarian identity.[31]

The Slovak response to the grievances articulated by ethnic Hungarians is rooted in the long history of Slovak-Magyar relations and the continued mutual distrust between the two groups. The Slovaks still suffer from the phobia that the Hungarians are seeking to annex part of their territory. Their fear is based on historical precedence, stemming from the oppressive nationalities policy of the Austro-Hungarian empire, irredentist attempts after World War I, the annexation of Slovak territory as a result of the Vienna Arbitration decision in November 1938, and the military incursion into the designated new Slovak state in March 1939. Although the first few months following the Velvet Revolution produced an atmosphere of friendship and cooperation between the Slovaks and Magyars primarily because they both shared the common goal of stripping the communists of their monopoly of power, the honeymoon lasted only until the June 1990 elections. During that brief period, one of the Hungarian political parties (the Hungarian Independent Initiative) was a member of the ruling coalition, ethnic Hungarians held key positions in both the Slovak and federal governments, and there were regular contacts between the Hungarian and Slovak political leaders as well as between the president of the Slovak National Council, F. Miklosko, and the president of Hungary, A. Goncz. Former dissident Czech political leaders like Vaclav Havel played a very positive role in the creation of an atmosphere of tolerance and cooperation between the Slovaks and ethnic Hungarians.

Most supporters of democratization and economic reforms in Czechoslovakia thought that the federal system was a guarantee for achieving full cooperation between the Slovaks and Magyars. Perhaps for this reason, when the issue of the demise of the federal republic surfaced in 1992, leaders of the Hungarian political parties were strongly opposed to the idea of two separate states. As we have already pointed out, however, the desire for Slovak national identity within an independent Slovak state was greater than that for inexperienced virtues of democratic equality and human rights. As Slovak nationalism mounted, so did the reaction of the ethnic Hungarians. The manifestation of power by MDS and SNP in the 1992 elections justified the change of policy in Slovak-Magyar relations from consensual to confrontational. That policy was supported with certain ups and downs by the overwhelming majority of the Slovak population, and politicians on both sides, recognizing the sensitivity and emotionalism involved in the Hungarian issue, have exploited it whenever it has been to their advantage. In early April 1998, for example, Jan Slota, the chairman of the SNP at Zilina, called for changing the Slovak Constitution so that only "Slovak public schools" would exist in Slovakia and the citizenship would be modified in a way that "every citizen of Slovakia be defined as a Slovak."

Among the additional ethnic minorities in Slovakia, only the Romanies were considered a legitimate minority because the Czechs, Germans, Poles, Ruthenian-Ukrainians, Jews, Bulgarians, and others represent less than 2 percent of the total population. The Magyars, Romanies, and to some extent Jews are considered to be problem minorities. In an October 1993 poll, almost 90 percent of Slovak citizens had a negative attitude toward the Romanies. Because of their racial characteristics and different way of life, the Romany minority was treated differently not only in Slovakia but also in the Czech Lands. The social stigma attached to Gypsies made the Romanies undesirable members of the Slovak society; in that same poll, 79 percent of respondents stated that they would be opposed to Romanies as neighbors.[32] The low level of education and lack of professional skills kept Romanies out of competition in the marketplace: Unemployment among them was extremely high, and that has, of course, resulted in crime. A large percentage of Romanies in Slovakia have accumulated extensive criminal records, which has caused further condemnation of them. Tensions have led to violence between the Romanies and groups of young Slovak "skinheads." Racially motivated attacks on Romanies, resulting in homicide, have been committed by members of these groups in several cities and towns since 1993. In July 1995, for instance, in Ziar nad Hronom a gang of skinheads beat up a young Romany man and then poured gasoline on him and set him on fire. The victim later died in the hospital.

While the authorities investigated and politicians issued statements, the council for ethnic minorities—a government overseeing agency—adopted new recommendations, but none of the Romany demands was met. Instead of an ombudsman, the government created a commission for a group of people requiring special care headed by a non-Romany. Finally, in September 1995, after the government made it conditional that it would negotiate with the Romanies only as a single entity, six Romany political parties formed the Union of Romany Political Parties. However, the Union was not joined by the Romany Independent Initiative (RII), the oldest and strongest party, established in 1989; its chairman, who at that time was a member of the council for ethnic minorities, was accused by the new union of treason by serving non-Romany interests. In the meantime, nongovernmental organizations in Slovakia were trying to fill the void in promises made by the government, especially in educational projects. For example, at the urging by some European nongovernmental and human rights organizations in the spring of 1998, the Komensky (Comenius) University in Bratislava decided to postpone the deadline for Romanies applying for study at some of its faculties (colleges) in order to give them more time to prepare for entrance exams. According to unofficial reports, in 1998 there were only two Romany students out of 24,528 registered at the university.

Jews are the smallest ethnic minority in Slovakia today. Although in the 1991 census only 350 people claimed Jewish ethnicity because of religious identity, it can be assumed that there are approximately 5,000 to 7,000 people with a Jewish background in Slovakia compared with 89,000 when the 1940 census was taken. More than 60,000 Slovak Jews were murdered in Nazi extermination camps, with the assistance of the puppet Tiso regime and its supporters. The revival of "Tisoism" in the

1990s has revived interest in the sensitive "Jewish question," which covers attitudes of the general public toward the 1939–1945 Slovak state and the present Jewish minority. Although the Slovak parliament in 1993 passed a law on the restitution of Jewish property, public opinion polls taken the same year indicated that anti-Semitic attitudes were more prevalent in Slovakia than in Hungary or the Czech Republic but slightly less common than such attitudes in Austria.[33] According to the *Global Report on Slovakia*, anti-Semitic articles are published in the tabloid weekly *Zmena* (Change) and the Slovak National Party's daily *Slovenska republika* (Slovak Republic). Both papers were recipients of the government's Ludovit Stur prize for journalism in 1995. The Central Union of Jewish Religious Communities lodged several protests against newspapers trying to rehabilitate and glorify officials of the Slovak state during World War II. A Jewish synagogue and cemetery were desecrated and some officials of the SNP made anti-Semitic remarks in public during the fiftieth anniversary of the end of World War II. Although the government disassociated itself from such statements, the Central Union claims that anti-Semitic feeling among some officials persisted, and only in April 1998 did the government's legislative council approve a bill to compensate Jews who were deported to Nazi concentration camps "on the territory of the former German Reich in the years 1939–1945." The bill would affect about 1,300 Slovak Jews who survived the Holocaust, their children, or families, who would receive an estimated 2,500 Kovuny (about $71.00) for each month spent in deportation.

The German minority in the Slovak Republic, though it is much larger than the Jewish minority, is more dispersed and assimilated than other groups. Ethnic Germans who survived the post–World War II persecution and were not deported from Slovakia refrained from asserting their cultural identity until the post–November 1989 period, when their cultural life showed signs of revival by organizing the Carpathian-German Association and pledging to revive German traditions, language, and culture. In August 1995, the association called for the annulment of the 1945 decrees, according to which all ethnic Germans were considered collectively guilty for crimes committed during World War II. They did not ask for the return of property expropriated during 1945–1948, but they did ask for financial compensation. Meciar's answer was to cut financial support to all ethnic minorities.

The problems facing the ethnic minorities are not the only indicator of the state of democratization in the Slovak Republic. Surveys in 1995 showed that most citizens were concerned about human rights violations and that people did not feel secure in talking freely about politics. Most survey respondents were frustrated with the state of democracy, and only 38 percent believed that freedom of speech, expression, and the press existed in Slovakia. Dissatisfaction with democratization was also noticeable in the frustration expressed with the political party system, which most thought was not a sufficient guarantee of democratic politics.[34]

ELECTIONS OF 1994
AND SOCIOPOLITICAL CONTINUITY

Frustration with the political party system in Slovakia dates back to the first day of independence and the original republican parliament, the Slovak National Council, elected in June 1992 as an integral part of the Czech and Slovak Federal Republic. On January 1, 1993, even though its legitimacy was in doubt, this body became the parliament of the independent, sovereign Slovak state because the same parliament remained in power until the elections of 1994. The Meciar government, originally formed after the 1992 elections, also remained in power. In June 1993, eight MDS deputies resigned after they criticized Premier Meciar for his authoritarian methods, and his government lost the majority support in parliament. Meciar and his party made an attempt to form a coalition with the SNP, and in October 1993, after long, complicated negotiations, both parties agreed to form a majority coalition in the NCSR and in the government by adding three ministers from the SNP. The political honeymoon between the MDS and SNP was short-lived. Divisiveness and splintering within the ruling MDS continued, and to Meciar's chagrin it carried over into the SNP, making Meciar's coalition government again a minority government.

To resolve the new government crisis, in his 1994 New Year address, President Michal Kovac proposed the creation of a broad coalition government that would override instability in the political parties. The ruling party, MDS, expressed no interest in such a coalition; on the contrary, the MDS leaders initiated a campaign against Kovac and tried to obstruct the smooth functioning of his office as well as his constitutional powers. The MDS in general, and Vladimir Meciar in particular, sought to grab as much power as necessary to build an authoritarian regime.

In his March 1994 state of the Slovak Republic address, President Kovac harshly criticized the negative developments in his country. Shortly after the speech, the NCSR forced Meciar's government to fall for the second time (the first time was in March 1991) and enabled the creation of the first grand coalition government, headed by Jozef Moravcik. The new government consisted of representatives from the Democratic Union (DU), the Christian Democratic Movement (CDM), and the Party of the Democratic Left (PDL). It was a coalition of the right and left, with the DU as a new liberal party made up of splinter groups from both the MDS and SNP. This government, supported by the Hungarian parties in Slovakia, had a comfortable majority and a great potential for speedy democratization. Even so, because of the insistence of the PDL (anticipating victory), the parliament agreed to schedule new elections in October 1994.

The relatively short duration of Moravcik's grand coalition government was a period of internal consolidation in the country. In spite of the varying views of its constituent parties, the government succeeded in stabilizing the political system and reactivating the previously obstructed economic reforms. By and large, the replacement of government elites created a consensual politics accompanied by problem-solving policymaking.

In the meantime, MDS, the main opposition party, mobilized its resources in preparation for the new elections. The hidden financial assets of the party were now used to help it regain power and continue the policies interrupted by Meciar's no-confidence vote in the NCSR in March 1994. At party meetings Meciar openly talked about steamrolling the political opposition. Although several political parties did not begin their campaign until June, others, including the MDS, started to campaign in March, on the day the parliament agreed to the election dates. Many of the parties lacked adequate organizations, however, as well as campaign workers and money to support a costly media promotion. They spent much of their time organizing meetings and producing a mail campaign (which worked in 1992) and not enough on door-to-door canvassing and the electronic media. Most of the party platforms were distorted or lacked full disclosure of information concerning timely issues. In many instances party platforms were not disclosed at all. As a result, voters relied on the sympathies or antipathies toward individual speech-making politicians rather than on substantive arguments on issues.[35]

The MDS had the money and skill to exploit the election campaign with the modern techniques of "telecracy." The evening news about the first day of the elections made Meciar and his party look like victims of persecution by the "grand coalition." As it turned out, Meciar and his family were not permitted to vote until the second day because their names were not on the list of registered voters. Meciar referred to the incident as a "plot," but other voters in a similar situation, including the head of the PDL and vice chair of CDM, called it an oversight in failing to register on time. The election campaign was watched on television by 78.5 percent of the Slovak citizens and 49 percent heard the radio coverage. Only 25 percent attended political gatherings, and it is unknown what percentage of attendees heard the messages. It is known, however, that the evening news on television on the first day of elections compelled many to go to the polls and vote for the "underdog" (Meciar) and his party.

While MDS spent a total of 9.3 million Slovak koruny (about U.S. $330,000) on printed and electronic media on the campaign, other political parties spent much less: DU spent 6.3 million Sk, CDM 4.7 million, DP 3.5 million, SNP 2.8 million, Corrmon Choice 1.8 million, the Hungarian Coalition and the Christian Social Union 0.9 million, the Liberals 0.5 million, and the New Slovakia 0.5 million. In most instances the cost of the campaign had little to do with the outcome: for example, the DP, which spent the same amount on the media campaign as the SNP, received only 3.7 percent of the total vote; SNP got 5.4 percent. It should also be noted that only a few days before the elections, a large number of voters (estimates varied from 15 to 20 percent) had no preferences. Since the MDS-PPS (Peasants' Party of Slovakia) coalition received significantly more votes than predicted, it became obvious that many of the undecided votes were cast for the MDS-PPS coalition. Hence it can be argued that the MDS-PPS coalition not only outspent but also outvoted all its opponents.

The results of the fall 1994 parliamentary elections deserve a close look. In spite of the amended election law of February 26, 1992, which raised the minimum required limit of total votes from 3 to 5 percent for single parties, 7 percent for coalitions of two or three parties, and 10 percent for coalitions of more than three parties, the number of participating political parties and movements did not diminish as anticipated.[36] In the spring of 1994 about sixty political parties and movements were registered in the Slovak Republic. About half of these entered into the election campaign, most of them as part of coalitions or on the candidate lists of larger parties. The second amendment to the election law did not result in any major change in regard to preconditions for the entrance of the political parties or coalitions into the parliament.[37] As the campaign wore on, many small parties created ad hoc coalitions or placed their candidate on the lists of larger, more powerful parties in order to increase their chances for representation. These election tactics were largely responsible for the decrease in the number of political parties and coalitions participating in the 1994 elections from thirty-one to eighteen (one, the Liberals, pulled out shortly before the elections).[38] Of the eighteen political parties and coalitions participating in the elections, seven managed to pass the threshold necessary to be represented in the NCSR (see Table 15).

The seven political parties and/or coalitions that together won 87 percent of the valid votes actually represented sixteen political parties

TABLE 15

RESULTS OF THE 1994 ELECTIONS FOR THE NATIONAL COUNCIL OF THE SLOVAK REPUBLIC

Political party or coalition	Percent of votes	Nonparliamentary seats
MDS and PPS	34.96	61
Common Choice (PDL, SDPS, PG, and AM)	10.41	18
Hungarian Coalition (HCDM, Coexistence, and HCP)	10.18	17
CDM	10.08	17
DU	8.57	15
AWS	7.34	13
SNP	5.40	9
Total	86.94	150

KEY: MDS, Movement for a Democratic Slovakia; PPS, Peasants' Party of Slovakia; HC, Hungarian Coalition; HCDM, Hungarian Christian-Democratic Movement; HCP, Hungarian Civic Party; AWS, Association of Workers of Slovakia; CDM, Christian Democratic Movement; DU, Democratic Union; SNP, Slovak National Party; PDL, Party of the Democratic Left; SDPS, Social Democratic Party of Slovakia; PG, Party of the Greens; AM, Agricultural Movement.

SOURCE: Grigorij Meseznikov, "Domestic Political Developments and the Political Scene in the Slovak Republic," in Martin Butora and Peter Huncik, eds., *Global Report on Slovakia: Comprehensive Analysis from 1995 and Trends from 1996* (Bratislava: Sandor Marai Foundation, 1997), p. 11.

and movements.[39] Nine had entered into the parliament in three election coalitions,[40] three parties placed their candidates on the lists of three other parties forming a crypto-coalition,[41] and only two parliamentary parties ran on separate lists.[42] In other words, besides one large political movement, MDS, and four intermediate parties (with more than ten deputies), there were also three small parties (with five to ten deputies) and eight miniparties (with one to three deputies).[43]

The MDS-PPS coalition win, with almost 35 percent of the total vote, was almost 10 percent higher than predicted. The PDL, in the framework of Common Choice, barely gained parliamentary representation. That made MDS still the dominating power on the Slovak political scene, with weaker adversaries on the right (CDM) and the left (Common Choice and especially PDL). Though the Hungarian party coalition, with the same number of seats as CDM, also leaned toward the right of the center, the ethnic interests of its policy negated most of its ideological orientation in favor of nationality rights. Its Slovak counterpart, the SNP (with only nine seats), though also a predominantly nationalist party, combined rightist rhetoric with leftist pragmatism. Only the DU, with fifteen seats, maintained a strong liberal posture and a strong commitment to democratic values, including privatization, civil liberties, and individual rights. Like the AWS, the two farmers' parties remained anachronistic as "class" parties of the interwar times. In the final analysis, Slovakia's 1994 parliamentary elections were a contest between the principles of democracy and consensus and those upholding populism, nationalism, and/or extremism.

In spite of its impressive victory, the MDS-PPS was unable to form a government because of the lack of the required majority, so Meciar expanded his coalition to include the nationalist SNP and the nonstandard, chaotic, populist party of the left—AWS. Members of this coalition differed in their proclaimed political ideas, but they were very similar in their common authoritarian understanding of politics, and during the night-long session of November 3–4, 1994, the new coalition usurped the power of all parliamentary functions and committees to assure absolute control of legislation. In addition, the new Meciar coalition appointed its people to the state administrative boards for television and radio broadcasts, thus assuming control of the most influential communications media.

Meciar's government wasted no time in showing society who was in charge of the country.[44] The coalition government first attacked President Kovac, elected in 1992 for a five-year term. Kovac's parliamentary address, delivered in March 1994, singed the ears of Vladimir Meciar, and very shortly thereafter, Kovac was deprived of the power to appoint the director of the secret service, officially known as the Slovak Information Service (SIS). To make matters worse, the parliament, following the government's recommendation, appointed Ivan Lexa, Kovac's archenemy, to the post. Lexa immediately provided the requested ammunition to launch an attack on the president with the aim of removing him from office. At the same time, the Meciar government introduced a new administrative policy leading to centralization of power and an opportunity to appoint "his own people" to various posts. The coalition government sought to achieve a qualified majority of 90 (out of 150) votes in the NCSR (the number required to remove the president from office), to change the Constitution, and to establish an authoritarian regime. Although these goals remained only wishful thinking, the Meciar coalition government embarked on a road toward authoritarian policies that inevitably contributed to the slowdown and in some instances a reversal of the democratization process. The country was still not a democracy, nor had it begun as one. In the post–November 1989 elections, the political parties and movements and their coalitions—MDA, AWS, and SNP—whose ambiguous and obscure programs did not easily fit the standard left-right continuum characterized by a confrontational style of politics—and because of their condemnation of pluralist democracy—gained 48 percent of the total vote. The so-called standard political parties—HC, CC, CDM, and DU—with clear-cut profiles that could easily be identified on the left-right continuum obtained only 39 percent of the vote. Thus it can be argued that political parties with plebiscitary characteristics were placed at the helm of political power in Slovakia during the momentous period of democratization. Analysts and prognosticators in Slovakia and abroad agreed that after the 1994 elections, Slovakia had reached the stage of democratization other Central European countries had already achieved during the first postcommunist transitional elections.[45]

The struggle for power in Slovakia after the 1994 elections thus became not so much a contest to determine which political party, movement, or coalition would rule the country but rather a competition between the organized political forces with a democratic orientation and those with an authoritarian, social-populist, and nationalist agenda. According to some political observers, Meciar's comeback and the creation of the MDS alliance with the radical nationalist SNP and antireform AWS resulted in a new political platform of authoritarianism that embodied both the prewar traditionalist nationalist populism and postwar socialist collectivism. The struggle for a sovereign Slovak state ruled by law, constitutional guarantees, and decisions of a parliamentary democracy following the principle of fair play inspired a large spectrum of the society to voice its opinion not only in organized political parties but also in what is known as the "third sector"—voluntary organizations. By December 1994, six months after the elections, 15 percent of Slovakia's citizens were members of various nongovernmental associations and societies. The number of these organizations had grown from zero in 1989 to almost 6,000 in 1993 and 9,800 by the end of 1994. Most of them were in the capital city of Bratislava; elsewhere in Slovakia participation in voluntary organizations was (and remains) about 12 percent lower.[46] In time, it is to be expected, these organizations, associations, and societies will become the missing link of the Slovak civil society, articulating values, preferences, and interests that no politicos, party leaders, or bureaucrats can ignore. For the present, however, many people in Slovakia still tend to rely on already formed stereotypes and behavior patterns implanted during the communist era rather than on the changing conditions affording individual freedom of choice, economic opportunities, and self-reliance. According to a survey taken in June 1994, 68.6 percent of the respondents (graduates of secondary schools) believed that the state had a decisive role in securing human rights, but only 49.7 percent of them found it obvious for citizens to respect the rights of minorities. Similarly, 88.8 percent of young people thought that the state had a responsibility to find and guarantee employment for them after they finished the required education. Views regarding the role of the state in securing suitable housing and medical care for all were very similar.[47]

Meciar and his associates were keenly aware of the country's transformational weakness, and they used it to the maximum. By and large, they were not enthusiastic about the existence and growth of voluntary organizations because one mission of some nongovernmental organizations (NGOs) was to monitor the democratization process. Accordingly, in 1994, half of the nonprofit organizations applying for state subsidy were allotted only 25 percent support. At the same time, not a single one of the 250 state-owned social welfare institutions was privatized. A large number of nonprofit organizations depended on financial support from abroad, which, of course, made them suspect in the eyes of the government. In the summer of 1995, for example, the Open Society Fund, supported by the American (Hungarian-born) George Soros and registered in Slovakia, came under attack by the Meciar government because Soros made some critical statements regarding the progress of democratization in the country. One member of the ruling coalition, Anna Malikova, branded the Open Society Fund an enemy and asked the general prosecutor to review its activities.

There were numerous other examples of the "enemy phobia" practiced by government officials against thousands of small, publicly beneficial organizations, associations, foundations, and clubs. Actions included nonparticipation in events organized by environmental NGOs, the termination of an agreement of cooperation with the Slovak Academic Information Agency, and attacks on the U.S.-based Foundation for a Civic Society for misusing the Internet.[48] Slovakia still had no regulatory laws on foundations and nonprofit organizations—only provisions in the constitution guaranteeing the basic freedoms (of expression, assembly, and association) applicable to these organizations. Nongovernmental associations in the "Gremium of the Third Sector" (GTS, established in Bratislava in April 1995) protested against the heavy-handed tactics of the Meciar government and brought the matter to the attention of the European Union, which expressed concern over the government's actions in a diplomatic note.[49] Without inviting representatives of the Gremium, the Ministry of Justice drafted a legislative proposal and sent copies to both the GTS and the Slovak Humanitarian Council for their comments. Those comments were ignored, and the government proceeded with its plan to enact the unchanged proposal into law. By mid-January 1996, GTS launched a national protest campaign and solicited the cooperation of the Confederation of the Trade Unions and the Association of Employer Unions and Cooperatives of the Slovak Republic to meet with the third sector delegates and offer their support. The GTS objected to provisions in the proposal, such as the screening of a foundation by a central state authority before it could be registered or requiring that registration be carried by the Ministry of the Interior rather than by the independent courts. Such issues raised concerns of abuse not only by the GTS but also by the Washington-based International Center for Not-for-Profit Law (ICNL).[50] During this tug-of-war between GTS and the government, 430 articles dealing with the protest campaign appeared in the Slovak press, and according to a public opinion survey conducted in February 1996, 52 percent of the respondents followed the debate. By the end of May 1996, 80 percent of the people in Slovakia supported the existence of foundations. As public support for the NGOs increased, the government took a more conciliatory stance. Premier Meciar on the Slovak Radio program *Radiozurnal* argued that there was no such proposed law, and the Ministry of Justice began to refer to its proposal as a "working draft."

Nevertheless, the government approved the proposed law on foundations and referred it to the NCSR, which passed the law on May 26, 1996. On June 5, 1996, President Kovac returned the law on foundations to parliament for further discussion, with the explanation that it was too restrictive and did not correspond to the actual situation of the majority of foundations in Slovakia. According to Kovac, the law was not in harmony with the model developed by the European Foundation Center and therefore widened the gap between the Slovak legal system and that of the EU and its members.[51] Ambassadors of the European Union, the United States, and Canada—the three main supporters of civil society in Slovakia—showed great interest in the matter and discussed the law with government officials and parliamentary representatives. In the latter part of June 1996, the parliament passed the government bill on foundations for a second time without the changes requested by GTS. Government officials claimed that "a compromise had been reached." The process of enactment of the law on foundations is a good example of the complex struggle for a civil society in Slovakia.[52]

ECONOMIC REFORMS AND PRIVATIZATION

Before Slovakia became an independent state in 1993, it possessed all but one condition necessary for successful completion of the economic reform program initiated by the federal parliament of the Czech and Slovak Federal Republic in September 1990. It had a prudent macroeconomic policy, low inflation, a modest debt, and a skilled and competitively priced labor force. The shift from a seller's market to a buyer's market had occurred, though there had been almost no progress in privatization primarily because, under the still prevailing system of state-controlled ownership, many enterprises seemed reluctant to change. By the end of 1992, only 30 percent of all property potentially suited for privatization had in fact been privatized. Meciar and the other leaders of MDS, which had been the leading opposition party since April 1991 when it bolted from the Public Against Violence (PAV), were strongly opposed to the restrictive monetary and fiscal policy advocated by the economic reform scenario, mainly on the grounds that the economic reform program would not work in Slovakia because it had been drawn up in the Czech Republic where conditions were quite different. In Slovakia, critics pointed out, the programs had brought a greater economic decline, a higher level of unemployment, and a low level of foreign investment; they failed to mention that these negative factors and variables were not so much a consequence of the economic reform process as they were a result of economic distortions caused by a communist-planned economy. The legacy of heavy industries ill suited to Slovakia's competitive advantages, weak banks, and unsustainable transfer payments were some of the unresolved problems that authoritative decision makers still had to face in 1993 in the independent Slovak state.

Yet there was a compelling urgency for decisions about the structural changes to determine the nature of future economic recovery. An estimate by the World Bank suggested that a rapid comprehensive reform program in 1993 could have boosted the per capita income about 25 percent higher by the year 2000.[53] Instead, the Meciar government, in spite of its earlier criticism of the reform process, created an atmosphere of uncertainty because it offered no workable alternative. Though macroeconomic performance improved steadily, privatization continued to move at a snail's pace. It is worth noting that the greatest improvement in macroeconomic performance, which also satisfied most of Slovakia's IMF- (International Monetary Fund) improved targets, was accomplished by the six-month interim "grand coalition" government headed by Jozef Moravcik, when annual inflation fell from 23 percent in 1993 to 13 percent in 1994. Although unemployment remained the same, the gross domestic product (GDP) reversed itself from minus 4 to plus 4 percent, and the budget deficit in 1994 was around half that in 1993. Furthermore, Slovakia's more than $800 million deficit in 1993 was transformed into a nearly $200 million trade surplus in 1994, and within one year, by the end of September 1994, the foreign currency reserves of the National Bank of Slovakia (NBS) had tripled. The Moravcik "grand coalition" government went as far as preparing property worth about $2 billion for the second wave of "coupon privatization" and sold, according to U.S. Central Intelligence Agency estimates, participation in the program to over 80 percent of Slovakia's eligible citizens. However, the early parliamentary elections held September 30–October 1, 1994, which gave the MDS-PPS coalition a resounding victory, also put the second wave of coupon privatization on hold and suspended sales of thirty-eight firms until the new government under Vladimir Meciar could evaluate the defeated Moravcik government's decisions in early 1995.

In the fall of 1995, favorable developments in the national economy prompted the Meciar government to adopt a macroeconomic policy of maintaining and gradually improving the growth in economic productivity in order to achieve a 5 percent annual growth rate of the GDP (in constant prices), reducing the rate of unemployment to less than 13 percent, keeping the rate of inflation at or below 10 percent, and making the state share of the budget deficit no more than 3 percent. Toward these ends, the government initiated and the parliament approved a new price law. This law, which constituted a major change in economic reform, gave the government the power to regulate, control, and direct not only prices regulated since January 1, 1990 (about 5 percent), when the initial economic reform was launched, but also prices that had already been liberalized (about 95 percent of them). The new law was designed to regulate market imbalances by preventing specific price increases.

Although critics argued that the new price law was a step backward, the Slovak economy continued to improve. By the end of 1995 the gross domestic product had grown by a revised 6.8 percent in constant prices compared with 14.8 percent the previous year. Final government spending increased by 1.6 percent, and household spending also grew by 3.14 percent; the fastest growth—5.8 percent—took place in gross fixed capital investment. Private sector share during 1995 was around 60 percent. The share of market services fell moderately to 41.03 percent, the share of industry fell to 28.06 percent, and the share of nonmarket services fell to 5.6 percent. The only item whose GDP share increased from 5.2 to 9.5 percent was the category of "other," meaning indirect taxes, duties, banking service charges, and profits and losses from stocks held.[54]

Macroeconomic development continued during 1996. The GDP grew by 6.9 percent. On the supply side this growth included an increase in value-added market services by 7.9 percent and an increase in value-added nonmarket services by 28.6 percent. On the demand side, the structural change caused a noticeable decrease in foreign demand for Slovak goods, which resulted in an unfavorable balance of trade and a sizable deficit of 614.3 billion Slovak koruny (Sk) compared with 9.4 billion Sk surplus in 1995. In constant prices government spending in 1996 increased by 214.2 percent, household spending grew by 7.2 percent, and the gross fixed capital investment increased by a whopping 32.8 percent.[55]

Similar positive results were recorded by the Statistical Office of the Slovak Republic in the areas of unemployment and inflation. Although unemployment hovered between 14.4 percent in 1993 and 12.8 percent in 1996, in February 1997 it rose to 13.7 percent; in May 1997 it dropped to 12.3 percent. Inflation declined steadily after 1993: in 1996, Slovakia had the lowest inflation among the postcommunist countries—having fallen from 9.9 percent in 1995 to 5.8 percent in 1996. The reasons for this success were attributed to the prudent monetary policies of the National Bank of Slovakia that postponed price liberalization in the areas of fuel, energy, water, gas, and rent and also limits on the growth of money supply. Inflation in the first half of 1997 was still under control—it showed only a modest 6.2 percent inflation growth.[56] Price control is very often not a guarantee for continued decline in the inflationary trend when the growth in real wages outpaces labor productivity, as it did in 1996. The index of real wages in 1996 stood at 107.2 vs. 104.2 for labor productivity—a ratio that by itself was inflationary and as such could account for the negative influence on Slovakia's exports—and the fast growth of real wages as a sign of overheating in the Slovak economy was also pointed out by the fact-finding mission of the IMF in October 1996.[57] Although the IMF encouraged the Slovak government to adopt a more stringent fiscal policy for 1997, Premier Meciar and his parliamentary coalition passed the 1997 state budget with a projected fiscal deficit of 19 billion Sk—far greater than expected by the IMF. A World Bank mission's findings issued in December 1996 resembled those of the IMF, but this optimism was conditional on such requirements as the need for structural adjustments and the elimination of the current account deficit and unprofitable activities that wasted scarce economic resources.[58] Practically the same findings, criticism, and recommendations were presented in a detailed study of economic development in the Slovak Republic by the Organization for Economic Cooperation and Development (OECD) in September 1996.[59]

On the other hand, although the prognosis for macroeconomic development in the Slovak Republic in 1997 looked promising, the lack of liquidity posed a chronic problem. According to the premier's economic adviser, Peter Stanek, although 60 percent of Slovak businesses traded profitably, they were unable to repay bank loans, fund their expansion needs, or establish distribution networks. By mid-1997, Slovakia's banks and enterprises had piled up a debt of 220 billion Sk ($6.3 billion)—roughly one-third of the GNP; of the 300 billion Sk ($9.9 billion) bank loan total in early 1996, about 90 billion Sk ($2.99 billion), or 30 percent, were considered bad debts. This lack of liquidity in the banking system became a circular problem: Banks could not make loans to new clients, while at the same time banks that held title to numerous factories as collateral were unable to sell them because there were no credible buyers. And many companies that were denied bank loans had no choice but to fund their investments out of cash flow or through the sale of their assets. Investment banks considered such companies a risk and therefore opted to invest their capital in state bonds and notes.[60]

Just how bad has it been for business? During the first half of 1997, the trade deficit continued to grow to about 30 billion Sk, or 5 percent of the projected GDP. The growing trade deficit encouraged some foreign investors to attempt a run on the Slovak currency, but the NBS weathered the attack and the exchange rate and the currency regime remained unscathed. To deal with the growing trade deficit, in April and July 1997, the government enacted a system of import deposits designed to restrict imports and reintroduced a 7 percent import surcharge as well as comprehensive price regulation on the public and private sectors of the economy. It also increased certain consumption taxes and administrative fees and raised all energy prices.

Still another measure devised for alleviating the liquidity problem was the Law on the Revitalization of Enterprises, which the NCSR passed in the first half of 1997. This law gave the government authority to cancel the debts of certain enterprises, and it was skillfully applied to enterprises whose workers and managers were more loyal to the governing coalition than the legitimate taxpaying entrepreneurs. The practice of patronage and cronyism in the Slovak Republic was not necessarily unknown to the Meciar government, of course, nor was money laundering. In the late spring of 1998, for example, Premier Meciar publically appealed to "citizens who acquired money on the black market and have it hidden from taxation" to purchase long-term state bonds issued by the government through the National Bank in order to deal with the problem of liquidity in the Slovak Republic.[61] Meciar's appeal to the "money launderers" seems to have been a desperate move to rectify the mistakes contained in the "revitalization" law, which gave the government power to prop up favored bankrupt firms—and further increased the budget deficit.[62] The economic fallout from Meciar's ill-conceived policies and statements has been particularly noticeable in the area of foreign investment where at the end of 1996 Slovakia ranked eighth (after Hungary, Poland, the Czech Republic, Russia, Romania, Slovenia, and Estonia) among the postcommunist countries.[63]

The shortage of foreign investment was also the result of the unpredictability of future political and economic developments and, of course, of the poor record of privatization. After a preparatory period in 1990, reform measures of private sector development were launched on January 1, 1991. Although more than 9,300 small shops, or over 80 percent of the total in Slovakia, were privatized before the country became an independent state, the privatization of large enterprises was much slower. Here the process included various methods such as vouchers, replaced in 1995 by bonds, direct placements, cash auctions, and competitive bidding, which took place in two "waves." Complex privatizations—energy, health services, and agriculture—were postponed to the second wave. By November 1991 there were 751 enterprises in the first wave of large privatization, with a book value of 167 billion Kcs (Czecho-Slovak koruny). Investment Privatization Funds dominated large owners in the first wave of privatization, controlling over 70 percent of the coupons. In that category the single largest owner of enterprises was the National Property Fund (NPF), a fund created by law and responsible to the SNC. In 1993 NPF owned 517 enterprises and a controlling interest in 60 additional companies.[64] In March 1994, as part of an effort to depoliticize the NPF and eliminate the government's role in appointing NPF officers, an amendment to the privatization law was passed calling for all board members to be appointed by parliament. After the 1994 elections, the victorious Meciar coalition took advantage of this change in the privatization law to appoint its own people in all positions within the NPF, and the NPF soon began to carry out direct sales for token prices to buyers who were close to or recommended by the government coalition leaders. In practice, NPF sold the enterprise on the block to a newly formed "employees' corporation" headed by the same managerial group of the old company but now "privatized," which meant that the majority of company stocks (newly issued) were owned by managers and only a small portion of the shares were held by the rest of the employees.

This method of transfer of state property through privatization guaranteed not only continuity in the economic performance of the company but political loyalty toward the benefactors of the regime. As a result, during the first eight months of 1995, 232 sales were carried out, of which only three (representing 1.3 percent) were made to foreign investors. It should be noted that, although before the end of 1992, 30 percent of all property designated for privatization was in fact privatized, between 1992 and March 1994 only 3.2 percent of such property was privatized. Furthermore, according to a study by the OECD, at the end of 1995 only 41.5 percent of state property in the Slovak Republic was privatized, compared with 81 percent for the Czech Republic.[65] At the end of 1997, the private sector share of GDP in Slovakia stood at 77.4 percent compared with 58.2 percent on December 31, 1994—three months after the Meciar coalition came to power. The Statistical Office of the Slovak Republic reported that at the end of 1997, out of 48,944 economic entities, 47,332 were private and 1,612 were public.

Since the law on privatization does not stipulate that privatization decisions must be subject to public scrutiny, NPF officials saw to it that their decision-making process was as far from public scrutiny as possible. Decisions on privatization were frequently made known by the government only several weeks after the fact. The privatization process is still regarded as an abuse of the democratic process that violates business ethics and rules. To no one's surprise, in the second half of 1995 the last powers of the Ministry of Privatization were transferred to the NPF.

SLOVAKIA'S FOREIGN AND NATIONAL SECURITY POLICY

In 1993, newly independent Slovakia lacked experienced diplomats, a skilled staff, adequate facilities, and the skills and tools necessary for the effective conduct of foreign policy. By the end of 1996 the central office of the Slovak Ministry of Foreign Affairs (SMFA) had 443 employees in addition to another 652—including 273 diplomats—working abroad.[66] Most of the appointed diplomats and higher echelon officers of the SMFA were political party loyalists serving the interests of their benefactors. Those who were disloyal rather than incompetent were automatically replaced or fired. In less than five years the Slovak Republic had six foreign ministers—a turnover that does not bode well for stability and continuity of the conduct of foreign policy. But the SMFA, though it carries the chief responsibility for the conduct of foreign policy, is not the most powerful institution in the decision-making process; the office of the president, the NCSR, and, especially, the office of the premier are also involved. As leader of the coalition government, the premier can use his or her power in foreign policy formulation much more effectively than either the president of the Slovak Republic or the president of the NCSR. As noted earlier in this chapter, during the intense polarization of Slovak domestic politics, Premier Meciar was able to constrain the powers of President Michal Kovac, primarily because of Meciar's political rather than constitutional powers. After March 4, 1998, when Kovac's term expired, Meciar assumed most of the powers of Slovakia's vacant presidency, including those pertaining to foreign policy.

The official foreign policy goals of the new Slovak state were to strive for achieving the conditions necessary for full membership in the EU and other European regional organizations; strengthen Slovak national security through membership in the security structures of Western Europe; engage in mutually advantageous economic cooperation with its neighbors, the EU and G-7 countries as well as the Russian federation; promote the Slovak Republic as a reliable partner in various governmental and nongovernmental international organizations; and adhere to the resolution of human rights issues and seek adoption of a European standard for the protection of national minorities. In a program announcement after the 1994 parliamentary elections, the Meciar government expressed its priority to gain full membership in both the EU and NATO "around the year 2000."[67]

The intent and desire to become a member of the EU was made official at a June 27, 1995, Council of Europe (CE) meeting in Cannes, when Meciar submitted the request for admission to French president Jacques Chirac. Although Slovakia was first among the ten applicants (later Cyprus became the eleventh), it was not considered among the six candidates chosen to become members of the EU probably in 2002.[68] In July 1997 the European Commission (CE, an independent executive organ of the EU) published a series of evaluation reports about the applicants for the December summit conference. In these evaluations not one of the ten associate countries completely satisfied the economic criteria for EU membership. The Slovak Republic was the only country that failed to meet both the economic and political criteria. Attempts by an official Slovak delegation to convince Sir Leon Brittan, deputy chairman of the EC, that the reports were in error failed.[69] After the Luxembourg summit conference, Slovakia was relegated to the next round of five countries (Bulgaria, Latvia, Lithuania, Romania, and Slovakia), with whom the EU would be working closely—that is, offering expanded political and economic assistance—with an eye toward *eventual* membership. Premier Meciar's perception four months after the rejection of membership into the EU was quite optimistic. In a radio interview on April 3, 1998, Meciar boasted that the Slovak government's goal concerning "the integration into the EU has been completely fulfilled," and he maintained that not political but economic conditions were decisive and that no one could argue that Slovakia was undemocratic.[70] Yet on the same day, one of the opposition leaders, deputy chairman of the PDL Peter Weiss, contradicted Meciar's optimism, saying, "Slovakia's integration into the EU will depend on the future cabinet after the autumn [1998] elections."[71]

Slovakia's failure to integrate into Western security structures, especially the North Atlantic Treaty Organization (NATO), was equally a failure of the government's own doing. On January 1, 1993, Slovakia inherited certain rights and obligations of the previous Czecho-Slovak regime, including membership in the Visegrad Group, dating from February 1991, when Slovakia was still part of the Czech and Slovak Federal Republic. Presidents Vaclav Havel and Lech Walesa of Poland and Premier Jozsef Antall of Hungary met in the Hungarian town of Visegrad and after several days of consultation issued a declaration stating that their countries' goal was total integration into the European political, economic, security, and legislative order. Toward that end they pledged cooperation among their own countries and close relations with European institutions, and the three East Central European states known as the Visegrad Group held regular meetings to coordinate policies toward the former Soviet Union, NATO, the European Community, the crisis in Yugoslavia, and military reforms.[72] During the transition period, between the postelections of 1992 and January 1, 1993, the Meciar government opted to become the fourth member of the Visegrad Group. But on the first day of Slovak independence Meciar expressed his preference first and foremost to uphold close relations with Russia and Ukraine. When Foreign Minister Milan Knazko argued for integration with the West, Meciar replaced him with Jozef Moravcik. At that time, Meciar still theorized about three possible choices of Slovak foreign policy: to remain neutral, move toward NATO, or act within a new Central European Security. We do not know what prompted Meciar to change his mind, but two months after Moravcik's appointment, he joined Moravcik and President Michal Kovac in pursuing a policy of closer ties with the West in general and membership in the EU and NATO in particular.[73]

In the security area, however, Slovak coalition leaders were less even-handed. Before the Slovak-Russian treaty was signed in August 1993, the Slovak government supported a provision (similar to the 1926 German-Soviet friendship and neutrality treaty) binding the two states not to make their territory available to other states in the event of a conflict with a third party. Owing to strong criticism from the opposition that Slovakia's sovereignty was at stake, the draft treaty was revised and a separate military agreement was signed calling for close security ties and the delivery of Russian military supplies to Slovakia. As a result, in November 1993, Russia made several arms deliveries (including aircraft), spare parts, and ammunition as a partial repayment of debts to Slovakia.[74] Meciar's government made similar overtures toward Romania and the Ukraine but with a strong emphasis on minority issues, both countries having a large Hungarian minority. After mutual visits between Meciar and President Ion Illiescu, in September 1993, the Slovak Republic and Romania signed a bilateral cooperation treaty, including a commitment to coordinate policies on ethnic minorities.[75] Ukraine refused to agree to Slovakia's request to sign an agreement on cooperation on minority issues, but in October 1993 it signed a bilateral cooperation treaty and a military cooperation agreement.[76] While the Meciar government was courting its old masters in the Kremlin and building a new type of "Little Entente," at the same time it was indicating its desire for NATO membership and military cooperation with the West. In February 1994, Slovakia became one of the first countries—one month before the Czech Republic—to join NATO's Partnership for Peace (PFP) program, and on November 25 it signed an agreement (among the first nine members) detailing the Individual Partnership Program for Slovakia.[77]

After the September-October 1994 elections in which Meciar regained his position as premier, Meciar and his new coalition partners, SNP and AWS, reintroduced the idea of neutrality as a possible course for Slovakia—in what was meant to reassure the Russians that, though it was joining NATO, it would remain a loyal friend of Moscow. As proof, in March 1995, before accepting an offer from the European Bank for Reconstruction and Development (EBRD) to borrow $300 million for completing the Russian-designed Mochovce nuclear station, Slovak finance minister Sergej Kozlik insisted that the Russians play a partnership role in the project; EBRD rejected the conditions.[78] At about the same time, Slovakia and Russia signed more than a dozen trade and economic agreements, including a controversial agreement on visa-free travel that caused noticeable alarm among the neighboring countries. Of greater significance was the arms-for-debt deal to repay Moscow's estimated $1.5 billion arrears to Slovakia.

It became obvious that Russia's interest in Slovakia was more than just strategic. Slovakia earns approximately $350 million a year in transit fees from the pipelines that carry Russian natural gas across its territory to customers in the West. Furthermore, Russia is the main provider of oil to Slovnaft, Slovakia's leading refiner and distributor. As long as close economic and military ties with Russia did not clash head-on with Slovakia's interest in seeking integration into Western European structures, especially NATO and the EU, the Slovak government faced an unencumbered road to "bridge-building" between the East and the West. But as soon as the Russian government showed its displeasure with the Western policy of eastern expansion under NATO, Slovak political leaders began to waver.[79]

The numerous warnings from the EU and the United States concerning the coalition government's disregard for democracy, human and minority rights, and principles of law created a superficial rift in the coalition: while the leaders of the SNP and the AWS opposed the enlargement of NATO and Slovak membership in it, Meciar's majority party, the MDS, ignored the views of its coalition partners and emphasized the government program as the official policy of the Slovak Republic—meaning that becoming a full member of NATO was still the priority of Slovak foreign policy. Thus, the president of the Slovak Republic, Michal Kovac, as well as the leaders of the opposition parties enthusiastically campaigned for Slovakia's membership in NATO, while Premier Meciar and his coalition parties—intentionally or unintentionally—continued to chip away at Slovakia's case for membership. After the first and second rounds of Slovakia's consultation with NATO representatives in May and June 1996, for example, Meciar blamed Kovac for slowing down the process of Slovakia's integration into the Western alliance. Three months later, in a radio interview, Meciar declared that the possibility of joining NATO would be decided by a referendum to be initiated by the coalition majority in the NCSR.[80] By then, however, the chances for joining NATO in the first wave were getting weaker.[81] Hence, Meciar and his coalition partners probably surmised that, whatever the results of the referendum, the blame for not becoming a NATO member would fall on either the voting public or the Western leaders, but not on Meciar or his coalition partners.

In February 1997, the NCSR passed a resolution directing President Kovac to call a referendum on Slovakia's membership in NATO. The referendum prepared by the coalition majority in parliament included three questions: "Are you in favor of joining NATO?" "Are you in favor of placing nuclear weapons within the territory of the SR?" and "Are you in favor of stationing foreign troops within the territory of the SR?"[82] When President Kovac received the NCSR version of the referendum, he was urged by the opposition leaders—who since January 1997 had gathered more than 500,000 of the 350,000 required signatures for a referendum on direct election of the president but had been ignored by the coalition majority—to add a fourth question on the direct election of the president. Kovac complied and in so doing was accused by the Meciar government of obstructing the referendum process. The government filed suit in the Constitutional Court of the Slovak Republic (CCSR) seeking to separate the two issues on the grounds that a referendum could not change the Slovak Constitution. In the meantime the government instructed Minister of the Interior Gustav Krajci to remove the added fourth question on direct presidential elections and to reprint 4.5 million ballots. On May 21, 1997, two days before the vote on the referendum, the CCSR ruled that the Constitution of the Slovak Republic could be changed by a referendum; President Kovac insisted on an official referendum with four rather than the initial three questions.[83] One day before the referendum voting, the Central Referendum Commission (the official body overseeing the referendum process) refused to endorse the new ballots with only three questions and declared them illegal. On the eve of the referendum, opposition leaders appealed to the voters not to vote if they received the so-called "official" ballots with only three questions, and President Kovac assured the citizens in a radio address that he would vote only on a ballot with all four questions. Voters—either confused or uninterested—shunned the referendum: only 9.53 percent of registered voters turned out. Premier Meciar declared the results of the referendum invalid; the Central Referendum Commission (CRC) branded the referendum an impediment and demanded that Minister of the Interior Gustav Krajci be immediately indicted on criminal charges. The only official who submitted his resignation on May 26, the first day of "postnational chaos," was Foreign Minister Pavol Hamzik, a career diplomat and an ardent supporter of Meciar's government. In his statement Hamzik acknowledged that the circumstances surrounding the referendum limited his ability to "achieve Slovakia's foreign policy goals."[84]

Although NATO officials were critical of the referendum's question about "placing nuclear weapons within the territory of the SR" as a precondition for membership in the organization, the ruling coalition responsible for the preparation of the ballot justified it on the basis of a declining public opinion of confidence in NATO between October 1993 and January 1997. Only 39 percent of the respondents in a poll taken in 1997 showed confidence in NATO, compared with 45 percent in 1993. The opposition critics argued that the timing of the referendum and the wording of the ballot indicated a government move to shift the blame from its own foreign policy failures onto the citizens of Slovakia.[85] Surveys taken immediately after the "obstructed" referendum showed that 57 percent of citizens would have participated had the ballot with all four questions been made available and that 71 percent of these would have voted for Slovakia's membership in NATO.[86] However, these optimistic figures remained only a matter of conjecture. The fact remains that at the July 8–9, 1997, NATO summit meeting in Madrid, Slovakia not only was bypassed for the first wave of NATO enlargement but was not even mentioned among the most likely candidates for the projected second wave.[87]

On July 14, 1997, U.S. Ambassador Ralph Johnson explained to a select Slovak audience why the United States could not support Slovakia's NATO membership at that time. Simply put, the reason was "concern about Slovakia's democratic development." He reminded the audience that the United States and members of the EU had routinely "expressed reservations about certain aspects of Slovakia's democracy to the highest level of the Slovak government." The two areas in which antidemocratic developments had taken place, according to Johnson, were "the intolerant and unfair treatment of those with opposing points of view" and "the increasing centralization of power." He made it clear that the United States viewed the ruling coalition's conduct during the

May 23–24 referendum as a "step backward" from the democratic record of free and fair elections in Slovakia since 1989. He openly criticized the treatment of the Hungarian minority in Slovakia and the media
coverage of the recent kidnapping of the former president's son, Michal
Kovac, Jr., as well as the murder of one of Kovac's kidnappers before he
could testify and the explosion outside the home of Deputy Frantisek
Gaulieder, whose mandate was illegally revoked by the ruling majority
in parliament. Finally, Ambassador Johnson reassured the Slovak citizens that the United States was committed to aid and assist all those in
Slovakia who supported democracy and free markets in order to ensure
the SR's rightful place in Europe.[88] Similar criticisms, and at the same
time reassurances, were expressed by officials of other Western states,
especially those in Europe.[89]

Although Slovakia continued as one of NATO's twenty-one partner
countries, on March 4, 1998—one day after assuming most of the powers of Slovakia's vacant presidency—Premier Vladimir Meciar canceled
a referendum for seeking NATO membership and holding direct elections for president. His coalition majority in parliament endorsed his
decision one month later.

Since Slovakia's foreign policy is greatly affected by the situation in
the neighboring countries, especially the fellow members of the Visegrad
Group, the proponents of the so-called Slovak "Eastern" or "neutrality"
policy must have been disappointed when in 1997 the other three members of the Visegrad Group became members of NATO. Slovakia's ability to cooperate with other countries is still judged by how well it main-
tains amiable relations with its neighbors, especially the Czech Republic
and Hungary.

From the first day of independence, officials of the Slovak and Czech
Republics committed themselves to promote the highest cooperation between the two new states. They entered into what in diplomatic language is known as "special relations." The record for the six years since
Slovakia's independence has shown that relations between the former
partners in the Czecho-Slovak federation have been more "chilling"
than "special." During the first two years of diplomatic relations between the two countries, Czech officials criticized their Slovak counterparts for using protectionist measures against Czech imports, for exaggerated border claims, violation of the 1993 agreement on payments
between the two countries and then its termination in September 1995,
as well as for Meciar's abusive language against Czech officials, espe-

cially President Havel. Slovak officials placed the blame on the Czechs, and thus the dialogue in several instances turned into innuendo, name-calling, and denunciation. During this period there were occasions for meetings between the two premiers, like the one on June 27, 1995, at the Cannes summit, where issues could be clarified and "misunderstandings" between the two governments smoothed over; but there were no official periodic meetings either between the heads of the two states or between their premiers, and meetings at the ministerial or lower bureaucratic levels took place on a haphazard basis. Nevertheless, before September 1998 Slovak-Czech relations were officially termed satisfactory, but not "special" and amicable.

During the Meciar regime Slovakia's relations with Hungary have been cordial, but not friendly. As early as January 1993, the Council of Europe reported violations of minority rights in Slovakia, which included the forcible removal of Hungarian-language place signs, a ban on the use of Hungarian first names in birth registers, and a proposed gerrymandering of administrative districts to weaken the political representation of the Hungarian minority. The government of the independent Slovak Republic promised to correct the situation, and six months later Slovakia was admitted to the CE. However, the government failed to make good on the promise.[90] The dispute between the Slovak government and the leaders of the Hungarian minority in Slovakia, which persisted into 1998, was the primary cause for preventing the signing of a bilateral cooperation treaty on March 19, 1995, guaranteeing the existing Hungarian-Slovak border. After signing the treaty, it took more than a year (March 26, 1996) to ratify the document. This did not improve Slovak-Hungarian relations[91] because the coalition majority in parliament added an amendment to the treaty asserting that the Slovak side did not recognize the concept of "collective rights" for its Hungarian minority.

Another thorny issue contributing to strained Slovak-Hungarian relations since Slovakia's independence in 1993 was the Gabcikovo-Nagymaros dam, a joint hydroelectric power project on the Danube River initiated by the two countries under communist regional planning in 1977. In 1989 Hungary abandoned the project, and three years after the communist collapse, on March 24, 1992, the parliament of the Republic of Hungary unilaterally abrogated the 1977 treaty, declaring it invalid as of May 19, 1992.[92] The newly elected government of Vladimir Meciar, without an explicit endorsement from the federal government, responded by unilaterally diverting the Danube in October 1992, thereby reducing the waterflow into Hungary and provoking a crisis as Hungary's wetlands dried up, imperiling local agriculture and the region's unique fauna and flora. The Danube's waters were channeled through a suffocating, sealed canal into a stagnant reservoir, which caused the drinking water in Budapest and other communities to become dangerously contaminated. The Hungarian government also claimed that Slovakia's Gabcikovo power plant was seismically unstable and unable to cope with winter ice.

After many charges and countercharges between the two governments and the intervention of the Danube Commission, UN secretary-general Boutros-Ghali, and even the pope, on October 28, 1992, British prime minister John Major brokered a tripartite agreement (Hungary-Czecho-Slovakia-EC). According to this agreement, all work on the dam was halted on a specified date established by the EC, Slovakia had to restore 95 percent of the Danube water in the old bed and refrain from operating the power plant, and it had to submit the dispute to the International Court of Justice (ICJ).[93] Although the agreement, also known as the London Protocol, temporarily prevented the crisis from further escalation, it failed to resolve the main issue because Slovakia failed to redivert the water or stop the operation of the power plant. Accordingly, the case was submitted to the ICJ on July 2, 1993, for adjudication. There were three issues before the high court: (1) whether Hungary was permitted to suspend work unilaterally on the Gabcikovo-Nagymaros project in 1989, (2) the legality of the "Variant C" plan introduced by the Slovak government in October 1992, and (3) the legality of the termination of the treaty of 1977 by Hungary in March 1992.

After intensive hearings and examination of the disputed project and territory, on September 25, 1997, the high court delivered its judgment on the protracted dispute between Hungary and Slovakia over the construction and operation of the Gabcikovo-Nagymaros dam and found both states in breach of their legal obligation. In its judgment, the ICJ found that (1) Hungary was not entitled to suspend and subsequently abandon its part of the works on the dam project, as laid down in the treaty signed in 1979 by Hungary and Czechoslovakia and related instruments; (2) Czecho-Slovakia was entitled to start, in November 1991, preparation of an alternative provisional solution—called "Variant C"—but not to put that "solution" into operation in October 1992 as a unilateral measure; (3) Hungary's notification of termination of the 1977 treaty and related instruments on May 19, 1992, did not legally terminate them (and that they were consequently still in force and governed the relationship between the parties); and (4) Slovakia, as successor to Czecho-Slovakia, became a party to the treaty of 1977.

Finally, as for the future conduct of the parties to the dispute, the ICJ found that (1) Hungary and Slovakia must negotiate in good faith in light of the prevailing situation and must take all necessary measures to ensure the achievement of the objective of the 1997 treaty, (2) each party must compensate the other party for damage caused by its conduct, and (3) the accounts for the construction and operation of the works must be settled in accordance with the relevant provisions of the 1997 treaty and its related instruments. The court also held that newly developed norms of environmental law were relevant for the implementation of the treaty and should be incorporated in several articles of the treaty. It further said that the parties must find a satisfactory solution for the volume of water to be released into the old bed of the Danube and into the side-arms of the river.[94] In Bratislava, the ruling by the ICJ was hailed as a victory for Slovakia, and on February 28, 1998, Hungary and Slovakia agreed in principle to build a new Danube River dam, which would eventually give new light to the controversial Gabcikovo hydroelectric plant. Two months later, however, the Slovak parliament adopted a resolution instructing the Meciar government to seek intervention by the EU to "persuade" Hungary to comply with the high court's decision. Slovak environmentalists have continued to criticize the dam. They have pointed out that the Slovak authorities failed to consult with ecology experts and viewed the project only from their technocratic point of view, whereas neighboring authorities in Austria and Hungary declared the neighboring Danube area to be national parks.

Possibly the most valuable neighbor of the Slovak Republic is Austria. As the only EU member sharing a common border with Slovakia, Austria is one of its largest foreign investors and trading partners. Nevertheless, from 1995 on, Austro-Slovak relations under Meciar were only cordial. The reason for that can be found in Slovakia's national disposition and the idiosyncracies of the country's foreign policy. In February 1995, after the European Bank for Reconstruction and Development (EBRD) approved a loan of DM 260 million to Slovakia to complete the nuclear plant at Mochovce, the Austrian parliament opposed the project because of the security risk involved and threatened to withdraw from EBRD. When Meciar and Foreign Minister Schenk visited Austria on March 4, 1995, Chancellor Franz Vranitzky made a loan offer to Slovakia of half a billion Austrian shillings to build a nonnuclear alternative power plant. Meciar's coalition government decided instead to cancel the loan from EBRD, and in April 1996 it concluded a delivery contract with Skoda Prague, consortium EUCOM (Siemens/Framatome), and Russian and Slovak suppliers to complete the nuclear plant at Mochovce; the following month, the government of the Slovak Republic received loans in the total amount of 28.86 billion Sk ($849 million) from Czech, French, German, and Slovak banks. Disregarding Austrian warnings, Slovak government officials justified the completion of the project by claiming that all West European security standards had been met.[95]

Another trouble spot in Austro-Slovak relations revolves around the constantly changing rules for doing business in the Slovak Republic. In 1995, Austria, like several other foreign investors in Slovakia, was eliminated from participation in the so-called bidding for enterprises by a simple act of the abolition of the second wave of the voucher privatization by the Meciar government. The Austrian investors considered this act a violation of the Austrian-Slovak Agreement on the Bilateral Protection of Investment and of the association agreement of Slovakia with the EU. As a result, Austrian investment companies lost millions of dollars in privatization funds backed by Austrian capital.

Austro-Slovak relations became strained again in 1996, when the son of the former president of the Slovak Republic, Michal Kovac, was abducted in Bratislava and dumped into the lap of Austrian authorities for trial in Germany. Instead of extraditing Michal Kovac, Jr., to Germany, the Austrian government and the Superior Regional Law Court in Vienna became suspicious of the Slovak government's involvement in the abduction and consequently released Kovac and permitted him to return to his country. An exchange of protest notes between Bratislava and Vienna followed, and the relations between the two neighboring countries worsened.[96] Nevertheless, there were also numerous positive accomplishments by the two Central European states, such as the development of an infrastructure to secure the open and efficient transport of goods. In this respect the building of a new Bratislava-Vienna-Budapest superhighway and the promotion of the Vienna and Bratislava airports to conduct joint marketing were well received in both countries.

On the whole, Slovak foreign policy under Meciar had a relatively poor record. Its main policy goals—membership in the European economic and security structures—suffered a serious setback in 1997. Slovakia's relations with its neighbors had not improved since 1995. The self-aggrandizing argument that the Slovak Republic possessed geostrategic significance in East Central Europe that the West could not ignore and that economic stability in the country was more important to the world than human rights, tolerance of the opposition, and the observance of democratic rules and procedures proved to be wrong and thus backfired on the Meciar government. It would appear that Slovakia, for most of its seven years of independence, lacked a coherent and consistent foreign policy. If it is true that any foreign policy is to a great extent a reflection of the domestic policy of a nation, then the blame for the lack of success can be clearly placed at the doorstep of the ruling majority under the leadership of Vladimir Meciar.

14 The End of "Democratic Tyranny"?

Because the Velvet Revolution in November 1989 failed—perhaps inevitably—to uproot the vestiges of authoritarianism, the new Czecho-Slovak "democracy" included communist features, and these vestiges were carried into Slovakia's government after its Velvet Divorce in 1992. For example, after the 1992 separation, the Movement for a Democratic Slovakia (MDS) acted as if it had a mandate to use certain authoritative and nationalist measures in the independent Slovak Republic. Starting on January 1, 1993, Slovakia under Vladimir Meciar (MDS's leader) experimented with "democratic tyranny," a form of democratic transformation described by Alexis de Tocqueville more than a century and half before. Except for a brief interlude between March and September 1994, when a broad coalition government led by Jozef Moravcik replaced divisive politics with consensual politics, Meciar and MDS held power from 1992 until October 1998. Referred to as "Meciarism," that period is equated with an authoritarian political machine supported by corruption, patronage, subterfuge, and disregard for democratic rules.

The comments and observations in this chapter are by no means conclusive because the stage of Slovak history is never ending—only the scenes, the characters, the actors, and the audiences are different inasmuch as they represent only seven years in the millennium of Slovak history, the period since the independence of the Slovak state in 1993.

Meciar's political machine exalted Slovak nationalism by institutionalizing his monopoly of power in the executive and legislative branches of the government and, through the tyranny of the majority, imposed Meciar's will on the political minority and society as a whole.

"MECIARISM" IN SLOVAK POLITICS AND ECONOMY

Although symptoms of Meciarism in Slovakia were present immediately after the 1992 elections, they became more obvious shortly after the 1994 parliamentary elections. During the infamous night of November 3, 1994, MDS, in cooperation with its coalition partners, the Slovak National party (SNP) and the Workers Association of Slovakia (WAS), violated the rules assuring the parliamentary opposition meaningful participation in the key institutions of government, from proportional representation on parliamentary committees to inclusion in bodies monitoring and supervising important state functions. As a result of personnel cleansing, MDS usurped the power of the state, creating an institutionalized monopoly of rule in the country that intentionally prevented the minority parties from exercising their democratic role. Any obstacle or person that stood in the way of the ruling coalition headed by Party Chairman and Premier Meciar had to be, and in most instances was, removed. That credo was also applied to Michal Kovac, who before his election to the presidency had been a loyal member of the MDS. After Kovac refused to become a team player in the Meciar coalition, the MDS repeatedly called on him to resign "because he failed to respect the results of the election, engaged in polarizing the country, presented Slovakia in a bad light abroad, and so on."[1] Finally, in August 1995, the council of MDS expelled Kovac from the movement and with the assistance of its coalition partners launched a smear campaign against him.

When that failed, another tactic was tried. On August 31, 1995, Kovac's son, Michal, Jr., was kidnapped by unknown persons and taken to neighboring Austria. At that time young Kovac was under indictment in Germany for his alleged involvement in the "Technopol case" and subject to apprehension by Interpol. But when the Austrian officials determined that the Slovak Information Service (SIS) was involved in the abduction, they sent Michal back to Slovakia. A criminal investigation of the abduction conducted in Bratislava also implicated SIS employees, but under pressure from MDS the investigators from the Slovak Police Force who made this disclosure were suddenly relieved of their positions. Premier Meciar, supported by the director of the SIS, Ivan Lexa, defended the action. Neither President Kovac nor the leaders of the opposition could do anything about the stalled criminal investigation because the parliamentary Special Control Organ responsible for overseeing the activities of the SIS was staffed solely by MDS members. In spite of continuing pressures, President Kovac persevered in his function as head of state and kept up his criticism of Meciar's method of operation.[2]

The failure to make a thorough investigation of the August 1995 kidnapping of Kovac's son led to several public protests against the Meciar government. In the spring of 1996, opposition members of parliament and an infuriated public in the streets asked for the resignations of Interior Minister Ludovit Hudek, SIS director Ivan Lexa, and Prosecutor General Michal Valo. In May 1996, after a strong public rally, the ruling majority in parliament allowed a debate of censure against the interior minister, but Hudek remained in the office until August 17, 1996, when he resigned along with two other ministers in the first and only cabinet reshuffle. Neither Lexa nor Valo was removed from office even though they failed to pursue an investigation of the 1996 car-bomb slaying of Robert Remias, a businessman who reportedly had evidence implicating the intelligence service in the Kovac kidnapping.

Meciar's power monopoly did not show signs of weakening. In 1997 Meciar successfully blocked the opposition's attempt to combine a vote on direct election of the president with a referendum on Slovakia's membership in NATO. This fiasco, discussed at length in Chapter 13, seemed to reassure Meciar that his concept of power—meaning no power to the people—and his notions on foreign policy—meaning continuing close relations with Russia and the East—were what the Slovak people ought to have, whether they liked it or not.

In March 1998, shortly after Kovac's term in office expired, Meciar used his new powers to stop another investigation of the kidnapping of Michal Kovac, Jr., and the murder of Robert Remias. The kidnapping case was reopened in June 1998 by Jozef Satek, former director of the regional office of investigation of the Bratislava police department.

In response to this investigation, Meciar granted amnesty to the Interior Ministry officials who sabotaged the 1997 referendum. And Meciar neither recalled nor censored other ministers accused of violating their power in office, among them Minister of Culture Ivan Hudec, Minister of Agriculture Peter Baco, and Minister of Education Eva Slavkova. As a result of these actions (and inactions), the Slovak people became ever more convinced that Meciar and his coalition partners had broken state laws and violated basic principles of democratic rule.

Perhaps the most bizarre case of Meciarism was the treatment of an MDS deputy who attempted to leave his parliamentary party club but was removed from the parliament against his own will. In November 1996, the Immunity and Mandate Committee received a letter of resignation, allegedly signed by Frantisek Gaulieder, along with two other letters, also by Gaulieder, which stated that he did not wish to resign. Since the date of resignation appeared to have been added with a different typewriter, the conclusion was drawn that MDS members were required to sign an undated letter of resignation that could be used for disciplinary purposes (an action precluded by the constitution). In spite of the questionable validity of this letter, the Immunity and Mandate Committee (dominated by MDS 10 to 5) voted to accept Gaulieder's "resignation" and thus remove his mandate. On December 4, 1996, over Gaulieder's protest, his seat was assigned to another member of MDS. Two days after Gaulieder's mandate was revoked, a bomb exploded outside Gaulieder's family home in Galanta. In July 1997 the Constitutional Court decided that the expulsion of Frantisek Gaulieder from parliament violated his legal rights, but in a television address Meciar scoffed at the court, saying that "its recommendation is not binding."[3] The court also stated that it could not correct the injustice; that could only be done by parliament. Three months later—September 1997—the opposition deputies succeeded in calling a special session of parliament to discuss the Gaulieder case, but the ruling majority deputies boycotted the session and the proposal to return Gaulieder to parliament failed for lack of a quorum. Meciarism was also evident in the case of Emil Spisak, who, according to the election laws and the decision of the Slovak Constitutional Court, was entitled to succeed a deceased SNP deputy, Bartolomej Kunc. But in January 1998 Spisak was denied the seat in parliament because he had opted to leave SNP in the meantime.

Though the parliamentary opposition attempted on several occasions to remove Vladimir Meciar and several of his loyal ministers from the government through a vote of no confidence, the majority always prevailed, and it also voted down most of the legislative proposals submitted by the opposition as soon as they were introduced, without an adequate hearing. It is not surprising, therefore, that in his July 1998 report about the governmental program, Meciar remarked that (former) President Kovac's negative and destructive attitude toward his government and parliament had harmed national interests: "L'état c'est moi."[4]

The longer Meciar remained in office, the more arrogant his abuse of power became. In March 1998, after Kovac's term as president had expired and Meciar as premier assumed some of the powers of the president, Meciar explained his abrogation of the 1997 referendum with a proviso that if by June 1998 no new president was elected in the NCSR, he would submit to the parliament a proposal to amend the constitution so that the president could be selected by direct elections at a time when parliamentary elections were held. Shortly after this commitment, the government established a commission, headed by Meciar, for changing and amending the constitution. In June the government submitted two proposals, neither one, of which, as promised, called for direct election of the president. The NCSR adopted the first version, according to which some of the presidential powers would be transferred to the chairperson of the parliament. As a result, from March until October 1998, Premier Merciar assumed all presidential powers. Not until mid-January 1999 did parliament approve direct elections of the president. The accepted proposal was prepared by the coalition government of Mikulas Dzurinda—not Vladimir Meciar.

There were many other deceptions, falsehoods, vendettas, and infractions committed by the Meciar government during the seven months of rule without a president. In April 1998, the Meciar government condemned a letter issued by the Catholic bishops criticizing the political situation in Slovakia as biased and harmful to the national interests because it created social tension and polarization.[5] In August 1998, the Meciar government antagonized the Association of Slovak Soldiers when it recalled the chief of staff of the Slovak Armed Forces, General Jozef Tuchyna, and appointed Marian Miklus as his successor. The association declared the government decision invalid and criticized the appointment of new generals, among whom were individuals implicated in questionable transactions concerning the repayment of the Russian debt.[6] The Meciar government was also actively engaged in blocking television and radio broadcasts of independent stations that refused to propagate the Meciar line.

In order to make Vladimir Meciar look like a man in peril for his convictions, his government floated rumors that there was a plot, originated from abroad, to assassinate him. The plot was mentioned by such notables as Minister of the Interior Gustav Krajci and the director of Special Police Forces, Tibor Kralovic, and the Ministry of the Interior solicited the aid and cooperation of Interpol. The director of the Slovak section of Interpol, Rudolf Gajdos, thought the assassination plot was probably a political ploy, which cost Interpol much time and wasted energy.[7]

Meciar's privatization policy was another exclusive MDS province. The National Property Fund (NPF), which was in charge of privatization, was in the hands of MDS appointees, and their arbitrary decisions sold many profitable companies to MDS supporters under the cover of unknown companies, many of which came into being only a few weeks before the privatization.[8] In order to appear legitimate, the ruling majority made its own rules and laws to use privatization as an instrument of building a power base in society. In February 1996, parliament passed the fourteenth amendment to the law on large-scale privatization, according to which new company owners were not obligated to permit employees' participation. Even if the employees were given the right to participate in privatization, their maximum share was limited to 10 percent of the 34 percent established before this amendment was passed.

In March 1996, parliament approved an income tax law, previously vetoed by President Kovac, according to which reinvestments of profit were tax deductible. Another discriminatory law, passed in November 1996, was the law on securities, which permitted shareholders to remain anonymous and gave joint-stock companies the chance to halt public trading in their shares. The president also vetoed this piece of legislation, and again Meciar's majority in parliament overrode the veto.[9]

Efforts of the opposition to block this sort of privatization by appealing to the Constitutional Court of Slovakia or by seeking a change in the composition of the NPF board of governors were equally unsuccessful. For example, they challenged the process of direct sales of state companies to the NPF as unconstitutional; in November 1996 the high court agreed, but because it also ruled that there was no legal way to invalidate all NPF decisions made since November 1994 because decisions could not be applied retroactively, NPF continued with privatization. Since Meciar's coalition in parliament had the necessary majority to control legislation, the executive had unlimited reign over privatization. If the president vetoed a bill, the ruling coalition could override it by a simple majority, which happened quite frequently. Thus the Constitutional Court was the last resort for the opposition, but it could not reverse the harm done by privatization, which put in jeopardy both economic reforms and the democratic process.

The law on privatization did not stipulate that privatization decisions must be subject to public scrutiny, and officials of NPF saw to it that their decision-making process was as far removed from public scrutiny as possible; decisions on privatization were frequently made known by the government only several weeks after the fact. As a result, the privatization process is still viewed as an abuse of the democratic process, violation of business ethics, and favoritism. To no one's surprise, the remaining powers of the ministry of privatization were transferred to the NPF in the second half of 1995.

Infringement upon the inviolability of private ownership by the state because of political considerations is well documented in the case of the First Slovak Investment Company (FSIC), whose operating license was revoked on March 31, 1995, by the Ministry of Finance after it carried out an audit of the company. First Slovak Investment Company was probably the strongest private Slovak investment company; it administered an open dividend fund, *Sporofond*, and was well known for its support of laissez-faire democracy and freedom of the press. It did not support the Meciar coalition government. Shortly after the Ministry of Finance revoked FSIC's license, the property previously administered by the company was transferred to two other investment companies, one of them the Harvard Investment Co., known for its close connections with the coalition leaders. The shareholders reacted by filing two lawsuits: one for the violation of their ownership rights and another for reparations arising from the devaluation of their funds that resulted from the state's intervention. At the end of 1995, the supreme court reversed the decision on the revocation of the license by the Ministry of Finance as unlawful. The government continued to harass FSIC and refused to release the property under its administration. In February 1996, the Ministry of Finance ordered another audit of FSIC and within a few days charged the company with unspecified violations of the law on investment companies and securities exchanges. The management of FSIC perceived the audit as an excuse to invoke the sanctions and thus prevent FSIC from demanding restitution for damages caused by the revocation of their license.[10] AG Banka, which became one of the custodians of FSIC assets, declared bankruptcy in 1999, and in mid-January 2000 its overseers returned all retrievable assets to FSIC in the amount of over one billion Slovak koruny, or about 63 percent of the original value.[11]

The disenfranchisement of FSIC in the spring of 1995 was in many ways a prelude to the sudden cancellation of voucher privatization and its replacement by the bond method in July 1995. Since the end of 1994, representatives of the government and their media had accused investments funds and companies of violating the interests of small shareholders and investors. The new privatization scheme was supposed to separate the "good companies"—those supporting the government coalition policies—from the "bad companies"—those critical of the coalition policies. Cancellation of voucher privatization meant a loss of almost all resources that the "bad companies" invested in the second wave. These funds and companies included several foreign investors, especially some from neighboring Austria. In December 1995, EPIC, an Austrian financial company that had an investment fund in Slovakia, announced that it intended to sue the Slovak government for having canceled voucher privatization without proper notification and due process of law, an act that had resulted in the loss to the company of 65 million Austrian shillings; EPIC based its case on the Austrian-Slovak Agreement on the Bilateral Protection of Investment and on the association agreement of Slovakia with the European Union. Eight additional privatization funds backed by Austrian capital incurred similar losses.[12]

Examples of haphazard operation by the NPF—or more bluntly put, the unknown rules used for the selection of buyers of privatized property—are also evident from the privatization of 51 percent of shares of the joint-stock company Slovenske Liecebne Kupele (Slovak Recuperative Spas) at Sliac and Kovacova. It was acquired in October 1995 by the joint-stock company Corvas of Piestany at a price much lower than that offered by the competitive bidder, the township of Kovacova. However, a closer scrutiny of the transaction revealed that one of the associates of the winning bid was V. Sobona, a former minister of health care and the 1994 campaign manager of Meciar's Movement for a Democratic Slovakia. It was the same Sobona who in 1992 campaigned for the state to retain a majority control in spas because in his view that was the only way to preserve the medical character of the spas.[13]

A similar scandalous sale of 51 percent of the shares of the lucrative and well-known Slovak Rehabilitation Spa Piestany (SRSP), a joint-stock company, came to light in the summer of 1996. The book value of the company was 1.6 billion Sk, but the NPF sold the shares to an employee joint-stock company—Association of Employees of the Piestany Spa (AEPS)—for only 302 million Sk. Shortly after the sale, the Supreme Audit Office discovered multiple legal violations in the founding of AEPS, and as a result, at the end of January 1997, the shares of SRSP were transferred from AEPS to a firm called Vadium Group, founded by the general director of Devin Banka, Karol Martinka, who had become manager of the bank in early 1995 after the Russian shareholders gained control of it. Martinka's closest collaborator became state secretary of the Ministry of Finance, and his wife became the closest collaborator to Premier Meciar at the Office of the Government. In 1997, the former head of intelligence of the Slovak secret service (from 1993 to 1995) alleged that the bank was an intermediary for Russian influence and that it was closely connected to Vladimir Meciar, not only through Mrs. Martinkova but through direct contact with the bank's chairman, a Mr. Gorodkov.[14]

The "give-away" privatization of state-owned property to Meciar's political cronies continued until the last day of his rule in October 1998. The early knavery purported by the NPF included disregard for contractual obligations in the privatization sale of 51 percent of shares of Novacke Chemicke Zavody to the INEKON company in the Czech Republic, the sale of 39 percent of shares of the joint-stock company Slovnaft to the joint-stock company Slovintegra, established by the nineteen managers of Slovnaft; and the sale of the remaining 45.9 percent of shares of Nafta Gbely, one of the most prosperous enterprises in Slovakia.[15] The shares were sold to Druha Obchodna, whose owners included high MDS officials such as Ivan Gasparovic, chairman of the parliament, Augustin Marian Huska, vice chairman, Sergej Kozlik, vice premier, and Anna Nagyova, a former assistant to the premier. When these party officials were asked to substantiate their involvement, they denied any complicity and the spokesmen for the company refused to identify the real owners, calling that a trade secret.[16] The direct loss to the state treasury from this sale was estimated at 3 billion Sk.

These examples of "sham privatization" practices are only an illustration of the 150 or so transactions that took place in 1995 and cost the state treasury billions of Slovak koruny. One of the reasons for such practices was the ruling majority's ability to prevent the opposition from revising the composition of the NPF or its rules of operation. Apparently to do so was consistent with the achievements of the Slovak "economic miracle." According to some reports in the print media, coalition party leaders or their family members allegedly were involved in privatization projects or were offered positions of trust in the NPF or certain profitable enterprises where the state is a co-owner.[17] There were also reports of connections between the so-called mafia and the privatization process. One report described the case (in 1997) of an abandoned sugar mill near Nitra in which the representative of the Ministry of Privatization who handled the sale to the new owner made approval conditional on the deposit of half the sales price and then returned after the sale was approved to demand approximately the same amount (5 million Sk), with the explanation that the new owner (buyer) would make "plenty and the party also demands its share." The report (in *Americke Listy*) went on to describe threats and intimidation involving the mafia, which so frightened the new owner that he left the matter in the hands of his trusted manager and fled the country with his family to find refuge somewhere abroad. His manager, under duress, had to sign papers authorizing the member of the Slovak mafia to transact business in the privatized old sugar mill. Although the authorities—the local police and the office of the district attorney—were fully informed about the case, the mafia continued its activities without retribution.[18]

The MDS's disregard for law and order was reflected in an increasing feeling of insecurity and helplessness among the citizenry. According to public opinion polls taken before the 1998 elections, 84 percent of Slovakia's citizens thought that crime in Slovakia was increasing and personal security was decreasing. People's concerns about the rise of racketeering and blackmailing against entrepreneurs by members of the Slovak mafia ranked highest among the ten leading issues of concern. Racketeering was directed against a relatively small group of people—primarily those engaged in business—but the lawlessness in the country and the seeming indifference of the police to the problem had a chilling impact on how citizens viewed their personal safety and the security of their property.

The deteriorating conditions in Slovakia after the 1994 elections have been well documented in public opinion surveys. In response to surveys conducted by FOCUS in December 1994 and by the Institute for Public Affairs in October 1997, 54 percent of the respondents felt that life was better *before* rather than after 1989. This group of disenchanted respondents included mostly people from rural areas over age sixty, pensioners, unskilled workers, people with lowest levels of education, and the unemployed. Immediately after the 1994 elections, 53 percent of citizens believed their children would have better prospects than they would have had under pre-1989 socialism; in 1997, only 34 percent held this opinion. Most Slovak citizens (83 percent in October 1997) still believed that the government should be responsible for providing every citizen with a job and a "decent" standard of living. Only 11 percent felt that this was every individual's responsibility. Similarly, only 40 percent of respondents believed that privatization of the economy was beneficial to the development of the national economy; 43 percent felt it was harmful. Most Slovaks not only believed in state paternalism but also associated the privatization process with "clientleism and corruption." The number of respondents claiming that "people in Slovakia become rich mainly through dishonest methods" increased from 86 percent in 1994 to 91 percent in 1997.[19]

In 1997, the Meciar coalition followed the guideline that government regulation of the financial infrastructure in the key industries was necessary in order to allow free competition in the marketplace at the grassroots level. As a result, the production and distribution of goods and services in Slovakia were driven to a large extent by government regulations rather than by incentives and rewards created by human nature.

Arbitrary actions of the government persisted and hampered capital investment because of the lack of assurance that any rewards would be legally protected. Also missing was the rule of law by an impartial judiciary and its associated rights giving consumers the guarantee that market prices would be determined by supply and demand rather than by government fiat. In many liberal democracies these rights function as an instrument to pressure political leaders to yield to the dictates of an effectively functioning market system, but in Slovakia under Meciar it was the will of the ruling coalition government that dictated the functioning of the market system. The economic success that lasted in Slovakia from 1994 to 1996 was only temporary and can be attributed to a transition from a low technological base to the adoption of more advanced technology. This opened Slovakia's economy to world competition while still mandating most of its output through government directives. Partial planning by government technocrats may appear to be successful for a time, but in the long run, as Alan Greenspan has pointed out, only sophisticated market mechanisms can successfully gauge the preferences of consumers and the evolving technologies of production.[20] Recent economic data reveal that government-induced investments led to gains in output for a number of years because of low real wages and low productivity; however, domestic consumers and export customers often passed over many of the goods and services that Slovakia produced. As a result, after 1997 Slovakia experienced an increase in defaulting companies, a decrease in foreign investment, and a buildup of nonperforming bank loans.

Slovakia was unable to attract foreign direct investment (in the years 1989–1996, only $623 million) primarily because of Meciar's "crony capitalism" approach to privatization, his attitude on market reform, and his resistance to foreign ownership in Slovak banking and industry.[21] The Meciar formula for privatization was to abandon voucher privatization in favor of a management buyout program on easy terms (10–20 percent down with government-generated loans), with the balance payable in installments over a long period of time. These installments were then reduced by additional (tax-deductible) investment that the managers put into the business. This method of privatization allowed sales of state property in Slovakia to be a *private* matter between Meciar's cronies and NPF. As a result, many foreign investors were kept out of Slovakia.

POLITICAL PARTIES AND THE SEPTEMBER 25–26, 1998, ELECTIONS

Multiparty systems in a parliamentary democracy, such as the one instituted in Slovakia, necessitate electoral alliances and cabinet coalitions to provide a measure of coherence. From 1993 on, Meciar and his party maintained a cabinet coalition, but electoral alliances were not so common. The first meaningful electoral alliance did not emerge until the summer of 1997.

In 1996, the growing dissatisfaction of voters with the ruling coalition enabled opposition parties to gain steady support. Between October 1994 (the third parliamentary elections) and April 1998, support for the ruling coalition and the parliamentary opposition changed from 47.7 percent favoring the ruling coalition and 39.3 percent favoring the opposition to 31.5 percent for the ruling coalition and 61 percent for the opposition.[22] After September 1995, popular support for the opposition was significantly higher than support for the ruling coalition, yet because of the heterogeneity of the nonruling political parties and the strong self-interest among their leaders, the fragmented political opposition was unable to assert itself in parliament as a unified successful power—that is, not until January 1997, when a successful petition drive for a referendum on direct election of the president took place. The drive was joined by all major opposition parties except the Party of the Democratic Left (PDL). Cooperation on other issues soon followed. In the meantime, leaders of the Christian Democratic Movement (CDM), the Democratic Union (DU), and the Democratic Party (DP) unofficially created the so-called Blue Coalition, which in the spring of 1997 led to negotiations with the leaders of additional parties and the creation of what journalists nicknamed the Rainbow Coalition. Finally, in July 1997 the chairmen of the CDM, DU, DP, the Social Democratic Party of Slovakia (SDPS), and the Party of the Greens (PG) signed an agreement to form a joint electoral alliance called the Slovak Democratic Coalition (SDC).

The Slovak Democratic Coalition gained overwhelming endorsements and support from individual member parties and their rank-and-file membership. The immediate reaction to the formation of SDC among the electorate was a shift of undecided voters among the parties of the alliance to SDC as well as a move of many undecided eligible voters and some supporters of PDL and the Hungarian Christian-Democratic Movement (HCDM) to SDC. A public opinion poll in July 1997 showed MDS with 27 percent and SDC with 34.2 percent support. By October 1997 the support for MDS had dropped to 25.2 percent while SDC's support stood at 31.1 percent.[23]

Of course, the ruling coalition in the government and parliament did not sit idly by and watch their influence diminish. After SDC was registered with the Central Election Commission (CEC) as a legitimate electoral entity for the forthcoming September 25–26, 1998, parliamentary elections, MDS attacked CEC and threatened to change the existing election law if CEC did not rescind its decision and declare SDC a coalition instead of a party. On May 20, 1998, the ruling coalition amended the election law to state that every political party, whether in a coalition or not, must receive 5 percent or more of the total votes cast in an election.[24] In practice it would have meant that SDC would need at least 25 percent of all votes (5 percent for each of the five party members) in order to qualify for representation in the NCSR. The SDC at once challenged this demand by MDS before the Supreme Court, which on August 14, 1998, ruled against MDS, thus enabling the SDC alliance to participate in the September 1998 elections as one party.[25]

In January 1998 a new political party, the Party of Civic Understanding (PCU), was organized. The chairman of the new party was a high-ranking member of the former Communist Party of Slovakia who from 1989 until June 26, 1990, had served as chairman of the Slovak National Council and since 1994 had been mayor of Kosice. This new party gained not only visibility but endorsement from a new class of "privatizers." In April 1998, when the party was officially registered with CEC, the PCU leaders emphasized their support for law and order, social justice, a consensus-seeking political style, and Slovakia's integration into NATO and EU; its support hovered between 13.4 percent (in April) and 16.5 percent (in July). But at whose expense? Surveys taken during that period revealed that as soon as PCU came into existence, SDC's support declined from 32.5 percent in February to 21.2 percent in July 1998, while the support for MDS rose from 22.7 percent to 25.9 percent.[26] It would appear that while the support for the five major parties remained constant after the creation of PCU, support for SDC suddenly declined and remained in the low 20 percentiles. The only consolation for SDC was the promise made by the PCU representatives "to cooperate mainly with the opposition, in order to defeat Meciar, and to reach a constitutional majority of the current opposition parties after the 1998 elections."[27] The main reason for SDC's decline in popular support after February 1998 (when PCU came into existence) may have been its lack of cohesion. As a relatively new political organization, SDC functioned more like an opposition bloc or election alliance than a disciplined political party. The leaders of the five former political parties in the SDC appear to have been too preoccupied with "consensus-seeking" procedures of decision making and too little concerned with building a solid base of followers.

Meanwhile, the cohesion of the ruling majority was also weakening. Disagreements on certain policy issues after 1997, like privatization and the aspiration for power among the leaders of the coalition parties, had caused the followers of the SNP and AWS to distance themselves from MDS. The ruling coalition's relations became asymmetrical: MDS followers were more sympathetic to SNP and AWS than vice versa. The unifying platform of the ruling coalitions followers in 1998 was its distance from the Party of the Hungarian Coalition (PHC) and SDC. While the supporters of the ruling coalition saw themselves a middle distance from the PDL, the adherents of PDL felt themselves a great distance from MDS, SNP, and PHC. Interestingly, by late 1997 relations among

SDC's party adherents had higher levels of cohesion than existed among the ruling coalition parties of MDS, SNP, and ASW.[28]

With President Kovac out of the way and most of the powers of the president usurped by the ruling coalition government, Vladimir Meciar embarked on a final journey to legitimize his monopoly of power at the ballot box during the parliamentary elections on September 25–26, 1998. Toward that end, in May 1998, the ruling coalition in parliament passed new amendments to the election law, which by reducing Slovakia's four electoral districts into one made it possible for Meciar's name to appear as a candidate on every ballot in the country. The same law increased the authority of the Ministry of the Interior to provide supervisory functions by using police and military units at the voting places. The law also increased the possibility that private media coverage of the elections would be unfairly and excessively restricted, and it made no provisions for domestic election observers. Although the new local election law was challenged in the Slovak Constitutional Court, its chairman, Milan Cic, refused to hear the case before the parliamentary elections, but on October 15, 1998, the Slovak Constitutional Court decided that many provisions of the recently amended local election law were at variance with the constitution. Cic hinted that, in order to permit the local elections scheduled for November 13 and 14 to take place, the new law would not be published in the *Law Digest* until after the elections so that the elections could be held under the currently valid law. The court described as unconstitutional the introduction of ethnic quotas for the division of mandates in municipal and communal councils and the banning of television and radio—with the exception of local stations—from taking part in the election campaign. It also called unconstitutional the requirement that an election candidate show proof of at least one year's residence in the town where the candidate was running. The provision that made it impossible for a candidate whose candidacy had been rejected to attend the court dispute over his or her case was also ruled unconstitutional.[29]

Officially the parliamentary election campaign started thirty days before the election day on September 25, 1998. Seventeen political parties and movements were competing for 150 seats in parliament. The official campaign airtime in the public media for the seventeen parties was twenty-one hours; however, because of the controversial new election law, throughout the campaign, the state Slovak Television (STV) gave the ruling coalition government and its parties 63.2 percent of its overall news coverage time, and only 13.4 percent for the four opposition parties. Memo 98, a nongovernmental organization made up of the Helsinki Citizens' Assembly and the Association for Support of Local Democracy, found that almost all coverage of the government (MDS and SNP) was presented in a favorable light and almost all coverage of the opposition was negative.

The progovernment bias in covering the election campaign became quite obvious in late August when the privately owned television station Markiza, a strong supporter of the government opposition, was abruptly taken over by Gamatex company, which owned 51 percent of its shares. This action, supported by the SIS and the Interior Ministry, resulted in the dismissal of its director, Pavol Rusko, and more than twenty employees. Broadcasts were suspended briefly. The reason for the takeover was obvious: Gamatex's bosses, Stefan Agh and Marian Kocner, were close friends of Vladimir Meciar. In mid-September, Markiza employees managed to broadcast a teletex appeal to viewers, asking them to come to the station. They did. They physically overcame the security guards and retook control of the station with the assistance of the crowds who responded to the appeal. Spontaneous rallies appeared in five major cities of Slovakia with crowds chanting, "Give us back our Markiza!" During the crisis, all Slovak opposition leaders also came to TV Markiza to show their support for the independent station. On the second day of the ruckus, the state police arrived but took no action.[30] Soon after order was restored, Markiza was fined 3.5 million Sk ($120,000) for televising the demonstration live, an act the Slovak Radio and Television Council said violated both the licensing agreement and the election law. In addition, Markiza was ordered to broadcast on three consecutive evenings a statement to viewers that it had broken the election law. And on September 23, a Bratislava regional court ruled that Marian Kocner should not have been given title to company shares.

The leaders of MDS were not overwhelmingly confident of victory, however, and they mobilized all their human and physical resources to secure a larger margin in 1998 than the one they achieved in 1994. As the campaign unfolded, it became more and more obvious that the divisions of left vs. right (reminiscent of 1990) or favoring vs. opposing Slovak independence (reminiscent of 1992) or liberal vs. conservative (reminiscent of 1994) had been replaced by two well-organized political forces: "Meciarism" vs. "anti-Meciarism."

The election campaign officially ended on September 23, 1998, leaving the required two-day cooling-off period before polls opened. The government decided to send 2,943 soldiers to reinforce the 20,000 policemen patrolling the 5,862 polling stations in more than 6,300 election wards. Also on September 23, three members of the European parliament, led by Jan Marinus Wiersma, left for Slovakia to join a larger Organization for Security and Cooperation in Europe (OSCE) parliamentary mission to observe the elections.

According to the Statistical Office of the Slovak Republic, 3,389,346 Slovak citizens cast their votes, which equaled 84.24 percent of participation—a new record for the four parliamentary elections since the Velvet Revolution. Although the election took place in an atmosphere of mistrust between the parties, the OSCE observers characterized the process as peaceful and orderly without any serious incidents.

The final official results of the election were released by the CEC on September 28, 1998 (see Table 16). Of the seventeen political parties, movements, and coalitions, only six met the required 5 percent minimum votes. Although MDS won a narrow victory over SDC as the leading single party, it lost the election because only the SNP was willing to enter into a coalition with MDS, which left Meciar's party short of the necessary majority to form a new government. That task was automatically shifted to the coalition of the four victorious opposition parties, which together gained 93 out of 150 seats in the new parliament—enough to guarantee them the constitutional changes they outlined in their campaign platforms, provided that one or more of them did not bolt and enter into a coalition with MDS. Vice Premier Sergej Kozlik

TABLE 16

RESULTS OF THE 1998 PARLIAMENTARY ELECTION

Parties	Votes (%)	Seats
Movement for a Democratic Slovakia (MDS)	27.00	43
Slovak Democratic Coalition (SDC)	26.33	42
Party of the Democratic Left (PDL)	14.66	23
Party of the Hungarian Coalition (PHC)	9.12	15
Slovak National Party (SNP)	9.07	14
Party for Civil Understanding (PCU)	8.01	13
Others	5.81	0
Total	100.00	150

SOURCE: *Narodna obroda*, September 28, 1988, and *Statisticky urad SR*, 1998.

announced that MDS as the single majority party "will act as the victor and in addition to its existing coalition partner—the SNP—MDS will also approach the leaders of both the PDL and the PCU in order to form the new government."[31]

In spite of the declaration on September 27 by the four opposition parties that they would maintain solidarity and determination to form the next government, a few days later leaders of the PDL made a few attempts to sound out their partners on issues close to their interests. The PDL leaders, such as Robert Fico, questioning the loyalty of the Hungarian minority, were trying to determine whether the new government could be formed without the inclusion of the PHC. PDL leaders thought that by keeping the coalition down to three parties they could gain more ministerial posts in the new government. When news of this leaked out, the Hungarian leaders were outraged; this innuendo reminded them of the same tactics used not long ago by Meciarism.[32] During the first few postelection days, when party leaders were jockeying for position, MDS's spokesman Jan Smerek made several overtures to the PDL leadership hoping to lure the party into a coalition with the MDS and the SNP, but these overtures were immediately rejected by PDL spokesman Lubomir Andrassy as well as by the party's leader, Jozef Migas. Similar rejections came from the PCU.

It took Vladimir Meciar three days after the votes were in to appear on Slovak Television to say with tears in his eyes that he would not try to form a new government and would resign as premier on October 29, 1998, the day on which the newly elected parliament convened. At the end of the broadcast he sang a short song to the viewers: "Farewell, I leave you. I never hurt, I never hurt any of you." The victorious opposition leaders considered such a late date of resignation—although constitutionally acceptable as the last day within the thirty-day limit—an insult to the nation. Even though the Meciar coalition had lost the election and Meciar had promised to step aside from politics, on October 3 the MDS meeting in Krajne confirmed that Meciar would continue as chairman of his party. Meciar then made several hasty appointments of new ambassadors, although the victorious opposition called on the new appointees to wait and see whether they would be approved by the new government.

Meanwhile, on October 6, PDL thought better of its idea of forming a new government without the PHC; after a meeting, the two parties issued a joint statement reaffirming their committment to the statement from the democratic roundtable of September 27, according to which "SDC, PDL, PHC and PCU expressed their determination to create . . . a new Slovak government for the next four years."[33] Apparently, it had dawned on the leaders of the PDL that the country was in grave economic difficulties and that an absolute majority in the parliament with PHC's participation in the government was not only a precondition to the future success of Slovakia but also a necessity. One week after the joint statement, Bela Bugar for the PHC and Pavol Hamzik for the PCU called for speedier talks on the formation of a new cabinet and for a coalition agreement to be signed before October 29—the last constitutionally sanctioned date for the new parliament to meet in session.

The leader of the SDC, Mikulas Dzurinda, made it known that the organization and makeup of the parliament would meet democratic standards; Meciar used the opportunity to claim the post of the speakership in the new parliament based on the principle of proportional representation. Dzurinda's response was brief and to the point: "I would have been delighted to hear you utter such a statement on the night of November 3–4, 1994. Had you followed such guidelines during the last four years, without any doubt Slovakia would have been far more advanced in democracy."[34] Meciar's defeated coalition partner Jan Slota, speaking for the SNP, also demanded a vice chair position in parliament and chairmanship of the committee on defense and the overseeing committee on SIS. As late as October 26, the party leaders of SDC and PDL, who were still negotiating the formation of the new coalition government, revealed that they would be willing to see their coalition partners, the PHC and the PCU, acquire more than two ministerial positions each. Finally, after marathon negotiations, in the early hours of October 28, the coalition partners announced their formula for the cabinet: 9:6:3:3—the numbers reflecting the votes for the parties in the recent election.[35]

The agreement designated Mikulas Dzurinda (SDC) as the new premier. The four deputy premiers were Lubomir Fogas (PDL) in charge of legislation, Pal Csaky (PHC) in charge of ethnic minorities and human rights, Ivan Miklos (SDC) in charge of economy, and Pavol Hamzik (PCU) in charge of European integration. In addition, the SDC was given the following ministerial posts: foreign affairs (Eduard Kukan), economic (Ludovit Cernak), interior (Ladislav Pittner), culture (Milan Knazko), transport and communications (Gabriel Palacka), justice (Jan Carnogursky), and health (Tibor Sagat). The PDL received the ministries of finance (Brigita Schmoegnerova), defense (Pavol Kanis), agriculture (Pavel Koncos), education (Milan Ftacnik), and social affairs (Peter Magvasi). The PHC was assigned the ministries of the environment (Laszlo Miklos) and construction and public works (Istvan Harna). The PCU received the ministry of privatization (Maria Machova).[36]

The four-party coalition also agreed to nominate Jozef Migas (PDL) for the speaker of the new parliament and Pavol Hrusovsky (SDC), Bela Bugar (PHC), and Igor Presperin (PCU) for deputy speakers. The new opposition—MDS and SNP—was given one of the four deputy speaker posts in the new parliament. According to the leader of the SNP, Jan Slota, his party's first choice for the position of the deputy speaker of parliament was Marian Andel; if he failed to receive the required votes, A. Malikova was the second choice. Neither Meciar nor any other representative of the MDS attended the organizational meeting of the new parliament, although the party leaders were in the building holding their parliamentary club meeting at that time. The outgoing speaker, Ivan Gasparovic (MDS), said it was not necessary for MDS to attend the organizational meeting because the MDS leaders had already submitted the names for the speaker of the parliament (Peter Brnak) and the names for the five committee chairs (constitutional-legal, financial, agricultural, defense, and social).

In the absence of the MDS representatives, the four-party coalition also announced that the SDC would chair five committees: defense (Vladimir Palko), integration (Frantisek Sebej), economic (Jaroslav Volf), human resources (Ladislav Ambros), and education and science (Lubomir Harach). The PDL was designated to chair three parliamentary committees: constitutional-legal (Ladislav Orosz), foreign affairs (Peter Weiss), and mandate and immunity (Viliam Sopko). The PHC was designated to chair two committees: finance (Istvan Hama) and human and civil rights (Laszlo Nagy). The PCU was also given two committee chairs: agriculture (Maria Kadlecikova) and public administration (Dusan Kovacic). At the same time the four-party coalition made an offer to the new opposition parties (MDS and SNP) to chair four standing committees: health, culture and the media, reconciliations, and social relations, as well as two special committees: one for overseeing the SIS and the other the military intelligence. Should the MDS refuse to accept any of the offered chairmanships, according to the SNP leader Jan Slota, his party would be willing to fill those positions.[37]

AFTER TEN YEARS,
AN ARDUOUS BEGINNING

The new Dzurinda government was sworn in during the inaugural session of parliament on October 29, 1998, the day after the victorious party leaders signed an agreement on the composition of the coalition government. It was a festive occasion filled with great optimism and jubilation. The new "coalition of coalitions" united ten of the seventeen political parties, whose reason for coming together was to deny Meciar another four years of authoritarian rule. The diversity of the new coalition government, manifested in different size, ideological orientation, and minority participation, had delayed its formation up to the final moment, and some Slovak pundits predicted that such a disparate government would need a strong opponent to keep it united. But since neither Meciar nor the SNP was willing to participate constructively in the political process, the new coalition of coalitions found itself from the very beginning wrangling with one another rather than with the opposition.

The members of the new coalition government realized that the next four years, 1998–2002, would be difficult because of the disarray caused by Meciarism and because of the urgent need to tackle such major problems as the vacancy in the office of the president, the deteriorating fiscal and economic situation in the country, abuses in privatization and ownership practices, the loss of respect for law and constitutionalism, the cumbersome system of state institutions, the disregard for minority rights, and the rise in crime and corruption. During the first few months of the new government, it became evident that there were disagreements on some of these issues, not only among the members of the government but among the parties. The coalition parties well knew that in giving them an overwhelming majority, the voters expected them to resolve most of the problems created by Meciarism on a consensus basis, and the October agreement that recognized those expectations was a pledge of harmony to implement their campaign promises and commitments. In other words, before the Dzurinda coalition assumed power, the new leaders were in agreement about the fundamental issues and the remedies required to eliminate the vestiges of Meciarism and restore democratic principles in the country.

The Dzurinda coalition's program presented to the parliament in

November included the acknowledgment of a mandate to change the social conditions in Slovakia within a framework of national revival supported by effective democratic institutions, economic modernization, and expanded Slovak participation in the global community. More specifically, the goals included the strengthening of the competitive economic system; the creation of opportunities for a higher standard of living; improved conditions for justice and freedom; protection of the citizens' lives, health, and ownership; a critical evaluation of the conditions inherited from the Meciar government; the creation of a legal framework for the prevention of any discrimination against citizens; and the inclusion of Slovakia into the OECD, NATO, and the EU. The Dzurinda government also promised immediate intervention against organized crime, a review of the effectiveness of the constitution and proposals for constitutional changes, the introduction of direct elections for the head of state, election reforms, and the strengthening of the independence of the judiciary and the prosecutors.

In early February 1999, when the heads of the various ministries finished their evaluations of the state of affairs in their particular sectors of the government, the Dzurinda government issued a *Black Book* that presented an analysis of economic and social conditions in Slovakia after Meciar. Two months earlier, Premier Mikulas Dzurinda had nullified all amnesties granted by his predecessor in March 1998 to the persons implicated in the abduction of Michal Kovac, Jr., and to the person who prevented the passage of the referendum in May 1997. At the same time, the Ministry of the Interior under Ladislav Pittner reopened the investigation into the abduction case. In response, the opposition, headed by MDS, unleashed a strong criticism against the new coalition government. While Dzurinda was defending his decision against the opposition, some leaders of the ruling coalition from the PDL openly complained that Dzurinda as premier and temporary president failed to consult with the rest of the coalition partners before announcing his decision. The MDS arguments about the misuse of Dzurinda's powers were similar to those used by the opposition against Meciar in 1998, except that whereas Meciar tried to protect the criminals, Dzurinda was trying to bring the criminals to justice. The state secretary of the Ministry of Justice, Jan Mazak, recognizing that under democracy there was no institution in the country that could strip Meciar of his right to remain silent, recommended that investigators resign from their positions before they offered Meciar's testimony into evidence. However, this recommendation did not satisfy the investigators because by August 1999 the director of the investigation department at the Ministry of the Interior, Jaroslav Ivor, sought approval in the parliament to indict the former director of SIS, Ivan Lexa, for alleged criminal acts committed against the state and its people in connection with the 1995 abduction of Michal Kovac, Jr. Ivor also asked the parliament for permission to interrogate former premier Meciar and former president Michal Kovac. He added that the latter had already offered full cooperation in this case.[38] The request for Meciar's testimony was based on a telephone conversation between Ivan Lexa and former Devin Banka director Karol Martinka, which supposedly implicated Meciar in influencing the investigation of the abduction of Michal Kovac, Jr.

Although the parliament approved the request to relieve Meciar of his secrecy oath and thus allow the police to question him about the abduction and about the contents of an SIS report dated May 26, 1995, which elaborated three ways the government could remove former president Kovac from office,[39] Meciar insisted that he would not testify and that the parliament had no right to force him to do so. He said he would go on a hunger strike if detained and questioned. The MDS joined Meciar by promising to call for a no-confidence vote in Interior Minister Ladislav Pittner and to organize mass protests.

In the meantime, on December 20, 1999, the First Senate of the Slovak Constitutional Court in Kosice rendered an opinion in the case of Jaroslav Svechota, former vice director of SIS, who was being investigated by a criminal section of the Ministry of the Interior and the regional office of the procurator in Bratislava in connection with the 1995 abduction of Michal Kovac, Jr. According to the presiding judge, Tibor Safarik, both institutions violated Svechota's constitutional rights because he had received amnesty. The court decision based its reasoning on the rule of irreversibility of constitutionally sanctioned decisions rendered by heads of state. Dzurinda's nullification of the amnesties in the Kovac case issued by Meciar was in conflict with the rule because, according to Judge Safarik, the constitution does not allow a constitutional decision to be voided retroactively.

Not so, according to a long list of leading Slovak constitutional lawyers, who vehemently disagreed with the opinion of Safarik's court. In their response, the constitutional lawyers stated that it should have been equally impossible for the court to accept the explanation of the past effectiveness of the constitution as recommended by the representatives of MDS in the NCSR. They also pointed out that it was wrong for the court to rely on a constitutional precedent for explaining Dzurinda's decision about the nullification of Meciar's amnesties when such provisions were not yet included in the constitution. According to the critics, Svechota's appeal to the constitutional court should have been rejected because he failed to exhaust all other remedies available to him in the Slovak legal system. They rejected the argument that Safarik's decision was also applicable to Ivan Lexa and others involved in the Kovac case. The critics maintained that the constitutional court could decide cases beyond the scope of the person who lodged the complaint.[40]

Shortly after the court decision and the criticism expressed by the leading constitutional lawyers, the party leadership of the Christian Democratic Movement (CDM) decided to request that Minister of Justice Jan Carnogursky introduce a constitutional law according to which the amnesty issued by Meciar could be nullified and the abduction of Michal Kovac, Jr., investigated. Although the vice chairman of MDS, V. Tkac, dismissed this move as legal nonsense, most party leaders of the "coalition of coalitions" in power expressed support for the proposal, though they were not clear about its stipulation.[41] In early January 2000 such a proposal was prepared with the stipulation that Meciar's and Dzurinda's decisions about amnesties both be nullified. Since the legislative council of the government would not support such a proposal, by the end of January it became obvious that the CDM proposal would fail.[42] Whatever the future course of action will be, one thing is clear: the legal and political tug-of-war between the pro- and anti-Meciar groups will continue for a long time to come. For the time being, the anti-Meciar lawmakers will have to struggle over Slovakia's transition from a totalitarian system to a democratic one.

As for Ivan Lexa, Gustav Krajci, and company, justice has not yet caught up with them, although Lexa, the former director of SIS, has been in and out of jail since April 15, 1999, when he was taken into pretrial custody. On June 20, 1999, Lexa's boss, the former minister of the interior Gustav Krajci, was indicted on charges that he interfered with the May 1997 referendum on direct presidential elections and NATO membership, that he abused the public trust vested in his office, and that he willfuly falsified and changed the public ballot. As of January 2000, Krajci had not been tried or convicted.

In the fall of 1998, the new Dzurinda government also had to face the urgent and critical problem of economic and financial disaster inherited from the Meciar period. Four years of Meciarism resulted in rising debt to foreign lenders, massive fiscal deficits, a weakened Slovak koruna, fraud, and rising unemployment. The reserves of the National Bank of Slovakia in mid-September 1998 were as low as 50,000 Sk. Fifty percent of the loans were government loans and corporation loans with state guarantees—a higher figure than in the neighboring countries. With a shortfall of almost 20 billion Sk in the state budget, 1998 was the worst year for the Slovak economy since its independence. The total foreign debt reached 11.8 billion, and the balance of trade was a minus 3.2 billion. Slovakia had become a debtor nation.[43] The reasons for the higher than planned state budget deficit were the extravagant capital expenditures on large infrastructure projects and lower revenue taxes from the value-added and consumption taxes.

To tackle the financial problems, on October 1, 1998, the National Bank of Slovakia introduced a free floating system by abolishing the fluctuation of the Slovak koruna and canceling its fixed regime, which had been pegged to a mark/dollar currency basket. As a result, the koruna was devalued by 17 percent before it stabilized and lost only 13.83 percent of its value by the end of 1998. The change in fiscal policy probably saved Slovakia from a currency crisis and a declaration of insolvency. Because of the new currency policy, Slovakia was now able to lower its interest rate and banks were able to finance the growing demand for loans. When, in spite of these efforts, the state-owned banks had far worse results in 1998 than in 1997, the Dzurinda government initiated a bank restructuring program for the three major state-owned banks—Vseobecna Uverova Banka, Investicna a Rozvojova Banka, and Slovenska Sporitelna—which represented about half of the total assets and nearly 64 percent of the total loans in the Slovak bank market at the end of Meciar's rule. The nonperforming loans of the three banks amounted to about 100 billion Sk of the over 130 billion Sk in bad loans held by the entire Slovak banking sector.[44] The government projection for the completion of the restructuring of the three state-owned banks was set for the end of the year 2000. After that a full privatization of the banks should commence.

Since Slovak membership in both the EU and OECD were priority objectives of the Dzurinda government, on January 7 and May 31, 1999, two austerity packages were introduced in order to restore fiscal discipline, reduce budgetary expenditures, increase revenues, raise the value-added tax, impose an import surcharge, and deregulate prices leading to increased state revenues. The price for Dzurinda's belt-tightening program was a rise in unemployment from 13.9 percent in 1998 to 17.7 percent in 1999, a reduction in GDP from 6.1 to 2.4 percent, an increase in inflation from 6.2 to 14 percent, a reduction in both exports and imports, a huge reduction in the unfavorable balance of trade from a minus $122.8 million to a minus $65 million, a favorable current account balance from a minus $1.244 billion to $764 million, a reduction of interest rates from 28.4 to 14.5 percent, and a currency exchange devaluation of the Slovak koruna from 35.9 in 1998 to 41.6 for $1.00 in 1999.[45]

In spite of the hardship caused by high unemployment and price increases in the cost of living, the young Dzurinda government persevered in forging ahead with economic and fiscal policies it hoped would transform the economy into a viable, modern, competitive system with an assured place in the global economy. With this objective in mind, the austerity program of the Dzurinda government was followed by two important legislative acts. On September 16, 1999, parliament passed the law on strategic companies canceling the not-for-sale status of state monopolies, paving the way for their privatization. And on November 24, 1999, parliament approved a law cutting the corporate tax rate from 40 percent to 29 percent. These and other actions were considered to be long overdue and essential for the transformation of the Slovak economy into a respectable market economy. In about one year the Dzurinda government had succeeded in a macroeconomic turnaround, bringing Slovakia back from the brink of disaster to the verge of respectability. However, in order to avoid high inflation, economists argue that the government will have to press ahead with price deregulation, cutting state budget expenditures and, within the third austerity package approved at the end of 1999, to reform social benefits, pension schemes, and the school and health sectors, and to reduce the size of the huge government bureaucracy.[46] The balance sheet of economic achievements during the first year of the Dzurinda government offers a mixed picture. Although economists and intellectuals in Slovakia praise Mikulas Dzurinda for grappling with the unsolved economic and fiscal problems inherited from the Meciar government, most of the population is unhappy about rising unemployment; increased prices of commodities, rent, and fuel; and lower real income. Even so, most Slovaks see no other alternative because they do not wish to return to the economic policies of the Meciar period.

Another compelling effort of the Dzurinda government to repair damages inflicted by the Meciar regime was to fulfill the promises made in the election campaign with regard to just and transparent privatization processes. It did not take long for the public to discover that privatization strengthened not the economy but the political parties that were in power. Before the parliamentary elections in 1998, almost all opposition political parties cited the need to reexamine the legality of Meciar's privatization practices with an objective of recovering state losses. His promise to the voters was also included in the declaration of the program issued by the victorious "coalition of coalitions." In 1998 the reconstituted NPF began to implement these practices, but not for long. Although the Dzurinda-appointed NPF filed several charges against former NPF members for knowingly defrauding the state, privatization—which is still a scareword in Slovakia identified with corruption and crime—was in 1999 still criticized for the lack of transparency, machinations behind the scenes, and shady dealings. Examples of the problems with privatization include Slovenske Telekomunicacie, GSM 1800, and Nafta Gbely.

Slovenske Telekomunicacie was the first company to permit a foreign bidder to enter into a Slovak strategic partnership and to acquire up to 49 percent shares in ownership. The controversy developed when telecom minister Gabriel Palacka in April 1999 selected the giant Deutsche Bank as the head of a consortium to advise on privatization of Slovenske Telekomunicacie. The other members of the consortium selected by Deutsche Bank included financial analysts Slavia Capital and Wood & Comp. and legal advisers White and Case to advise on the sale of a minority share in Slovenske Telekomunicacie to a strategic partner. Palacka and Deutsche Bank were criticized by the media for alleged personal ties between economy minister Ludovit Cernak and Slavia Capital.[47] Firms that lost the potential contract with Deutsche Bank spoke of a "conspiracy theory." In August, when it was discovered that the tender had violated the Slovak commercial code as well as other nontransparent procedural violations, telecom minister and SDC member Gabriel Palacka had to resign.[48] A similar nontransparent violation occurred in the selection of the operator of the mobile network Globtel GSM 1800, where the Telenor company was excluded from competitive bidding.

The most controversarial case involving high governmental officials is the privatization of Nafta Gbely, an oil refinery. In 1997, in spite of Premier Meciar's denial, it became known that Vladimir Poor, head of the regional organization of MDS in Trnava, was one of the owners of Druha Obchodna, which controlled Nafta Gbely. In early 1999 Poor announced that he planned to sell his shares in Druha Obchodna, and a short time later Premier Dzurinda announced that his government was working on the return of part of the assets of Nafta Gbely to NPF.[49] During legal scrutiny of the sale of 45.9 percent of shares of Nafta Gbely (500 million Sk valued at 3.2 billion Sk) to the undisclosed owners of Druha Obchodna, it became obvious that it was in violation of the privatization act of 1991 because all shares were sold to private owners and the action violated the commercial code and price laws. In the beginning of March 1999, after NPF brought charges against Druha Obchodna, the executive officers of the two institutions agreed that Druha Obchodna would return 40.9 percent and keep 5 percent of the Nafta Gbely shares. That deal would have permitted Vladimir Poor to retain part of his shares in Nafta Trade, a subsidiary of Nafta Gbely, which he controlled. In the meantime, Poor sold another subsidiary of Nafta Gbely, Arad, to unknown buyers, who turned out to be the refinery company Konsorcium IPB-A11, which represented the Cincinnati-based Cinergy Company. After it was learned that four imposters from Moravia (the Czech Republic) dealing with Economy Minister Ludovit Cernak had presented themselves as representatives of Cinergy Global Resources, the Dzurinda government ruled the sale invalid and promised to take legal action. Then in August 1999, lawyers representing Vladimir Poor submitted to the MPF a written statement in which Poor stated that he had canceled all contracts for the sale of the Nafta Gbely refinery to Konsorcium IPT-K11. The lawyers and MPF agreed that Poor's 45.9 percent stake in Nafta Gbely would be transferred back to MPF in an out-of-court settlement.[50] Finally, just before Christmas Day in 1999, the Dzurinda government approved the sale of a 45.9 percent package of Nafta Gbely shares to Slovensky Plynarensky Priemysel.

The fallout from the Nafta Gbely privatization process during the Dzurinda administration resulted in several casualties. At the end of June 1999, the president Ludovit Kanik and vice president Ladislav Sklenar of NPF were asked to resign. Kanik refused to do so unless the cabinet admitted that its censure of him was "a purely political matter"; he placed the blame on Economy Minister Ludovit Cernak for failing to secure all Nafta Gbely shares for the government.[51] This was also the feeling of the deputy premier for economy, Ivan Miklos. Premier Dzurinda blamed primarily the top leaders of NPF. By mid-October, the evidence against Ludovit Cernak in the Nafta Gbely case and other affairs was convincing enough to force Cernak's resignation. He was replaced by Lubomir Harach.

Although the Dzurinda government was praised for its early efforts to introduce democratic changes into the privatization process and to rectify some of the damage done by the Meciar regime, people began to lose their optimism. By mid-1999, after the media exposed scandals, incompetence, greed, corruption, and even mafia ties to privatization,[52] the embittered public lost confidence in the new regime and began to equate it with the Meciar government. If privatization was supposed to contribute to the restructuring of the Slovak industry and thus to the improvement of its output, then privatization in Slovakia has failed. Most of the new business owners are bureaucrats and politicos who have no business experience or management expertise, and they run outmoded and uncapitalized enterprises on an artificial basis, causing depreciation in their values and usefulness. Privatization has become a source of personal greed and temporary enrichment mostly for those in power.[53]

One positive action that has fulfilled election promises has been to give voters the right to elect their president directly. As promised, in January 1999, parliament approved a constitutional change mandating direct presidential elections, and in March it approved the procedural requirements for electing the head of state. At the same time the speaker of the NCSR, Jozef Migas (PDL), announced the date for the first round of elections as May 15, 1999, with May 29 for a second round if one was needed. Ten candidates met the legally prescribed requirements. Three candidates (Rudolf Schuster, Vladimir Meciar, and Jan Slota) were nominated by NCSR deputies; the remaining seven, including Michal Kovac, were registered by petitions. The last-minute nomination of Meciar by MDS upset the campaign strategy of all the other candidates by 180 degrees. They now had to make certain that Meciar did not win the elections by default or because of squabbling among the other candidates. After an initiative by the SDC to form coalitions among the anti-Meciar candidates, known as "three for one," failed, Michal Kovac withdrew his candidacy and asked for support for Rudolf Schuster.

No candidate received the required 50 percent of votes in the first election on May 15. The two candidates with the highest number of votes—Rudolf Schuster with 47.3 percent and Vladimir Meciar with 37.2 percent—became designated candidates for the second round on May 29. These results indicated that the voters in Slovakia were polarized into two major blocks: one for the "coalition of coalitions," the other for the Meciar coalition. The rest of the candidates were not considered pivotal or sufficiently unified to represent a swing bloc. The second round was therefore viewed primarily as a plebiscite for or against Meciar's return to power. On May 29 the 75.45 percent of voters who participated in the first direct presidential election cast 57.18 percent of their votes for Schuster and 42.8 percent for Meciar.[54] The coalition of coalitions was jubilant about Schuster's victory and hopeful that this was Meciar's last hurrah; MDS spokesmen and several prognosticators felt that Meciar, with 1.3 million votes, had actually gained strength when compared with the September 1998 election results. Opinion polls showed that the privatization scandals, the two austerity packages, and other problems plaguing the Dzurinda coalition had made MDS once again the most popular party in the country.[55] In his inaugural speech President Schuster emphasized more than once that he planned to represent not only the alliance of parties that supported him but also the opposition.

Another successful achievement for the Dzurinda government in 1999 was the extended European Union invitation to begin negotiations for entry into its body. Slovakia, like Romania, Bulgaria, Lithuania, Latvia, and Malta, now has the opportunity to prepare for accession by fulfilling the twenty-nine "chapters" of the *acquis communautaire*, a body of legal and administrative standards common to EU countries. Slovakia's EU negotiator, Deputy Foreign Minister Jan Figel, has projected 2005 as the year when all twenty-nine chapters of the *acquis* will be more or less compatible with Slovakia's preparatory work for accession; Premier Dzurinda would like to see it done by 2003 so that Slovakia could be admitted to the EU at the same time as the three other members of the Visegrad Group (Czechoslovakia, Hungary, Poland), which began EU entry negotiations in April 1998.[56] Dzurinda's eagerness and enthusiasm were noticed by President of the European Commission Romano Prodi on his visit to Bratislava on January 20, 2000: when Dzurinda's government began to suggest that the EU might begin to negotiate as many as fifteen chapters of the *acquis*, Prodi jokingly remarked that it looked like the number of chapters for Slovaks was "more important than sex." Even so, Prodi announced that the EU would open no more that five of the *acquis'* total thirty chapters with Slovakia in February 2000.[57]

In spite of tremendous handicaps, in the short space of one year the

Dzurinda government regained the credibility and support in the global community that the country lost during the Meciar period. Foreign Minister Eduard Kukan was optimistic. Potential for membership in the OECD in the near future and NATO by 2001 or 2002 are promising.[58] Of course, whether these and many other expectations will be realized will depend on the stability, cooperation, and leadership of the coalition of coalitions in government and the success of democratic transition in Slovakia.

CAN THE COALITION OF THE COALITION GOVERNMENT PREVAIL?

In October 1998, when the eight coalition parties were declared the overwhelming winners of the parliamentary elections, their respective leaders were aware that stability was an essential requirement for the success of their newly elected government. They signed a pledge to that effect. They pledged to adhere to the agreed rules in inter- and intra-coalition relations, to work toward the smooth functioning of parliamentary democracy, and to agree on foreign policy. They also were aware that taking opposing stands on key socioeconomic issues or exercising self-aggrandizement at the expense of coalition policy would be harmful to the stability of the coalition.

From the time its first bill was introduced in parliament, the Dzurinda coalition government expected the opposition parties (MDS and SNP) to engage in constructive criticism within the political process. But with Meciar absent from the political arena, the government found itself debating bills and programs largely within the coalition itself. These internal squabbles meant that the ruling coalition was unable to speak to voters with a unified voice or to be effective in promoting austerity measures, language law reform, privatization of strategically important enterprises, and so on. In March 1999, for instance, agriculture minister Pavel Koncos (PDL) threatened to sue PHC leader and deputy speaker of parliament Bela Bugar for libel during a dispute over the directorship of the Land Fund. On July 10, 1999, "after parliament had approved a PDL-amended minority language law over the objections of PHC, PDL deputies rose and joined the opposition (MDS and SNP) members in signing the nationalist song 'Hej Slovaci,' in apparent provocation of their Hungarian colleagues."[59]

On other occasions the squabbles turned into more serious disputes and disagreements, visibly dividing the coalition into splinter groups. But by then Vladimir Meciar had emerged from seclusion and as MDS leader was directing his party to exploit the divisions in the government coalition. With public opinion polls showing 30 percent support compared with 13 percent for the SDC, MDS was making predictions that Meciar would return to power, replacing a Dzurinda government plagued by disunity and scandals. The reference was to such occurrences as the disagreements among the five party leaders within the SDC (CDM, DU, DP, PG, and SDPS) on deciding what policies their deputies should or should not support while the coalition partners (PDL, PHC, and PCU) were left guessing. The scandals referred to the privatization debate when the DP faction of the SDC declared that it would not support Premier Dzurinda's decision to remove NPF president Ludovit Kanik in the Nafta Gbely case. As a result of the dispute over Kanik's removal, eighteen SDC deputies (from the CDM) opposed the government position and another eight (from the CDM) voted against new privatization. In March 1999, eight and in May still more Christian Democrat deputies left in protest at having to support Rudolf Schuster for president. The SDC was also divided on the drafting of the law on privatization of strategic industries, which would have allowed the sale of state utilities and banks to foreign investors. The PDL insisted that state ownership of certain utilities be guaranteed by law; the DP members of the SDC refused to accept anything less than full privatization. Even a compromise law was refused by six deputies.[60]

By September 6, 1999, the situation within the SDC coalition party was so frustrating that its chairman, Premier Dzurinda, decided to return to his former Christian Democrat party (CDM); his explanation for the move was concern for how the party was being run by his former political rival, justice minister and CDM chairman Jan Carnogursky. Dzurinda was referring to the latest public opinion polls, which placed CDM behind PDL, the former communist party. Dzurinda claimed that he never intended to build SDC into a separate party, and certainly the trend within the SDC since the parliamentary elections of 1998 has been for members of the coalition to resume their former political identities. The other three members of the ruling coalition—PHC, PDL, and PCU—are concerned that if SDC splits into its five founding members, the coalition agreements signed as a party in November 1998 may become invalid. It is no wonder that MDS has renewed its desire to have early parliamentary elections in Slovakia.[61]

Following this new crisis, the logical questions of who will make policy and how in the SDC camp in the future became moot. Although under the Slovak parliamentary system each party has a deputies club to which all its MPs belong, the SDC deputies club was, for all practical purposes, window dressing long before this crisis erupted. The spokesmen of the SDC may pretend that their party is united, but they know that it is fragmented. Rumblings from both PCU and PDL were heard as early as mid-September 1999. Since the three coalition partners could not rule with the SDC, no matter how unauthoritative or unsuccessful, they have had no choice but to tolerate the status quo. But for how long?

Although the general public was made to believe that the political scene in Slovakia was calm and stable, behind the scene, politicians of all orientations were scampering around to find their niche in the shifting political power constellation. The situation became so fluid that even MDS contemplated transforming itself from a movement into a party. However, most party leaders in the coalition of coalitions government expressed no interest in negotiating with MDS as long as Vladimir Meciar was its head. On December 23, 1999, in an attempt to quell further rumors and speculations about the weaknesses of the ruling coalition, all five member parties of the SDC as well as its leader, Mikulas Dzurinda, signed an agreement "to agree." The agreement called for support of the Dzurinda government, the creation of a six-member council to meet at least once every two months to discuss all political questions its members felt necessary, and a pledge not to break up the SDC parliamentary club. But it remained unclear whether the agreement meant a return of the SDC party to a five-member coalition of parties or its continuance as a single party, which signed the coalition agreement with PDL, PHC, and PCU in October 1998. The former status, of course, could have created all sorts of legal complications. Thus, some observers concluded that the agreement was primarily a public relations ploy to improve SDC's image among the voters.[62]

The guessing game about Dzurinda's hedging whether or not SDC is a party or a coalition of parties was clarified on January 17, 2000. On that day, he announced the creation of a new political party, the Slovak Democratic and Christian Union (SDCU), which he would like to use in the 2002 parliamentary elections. Until then, according to the premier, SDC should maintain status quo. The declaration about the aims to retain the continuity of the SDC and the creation of the new party was signed by eleven politicians from all coalition parties in the SDC except the DP.[63] Although the followers of a spontaneous initiative known as the Association of Voters for SDC (established nine days later) were jubilant at having finally been able to speed up the transformation of SDC into a creditable political party, the party leaders in the SDC coalition considered the move destabilizing for SDC and devisive of the democratic forces in Slovakia.[64] With this new division in the leadership ranks of the SDC, it became questionable whether the six-member leadership council of the SDC, created on December 23, 1999, would still have any validity. Thus it was surmised that hereafter Premier Dzurinda would have to seek support for his government from the leadership councils of the coalition parties or directly from the parliamentary clubs of the parties within the SDC, even though the parliamentary club of the SDC remained intact. With the exception of the Party of the Greens (PG), the majority of the forty-two deputies in other coalition parties of the SDC parliamentary club were against Dzurinda's initiative. So were the leaders of the opposition parties (MDS and SNP). According to the vice chairman of the MDS, V. Tkac, Dzurinda's announcement of the creation of SDCU signified the collapse of the SDC and therefore the call for early elections was justifiable. Similar reaction came from the chairwoman of SNP, A. Malikova, who recently replaced Jan Slota; she accused Dzurinda of covering up the chaos and mistakes committed by SDC.[65]

Prompted by these events, on February 1, 2000, President Schuster met with Vladimir Meciar for the fourth time since taking office. According to Meciar, they spent two hours discussing a possible referendum on early parliamentary elections, during which Schuster promised to seek advice on the legality of the question to be put to voters. Shortly after the meeting, MDS announced its petition drive to collect the required 350,000 signatures in order to force the hand of the president to call a referendum. The previous attempt by MDS to nullify the June 1999 passage by parliament of a minority language law failed when Schuster declared that the referendum question was against the constitution. This time Schuster's response to Meciar's initiative was that, though he did not support early elections, he did not have the right to prevent them. Legal experts were critical of President Schuster for promising Meciar to seek legal advice on the referendum question, which would amount to taking responsibility for a plebiscite on himself.

Critics have also argued that the Slovak Constitutional Court (SCC) could only render opinions on cases that had been referred to it on the basis of a dispute or complaint and not on the basis of a friendly request for advice. Furthermore, the government would be prohibited from challenging the legality of a referendum approved by the president on the basis of the court's previous ruling; the law also forbids the president to consult with SCC members on such matters.[66]

Although it is unlikely that a referendum on early elections would be successful, Meciar and his MDS are managing to create divisions in the ranks of the coalition by exploiting the democratic process and, by doing so, slowing down the progress of transition to democracy in Slovakia. There are several reasons for the failure of the referendum. According to a January 2000 poll by IVO, over 57 percent of Slovak citizens are not in favor of a referendum on early elections; the constitution requires 50 percent participation of registered voters for its results to be considered valid. Approval of a referendum would require a constitutional amendment to shorten parliament's term in office—highly unlikely when the Dzurinda government controls 92 of the 150 votes in parliament. Even so, while the coalition of the coalition government is growing more divided and weaker, the opposition parties headed by Meciar and Malikova are becoming more united and stronger.[67]

As a result of the increasing fragility of the ruling coalition, in August and October 1999, two new political parties (Party of the Democratic Center and the Direction Party) were added to the list of twenty-two organizations competing for votes. The Democratic Center is headed by Ivan Mjartan, former MDS member and Slovak ambassador to Prague from 1993 to 1998; Direction is led by Robert Fico, a former deputy for the PDL. Fico's party is more to the left, with a populist bend bordering on racist sentiments. Both party leaders met with Meciar in January 2000 and supported his goal of forcing early elections.[68] According to a public opinion poll taken in late January 2000 by Markant, MDS was leading the pack with 32.2 percent, followed by Direction with 14.3 percent, Dzurinda's SDCU 13.6 percent, PHC 8.0 percent, SNP 7.2 percent, PDL 5.3 percent, PCU 4.4 percent, Democratic Center 3.7 percent, CDM 2.7 percent, DP 2.7 percent, DU 2.4 percent, Communist Party of Slovakia 1.5 percent, Workers Association of Slovakia 0.7 percent, PG 0.5 percent, SDPS 0.2 percent, and others 1.7 percent.[69] As this survey shows, the present coalition of coalitions government could muster no more that 41.8 percent of the responses, leaving the two opposition parties (MDS and SNP) with 39.4 percent. If this is an indication of things to come, any future coalition group will have to count on Fico's Direction Party for the decisive swing vote. The question is, What will the Dzurinda coalition government do to improve its stand in the political arena before the next scheduled parliamentary elections in 2002?

Although the answer may be a complex one, it is couched in a simpler, more general question: Do the citizens of Slovakia want to become an integral part of the European Community, or do they want to live in isolation as a separate sovereign nation? If they choose the former, then the question is, How soon do they want to become full members of the EU, NATO, OECD, and other international governmental organizations? The answer to that is also relatively simple: the requirements for entry into the EU are spelled out in the twenty-nine chapters of the *acquis communautaire*. It should be remembered that Slovakia was not invited to begin negotiations on entry to the EU before 1999 because of Meciarism. Should Vladimir Meciar return to power in 2002 or before, it is doubtful that Slovakia could successfully complete the requirements contained in the twenty-nine chapters of the *acquis* for admission into the EU. Politicians must be aware of these facts, and it is up to them to educate the public about what the choices are for the future of Slovakia.

Notes

INTRODUCTION

1. Stanley Z. Pech, "New Avenues in Eastern European History," *Canadian Slavonic Papers* 10, no. 1 (1968) 14–15.

2. See *Thirteenth Census of the United States Taken in the Year 1910: Volume I, Population* (Washington, D.C., 1913), p. 961, and *Fourteenth Census of the United States Taken in the Year 1920: Volume II, Population: General Report and Analytical Tables* (Washington, D.C., 1922), p. 973.

3. For further details, see M. Mark Stolarik, *Immigration and Urbanization: The Slovak Experience, 1870–1918* (New York: AMS Press, 1989), pp. 1–27.

4. Jan Sveton, "Slovenske vystahovalectvo v obdobi uhorskeho kapitalizmu" (Slovak emigration during the period of Hungarian capitalism), *Ekonomicky casopis* (Economic Journal 4, no. 2 (1956): 171–79.

5. These are estimates developed by M. Mark Stolarik, *Slovaks in Canada and the United States, 1870–1990: Similarities and Differences* (Ottawa: Chair in Slovak History and Culture, University of Ottawa, 1992), pp. 10–11.

6. Carol Skalnik Leff, *National Conflict in Czechoslovakia: The Making and Re-Making of a State, 1918–1987* (Princeton, N.J.: Princeton University Press, 1988).

7. Mikulas Sprinc, "Slovenska Liga v Amerike od 1939–1947" (The Slovak League in America from 1939–1947), in Mikulas Sprinc, ed., *Slovenska Liga v Amerike styridsatrocna* (The Slovak League in America forty years old) (Scranton, Pa.: Slovenska Liga v Amerike, 1947), pp. 68–69.

8. Joseph M. Kirschbaum, *Slovaks in Canada* (Toronto: Canadian Ethnic Press Association of Ontario, 1967), pp. 408–9, cited in Stolarik, *Slovaks in Canada* (Toronto: Canadian Ethnic Press Association of Ontario, 1967), p. 14 n. 85.

9. For details of the earlier period, see Stolarik, *Slovaks in Canada,* p. 15.

10. Dr. Joseph M. Kirschbaum, who settled in Canada, was Tiso's Ambassador to Switzerland. His son, Stanislav J. Kirschbaum, was raised and educated in Canada and is now professor of political science at York University.

11. Jiri Pehe, "Émigrés in the Postcommunist Era: New Data, New Policies," *Report on Eastern Europe* 2, no. 17 (April 26, 1991): 14.

12. Stolarik, *Slovaks in Canada,* p. 15.

13. G. E. Mitton, *Austria-Hungary* (London: Adam and Charles Black, 1914), p. 70.

CHAPTER 1

1. Evidence about the Slavs was related by Procopius from Kaisareie in his volume about the wars, *Hyper ton po lemon logoi* (Books about the wars).

2. Alexander Avenarius, *Die Awaren in Europa* (The Avars in Europe) (Bratislava: Veda, 1974); Zlata Cilinska, "The Development of the Slavs North of the Danube During the Avar Empire and Their Social-Cultural Contribution to Great Moravia," *Slovenska archeologia* 31 (1983): 237–76.

3. "Letopis Nestora" (Nestors chronicle), in *Monumenta Poloniae historica,* vol. 1 (Warsaw: Panstwowe wydawnictwo nauk, 1960).

4. *Fredegarii Chronicorum Liber Quartus cum Continuationibus* (The fourth book of the Chronicle of Fredegar with its continuations), trans. from Latin by J. M. Wallace-Hadrill (London: Thomas Nelson and Sons, 1960).

5. *Magna Moravia, Sbornik k 1100 vyroci prichodu byzantske mise na Moravu* (Great Moravia, an anthology of the 1000th anniversary of the arrival of the Byzantine mission into Moravia) (Prague: Statni pedagogicke nakladatelstvi, 1965); Matus Kucera, "Grossmaehren und die Anfaenge unserer nationalen Geschichte" (Great Moravia and the beginnings of our national history), *Studia historica slovaca* 16 (1988): 65–119; Peter Ratkos, "The Territorial Development of Great Moravia (Fiction and Reality)," *Studia historica slovaca* 16 (1988): 121–55; Oldrich Tuma, "Great Moravia's Trade Contacts with the

Eastern Mediterranean and the Mediating Role of Venice," *Byzantinoslavica* 46 (1985): 67–77.

6. Francis Dvornik, ed., *Les Légendes de Constantin et de Method vues de Byzance* (The legends of Constantin and Methodius as seen through Byzantinum) (Prague: Orbis, 1933); Frantisek Grivec and F. Tomsic, eds., *Constantinus et Methodius Thessalonicenses. Fontes* (Constantin and Methodius of Thesalonica. History) (Zagreb: 1960); Zdenek R. Ditrich, *Christianity in Great Moravia* (Groningen: Wolters, 1962); Frantisek Grivec, *Konstantin und Methodius Lehrer der Slawen* (Constantin and Methodius as teachers of the Slavs) (Wiesbaden: Harrasowitz, 1960); Matus Kucera, "Written Culture in Great Moravia and Its Impact on the Slav Nations," *Human Affairs* 2, no. 1 (1992): 71–76.

7. Jan Dekan, *Velka Morava. Doba a umenie* (Great Moravia. Age and the arts) (Bratislava: Tatran, 1976).

8. Cf. Peter Ratkos, ed., *0 pociatkoch slovenskych dejin* (About the beginnings of Slovak history) (Bratislava: Slovenska akademia vied, 1965); Balint Homan, *Geschichte des ungarischen Mittelalters* (History of the Hungarian Middle Ages), 2 vols. (Berlin: Verlag Walter de Gruyter, 1940); Peter Vaczy, *Die erste Epoche des ungarischen Koenigtums* (The first epoch of the Hungarian kingdom) (Pecs: Danubius, 1935).

9. See R. Hoffmann, "Geschichtliches und Bergmaenisches aus der kgl. freien Bergstadt Kremnitz," in *Mitteilungen der Sektion f. Naturkunde* (Vienna), vol. 11 (1899); L. Grauss, "Aus der Vergangenheit des Goellnitzthaler Bergbaues," *Zipser Jahrbuch 1938*.

10. See Elisabeth Galantai and Julius Kristo, eds., *Johannes de Thurocz: Chronica Hungarorum*, vol. 1 (Budapest: Akademiai kiado, 1985).

11. Ibid.

12. Alfred Kohler, "Von die Jagiellonen zu den Habsburgen" (From the Jagellons to the Habsburgs) in *Slovensko a Habsburgska monarchia v 16.–17. storoci* (Slovakia and the Habsburg monarchy in the 16th and 17th centuries) (Bratislava: Oesterreichisches Ost und Suedosteuropa Institut, 1994).

13. Jan Tibensky, *Dejiny Slovenska slovom i obrazom* (History of Slovakia in words and pictures), vol. 1 {Bratislava: Osveta, 1973), p. 170.

14. David P. Daniel, "The Reformation and Eastern Slovakia," *Human Affairs* 1, no. 2 (1991): 172–86.

15. Z. Angyal, *Ursachen, Verlauf und Ergebnis des Aufstandes Bocskay* (Reasons, duration, and events of the Bocskay uprising) (Budapest, 1916).

16. Sandor Szilagyi, ed., *Actes et documents pour servis de l'histoire de l'alliance G. Rakoczy avec les Françaises et les Suedois dans la guerre de Trente ans* (Budapest, 1873).

17. Vojtech Kopcan, "Der osmanische Krieg gegen die Habsburger 1663–64 (in Hinblick auf die Slowakei)" (The Ottoman war against the Habsburgs in

1663–64: With regard to Slovakia), *Asian and African Studies* 2, no. 2 (1993): 169–89.

18. Peter Ratkos, "Die slowakische Bauern im Klassenkampf von 1526 bis 1785" (The Slovak peasants in class struggle from 1526 to 1785), in *Der Bauer in Klassenkampf* (Berlin: Akademie Verlag, 1975), pp. 429–47.

19. Ignac Acsady, *Der Befreiungskrieg oder Ungarns Befreiung von der Tuerkenherrschaft* (The Liberation War or Hungary's liberation from the Turkish rule) (Budapest, 1909); Vojtech Kopcan, "The Last Stage of the Ottoman Rule in Slovakia," *Studia historica slovaca*, 15 (1986): 209–40.

20. *Dejiny Bratislavy* (The History of Bratislava) (Bratislava: Obzor, 1978).

21. See Pavol Horvath, "Der Character der Spaetfeudalismus in der Slowakei" (The character of late feudalism in Slovakia), *Slovanske historicke studie* 7 (1974): 78–101; Zsigmond Pal Pach, *Die ungarische Agrarentwicklung in 17.–18. Jahrhundert* (The Hungarian agricultural development in the 17th and 18th centuries) (Budapest: Akademiai kiado, 1964); Peter Ratkos, "Die slowakische Bauern im Klassenkampf von 1526 bis 1785"; J. Varga, *Typen und Probleme des baeurlichen Grundbesitzes in Ungarn 1767–1849* (Types and problems of peasant land ownership in Hungary, 1767–1849) (Budapest: Akademiai kiado, 1965).

22. Alfred Arneth, *Geschichte Maria Theresias*, 10 vols. (Vienna: Braumueller, 1863–1879); Gottfried and Gerda Mraz, *Maria Theresia. Ihr Leben und Ihre Zeit* (Maria Theresa. Her life and her times) (Munich: Sudetendeutsch Verlag, 1980).

23. Jozef Vlachovic, "Die Bergakademie in Schemnitz in XVIII. Jahrhundert" (The Mining Academy in Schemnitz [Kremnica] during the 18th century), *Studia historica slovaca* 2 (1964): 103–39.

24. See Jan Tibensky, *Slovensky Sokrates (Adam Frantisek Kollár)* (The Slovak Socrates, Adam Frantisek Kollar) (Bratislava: Tatran, 1983).

25. See Ferdinand Maas, ed., *Der Josephinismus. Quellen zu einer Geschichte in Oesterreich 1760–1830* (Josephinism. Sources of a history in Austria, 1760–1830), 5 vols. (Vienna: Herold, 1951–1957); M. Csaky, *Von Aufklaerung zum Liberalismus* (From proclamation to liberalism) (Vienna, 1982). In the Austrian section of the monarchy, slavery was abolished in 1781 by the Patent of Tolerance.

26. Vaclav Husa, ed., *Nase narodni minulost v dokumentech* (Our national past in documents) (Prague: Nakladatelstvi Ceskoslovenske akademie ved, 1954), pp. 530–33.

27. Kalman Benda, *A magyar jakobinusok iratai I* (Documents of the Hungarian Jacobins, vol. I) (Budapest: Akademiai kiado, 1957), pp. 1003–14.

CHAPTER 2

1. It is characteristic of the times in the Kingdom of Hungary that Bernolaks treatise, which codified the literary language of Slovak, was written in Latin.

2. See Istvan Fried, "Angaben zur slowakischen Kulturgeschichte (Anfang des XIX. Jahrhunderts)" (Lectures about Slovak cultural history, early XIX century) *Historicke studie* 35 (1994): 5–12.

3. Jan Hucko, ed., *Bratislava a pociatky slovenskeho narodneho obrodenia* (Bratislava and the beginning of Slovak national renaissance) (Bratislava: Obzor, 1992), p. 248.

4. Bohuslav Tablic, "Vlastenecke zadosti, Literarni priloha k Cisarsko kralovskym videnskym novinam 1815" (Patriotic requests, literary supplement to the imperial royal Viennese newspapers, 1815), in J. Hucko, ed., *Bratislava a pociatky*, p. 274.

5. See Horst Haselsteiner, "Die Haltung Stephan Graf Szechenyis in Krisenjahr 1832; zwischen Loyalitaet und Solidaritaet" (The position of Count Stephen Szecsenyi in the year of crisis 1832: Between loyalty and solidarity), *Historicke studie* 35 (1994): 13–21.

6. Jan Kollar, *Pamati z mladsich rokov zivota* (Memories from younger years of life) (Repr. Bratislava: Tatran, 1972): 219–29.

7. See Vladimir Matula, "The Conception and the Development of Slovak National Culture in the Period of National Revival," *Studia historica slovaca* 17 (1990): 150–89.

8. See Ludovit Stur, *Reci a state* (Lectures and essays) (Bratislava: Hviezdoslavova spolocnost, 1953).

9. Jan Tibensky, *Dejiny Slovenska slovom i obrazom*, p. 247.

10. See Stur, *Reci a state.*

11. The laws were published in *Slovenskje narodnje novini* (Slovak national gazette) on March 31, 1848.

12. For background on the Slovak revolution of 1848–1849, see the monumental work by Daniel Rapant, *Slovenske povstanie roku 1848–1849. Dejiny a dokumenty* (The Slovak uprising in 1848–1849. History and documents), 5 vols. (Turciansky Sv. Martin: Matica slovenska, 1937–1972).

13. From the Slovak translation in Bohumil Kosticky, ed., *Slovensko 1848–1948 v zrkadle pramenov* (Slovakia, 1848–1948 in the mirror of sources) (Martin: Osveta, 1983), pp. 4–25.

14. Albert Prazak, "Czechs and Slovaks After the Revolution of 1848," *Slavonic Review* 6 (1993): 118–29.

15. Dusan Skvarna, "Self-Reflections of Two Neighbours: Magyars and Slovaks," *Human Affairs* 3 (1993): 131–41.

16. See Arthur J. May, *The Habsburg Monarchy, 1867–1914* (Cambridge, Mass.: Harvard University Press, 1965); Julius Miskolczy, *Ungarn in der Habsburger Monarchie* (Hungary in the Habsburg monarchy) (Vienna and Munich: Herold, 1959).

17. For details of the Slavic idea, see Julius Mesaros, "Idee der slawischen

Schicksalsgemeinschaft in der slowakischen nationalen Bewegung in der zweiten Haelfte des 19. Jahrhunderts" (Idea about the fateful Slavic community in the Slovak national movement during the second half of the 19th century), *Historica* 10 (1965): 159–211; and T. Ivantysynova, "Die slawische Idee bei den Slowaken in der zweiten Haelfte des 19. Jahrhunderts" (The Slovaks' Slavic idea in the second half of the nineteenth century), *Slovanske studie 1992*, special issue.

18. See Pavel Hapak, "Fragen zur wirtschaftlichen Entwicklung der Slowakei am Begin des 20. Jahrhunderts" (Issues concerning the economic development of Slovakia at the beginning of the 20th century), *Studia historica slovaca* 15 (1986): 101–30; Jozef Faltus, "Development of Capitalist Industrialisation of Slovakia and Its Problems," ibid., 77–99.

19. The first step toward changing the kingdom into a Magyar state was to achieve a Magyar majority, and to this end, falsification of statistical data became an expedient avenue. See J. Sveton, *Statistische Madjarisierung* (Statistical Magyarization) (Bratislava: Wissenschaftliche Gesellschaft, 1944); Frantisek Vnuk, "Statistics and Politics," *Slovakia* 10 (1960): 21–28; Ladislav Deak, "The Slovaks in Hungarian Statistics," in Dusan Kovac, ed., *History and Politics* (Bratislava: Czechoslovak Committee of the European Cultural Foundation, 1993), pp. 93–104.

20. See Scotus Viator (Robert W. Seton-Watson), *Ungarische Wahlen* (Hungarian elections) (Leipzig: Dieterich, 1912).

21. Milan Hodza, "K aktivite Slovenskej narodnej strany," *Hlas* 4, September 1, 1901.

22. Robert W. Seton-Watson, *Slovakia Then and Now* (London: G. Allen and Unwin, 1931).

23. See Hans Beyer, "Bjornsterne, Bjornson und die Nationalitaetenfrage Oesterreich-Ungarns" (Bjornsterne Bjornson and the nationalities issue in Austria-Hungary), *Suedostforschungen* 19 (1960): 215–38; Robert W. Seton-Watson, *The Future of Austria-Hungary and the Attitude of the Great Powers* (London: Constable, 1907).

24. Alfred Francis Pribram, *Austrian Foreign Policy 1908–1918* (London: Gallen, 1923).

CHAPTER 3

1. See M. Mark Stolarik, "The Role of American Slovaks in the Creation of Czecho-Slovakia, " *Slovak Studies* no. 8 (1968): 7–82.

2. See Jaroslav Papousek, *The Czechoslovak Nation's Struggle for Independence* (Prague: Orbis, 1928); Stefan Osusky, "How Czecho-Slovakia was

Born," in Joseph M. Kirschbaum, *Slovakia in the 19th and 20th Centuries* (Toronto: Slovak World Congress, 1973), pp. 81–93.

3. See Robert W. Seton-Watson, *Masaryk in England* (Cambridge: Cambridge University Press, 1943). For the text of the memorandum, see *R. W. Seton-Watson and His Relations with the Czechs and Slovaks: Documents, 1906–1951* (Prague: Ustav T. G. Masaryka, 1995), 1: 209–15.

4. The text of the memorandum is in *R. W. Seton-Watson and His Relations*, pp. 223–35.

5. Ibid., p. 232.

6. See O. D. Koreff, *Milan Rastislav Stefanik: A Short Biography* (Cleveland: First Catholic Slovak Union, 1924).

7. On Stefanik's relation with Janin, see Dusan Kovac, "Deux hommes dans la Grande Guerre: Maurice Janin et Milan Rastislav-Stefanik" (Two men in the Great War: Maurice Janin and Milan Rastislav-Stefanik), *Guerres mondiales et conflits contemporains* (Great wars and contemporary conflicts), no. 169 (January 1993): 51–58.

8. Coverage of the Czecho-Slovak Legions in English is extensive. See, e.g., Henry P. Baerlein, *The March of Seventy Thousand* (London: L. Parsons, 1926); Gustav Baevar, *The Lost Legion: A Czechoslovak Epic* (London: S. Paul, 1939); John F. N. Bradley, *The Czechoslovak Legion in Russia, 1914–1920* (Boulder, Colo.: East European Monographs, 1991); Richard Earnest Dupuy, *Perish by the Sword: The Czechoslovak Anabasis and Our Supporting Campaigns in North Russia and Siberia, 1918–1920* (Harrisburg, Pa.: Military Service Publishing Co., 1939); Victor M. Fic, *The Bolsheviks and the Czechoslovak Legion: The Origin of Their Armed Conflict, March–May 1918* (New Delhi: Abhinav Publications, 1978); Edwin P. Hoyt, *The Army Without a Country* (New York: Macmillan, 1967); Rudolf Medek, *The Czechoslovak Anabasis Across Russia and Siberia* (London: Czech Society, 1929); Betty M. Unterberger, *The United States, Revolutionary Russia, and the Rise of Czechoslovakia* (Chapel Hill: University of North Carolina Press, 1989).

9. See Maria Holma-Oertel, "Die Slowaskei und die Slowaken" (Slovakia and the Slovaks), *Osteruropaische Zukunft* (East European future) (Berlin), October 1, 1916.

10. On the activities of the Maffia, see Emanuel V. Voska and William H. Irwin, *Spy and Counterspy* (New York: Doubleday, Doran, 1940).

11. See Ottokar Czernin, *Im Weltkriege* (In the World War) (Berlin-Vienna: Verlag bei Willstein, 1919).

12. Quoted in Jan Galandauer, *Vznik Ceskosolvenske republiky 1918* (The creation of the Czechoslovak Republic in 1918) (Prague: Svoboda, 1988), p. 288.

13. Ibid., pp. 297–98.

14. See Marian Hronsky, *Slovensko pri zrode Ceskoslovenska* (Slovakia during the birth of Czechoslovakia) (Bratislava: Pravda, 1988).

15. *Vznik Ceskoslovenska 1918, Dokumenty ceskoslovenske zahranicni politiky* (The creation of Czechoslovakia, 1918, Documents of the Czechoslovak foreign policy) (Prague: Ustav mezinarodnich vztahu, 1994), pp. 163–64.

16. Karol A. Medvecky, *Slovensky preverat* (The Slovak revolution), vol. 4 (Trnava: Vydal Spolok Sv. Vojtecha, 1931), pp. 36–61.

17. There are numerous studies in English focusing on the creation of Czechoslovakia from the beginning of World War I. See, e.g., Cestmir Jesina, *The Birth of Czechoslovakia* (Washington, D.C.: Czechoslovak National Council of America, 1968); William V. Wallace, "Masaryk, Beneš, and the Creation of Czechoslovakia: A Study in Mentalities," in Harry Nowak, ed., *T. G. Masaryk (1850–1937), Statesman and Cultural Force*, vol. 3. (New York: Macmillan, 1990); Zbynek A. Zeman, *The Break-up of the Hapsburg Empire, 1914–1918* (London: Oxford University Press, 1961).

18. See Andras Siklos, *Revolution in Hungary and the Dissolution of the Multinational State, 1918* (Budapest: Akademiai kiado, 1988).

19. See Jan Opocensky, *The Collapse of the Austro-Hungarian Monarchy and the Rise of the Czechoslovak State* (Prague: Orbis, 1928).

20. See J. Jahelka, "The Role of Chicago Czechs in the Struggle for Czechoslovak Independence," *Journal of the Illinois State Historical Society* 31 (December 1938): 381–410; Josef Kalvoda, "Masaryk in America in 1918," *Jahrbucher für Geschichte Osteuropas*, no. 27 (1979): 85–99; Victor S. Mamatey, *The United States and East Central Europe, 1914–1918: A Study in Wilson Diplomacy and Propaganda* (Princeton, N.J.: Princeton University Press, 1957); Victor S. Mamatey, "Masaryk and Wilson: A Contribution to the Study of Their Relations," in Robert B. Pynsent, ed., *T. G. Masaryk (1850–1937), Thinker and Critic*, vol. 2 (New York: Macmillan, 1989); Victor S. Mamatey, "The Role of President Wilson in the Foundation of Czechoslovakia," in Miloslav Rechcigl, Jr., ed., *Czechoslovakia, Past and Present*, vol. 1 (The Hague: Mouton, 1968).

21. See Victor S. Mamatey, "The Czechoslovak Agreement of Pittsburgh (May 30, 1918) Revisited," *Kosmas: Journal of Czechoslovak and Central European Studies* 2, no. 2 (1983): 41–48. See also *The Slovaks and the Pittsburgh Pact* (Chicago: Tylka Bros. Press, 1934).

22. See George J. Kovtun, *The Czechoslovak Declaration of Independence: A History of the Document* (Washington, D.C.: Library of Congress, 1985). The complete text was also published in a separate document under the title, *Declaration of Independence of the Czechoslovak Nation* (New York: Marchbanks Press, 1918).

23. Kovtun, *The Czechoslovak Declaration of Independence*.

24. Ibid.

25. J. Galendauer, *Vznik Ceskoslovenske republiky 1918*, p. 228.

26. Ibid., pp. 345–46.

27. Ibid.

28. See Josef Teichman, *Madari ve valce a po valce* (The Magyars before and after the war) (Prague: Melantrich, 1937), p. 118; Oszkar Jaszi, *A monarchia jovoje. A dualizmus bukasa es a Dunai Egyesult Allamok* (The future of the monarchy. The failure of dualism and the United States of the Danube) (Budapest: Magyarorszag Reszvenytarsasag, 1918); Fedor Houdek, *Vznik hranic Slovenska* (Origins of the borders of Slovakia) (Bratislava: Kniznica Prudov, 1931), p. 214.

29. For further details, see Public Law no. XXX about the self-rule of the Slovak Territory, issued on March 12, 1919.

30. David Hunter Miller, *My Diary at the Conference of Paris* (New York: Appeal Printing Co., 1924), vol. 4, Doc. 246, "Outline of Tentative Report and Recommendations. . . . For the President and the Plenipotentiaries," 17. Hungary, pp. 244–45, quoted in Ignac Romsics, "Edvard Benes a Ceskoslovensko-Madarska hranice" (Edward Benes and the Czechoslovak-Hungarian border), *Stredni Evropa* (Central Europe) 8, no. 27 (1993): 11 n. 12.

31. For a select number of Benes's memoranda presented at the Paris Peace Conference, see Rudolf Kucera, "Komentar" (Commentary), *Stredni Evropa* (Central Europe) 8, no. 25 (1992): 5–21.

32. Maria Ormos, *Padovatol Trianoning 1918–1920* (From Padua to Trianon, 1918–1920) (Budapest: Akademiai kiado, 1983), pp. 109–11. See also Istvan Borsody, *Magyar-Slovak kiegyezes* (Budapest: Officina, 1945), pp. 225–26, quoted in Romsics, "Edvard Benes," p. 12 n. 14; J. Klimko, "Uprava juznych hranic Slovenska po vzniku CSR," *Pravnehistoricke studie* (Historical-legal studies) 18 (1974): 50, quoted in Marta Romportlova, "Zacleneni Slovenska do CSR jako jeden z urcujicich faktoru ceskoslovensko-madarskych vztahu po prvni svetove valce" (Inclusion of Slovakia into Czechoslovakia as a determining factor of Czechoslovak-Hungarian relations after the First World War), *Casopis Matice Moravske* (Journal of the Moravian Society) 110, no. 1 (1991): 132.

33. *Zlata kniha Slovenska* (The golden book of Slovakia) (Bratislava: Milos Kolesar, vlastnym nakladom, 1929), p. 123. See also L. Lipscher, *K vyvinu politickej spravy na Slovensku v r. 1918–1938* (Concerning the development of political administration in Slovakia from 1918 to 1939) (Bratislava: VSAV, 1966), pp. 219–20.

34. Kucera, "Komentar," p. 7. Memorandum no. 1 is entitled "Czechoslovaks," no. 2 "The Territorial Demands of the Czechoslovak Republic," no. 3 "The German Problem in Bohemia," no. 4 "The Problem of Teshin-Silezia," no. 5 "Slovakia," no. 6 "The Problem of Magyar Ruthenians," no. 7 "The Lusitian Serbs," no. 8 "The Czech Upper Silesia," no. 9 "The Problem of the Kladno Area," no. 10 "Border Issues," and no. 11 "Rights to Restitutions for War Damages."

35. For documents pertaining to the rise and fall of the Hungarian Soviet Republic, see Bela Kun, *Valogatott foirasok es beszedek* (Selected sources and speeches) (Budapest: Kossuth Konyvkiado, 1966), vols. 1 and 2; and A Magyar Szocialista Munkaspart Kozponti Bizottsaganak Parttorteneti Intezete, *A Magyar munkasmozgalom tortenetenek valogatott dokumentumai: A Magyar tanacskoztarsasag 1919 marcius 21–1919 augusztus 1* (The Party Historical Institute of the Central Committee of the Hungarian Socialist Worker's Party, *Selected documents of the history of the Hungarian worker's movement: The Hungarian Soviet Republic March 21–August 1, 1919*) (Budapest: Kossuth Konyvkiado, 1959, 1960), vols. VIA and VIB.

36. Marta Romportlova, *Madarsko 1918–1938* (Hungary 1918–1938) (Brno: Universita J. E. Purkyne, 1973), pp. 10–17. See also Zsuzsa L. Nagy, *A parizsi bekeskonferencia es Magyarorszag 1918–1919* (The Paris Peace Conference and Hungary, 1918–1919) (Budapest: Kossuth, 1965).

37. Zsuzsa L. Nagy, "The Mission of General Smuts to Budapest, April 1919," *Acta Historica* (Budapest) 11, nos. 1–4 (1965): 163–85. See also Romsics, "Edvard Benes a Ceskoslovensko-Madarska hranice," p. 12.

38. Milos Gosiorovsky, *Prispevek k dejinam slovenseho delnickeho hnuti* (Contribution to the history of the Slovak workers' movement) (Prague: Rovnost, 1952), p. 65.

39. The way this situation was exploited by the communists is well described by Wilhelm Boehm, military commander of the Hungarian Red Army, in his *Im Kreuzfeuer zweier Revolutionen* (In the crossfire of two revolutions) (Munich: Verlag für Kulturpolitik, 1924).

40. See Ivan T. Berend, ed., *Magyarorszag Tortenete* (History of Hungary), vol. 2 (Budapest: Gondolat, 1966), pp. 346–47, and Romportlova, "Zacleneni Slovenska," p. 136 n. 25.

41. Peter A. Toma, "The Slovak Soviet Republic of 1919," *American Slavic and East European Review* 17, no. 2 (1957): 203–15.

42. *Cervene Noviny* (The red gazette), June 17, 1919, quoted in ibid., pp. 208–9.

43. Quoted in Ferdinand Peroutka, *Budovani statu* (The building of state) (Prague: Orbis, 1936), 2: 1002. See also Toma, "The Slovak Soviet Republic of 1919," p. 209.

44. See F. Bokes's article in *Kulturny zivot* (Cultural life), April 3, 1949, quoted in Gosiorovsky, *Prispevek k dejinam*, p. 71.

45. Jindrich Vesely, *O vzniku a zalozeni KSC* (About the origin and foundation of the Communist Party of Czechoslovakia) (Prague: Svoboda, 1953), p. 131.

46. Karol A. Medvecky, *Slovensky prevrat* (The Slovak revolution) (Bratislava: "Komensky," 1931), p. 131.

47. Quoted in Toma, "The Slovak Soviet Republic of 1919," p. 212 n. 19; original quotation in Vesely, *O vzniku*, p. 78.

48. For further details on the Hungarian revolution, see Franz Borkenau, *World Communism* (New York: W. W. Norton, 1939); Boehm, *Im Kreuzfeuer Zweier Revolutionen;* Oszkar Jaszi, *Revolution and Counter-Revolution* (London: P. S. King and Son, 1924); Rudolph L. Tokes, *Bela Kun and the Hungarian Soviet Republic* (Stanford: Hoover Institution on War, Revolution, and Peace, 1967).

CHAPTER 4

1. See "Ohlas SNR k bratom Slovakom z 3. novembra 1918," in M. Hronsky, *Slovensko na razcesti* (Slovakia at the crossroads) (Kosice: Vychodoslovenske vydavatelstvo, 1976), p. 97.

2. See *Zakon 64/1918 Zbierka zakonov a nariadeni o mimoriadnych a prechodnych ustanoveniach na Slovensku* (Public law 64/1918 collection of laws about special and temporary statutes in Slovakia).

3. Ferdinand Peroutka, *Budovani statu*, 1: 406. Also quoted in Stanley Kirschbaum, *A History of Slovakia: The Struggle for Survival* (New York: St. Martin's Press, 1995), p. 162 n. 17. It is interesting that Kirschbaum (pp. 160–63) identifies Srobar with the "Hlasists" and thus builds a case for a persecution of the Slovak Catholics by Czech Lutherans with Srobar as the leading executor of the Czech agenda to create one Czechoslovak nation loyal to Prague.

4. See "Uradne noviny ministra MPS Srobara" (Official news of MPS Srobar), in *Zlata kniha slovenska*, p. 206.

5. See *Zakon 37/1918 Zbierka zakonov a nariadeni* (Public law 37/1918 collection of public laws and decrees).

6. Tomas Garrigue Masaryk, *Svetova revoluce* (World revolution) (Prague: Cin, 1925), p. 533.

7. Eva Broklova, *Ceskoslovenska demokracie* (Czechoslovak democracy) (Prague: Sociologicke nakladatelstvi, 1992), p. 34 n. 3.

8. Peroutka, *Budovani statu*, 2: 1332.

9. Josef Macek, *Parlament zevnitr* (Parliament from within) (Prague: Ukoly, 1932), p. 18.

10. Otakar Klapka, *Samosprava a zrizeni zupni* (Self-government and the regional administrative system) (Prague: "Parlament," 1923), pp. 6–7, 113. See also *Zakon 210/1920 Zbierka o docasnej uprave politickej spravy na Slovensku* (Public law 210/1920 collection of laws and regulations about the temporary preparation of political administration in Slovakia).

11. See *Zakon 126/1920 Zbiarka zakonov a nariadeni zupnych okresnych uradov v republike Ceskoslovenskej* (Public law 126/1920 collection of laws

and regulations about the organization of administrative areas and district offices in the Czechoslovak Republic).

12. See Zakon 122/1927 *Zbierka zakonov a nariadeni o organizacii politickej spravy* (Public law 125/1927 collection of laws and regulations about the organization of political administration).

13. For the text and analysis of the document, see Eva Broklova, *Prvni ceskoslovenska ustava* (The first Czechoslovak constitution) (Prague: Ustav pro soudobe dejiny, 1992).

14. See *Zakon 122/1920 Zbierka zakonov a nariadeni ktorym sa stanovuju jazykove prava v republike Ceskoslovenskej* (Public law 122/1920 collection of laws and regulations regarding the establishment of rights to native language in the Czechoslovak Republic).

15. Milan S. Durica, *Slovensky narod a jeho statnost* (The Slovak nation and its statehood) (Bratislava: Alfa, 1990), p. 21.

16. When the Treaty of St. Germain was signed on September 10, 1919, for Austria's recognition of Czechoslovakia, Yugoslavia, Poland, and Hungary, these states were obliged to give guarantees of protection of minorities. According to this treaty, the signatories could use only one language designated as "official." Eva Broklova claims that "this was the reason for using the term Czechoslovak language in the document." See Broklova, *Prvni ceskoslovenska ustava*, documents nos. 5, 6, and 7.

17. See Eva Broklova, "Cesi a Slovaci 1918–1938" (Czechs and Slovaks, 1918–1938), *Sociologicky casopis* (Journal of sociology) 29, no. 1 (1993): 34. Before October 28, 1918, according to Edvard Benes, the problem of the Slovak nation in the official ideology of the Czechoslovak foreign policy did not exist because "the Slovaks are Czechs even though they use their dialect as their language." From the memorandum "Independent Czechia, 1915" in E. Benes, *Svetova valka a nase revoluce* (The World War and our revolution), vol. 3 (7th ed., Prague: Cin, 1935), doc. 69, p. 212, quoted in Broklova, *Ceskoslovenska demokracie*, p. 115 n. 2.

18. It should be noted that when the framers of the Czechoslovak constitution discussed proportional representation, they purposefully avoided the reference to minorities by using the term "nations" rather than "nationalities."

19. Durica, *Slovensky narod*, p. 5.

20. According to C. A. Macartney, in 1910 there were 7,468 Czechs in Slovakia; by 1921 their numbers had increased to 71,733. See his *Hungary and Her Successors* (London: Oxford University Press, 1937), p. 78.

21. Quoted in Alena Bartlova, "Boj o autonomiu Slovenska v rokoch 1918–1938" (The struggle for Slovak autonomy during the years 1918–1938), *Sbornik k dejinam 19. a 20. stoleti* (Journal of 19th and 20th century history) 13 (1993): 214.

22. See *Zakon 124/1920 Zbierka zakonov a nariadeni o zalozeni a pravo-*

moci senatu (Public law 124/1920 collection of laws and regulations about the creation and power of the senate).

23. Quoted in Frantisek Vnuk, "Slovakia in Pre-Munich Czecho-Slovakia, (1918–38)," in Joseph M. Kirschbaum, ed., *Slovakia in the 19th and 20th Centuries,* p. 103.

24. As early as October 30, 1918, Dr. Stodola at Turciansky Sv. Martin spoke about the indispensable need for solving the question of Slovak autonomy within the framework of Czecho-Slovakia. Stodola published several articles and books on the subject of the Swiss federal system. His treatise entitled *O samosprave Slovenska* (About self-rule of Slovakia) (Turciansky Sv. Martin: Knihtlaciarsky ucastinarsky spolok, odtlacok z Narodnych novin, 1921) became the platform for the newly created party he was heading, the Slovak National Party.

25. Brackett Lewis, *Facts About Democracy in Czechoslovakia* (Prague: American Institute in Czechoslovakia, 1937), p. 36.

26. See Severin K. Turosienski, *Education in Czechoslovakia* (Washington, D.C.: U.S. Government Printing Office, 1936), pp. 24–25.

27. Ibid., p. 58.

28. Lewis, *Facts About Democracy,* p. 37.

29. Turosienski, *Education,* p. 96.

30. Ibid., p. 107.

31. Ibid., p. 110.

32. Ibid., p. 180.

33. Lewis, *Facts About Democracy,* p. 49.

34. Anton Spiesz, *Dejiny Slovenska. Na ceste k sebauvedomeniu* (History of Slovakia. On the road to self-awareness) (Bratislava: Vydavatelstvo Respekt, 1992), p. 141.

35. For further details, see Macartney, *Hungary and Her Successors,* p. 78 ff.

36. See *Zakony 215/1919* (16.4.1919); *81/1920* (30.1.1920); *329/1920* (8.4.1920 a 28.6.1922). *Zbierka zakonov a nariadeni* (Public laws 215/1919; 81/1920; and 329/1920. Collection of laws and decrees).

37. See A. Spiesz, *Dejiny Slovenska,* p. 140; J. Faltus and V. Prucha, *Prehlad hospodarskeho vyvoja na Slovensku v rokoch 1918–1945* (Survey of agricultural development in Slovakia during 1918–1945) (Bratislava: Vydavatelstvo politickej literatury, 1967), p. 121.

38. Faltus and Prucha, *Prehlad,* p. 299.

39. See statements of the general secretary of the Central Association of Slovak Industry, Pavol Zatko, in *Slovensky dennik* (Slovak daily), April 27, 1937.

40. Juriga published his proposal of Slovak autonomy in *Slovenske ludove noviny* (The Slovak people's gazette) on June 10, 1921. Labay described his proposal about Slovak autonomy in the newspaper *Slovak* on June 19, 1921.

See also Karol Sidor, *Slovenska politika na pode prazskeho snemu 1918–1938* (Slovak politics on the floor of the Prague senate, 1918–1938), vol. 2 (Bratislava: Tlacou knihtlaciarne Sv. Andreja, 1943), pp. 34–35.

41. *Slovak*, June 24–July 3, 1921.

42. See *Tlac poslaneckej snemovne NSRC* (Printing of the parliamentary senate of the National Assembly of the Czechoslovak Republic) 1922, 1st Session, Proposal no. 3403.

43. See the decree of the president of the Czechoslovak Republic dated June 29, 1927.

44. *Slovak*, January 1, 1928.

45. For the legislative proposal by representative Andrej Hlinka submitted by Dr. K. Mederly on May 8, 1930, see Printing no. 425-IIIrd Session of the Senate, quoted in Sidor, *Slovenska politika*, 2: 34–35.

46. See *Program Slovenskej narodnej strany. Co ziada Slovensko* (Program of the Slovak National Party. What does Slovakia demand?) (Turciansky Sv. Martin: Knihtlaciarsky ucastinarsky spolok, 1932).

47. See *Zvolensky manifest z 16.10.1932* (Zvolen manifesto of October 16, 1932).

48. See Sidor, *Slovenska politika*, 2: 165–66.

CHAPTER 5

1. Marta Romportlova, "Zacleneni Slovenska," pp. 139–40.

2. For a sample of the literature about the Munich crisis, see George J. Kovtun, *Czech and Slovak History* (Washington, D.C.: Library of Congress, 1996), pp. 189–207.

3. See *Slovensky dennik* (Slovak daily), February 21, 1937.

4. For the proposal of A. Hlinka, K. Sidor, M. Sokol, J. Tiso, and others to revise the constitution of 1920 and grant autonomy to Slovakia (prepared by Frantisek Durcansky), see *Slovak*, June 5, 1938.

5. See the "Manifesto of the Slovak Nation," resolved at the HSLS meeting on October 6, 1938, in *Slovak*, October 7, 1938.

6. See the proposal submitted by representatives A. Hlinka (deceased), K. Sidor, M. Sokol, and J. Tiso to amend the constitution about the autonomy of the Slovak Land, dated November 22, 1938: *Tlace poslanecke snemovne NZRC 1938, tlac c. 1429* (Printings of the Parliament NZRC, issue no. 1429).

7. Jorg K. Hoensch, *Slowakei und Hitlers Ostpolitik* (Slovakia and Hitler's eastern politics) (Graz-Köln: Boehlau Verlag, 1965).

8. B. Kosticky, ed., *Slovensko 1848–1948. V zrkadle pramenov* (Slovakia 1848–1948. In the mirror of references) (Martin: Osveta, 1983), pp. 318–20.

9. Alexander Mach's memoirs have not been published, but they are catalogued in the archives of the Slovak Republic.

10. See *Narodohospodar Peter Zatko spomina* (Economist Peter Zatko remembers) (Liptovsky Mikulas: Tranoscius, 1994), p. 79.

11. See Pavol Carnogursky, *14. Marec 1939* (March 14, 1939) (Bratislava: Veda, Vydvatelstvo Slovenskej akademie vied, 1992).

12. *Slovensky zakonnik 1939*, zakon c. 1/39 (Slovak collection of laws, 1939, Law no. 1/1939).

13. Karin Schmid, "The Constitution of the Slovak Republic," in *Slovak Politics: Essays on Slovak History in Honour of Joseph M. Kirschbaum* (Cleveland: Slovensky ustav, 1992), pp. 191–220.

CHAPTER 6

1. For the history of the Slovak Republic, see, e.g., Victor S. Mamatey and Radomir Luza, eds., *A History of the Czechoslovak Republic, 1918–1949* (Princeton, N.J.: Princeton University Press, 1973), especially the chapter by Jorg K Hoensch; Yeshayahu A. Jelinek, *The Parish Republic. Hlinka's Slovak People's Party 1939–1945* (Boulder, Colo.: East European Monographs, 1976); Stanislav J. Kirschbaum, "The Slovak Republic and the Slovaks," *Slovakia* 29, nos. 53–54 (1980–1981): 11–38.

2. See two works by Joseph M. Kirschbaum: "International Recognition of the Slovak Republic," *Slovakia* 1, no. 1 (1951): 23–31; and "Diplomatic and Consular Relations of Slovakia with Neutral States," 23, no. 46 (1973): 111–22. See also Joseph A. Mikus, "The Diplomatic Service of the Slovak Republic, ibid. 2, no. 2 (1952): 38–41.

3. For Slovak-French relations, see P. Petruf, "Relations Between Slovakia and France, 1939–1948," *Human Affairs* 4, no. 1 (1994): 74–88.

4. For Slovak-Soviet relations, see Miroslav Licko, "The Development of Slovak-Soviet Relations During the Second World War," in Joseph M. Kirschbaum, ed., *Slovakia in the 19th and 20th Centuries*, pp. 281–99.

5. For Nazi Germany's policy toward Slovakia, see Yeshayahu A. Jelinek, "Slovakia's Internal Policy and the Third Reich, August 1940–February 1941," *Central European History* 4, no. 3 (1971): 242–70; and J. Low-Myron, "From Autonomous State to Protectorate: German Policy Toward Slovakia," *Historian* 26 (1964): 405–25.

6. Frantisek Vnuk, "Slovakia's Accession to the Tripartite Pact," *Slovakia* 9, no. 1 (1959): 6–19.

7. Valerian Bystricky and Stefan Fano, eds., *Pokus o politicky a osobny profil Jozefa Tisu* (An attempt at a political and personal profile of Joseph Tiso)

(Bratislava: Historicky ustav SAV, 1992). See also Theodoric J. Zubek, "Dr. Jozef Tiso, Controversial Personality," *Slovakia* 6, nos. 3–4 (1956): 15–24.

8. Yeshayahu A. Jelinek, "Storm-Troopers in Slovakia: The Rodobrana and the Hlinka Guard," *Journal of Contemporary History* 6, no. 3 (1971): 97–119.

9. See George J. Kovtun, *Czech and Slovak History,* chap. 17.

10. Yirmeyahu Oscar Neumann, *Im Schatten des Todes. Ein Tatsachenbericht vom Schicksalkampf des slowakischen Judentums* (In the shadow of death. A factual report about the fateful struggle of the Slovak Jewry) (Tel Aviv: Alamenu, 1956); L. Rotkirchen, *The Destruction of Slovak Jewry. A Documentary History* (Jerusalem: Yad va-shem, 1961); Frantisek Kuruc, "Vatikan, Slovensky stat a zidia" (The Vatican, the Slovak state and the Jews), *Stredni Evropa* (Central Europe) 6, no. 15 (1990): 52–69.

11. Pierre Blet, Robert A.Graham, Angelo Martini, and Burckhart Schneider, eds., *Actes et documents du Saint Siège relatifs à la Second guerre mondiale 1939–1945* (Official papers and documents of the Holy See pertaining to the Second World War, 1939–1945) (Vatican: Libreria editrice Vaticana, 1974), vol. 8, no. 199, pp. 345–47.

12. Ibid.

13. See two works by Ivan Kamenec: "Slovak Society and Antifascist Resistance During World War II Up to the Year 1943," *Studia historica slovaca* 14 (1985): 71–105; and "The Deportation of Jewish Citizens from Slovakia in 1942," in Dezider, Toth, et al., *The Tragedy of Slovak Jews* (Banska Bystrica: DATEI, 1992), pp. 83–98.

14. *Actes et documents,* vol. 8, no. 305, pp. 459–60.

15. J. S. Conway, "The Churches, the Slovak State, and the Jews, 1939–1945," *Slovak and Central European Review* 52, no. 126 (1974): 85–112.

16. *Actes et documents,* vol. 8, no. 199, pp. 345–47.

17. Ibid., vol. 8, no. 400, pp. 561–62, and no. 426, pp. 597–98.

18. Kamenec, "Slovak Society and Antifascist Resistance."

19. See Miroslav Ivanov, *The Assassination of Heydrich, 27 May 1942* (London: Hart-Davis and MacGibbon, 1973); Callum MacDonald, *The Killing of Obergruppenfuhrer Reinhard Heydrich* (London: Macmillan, 1989).

20. Cf. Stefan Osusky, *Beneš and Slovakia,* trans. from Slovak by Philip James Anthony (Middletown, Pa.: Jednota Press, 1943). About Osusky, see Konstantin Culen, "Osusky After March 14, 1939," *Slovakia* 9, no. 3 (1959): 75–80; and Frantisek Vnuk, "Stephen Osusky on March 14, 1939," *Slovakia* 9, no. 5 (1959): 65–75.

21. See Miroslav J. Licko, *1944 USA v Banskej Bystrici* (1944 USA in Banska Bystrica) (Bratislava: NVK International, 1944), p. 20; Peter Toma, "Soviet Strategy in the Slovak Uprising of 1944," *Journal of Central European Affairs* 19, no. 3 (October 1959): 291.

22. Smidke was a former deputy and chairman of the CPC; he headed the Czecho-Slovak communists in Moscow until his return to Czechoslovakia in April 1945.

23. SNR was the supreme organ of the liberation movement with legislative and executive powers in the insurgent territory after September 1, 1944. After the war, Benes prudently recognized the legality of the Council, which had 13 members (7 Democrats, 4 Communists, and 2 Social Democrats) and later increased to 41 and then to 50 (25 Democrats, 13 Communists, 10 Social Democrats, and 2 military commanders with no political affiliations). See Toma, "Soviet Strategy," p. 291 n. 9.

24. According to Edward Taborsky (Benes's former personal secretary), Smidke was supposed to have been Catlos's agent carrying a proposal to "solve the internal problems of Slovakia in harmony with Soviet interests." When Benes protested to Moscow against this type of negotiation "behind his back," V. Z. Lebedyev, the Soviet ambassador to the Czechoslovak government in London, informed him that the negotiations were conducted by the CPC and not by the Soviet government. See Taborsky, "Benesove moskovske cesty" (Benes's trips to Moscow), *Svedectvi* (Evidence) 1, nos. 3–4 (1957): 203. See also Jozef Jablonicky, "Neuspesna misia v Moskve (I)" (The unsuccessful mission in Moscow (I)), *Historie a vojenstvi* (History and militarism) 39, no. 2 (1990): 26–45, 33–43. See also Zdenek Valis, "Mise ze Slovenska do Sovetskeho svazu 1944" (The mission from Slovakia to the Soviet Union in 1944), *Historie a vojenstvi* 40, no. 2 (1991): 143–59.

25. Jablonicky, "Neuspesna misia v Moskve (III)" *Historie a vojenstvi* 39, no. 4 (1990): 23–24.

26. Vilem Precan, "Nacisticka politika a Tisuv rezim v predvecer Povstani (IV)" (Nazi politics and Tiso's regime on the eve of the uprising (IV)), ibid., no. 5 (1990): 21–23.

27. Jan Korcek, "K niektorym otazkam mocensko-represivneho aparatu slovenskeho statu—1943–August 1944" (Some questions about the power-repressive apparatus of the Slovak state—1943–August 1944), *Historie a vojenstvi* 41, no. 1 (1992): 46–77.

28. Samuel Faltan, *Partizanska vojna na Slovensku* (Partisan war in Slovakia) (Bratislava: Osveta, 1959), p. 70, quoted in Licko, *1944 USA*, p. 50 n. 9.

29. Precan, "Nacisticka politika," 39, no. 5 (1990): 20–21.

30. Miroslav Kropilak, "Vojenske operacie v Slovenskom narodnom povstani. Bojove akcie I. cs Armady" (Military operations in the Slovak national uprising. Military actions of the First Czechoslovak Army), *Historicky casopis Slovenskej akademie vied* (Historical journal of the Slovak Academy of Sciences) 5, no. 1 (1957): 8.

31. Josef Rodak, "Bojova cinnost prislusnikov vychodoslovenskych divizii po ich rozpade" (Battle activities of members of the eastern Slovak divisions

after their collapse), *Historie e vojenstvi* 41, no. 4 (1992): 63. See also Toma, "Soviet Strategy," pp. 291–92 nn. 10, and 12; Kropilak, "Vojenske operacie," p. 8 ff.; Precan, "Nacisticka politika," part I, *Historie a vojenstvi* 39, no. 2 (1990): 13, and part III, 39, no. 4 (1990): 12.

32. *Archiv Dukelskeho muzea* (Archive of the Dukla Museum), no. 72/91, quoted in Rodak, "Bojova cinnost," p. 67 n. 23.

33. Vilem Precan, *Slovenske narodne povstanie. Dokumenty* (The Slovak National Uprising. Documents) (Bratislava: VPL, 1965), pp. 390–91.

34. Jozef Jablonicky and Miroslav Kropilak, *Slovnik Slovenskeho narodneho povstania*. 2 vydanie (Dictionary of the Slovak National Uprising. 2nd ed.) (Bratislava: Epocha, 1970), pp. 222–25.

35. Licko, *1944 USA*, p. 25.

36. See "Message of the President of the United States Franklin D. Roosevelt to President Eduard Beneš About the Slovak Insurgents," in Jozef Lettrich, *History of Modern Slovakia* (New York: Praeger, 1955), pp. 390–91. Roosevelt's reference to "Czechoslovak comrades-in-arms" was, of course, in agreement with Beneš's perception of Czechs, Slovaks, and Czechoslovaks—they all represented one nation.

37. On December 16, 1943, Benes submitted to the Soviet government in Moscow a memorandum, prepared by the Czechoslovak government, about military issues; these were discussed with and approved by J. V. Stalin two days later. In Section II, paragraph 1, the Soviet Union agreed to provide considerable military aid shortly before and after the uprising had begun. It specified "light armor for about 50,000 soldiers of German type for which ammunition is manufactured on Czechoslovak territory. Arms to be delivered early, shortly before the uprising and after to be dropped by parachute at given places. . . . To engage the Soviet Airforce in bombing key German railroad and industrial centers on Czechoslovak territory: The targets to be designated at the appropriate time." The original document is in Russian on nine typewritten pages signed by V. M. Molotov. See Frantisek Janacek and Marie Michalkova, "Nezname dokumenty z Benesovy cesty do Moskvy, v roce 1943. Dokumenty" (The unknown documents of Benes's trips to Moscow in the year 1943. Documents), *Historie a vojenstvi* 41, no. 5 (1992): 162–67.

38. Licko, *1944 USA*, pp. 21–22. For further details of the military operations in SNP, see *Dejiny Slovenskeho narodneho povstania, zv. 3. Dokumenty* (History of the Slovak National Uprising, vol. 3. Documents) (Bratislava: Pravda, 1984); Precan, *Slovenske narodne povstanie. Dokumenty* (1965); *Vojenske dejiny Slovenska, IV. diel* (Military history of Slovakia, 4 vols.) (Bratislava: Ministerstvo narodnej obrany, 1997); *Dostojnici a staby povstaleckej armady* (Officers and staff of the resistance army) (Banska Bystrica: Muzeum SNP, 1994).

39. See S. Grachev, *Pomosh SSSR narodam Chekhoslovakii v ikh borbye za svobodu i nezavisimost* (USSR's help to the peoples of Czechoslovakia in their

struggle for freedon and independence) (Moscow: Gospolitizdat, 1953), p. 163. See also Zdenek Fierlinger, *Ve sluzbach CSR* (In the service of the Czechoslovak Republic), vol. 2 (Prague: Delnicke nakladatelstvi, 1949), p. 358.

40. Sverma lost his life during the uprising in 1944. His widow, Marie Svermova, in 1949 was denounced as a spy and arrested. Slansky, who in 1945 became secretary-general of the CPC, was arrested in November 1951 on a charge of being a spy in the pay of Western imperialists. He was tried in November 1952 and hanged a few days afterward.

41. B. Pavlik, *Kommunisticheskaya partiya Chekhoslovakii v borbye za svobodu* (The Communist Party in the struggle for freedom), trans. from Czech by T. A. Yegerev and N. N. Sokolov (Moscow: Izd-vo inostrannoi literatury, 1951), p. 198.

42. Jozef Jablonicky, "Za cest generala Viesta" (In honor of General Viest), *Historie a vojenstvi* 39, no. 4 (1990): 99; ibid., p. 99 n. 4, quoting Ferdinand Beer et al., *Dejinna krizovatka* (Historical crossroads) (Bratislava: Vydavatelstvo politickej literatury, 1964), p. 423.

43. Ibid., p. 100 n. 8, quoting Vilem Precan, *Slovenske narodne povstanie. Dokumenty*, pp. 714–15.

44. Quoted in Licko, *1944 USA*, p. 104 n. 24.

45. Ibid., n. 25.

46. Ibid., pp. 25–26 n. 4.

47. Precan, *Slovenske narodne povstanie. Dokumenty*, p. 755.

48. Jablonicky, "Za cest generala Viesta," p. 102.

49. Peter Toma was one of the thousands who experienced this exodus until ` his capture by a French SS battalion three days later near Prasiva.

50. For further details about the capture, interrogation, and execution, see Jablonicky, "Za cest generala Viesta," pp. 109–14.

51. Licko, *1944 USA*, p. 29. See also Stefan Pazur, ed., *Fasisticke represalie na Slovensku* (Fascist reprisals in Slovakia) (Bratislava: Obzor, 1982).

52. Licko, *1944 USA*, p. 30.

CHAPTER 7

1. About the problems of the First Czechoslovak Army Corps, see Ludvik Svoboda, *Z Buzuluku do Prahy* (From Buzuluk to Prague) (Prague: Mlada fronta, 1960).

2. Winston S. Churchill, *The Second World War: Triumph and Tragedy* (Boston: Houghton Mifflin, 1953), pp. 506–7.

3. Ibid., p. 507.

4. Vlasov and thousands of his soldiers surrendered to the Americans, who

later handed them over to the Soviet authorities, at the request of the latter. Vlasov and his officers were later executed.

5. Karel Kaplan, "Ceskoslovensko po druhe svetove valce" (Czechoslovakia after the Second World War), *Historicky obzor* 1, no. 1 (1990): 7.

6. Ibid.

7. Ibid.

8. See Milos Klimes et al., eds., *Cesta ke kvetnu. Dokumenty o vzniku a vyvoji lidove demokracie v Ceskoslovensku do unora 1948* (The road to May. Documents about the origin and development of people's democracy in Czechoslovakia to February 1948) (Prague: Vydatelstvi CSAV, 1965), pp. 337–38, 410–14, 425–37. See also *Dokumenty moderni doby* (Documents of modern times) (Prague: Svoboda, 1978), pp. 474–94.

9. Klimes et al., *Cesta Ke Kvetnu,* pp. 337 ff.

10. Ibid. pp. 382–83.

11. Ibid., pp. 384–88.

12. Ibid., p. 366.

13. Ibid., p. 384.

14. Ibid., p. 427.

15. The composition was as follows: premier, Zdenek Fierlinger (Social Democrat); vice premiers, Klement Gottwald (Czech Communist), Viliam Siroky (Slovak Communist), Josef David (National Socialist), Msgr. Jan Sramek (Populist), and Jan Ursiny (Slovak Democrat); Jan Masaryk remained foreign minister; minister of national defense, Gen. Ludovik Svoboda; minister of interior, Vaclav Nosek (Czech Communist); minister of foreign trade, Hubert Ripka (National Socialist); minister of finance, Vavro Srobar (Slovak Democrat); minister of education, Zdenek Nejedly (Czech Communist); minister of justice, Jaroslav Stransky (National Socialist); minister of information, Vaclav Kopecky (Czech Communist); minister of agriculture, Julius Duris (Slovak Communist); minister of industry, Bohumil Lausman (Social Democrat); minister of trade, Ivan Pietor (Slovak Democrat); minister of transport, Gen. Antonin Hasal; minister of postal service, Frantisek Hala (Populist); minister of social welfare, Jozef Soltesz (Slovak Communist); minister of public health, Adolf Prochazka (Populist); supply minister, Vaclav Majer (Social Democrat).

16. Benes himself was proud to acknowledge his departure from the "rotten" liberal democracy and the inclusion of the higher phase of humanitarian democracy. See his *Democracie dnes a zitra* (Democracy today and tomorrow) (London: Kruh pratel ceskolovenske knihy v Londyne, 1941).

17. See Frantisek Janacek and Marie Michalkova, "Nezname dokumenty z Benesovy cesty do Moskvy v roce 1943. Dokumenty" (Unknown documents from Benes's trip to Moscow in 1943. Documents), *Historie a vojenstvi* 41, no. 5 (1992): 151–52.

18. "Benesuv archiv umisten ve Vojenskem historickem archivu, puvodni manipulace, rada: svetova valka, karton 278a" (Benes's archives, World War, carton 278a), quoted in Antonin Klimek, "Plany Edvarda Benese na povalecny vyvoj Ceskoslovenska" (Eduard Benes's plans for the postwar development of Czechoslovakia), *Stredni Evropa* 9, no. 30 (1993): 25 n. 3.

19. Charles de Gaulle, *Valecni pameti 1940–44* (War memoirs, 1940–44) (Prague: Nase vojsko, 1989), pp. 443–44, quoted in Klimek, "Plany Edvarda Benese," p. 25 n. 4.

20. Karel Kaplan, *Nekrvava revoluce* (Bloodless revolution) (Prague: Mlada fronta, 1993), pp. 42–43. For the full text of the nationalization decrees, see *Dokumenty moderni doby,* pp. 531–37. See also Vaclav Vrabec, "Znarodneni 1945" (Nationalization 1945), *Dejiny a soucasnost* (History and the presence) 13, no. 1 (1991): 48–59.

21. *Cas* (Times), October 31, 1945.

22. *Slovensky narodny archiv* (The Slovak National Archives), *fond 21, kartony 10–20* (fond 21, cartons 10–20). See also Dieter Blumenwitz, "Benesovy dekrety z roku 1945 z hlediska mezinarodniho prava" (Benes's decrees of 1945 from the view of international law), *Stredni Evropa* 8, no. 26 (1992): 22–30.

23. About the proposals of the underground resistance in Bohemia concerning the future treatment of Germans in postwar Czechoslovakia, see Vaclav Vrabec, "Vznik myslenky odsunu Nemcu v domacim odboji" (The origin of the idea to displace the Germans in domestic resistance), *Deiiny a soucasnost* (History and the presence) 12, no. 1 (1990): 50–53.

24. See Janacek and Michalkova, "Nezname dokumenty," p. 154. For the approved text of the memorandum about the transfer of Germans (with a brief reference to the Hungarians), see document no. 2, pp. 156–58.

25. For the details on the treatment of the German clergy and other religious matters, see Tomas Stanek, "Odsun Nemcu a Krestane (1945–1948)" (The transfer of Germans and Christians (1945–1948)), *Stredni Evropa* 7, no. 22 (1992): 121–31.

26. For details of this incident, see Tomas Stanek, "Co ste stalo v Usti nad Labem 31. cervence 1945?" (What happened at Usti nad Labem on July 31, 1945?), *Dejiny a soucasnost* 12, no. 2 (1990): 48–51. See also M. Veverkova, "Bila barva zbarvila nachem hnevu a krve" (The white color tainted with anger and blood), *Osidlovani* (Settlement), nos. 4/5 (1947): 93; O. Graaf's commentary in *Svet prace* (The world of work), September 20, 1945, p. 3; *Obzory* (Horizons), no. 9 (October 20, 1945); and *Obzory,* no. 10 (October 27, 1945).

27. *OA Prerov, Okresni soud Prerov, odd. c. IV. TkX 2282/447, list 81–83* (OA Prerov, District Court Prerov, section no. IV, TkX 2282/47, pp. 81–83).

28. According to the protocol prepared by Lt. Maj. Eugen Surovcik on August 21, 1945, at Levice, "At the request of Lt. Pazur, I gave him 20 soldiers with these words of advice: You know best what your dispositions are, what

you have to and what you don't have to do. If you are going to do something, do it at night in such a way and in a place where the civilians won't see it. As far as I know, the entire action was carried out unnoticed at night." *Archiv Federalniho ministerstva vnitra. 302-528-23* (Archives of the Federal Ministry of the Interior, 302-528-23), quoted in Tomas Stanek and Lubor Vaclavu, "Pripad Prerov 18. cervna 1945. Dokumenty" (The Case of Prerov, June 18, 1945. documents), *Historie a vojenstvi* 40, no. 3 (1991): 170.

29. For further details and documents, see Stanek and Vaclavu, "Pripad Prerov," pp. 168–75.

30. See the memoirs of Col. Anton Rasla, chief military procurator in the case against Lt. Karol Pazur, in *Archiv Muzea SNP*, Banska Bystrica, fond XII, prir. cis. 57/87, str. 69–70 (Archives of the SNP Muzeum at Banska Bystrica, fond XII, catalogue no. 57/87, pp. 69–70).

31. Ibid.

32. Stanek and Vaclavu, "Pripad Prerov," p. 172.

33. Ibid.

34. Thomas Garrigue Masaryk, *Idealy Humanitni* (Humanitarian ideals) (Prague: Cin, 1946), p. 57.

35. For additional data on German transfer, see Karel Kaplan, *Pravda o Ceskoslovensku 1945–1948* (Truth about Czechoslovakia, 1945–1948) (Prague: Panorama, 1990), p. 144 ff.

36. See, e.g., Alfred de Zayas, "Angloamericane a vyhnani sudetskych Nemcu" (Anglo-Americans and the expulsion of Sudete Germans), *Stredni Evropa* 8, no. 26 (1992): 61–66. See also Alfred de Zayas, "Vysidleni a pravo" (Displacement and law), ibid. 7, no. 21 (1991): 57–61.

37. *The Week in Germany*, May 2, 1997, p. 2.

38. "12.000 Madarov odtransportovanych do Ciech a na Moravu" (Twelve thousand Magyars deported to Bohemia and Moravia), *Cas* (Bratislava), November 15, 1945, p. 2, quoted in lmre Molnar, "Kapitoly z povalecnych dejin Madaru vysidlenych do Cech" (Chapters for postwar history of Magyars deported to Bohemia), *Stredni Evropa* 7, no. 19 (1991): 75.

39. Stefan Sutaj, "Poznamky ku kapitolam z povalecnych dejin Madaru vysidlenych do Cech" (Remarks to the chapters from postwar history of Magyars deported to Bohemia), *Stredni Evropa* 8, no. 26 (1992): 75.

40. For details, see Molnar, "Kapitoly," pp. 78–87. See also Juraj Zvara, *Madarska mensina na Slovensku po roku 1945* (The Hungarian minority in Slovakia after the year 1945) (Bratislava: Epocha, t. Pravda, 1969).

41. Sutaj, "Poznamky," p. 80 n. 11.

42. Hugh Seton-Watson, *The East European Revolt* (New York: Praeger, 1961), p. 182.

43. See Elo Rakos and Stefan Rudohradsky, *Slovenske narodne organy 1943–1968* (Slovak national institutions, 1943–1968) (Bratislava: Slovenska archivna sprava, 1973), pp. 554–57.

44. Seton-Watson, *The East European Revolt*, pp. 183–84.

45. According to official reports, about 70 percent of all offices of the prewar army (1939) were readmitted into service, but that included less than 50 percent of all generals and colonels. See Frantisik Hanzlik, "K problematice budovani dustojnickeho sboru Ceskoslovenske armady v roce 1945" (The problem of building the officer corps of the Czechoslovak army in 1945), *Historie a vojenstvi* 41, no. 6 (1992): 76–101.

46. Janacek and Michalkova, "Nezname dokumenty," p. 152. See also Ivo Duchacek, "The Strategy of Communist Infiltration of Czechoslovakia in 1944–1948," *World Politics* 2, no. 3 (April 1950): 354; Waldermar Gurian et al., *The Soviet Union: Background. Ideology. Reality* (Notre Dame, Ind.: Notre Dame University Press, 1951), pp. 69–70; Jiri Hronek, "Czechoslovakia: The Immediate Problems," *Central European Observer* 22, no. 4 (February 23, 1945): 59.

47. Zdenek Fierlinger, *Ve sluzbach CSR: Pameti z druheho zahranicneho odboje* (In the service of Czechoslovakia: Memoirs from the second resistance abroad), vol. 2 (Prague: Svoboda, 1949), pp. 595–96.

48. *New York Herald Tribune*, June 8, 1948.

49. For details, see Eric Johnston, "A Satellite is Born," *Reader's Digest*, September 1948, pp. 31–35.

CHAPTER 8

1. See Pavel Reiman et al., *Dejiny Komumisticke strany Ceskoslovenska* (History of the Communist Party of Czechoslovakia) (Prague: Statni nakladatelstvo politicke literatury, 1961), pp. 522–35.

2. Walter Wellman, "Prezident Benes mezi Vychodem a Zapadem (1943–1948)" (President Benes between the east and the west (1943–1948)) *Historie a vojenstvi* 39, no. 6 (1990): 112–19.

3. The next several pages are based on works by Jaromir Smutny, *Unorovy prevrat 1948* (The February 1948 coup d'état), vol. 1 (London: Ustav dr. E. Benese, Doklady a rozpravy c. 12, 1953), pp. 15–16; Lev Sychrava, *Svedectvi a uvahy o prazskem prevratu v unoru 1948* (Testimony and reflections about the Prague coup in February 1948) (mimeograph, London: Ustav dra. Edvarda Benese v Londyne, 1953); and Vrastislav Busek, *Pouceni unoroveho prevratu* (Lessons from the February coup) (New York: CS Publishing Co., 1954), whose account of the events is here summarized.

4. A. J. Jandacek, *Zivot za zeleznou oponou* (Life behind the iron curtain) (Chicago: Tiskarna Ceskych Benediktinu, 1948), p. 34.

5. Smutny, *Unorovy prevrat 1948*, p. 24.

6. Ibid., p. 25.

7. Bohumil Lausman, *Kdo byl vinen?* (Who was guilty?) (Vienna: Vorwarts, 1953), p. 160.

8. Hubert Ripka, *Czechoslovakia Enslaved* (London: Gollancz, 1951), pp. 238, 288. See also Ivo Duchacek, "The February Coup in Czechoslovakia," *Foreign Affairs* 2, no. 4 (July 1950): 511–32; Adolf Klimek, "Jak to delali" (How they did it), *Hlas Ceskoslovenska III (18)*, no. 2 (1953): 17.

9. Lausman, *Kdo byl vinen*, pp. 120, 124.

10. *Dejiny KSC*, p. 528.

11. John Brown, *Who's Next?* (London: Hutchinson, 1951), p. 156.

12. Jandacek, *Zivot za zeleznou oponou*, p. 45.

13. Lausman, *Kdo byl vinen*, p. 128; Jandacek, *Zivot za zeleznou oponou*, p. 49.

14. Lausman, *Kdo byl vinen*, p. 131.

15. Ibid., p. 135.

16. Ripka, *Czechoslovakia Enslaved*, p. 267.

17. Jandacek, *Zivot za zeleznou oponou*, p. 57.

18. Busek, *Pouceni*, p. 110.

19. Ibid., p. 115.

20. Peter A. Toma, "The Political Role of the Coup of February 1948 in the History of the Socialist Revolutions," in M. Rechcigl, ed., *Czechoslovakia Past and Present* (The Hague: Mouton, 1968), pp. 269–95.

21. Winston S. Churchill, *Closing the Ring* (Boston: Houghton Mifflin, 1951), pp. 452–53.

22. Ferdinand Peroutka, *Byl dr. Edvard Benes vinen?* (Was Dr. Edward Benes guilty?) (London: Masarykuv demokraticky Svaz, 1950).

23. Dana Adams Schmidt, *Anatomy of a Satellite* (Boston: Little, Brown, 1952), p. 110.

24. Peter Mares, "Unor ocima americkeho velvyslance v Praze. Prameny a dokumenty" (February through the eyes of the American ambassador in Prague. Sources and documents), *Dejiny a soucasnost* (History and the presence) 13, no. 2 (1991): 52.

25. A good sample of documentary evidence about Benes's attitude toward the Soviet Union after the signing of the Czechoslovak-Soviet Agreement About Friendship and Military Alliance of December 12, 1943, is contained in Antonin Klimek, "Plany Edvarda Benese na povalecny vyvoj ceskoslovenska" (Edward Benes's plans for postwar development in Czechoslovakia), *Stredni Evropa* 9, no. 20 (1993): 25–31.

26. For overviews of post–WWII developments in Czechoslovakia, see John F. N. Bradley, *Politics in Czechoslovakia, 1945–1990* (Boulder, Colo.: Westview

Press, 1991); and Hans Renner, *History of Czechoslovakia Since 1945* (New York: Routledge, 1989).

27. Vrastislav Busek, "Action Committees in the Czechoslovak National Socialist Party" in M. Rechcigl, ed., *Czechoslovakia Past and Present*, pp. 296–333; Vlastislav J. Chalupa, *The National Front in Czechoslovakia* (Chicago: Czechoslovak Foreign Institute in Exile, 1958).

28. For early totalitarian practices, see Vlastislav J. Chalupa, *Rise and Development of a Totalitarian State* (Leiden: H. E. Stenfert Kroese N.V., 1959); Ladislav K. Feierabend, "The Gottwald Era in Czechoslovakia," *Journal of Central European Affairs* 13, no. 3 (October 1953): 246–56; Zdenek Krystufek, *The Soviet Regime in Czechoslovakia* (Boulder, Colo.: Westview Press, 1981).

29. See Jiri Pelikan, ed., *The Czechoslovak Political Trials. 1950–1954: The Suppressed Report of the Dubcek Government's Commission of Inquiry 1968* (Stanford: Stanford University Press, 1971); Robert K. Evanson, "Political Repression in Czechoslovakia, 1948–1984," *Canadian Slavonic Papers* 28, no. 1 (1986): 1–21; Karel Kaplan, *Political Persecution in Czechoslovakia 1948–1972*, Study no. 3 of research project, "Crises in Soviet-Type Systems," directed by Zdenek Mlynar with a scientific counsel (Köln: INDEX e.V., 1983).

30. Karel Kaplan, *Report on the Murder of the General Secretary* (Columbus: Ohio State University Press, 1990); Louis Rapoport, *Stalin's War Against the Jews: The Doctor's Plot and the Soviet Solution* (New York: Free Press, 1990); Artur Gerard London, *On Trial* (London: MacDonald, 1970).

31. Karel Kaplan, *Prazske dohody 1945–1947. Sbornik dokumentu* (The Prague agreements, 1945–1947. Collection of documents) (Prague: Ustav pro soudobe dejiny ve spolupraci se Statnim ustrednim archivem, 1992).

32. Josef Kalvoda, "Czechoslovakia's Socialist Constitution," *American Slavic and East European Review* 20, no. 2 (1961): 220–36.

33. For observations on the political developments in Czechoslovakia, see H. Gordon Skilling's "Journey to Prague" series published in *Kosmas: Czechoslovak and Central European Journal*, vols. 5–8 and 11 for the years 1948–1968.

34. Jaroslav Krejci, *Social Change and Stratification in Postwar Czechoslovakia* (New York: Columbia University Press, 1972).

35. *Sjazd KSS v dnoch 23.–25. Novembra 1962* (Congress of the Communist Party of Slovakia during November 23–25, 1962) (Bratislava: Ustredny vybor Komunistickej strany Slovenska, 1962).

36. See Galia Golan, *The Czechoslovak Reform Movement: Communism in Crisis, 1962–1968* (Cambridge: Cambridge University Press, 1971); Jiri Kosta, "The Czechoslovak Economic Reform of the 1960s," in Norman Stone and Edward Strouhal, eds., *Czechoslovakia: Crossroads and Crises, 1918–1988* (New York: St. Martin's Press, 1989), pp. 231–52.

CHAPTER 9

1. Dusan Hamsik, *Writers Against Rulers* (London: Hutchinson, 1971).

2. Galia Golan, "Antonin Novotny: The Sources and Nature of His Power," *Canadian Slavonic Papers* 14, no. 3 (1972): 421–41.

3. Yeshayahu A. Jelinek, "National Tension as a Lever for Seizure of Power: Czechs, Slovaks, and Communists," *East Central Europe* 16, nos. 1–2 (1989): 71–88; Stanislav J. Kirschbaum, "Federalism in Slovak Communist Politics," *Canadian Slavonic Papers* 19, no. 4 (1977): 444–67; Kirschbaum, "Slovak Nationalism in Socialist Czechoslovakia," *Canadian Slavonic Papers* 22, no. 2 (1980): 220–46; Pavel Korbel, "Prague and the Slovaks," *East Europe* 12, no. 3 (1963): 6–12.

4. Z. Hejzlar, "Changes in the Czechoslovak Communist Party, 1966–68," in Vladimir V. Kusin, ed., *The Czechoslovak Reform Movement. 1968* (London: International Research Documents, 1973), pp. 109–32.

5. For a bibliography of works about Dubcek, see the study compiled by George J. Kovtun, *Czech and Slovak History* (Washington, D.C.: Library of Congress, 1996), p. 69.

6. For General Sejna's role in the planned military intervention against the proreform Czech and Slovak communists and other enemies of Novotny in December 1967–January 1968, see Alexander Dubcek's memoirs in his *Hope Dies Last*, edited and translated by Jiri Hochman (New York: Kodansha International, 1993), pp. 124–25, 138.

7. See G. Chand, "Economic Reforms and Their Meaning," in P. K. Sundarm, ed., *Whither Czechoslovakia? Essays and Documents on Czechoslovak Crisis* (New Delhi: Dawn Publishers, 1969), pp. 88–103; articles by Vaclav Holesovsky published in *East Central Europe* during 1964, 1965, 1967; and Vaclav Holesovsky and Gregor Lazarczik, *Czechoslovakia* (New York: Columbia University Press, 1968), especially parts I and II. See also Ota Sik, "Prague's Spring, Roots and Reasons: The Economic Impact of Stalinism," *Problems of Communism* 20, no. 3 (1971): 1–10; and Eugene Loebl, "The Perspectives of Reform," in Kusin, ed., *The Czechoslovak Reform Movement. 1968,* pp. 323–40.

8. For the role of the media, see Madeleine Korbel Albright, "The Role of the Press in Political Change: Czechoslovakia 1968" (Ph.D. dissertation, Columbia University, 1976); D. Havlicek, "Mass Media and Their Impact on Czechoslovak Politics in 1968," in Kusin, ed., *The Czechoslovak Reform Movement, 1968,* pp. 237–80; Frank L. Kaplan, *Winter into Spring: The Czechoslovak Press and the Reform Movement. 1963–1968* (Boulder, Colo.: Westview Press, 1977).

9. The declaration is reprinted in Andrew Oxley, Alex Pravda, and Andrew Ritchie, eds., *Czechoslovakia: The Party and the People* (New York: St. Martin's Press, 1973).

10. Arnulf Ivan Simon, "Czechoslovakia's KAN: A Brief Venture in Democracy," *East Europe* 18, no. 6 (1969): 20–22; Jaroslav Brodsky, "Czechoslovakia's 231 Club," ibid., pp. 23–25.

11. For Moscow's position, see Karen Dawisha, *The Kremlin and the Prague Spring* (Berkeley: University of California Press, 1980). See also Dubcek, *Hope Dies Last*, pp. 158–59.

12. Albania, one of the original eight members of the WTO, had by this time withdrawn.

13. Boris Meisner, *The Brezhnev Doctrine* (Kansas City, Mo.: Park College, Governmental Research Bureau, 1970). See also Dubcek, *Hope Dies Last*, pp. 167–70.

14. See Robert W. Dean, *Nationalism and Political Change in Eastern Europe: The Slovak Question and the Czechoslovak Reform Movement* (Denver: University of Denver Press, 1973).

15. *Kulturny zivot* (Cultural Life), May 3, 1968.

16. *Zbierka zakonov CSSR, Ustavnv zakon o ceskoslovenskej federacii, c. 143/1968 z 27. oktobra 1968* (Collection of laws in the Czechoslovak Socialist Republic, constitutional law about Czechoslovak Federation, no. 143/1968, October 27, 1968).

17. Milan J. Reban, "Czechoslovakia: The New Federation," in George Klein and Milan J. Reban, eds., *Politics of Ethnicity in Eastern Europe* (Boulder, Colo.: East European Monographs, 1981), pp. 215–46.

18. Peter A. Toma, "The Czecho-Slovak Question Under Communism," *East European Quarterly* 3, no. 1 (March 1969): 15–30.

19. I. William Zartmann, *Czechoslovakia: Intervention and Impact* (New York: New York University Press, 1970); *The Czech Black Book* (New York: Praeger, 1969); Barbara W. Jancar, "When the Soviets Invaded Bratislava," *East Europe* 17, no. 10 (1968): 2–9.

20. Published on August 21, 1969, in all Czech and Slovak daily newspapers.

21. Jaroslav Pelikan, ed. , *The Secret Vysocany Congress: Proceedings and Documents of the Extraordinary Fourteenth Congress of the Communist Party of Czechoslovakia, 22 August 1968* (New York: St. Martin's Press, 1971).

22. Cf. Zdenek Mlynar, *Nightfrost in Prague: The End of Humane Socialism* (London: Hurst, 1980).

23. For 31 years it was rumored, but denied, that the communist dogmatists from Czechoslovakia, headed by Vasil Bilak, wrote a letter to the Soviet party chief, Leonid I. Brezhnev, asking for Soviet military intervention against the Czechoslovak counterrevolutionaries. According to a documentary, "Vasil Vlastenec" (Vasil the Patriot), aired by Czech TV (CT2) on December 7, 1999,

and (CT1) on December 14, 1999, Boris Yeltsin in 1992 handed to Vaclav Havel such a document; the commander of the central group of the occupation forces in 1968, General Mayorov, testified that it was Bilak and his cohorts who called in the troops. See *SME*, December 23, 1999.

24. By then, the first phase of "normalization" had been put into motion. For a long list of references in English about the "Prague Spring", see the bibliography in George J. Kovtun, *Czech and Slovak History*.

CHAPTER 10

1. For "normalization," see Vladimir V. Kusin, *From Dubcek to Charter 77* (New York: St. Martin's Press, 1978); Milan Simecka, *The Restoration of Order: The Normalization of Czechoslovakia. 1969–1976* (London: Verso, 1984); Edward Taborsky, "Czechoslovakia's Abnormal 'Normalization,' " *Current History* 64, no. 381 (1973): 207–10; Otto Ulc, "The Normalization of Post-Invasion Czechoslovakia," *Survey* 24, no. 3 (1979): 201–13.

2. For the Husak era, see Edward Taborsky, "Czechoslovakia Under Husak," *Current History* 64, no. 381 (1973): 207–10; and Josef Josten, *Czechoslovakia: From 1968 to Charter 77: A Record of Passive Resistance* (London: Institute for the Study of Conflict, 1977).

3. Vladimir V. Kusin, "Husak's Czechoslovakia and Economic Stagnation," *Problems of Communism* 31, no. 3 (1982): 24–37.

4. Gordon H. Skilling, "Czechoslovakia and Helsinki," *Canadian Slavonic Papers* 18, no. 4 (1976): 245–65; Edward Taborsky, "Czechoslovakia After Helsinki," *Current History* 74, no. 436 (1978): 164–84.

5. For the dissident movement, see Vaclav Havel, "The Power of the Powerless," in William M. Brinton and Alan Rinzler, eds., *Without Force or Lies: Voices from the Revolution of Central Europe in 1989–90* (San Francisco: Mercury House, 1990), pp. 43–127.

6. *Charta 77 (1977–1989). Od moralni k demokraticke revoluci* (Charter 77 (1977–1989). From moral to democratic revolution), ed. by Vilem Precan (Bratislava: Cs. Stredisko nezavisle literatury, Scheinfeld-Schwarzenberg a ARCHA, 1990), p. 9.

7. Ibid., p. 12.

8. Some of Havel's better-known political writings include "Havel's Letters from Prison," *Cross Currents* 3 (1984): 87–106; *Open Letters: Selected Writings, 1965–1990* (New York: Knopf, 1991); and *Living in Truth: Twenty-two Essays Published on the Occasion of the Award of the Erasmus Prize to Vaclav Havel* (London: Faber & Faber, 1989).

9. Part of the dissident movement also included the rudimentary technique

of dissemination of the press and other publications. See Gordon H. Skilling, "Samizdat: A Return to the Pre-Gutenberg Era?" *Cross Currents* 1 (1982): 64–80.

10. In Slovakia, one signatory of the Charter was the writer Hana Ponicka. See Mary Hrabik-Samal and Z. Borska, "The Lukavica Notebooks," *Cross Currents* 9 (1990): 241–60.

11. About Eurocommunism and Czechoslovakia, see Jiri Valenta, "Eurocommunism and Czechoslovakia," *East Central Europe* 7, no. 1 (1980): 17–38.

12. See Sabrina Petra Ramet, "The Catholic Church in Czechoslovakia, 1948–1991," *Studies in Comparative Communism* 24, no. 4 (1991): 377–93; and Peter A. Toma, "Church-State Schism in Czechoslovakia," in Boris R. Bociurkiw, ed., *Religion and Atheism in the USSR and Eastern Europe* (New York: Macmillan, 1975), pp. 273–91.

CHAPTER 11

1. Data for the events in Prague and Bratislava, unless otherwise indicated, are derived from "Kronika nasho prebudenia. Retrospektiva novembrovych dni nasich narodov" (Chronicle of our awakening. In retrospect the November days of our nations); excerpts from the world and Czechoslovak press compiled by research workers of the Slovak Academy of Sciences, Institute of Modern History, Bratislava, as well as from Petr Proks, *Konec jednoho experimentu* (The end of an experiment) (Prague: H & H, 1993), pp. 58–63.

2. See SNC, *121 Uznesenie Slovenskej narodnej rady z 30 novembra 1989, cislo: 1187/989* (121st Resolution of the Slovak National Council on November 30, 1989, no. 118711989).

3. *Svobodne Slovo* (Free Word), January 24, 1990.

4. Vladimira Dvorakova and Gabriela Stechova, "Sjednana demokratizace" (Negotiated democratization), *Politologie dnes* (Politology today), no. 1 (1992): 46–59.

5. Jiri Kosta, "Oekoenoemische Aspekte des Systemswandels in der Tschechoslowakei" (Economic aspects of the changing system in Czechoslovakia), in Rudolph Deppe et. al., eds., *Demokratischer Umbruch in Osteuropa* (Democratic transition in Eastern Europe) (Frankfurt: Suhrkamp, 1991), pp. 302 ff.

6. Pavel Machonin and Miloslav Petrusek, "Jeste jednou ke koncepciam vyvoje socialni struktury v Ceskoslovensku" (More on the concepts of development of the social structure in Czechoslovakia), *Sociologicky casopis* (Journal of sociology) 27, no. 1 (1991): 90–96.

7. For further details concerning the conceptual differences between liberal-

ization and democratization, see Pietro Grilli di Cortona, "From Communism to Democracy: Rethinking Regime Change in Hungary and Czechoslovakia," *International Social Science Journal* 43, no. 2 (May 1991): 315–31.

8. Zora Butorova and Martin Butora, "Political Parties and Slovakia's Road to Independence," in Gyorgy Csepeli, ed., *From Subject to Citizen* (Budapest: Hungarian Center for Political Education, 1994), pp. 322–23.

9. For public opinion surveys on issues and political preferences during the liberalization process in Slovakia, see Z. Butorova, P. Frie, and T. Rosova, "Rok Po: vyvoj politickej sceny na Slovensku v zrkadle vyskumov" (The year after: The political developments in Slovakia as reflected in research), *Sociologia* (Sociology) 27, no. 6 (1991), quoted in Martin Butora, Zora Butorova, and Tatiana Rosova, "The Hard Birth of Democracy in Slovakia: The Eighteen Months Following the 'Tender' Revolution," *Journal of Communist Studies* 7, no. 4 (December 1994): 442–43.

10. V. Bacova and A. Zelova, "Etnicke mensiny na Slovensku" (Ethnic minorities in Slovakia), in *Slovensko kroky k europskemu spolocenstvu. Scenar socioalno-politickych suvislosti do roku 2005* (Slovakia, steps toward European society. A scenario of sociopolitical relations until the year 2005) *Collected Works,* vol. 1 (Bratislava: 1993), pp. 237–70.

11. Fedor Gal, *Z prvei ruky* (At first hand) (Bratislava: Archa, 1991), pp. 72–73.

12. Fedor Gal, "Problem cesko-slovenskych vztahov po novembri 1989 cez prizmu politiky" (The problem of Czecho-Slovak relations after November 1989 through the prism of politics), in *Dnesni krize cesko-slovenskych vztahu* (Contemporary crisis in Czecho-Slovak relations), *Collected Works* (Prague: 1992), pp. 21–22.

13. Gal, *Z prvei ruky*, pp. 71–73.

14. *Sloboda* 45, 2 (1990), p. 3.

15. *Sloboda*, 45, 3 (1990), p. 1.

16. *Pravda*, 71, 108 (May 10, 1990), p. 6.

17. Gal, *Z prvei ruky*, pp. 32–36; *Pravda*, 71, 119 (May 23, 1990), p. 3.

18. *Verejnost* (The public) 1, no. 13 (May 29, 1990), p. 4.

19. Jiri Pehe, "The Electoral Law," *Report on Eastern Europe* 1, no. 21 (May 25, 1990): 18.

20. *Svobodne Slovo*, April 20, 1990. Because CF and PAV as well as the Christian and Democratic Union and the Christian Democratic Movement had agreed to run independently but become coalition partners after the elections, the actual number of parties, movements, and coalitions came to 26.

21. *Pravda* (Bratislava), April 11, 1990, p. 1.

22. *Financial Times*, May 17, 1990.

23. Peter Martin, "The Election Campaign," *Report on Eastern Europe* 1, no. 24 (June 15, 1990): 17.

24. *Washington Post,* June 3,1990.

25. Martin, "The Election Campaign," pp. 17–18.

26. Ibid., p. 18.

27. Ibid., p. 19 n. 22; *The Guardian,* April 21, 1990.

28. Jiri Pehe, "Marian Calfa to Form New Government," *Report on Eastern Europe* 1, no. 26 (June 29, 1990): 5.

29. "Owing to a technicality, Havel swore in the new federal government twice. On June 27, the Czechoslovak federal government of 'national understanding' resigned, and a new government was sworn in. The same day, however, the Federal Assembly Presidium said that the resignation of the old government and the swearing in of the new one had not been carried out according to Constitutional Law (Article 71), whereby a new government may resign only after the constituent session of the new Federal Assembly. Because the government had resigned at 8:30 P.M. and the new one had been sworn in shortly after 9:00 P.M., that is, before the parliamentary session was over at 10:30 P.M., the resignation of the previous government was considered invalid. On June 29 the new government resigned and was sworn in by Havel for the second time." Radio Prague, June 28, 1990, 10:30 A.M., quoted in Peter Martin, "The New Governments," *Report on Eastern Europe* 1, no. 30 (July 27, 1990): 12 n. 1. It should also be pointed out that the first competitive elections leading to a new government and new institutional order along with restructuring did not conclude the democratization process, as some scholars, like Pietro Grilli di Cortona, have alleged. See di Cortona, "From Communism to Democracy: Rethinking Regime Change in Hungary and Czechoslovakia," p. 325.

30. *Praca* (Labor) 45, no. 149 (June 27, 1990).

31. *Verejnost* (The public) 1, no. 39 (June 28, 1990).

32. Ibid., July 3, 1990.

33. Peter Martin, "The Movements Present Their Programs," *Report on Eastern Europe* 1, no. 30 (July 27, 1990): 13–15.

34. Butora, Butorova, and Rosova, "The Hard Birth of Democracy in Slovakia," p. 445.

CHAPTER 12

1. Jiri Pehe, "Changing Configuration of Political Forces in the Federal Assembly," *Report on Eastern Europe* 2, no. 16 (April 16, 1991): 11–12.

2. Jiri Pehe, "Growing Slovak Demands Seen as Threat to Federation," ibid. 2, no. 12 (March 22, 1991): 6.

3. *Narodna obroda* (National revival), March 11, 1991.

4. *Pravda,* March 13, 1991.

5. Pehe, "Growing Slovak Demands Seen as Threat to Federation," pp. 8–9.

6. Jiri Pehe, "The First Weeks of 1991: Problems Solved, Difficulties Ahead," *Report on Eastern Europe* 2, no. 10 (March 8, 1991): 8.

7. The program was published in *Narodna obroda*, September 5, 1990.

8. For data showing the results of "equalization" of the economically active populations of the Czech and Slovak Republics during the 1970s and 1980s in education, work-complexity, managerial positions, earnings, and lifestyle, see Jaroslav Krejci and Pavel Machonin, *Czechoslovakia. 1918–92* (New York: St. Martin's Press, 1996), pp. 192–211. On the effects of Slovakia's asynchronical modernization during the socialist regime as well as the application of the unifying Soviet model, see Jiri Musil, "Ceska a slovenska spolecnost" (Czech and Slovak society), *Sociologicky casopis* 29, no. 1 (1993): 9–24.

9. S. Sikora, "Stop rychlej konverzii" (End to speedy conversion), *Narodna obroda*, January 8, 1991.

10. *Lidove Noviny*, December 28, 1990, p. 2.

11. *Narodna obroda*, January 3, 1991.

12. *Die Presse*, August 27, 1990.

13. Among the Slovak and Czech sociologists who participated in the research and survey analysis under the auspices of several Czech and Slovak research institutes were Vladimir Krivy, Zora Butorova, I. Dianiska, M. Dobrovodsky, P. Fric, T. Rosova, I. Radicova, E. Stehlikova, and O. Smidova. See Vladimir Krivy, "Slovenska a ceska definicia situacie" (Slovak and Czech definition of the situation), *Sociologicky casopis* 29, no. 1 (1993): 73–87.

14. Zora Butorova, "Premyslene 'ano' zaniku CSFR? Image stran a rozpad Cesko-Slovenska ocami obcanov Slovenska" (A deliberate 'yes' to the dissolution of the CSFR? The image of the parties and the split of Czecho-Slovakia in the eyes of the Slovak population), ibid., pp. 88–90.

15. Ibid., pp. 93–99.

16. *Pravda*, June 8, 1992.

17. *Ciele Hnutia za demokraticke Slovensko* (Goals of the movement for a democratic Slovakia) (1992 election poster).

18. *Tezy z uvodu volebneho programu Slovenskej narodnej strany: Slovensko 1992* (Theses from the introduction to the election program of the Slovak National Party: Slovakia 1992) (1992 election flyer).

19. See Vaclav Havel, *Letni premitani* (Summer reflections) (Prague: Odeon, 1991).

20. See *The Constitution of the Slovak Republic* (Bratislava: PRESSFOTO, the Publishing House of the Press Agency of the Slovak Republic, n.d.).

21. See *Usnesenie Ustavneho sudu c. 206/1993 Zbierky zakonov a usnesenie Ustavneho sudu 1993–1994* (Decision of the Constitutional Court no. 206/

1992 collected statutes, no. 5/1993 of the collected findings and decisions of the Constitutional Court 1993–1994). See also Lubor Cibulka, "Ustava SR s akcentom na postavenie prezidenta SR" (The Constitution of the SR with an emphasis on the role of the president of the SR), in *Aktualni otazky ceskeho a ceskoslovenskeho konstitucionalismu* (Timely issues concerning Czech and Czechoslovak constitutionalism) (Brno: Law Faculty of Masaryk University, 1993), pp. 85–94.

22. For the inconsistencies contained in the 1992 constitution, see Ernest Valko, "Legislation," in Martin Butora and Peter Huncik, eds., *Global Report on Slovakia: Comprehensive Analysis from 1995 and Trends from 1996* (Bratislava: Sandor Marai Foundation, 1997), pp. 76–77.

23. For a critical commentary and recommendations of the constitution, see Zdenek Koudelka, "Navrh na upravu slovenske ustavy" (A proposal for improving the Slovak constitution), *Politologicky casopis* (Journal of politology) 3, no. 1 (1996): 38–50.

24. Published in all Slovak daily newspapers on January 2, 1993.

25. For additional comparative data on the Slovak economy since the transition in 1993, see Butora and Huncik, eds., *Global Report on Slovakia.*

26. Zora Butorova and Martin Butora, "Political Parties and Slovakia's Road to Independence," in Gyorgy Csepeli, Daniel German, Laszlo Ken, and Istvan Stumpf, eds., *From Subject to Citizen* (Budapest: Hungarian Center for Political Education, 1994), pp. 329–30.

CHAPTER 13

1. Vaclav Havel, "The Power of the Powerless," in William M. Brinton and Alan Rinzler, eds., *Without Force or Lies*, p. 124.

2. Ibid., pp. 106–10.

3. Valerie Bunce, "The Struggle for Liberal Democracy in Eastern Europe," *World Policy Journal* 7, no. 3 (Summer 1990): 395–430, quoted in Tamara J. Resler and Roger E. Kanet, "Democratization: The National-Subnational Linkage," *In Depth* 1, no. 1 (Winter 1993): 12.

4. Grigorij Meseznikov, "Domestic Political Developments and the Political Scene in the Slovak Republic" in Martin Butora and Peter Huncik, eds., *Global Report on Slovakia: Comprehensive Analyses from 1995 and Trends from 1996*, p. 15.

5. Ibid.

6. Ibid.

7. See Article 102, paragraph (r) of *The Constitution of the Slovak Republic*, p. 57; Meseznikov, "Domestic Political Developments," p. 15.

8. See "The Preamble," *The Constitution of the Slovak Republic,* p. 15.

9. Radio Prague, April 27, 1990, 7:30 P.M.

10. See *Literarni Noviny* (Literary news), no. 5 (1990): 1, 3; *Nove Slovo* (New word), no. 21 (May 24, 1990): 5.

11. *Slovensky Dennik* (Slovak daily), July 30, 1990.

12. Martin Butora et al., "The Hard Birth of Democracy in Slovakia," p. 451.

13. *Elet es Irodalom* (Life and literature), December 15, 1989.

14. *Nepszabadsag* (People's freedom), January 15, 1990.

15. *Uj Szo* (New word), December 15, 1989.

16. *Nepszabadsag,* January 15, 1990.

17. *Magyar Hirlap* (Hungarian newspaper), January 27, 1990. For further details of the postcommunist development of the Hungarian minority in Czechoslovakia, see Edith Oltay, "Hungarian Minority in Slovakia Sets Up Independent Organizations," *Report on Eastern Europe* 1, no. 11 (March 16, 1990): 18–22.

18. *A Het* (The week), March 16, 1990.

19. *Uj Szo,* April 19, 1990.

20. Edith Oltay, "Hungarians in Slovakia Organize to Press for Ethnic Rights," *Report on Eastern Europe* 1, no. 22 (June 1, 1990): 22.

21. Ibid., p. 23, and *Magyar Hirlap,* March 2, 1990.

22. Ibid., and *Magyar Forum,* March 15, 1990.

23. Jan Obrman, "Language Law Stirs Controversy in Slovakia," *Report on Eastern Europe* 1, no. 46 (November 16, 1990): 14–15. It is interesting to note that, since SNP held only 22 seats in the SNC, 29 deputies of other parties apparently supported the more radical version of the law.

24. *Lidove Noviny,* October 26, 1990.

25. *Praca* (Labor), October 10, 1990.

26. Ondrej Dostal, "Minorities," in Butora and Huncik, eds., *Global Report on Slovakia,* p. 67.

27. Ibid., p. 68.

28. Vladimir Krivy, "Slovakia's Regions," in *Global Report,* pp. 297, 299–300.

29. Zora Butorova, "Public Opinion," in ibid., p. 280.

30. See Butorova, ibid., p. 281. See also Zora Butorova et al., *Current Problems of Slovakia After the Split of the CSFR—October 1993* (Bratislava: FOCUS, 1993).

31. For further details about a demographic analysis of the ethnic Hungarians in Slovakia, see Laszlo Gyurgyik, *Magyar merleg: A szlovakiai magyarsag a nepszamlalasi es a nepmozgalmi adatok tukreben* (The Hungarian scales: Slovakia's Hungarian population in the mirror of the census and people's mobility data) (Bratislava: Kalligram, 1994).

32. Martin Butora et al., *Slovensko Rok Po* (Slovakia a year after) (Prague: FOCUS, 1994), p. 52.

33. Martin Butora and Zora Butorova, "A Wary Approach: Attitudes Towards Jews and Jewish Issues in Slovakia," *East European Jewish Affairs* 23, no. 1 (1993): 5–20.

34. Zora Butorova, "Public Opinion," in *Global Report*, pp. 270–71. See also *Pravda*, March 23, 1996, and *Narodna obroda*, March 27, 1996.

35. Josef Kosta, "Some Characteristics of the 1994 Parliamentary Election Campaign," in Sona Szomolanyi and Grigorij Meseznikov, eds., *Slovakia: Parliamentary Elections 1994* (Bratislava: lnterlingua Publishing House, 1995), pp. 178–81.

36. See *Zakon SNR o volbach do SNR c. 179/1992 Zbierka, 41* (The law of the SNC about the elections into the SNC, no. 179/1992 collected, 41).

37. See *Zakon NR SR c. 157/1994 Zbierka* (The law of the NCSR no. 157/ 1994 collected).

38. *Narodna obroda*, August 2, 1994. See also ibid., September 22, 1994 (suppl.).

39. See *Volby do Narodnej rady SR konane 30.9 a 1.10.1994* (Elections to the NCSR, September 30–October 1, 1994) (Bratislava: Statistical Office of the Slovak Republic, October 1994), pp. 13–19, 93–97.

40. PDL-SDPS-PG-AM in the framework of the Common Choice; Coexistence-HCDM-HCP in the framework of the Hungarian Coalition; and the coalition of MDS-PPS.

41. PCCI on the candidates list of CDM, SGA on the candidates list of MDS-PPS, and NDP-NA on the candidates list of DU.

42. SNP and AWS.

43. Milan Zemko, "Political Parties and the Election System in Slovakia: Retrospective on the Last Three Elections to the Slovak National Council and the National Council of the Slovak Republic," in Szomolanyi and Meseznikov, eds., *Slovakia: Parliamentary Elections 1994*, p. 49.

44. Dusan Kovac, "Der gesellschaftliche Wandel (The social change) in H. Suessmuth, ed., *8. Leutherheider Forum* (The eighth Leutherheid forum) (Baden-Baden: Nomos, 1996), pp. 76–79; ibid., "Selbstständige Slowakei—das Land 'dazwischen' " (Independent Slovakia—the country "in-between"), *Europaische Rundschau* (European review) 22, no. 1 (1994): 81–88.

45. Sona Szomolanyi, "Does Slovakia Deviate from the Central European Variant of Transition?" in Szomolanyi and Meseznikov, eds., *Slovakia: Parliamentary Elections 1994*, p. 15.

46. Martin Butora and Zuzana Fialova, *Nonprofit Sector and Volunteering in Slovakia* (Bratislava: SAIA-SCTS and FOCUS, 1995), pp. 16–17.

47. Silvia Mihalikova, "Communitarianist Aspect of Election Behavior in Slovakia," in Szomolanyi and Meseznikov, eds., *Slovakia: Parliamentary Elections 1994*, pp. 164–65.

48. Butora et al., "Nonprofit Sector and Voluntarism in Slovakia," in *Global Report*, pp. 229–30. See also *Pravda*, January 19, 1996.

49. See 0. Dostal, "Vizitka slovenskej demokracie" (Proof of Slovak democracy), *SME*, November 14, 1995.

50. Butora et al., "Nonprofit Sector," p. 231.

51. See "Prezident vratil NR SR zakon o nadaciach" (The President returned the law about foundations to Parliament), *SME*, June 6, 1996.

52. See I. Samel, "Prezidentom vrateny zakon o nadaciach definitivne schvaleny" (The law on foundations returned by the president definitely passed), *Narodna obroda*, June 21, 1996; and "Parlament vyslal negativny signal do Europy" (The Parliament sent a negative signal to Europe), *SME*, June 21, 1996.

53. Kemal Dervis et al., *Slovakia: Restructuring for Recovery* (Washington, D.C.: World Bank, 1994), p. 1.

54. Ivan Miklos and Eduard Zitnansky, "Economy," in Butora and Huncik, eds., *Global Report on Slovakia*, p. 92.

55. Ivan Miklos and Eduard Zitnansky, "The Economy," in Martin Butora and Thomas W. Skladony, eds., *Slovakia 1996–1997: A Global Report on the State of Society* (Bratislava: Institute for Public Affairs, 1998), p. 103.

56. Ibid., pp. 104–5.

57. See *Sprava misie Medzinarodneho menoveho fondu* (Report of the mission of the International Monetary Fund) (Bratislava: Ministry of Finance of the Slovak Republic, 1996).

58. See *Slovakia: Country Economic Memorandum Mission. Aide Memoire* (Washington, D.C.: World Bank, 1996).

59. See OECD Economic Surveys, *Slovak Republic. 1995–1996* (Bratislava: Center for Economic Cooperation with the Economies in Transition, 1996).

60. See Anthony Axon, "Slovakia," *Business Europa*, no. 17 (June–July 1996), p. 6.

61. See Zita Sujova, "Meciarov navod na prianie spinavych penazi" (Meciar's instructions for money laundering), *Americke Listy* (American letters), May 7, 1998, p. 1.

62. See *The Economist*, August 16, 1997.

63. Miklos and Zitnansky, "The Economy," p. 108.

64. Dervis et al., *Slovakia*, pp. 46–47.

65. Miklos and Zitnansky, "The Economy," pp. 91, 106.

66. Miroslav Wlachovsky, Alexander Duleba, Pavol Lukac, and Thomas W. Skladony, "The Foreign Policy of the Slovak Republic," in Butora and Skladony, eds., *Slovakia 1996–1997: A Global Report*, p. 82.

67. *Pravda*, January 16, 1995, p. 8.

68. See "European Union Approves Plans for Expansion and 'Euro Club' at Luxembourg Summit," *The Week in Germany*, December 19, 1997, pp. 1–2.

69. *SME*, December 12, 1997. Early in July 1996, Meciar's coalition government was personally warned by two ministers of the EU—Michel Barnier and Werner Hoyer—about the disturbing domestic political developments and the authoritarian methods of Mr. Meciar, whose style was described as reminiscent of the methods used by the former communist regimes. This was the third warning by the EU. Zdenek Leiner, "Treti varovani" (Third warning), *Polygon*, no. 5 (August 5, 1996): 28.

70. See "CTK News from Slovakia, April 3," *CTK Czech News Agency*, Prague, April 8, 1998, 4:30 P.M.

71. Ibid.

72. Rudolf L. Tokes, "From Visegrad to Krakow: Cooperation, Competition, and Coexistence in Central Europe," *Problems of Communism* 40, no. 6 (November–December 1991): 111.

73. Andrew Cottey, *East-Central Europe After the Cold War* (New York: St. Martin's Press, 1995), pp. 85–86. See also S. Fisher, "Slovakia's Foreign Policy Since Independence," *RFE/RL Research Report* 2 (December 10, 1993): 28–29.

74. Cottey, *East-Central Europe*, pp. 86–87; Fisher, "Slovakia's Foreign Policy," p. 33.

75. Fisher, "Slovakia's Foreign Policy," p. 33.

76. "Slovak Ukrainian Military Agreement Signed," *RFE/RL News Briefs* 2 (October 25–29, 1993): 20.

77. Michal Kovac, "Slovakia and the Partnership for Peace," *NATO Review* 42, no. 1 (February 1994): 15–18. See also Cottey, *East-Central Europe*, p. 86.

78. See "Two-faced: Slovakia," *The Economist*, May 6, 1995, p. 50.

79. Greg Gransden, "Cosying Up," *Business Central Europe* 3, no. 21 (May 1995): 15–16.

80. *Narodna obroda*, October 15, 1996.

81. According to a poll conducted in the United States September 14–20, 1996, by the Program on International Policy Attitudes, support for Poland ranked the highest, 68 percent, then Hungary with 63 percent, and the Czech Republic 56 percent; support for Slovakia was only 50 percent—the third from the bottom. See Steven Kull, "The American Public, Congress, and NATO Enlargement," *NATO Review* 45, no. 1 (January 1997): 10. A similar survey published by the European Commission in March 1997 asked the question, "If these were a referendum on the question of your country's membership of NATO, would you vote for or against membership?" Romania and Poland were at the top with 76 and 65 percent for; Slovakia was at the bottom with only 27 percent of the respondents favoring membership, 30 percent undecided, and 19 percent against. See George Cunningham, "EU and NATO Enlargement: How Public Opinion Is Shaping Up in Some Candidate Countries," *NATO Review* 45, no. 3 (May–June 1997): 17.

82. Wlachovsky et al., "The Foreign Policy of the Slovak Republic," p. 97.

83. William Drozdiak, "Clash Between Slovak Leaders Disrupts NATO Referendum," *Washington Post*, May 25, 1997.

84. See *OMRI Daily Digest Slovak Selection*, May 27, 1997, pp. 1–2.

85. Zora Butorova, "Public Opinion," in Butora and Skladony, eds., *Slovakia 1996–1997*, p. 74.

86. Ibid.

87. See "Madrid Declaration on Euro-Atlantic Security and Cooperation" and "Building a New NATO for a New Europe," *NATO Review. Special Summit Edition* 45, no. 4 (July–August 1997): 1–3; and Wlachovsky et al., "The Foreign Policy of the Slovak Republic," p. 97.

88. See "Slovakia and NATO," Geocitizen's unofficial guide to Slovak politics: *GugtSp News*, August 10, 1997, pp. 1–5. For details of the kidnapping, see the section under "Meciarism" in chap. 14.

89. See Wlachovsky et al., "The Foreign Policy of the Slovak Republic," pp. 89–92.

90. Alfred A. Reisch, "Slovakia's Minority Policy Under International Scrutiny," *RFE/RL Research Report* 2 (December 10, 1993): 35–42. See also Cottey, *East-Central Europe*, pp. 88–89.

91. Eleonora Sandor, "The Slovak-Hungarian Basic Treaty," in Butora and Huncik, eds., *Global Report*, pp. 55–61. See also *SME*, May 5, 1996.

92. "Prohlaseni vlady Madarske republiky" (Declaration of the government of the Hungarian Republic), *Stredni Evropa* 8, no. 25 (1992): 149–71.

93. John Fitzmaurice, *Damning the Danube* (Boulder, Colo.: Westview Press, 1996), p. 105.

94. *ICJ Press Release* (The Hague), September 26, 1997.

95. Mikulas Huba and Lubica Trubiniova, "The Environment and Sustainable Development," in Butora and Skladony, eds., *Slovakia 1996–1997*, pp. 166–68.

96. *SME*, February 23, 1996.

CHAPTER 14

1. Grigorij Meseznikov, "Domestic Political Developments and the Political Scene in the Slovak Republic," p. 16.

2. Ibid.

3. *Americke Listy*, September 11, 1997.

4. *Narodna obrodna*, July 15, 1998.

5. *SME*, April 29, 1998.

6. *SME*, August 28, 1998.

7. *SME*, January 25, 1999.

8. Darina Malova, "Slovakia," *European Journal of Political Research*, 32, nos. 3–4 (1997): 484.

9. Ibid., p. 485.

10. Ivan Miklos, "Privatization," in Martin Butora and Peter Huncik, eds., *Global Report on Slovakia: Comprehensive Analyses from 1995 and Trends from 1996*, pp. 112–13.

11. *SME*, December 29, 1999, and January 18, 2000.

12. *MF Dnes*, December 1, 1995.

13. *SME*, December 13, 1995. See also Miklos, "Privatization," *Global Report*, p. 113.

14. *SME*, March 5, 1997, and Ivan Miklos, "Privatization," in Martin Butora and Thomas W. Skladony, eds., *Slovakia 1996–1997*, pp. 123, 125 n. 8.

15. *Pravda*, December 21, 1995; Miklos, "Privatization" *Global Report*, pp. 114–16; *Polygon* (Zurich, Switzerland) no. 6 (October 9, 1995): 4.

16. *Narodna obroda*, August 8, 1996. See also Miklos, "Privatization," in Butora and Skladony, eds., *Slovakia 1996–1997*, p. 122.

17. For further details, see Miklos, in Butora and Skladony, eds., p. 124; and Ivan Miklos, "Ekonomika a privatizacia" (The economy and privatization), in Sona Szomolanyi, ed., *Aky rezim sa formuje na Slovensku sedem rokov po?* (What type of regime is being formed in Slovakia seven years after?) (Bratislava: Friedrich Ebert Foundation, 1997).

18. See Zita Sujova, "ZIy sen" (Bad dream), *Americke Listy*, December 7, 1997, pp. 1–12.

19. Data in this paragraph are from Zora Butorova, ed., *Democracy and Discontentment in Slovakia: A Public Profile of a Country in Transition* (Bratislava: Institute for Public Affairs, 1998), pp. 21–36. Similar results were obtained by a USIA-commissioned survey in Slovakia. See Anna E. Sweeney, "Opinion Analysis: With Elections Around the Corner, Slovak Public Still Dissatisfied with Democracy," USIA Office of Research and Media Reaction, *News and Hot Issues* (American Embassy, Bratislava), August 27, 1998.

20. See "Remarks by Chairman of the Board of Governors of the US Federal Reserve System before the Annual Convention of the American Society of Newspaper Editors," held in Washington, D.C., on April 2, 1998.

21. For further details, see Colin Jones, "A Tested Leadership," *The Banker* 148, issue 865 (March 1998): 41–44.

22. See table 12 in Zora Butorova, Olga Gyarfasova, and Vladimir Krivy, "Parties, Institutions, and Politicians," in Zora Butorava, ed., *Democracy and Discontent in Slovakia: A Public Opinion Profile of a Country in Transition* (Bratislava: Institute for Public Affairs, 1998), p. 70.

23. See table 13 in ibid., p. 73.

24. See Act of the NCSR no. 187/1998 of May 20, 1998, amending and supplementing Act no. 80/1990 on Elections enacted by the SNC on March 16, 1990.

25. For background on the 1998 elections, see Martin Butora, Grigorij Meseznikov, and Zora Butorova, eds., *Slovenske volby '98: Kto? Preco? Ako?* (Slovak elections '98: Who? Why? How?) (Bratislava: Institut pne verejne otazky, 1999).

26. See FOCUS—Opinion Polls—in *Slovensko.com, Slovakia Daily Survey,* September 8, 1998.

27. Butorova et al., "Parties, Institutions, and Politicians," p. 74.

28. For details of relations between political parties, see ibid., pp. 76–80.

29. See "CTK News from Slovakia, October 15," *CTK Czech News Agency,* Prague, October 15, 1998.

30. See Miroslav Beblavy, "Who Won the Battle of Markiza TV?" *Prague Post Online,* September 23, 1998.

31. *Trend,* September 30, 1998.

32. *Slovak Spectator,* October 12–18, 1998.

33. *Central Europe Online,* October 7, 1998.

34. *SME,* October 9, 1998.

35. *Pravda,* October 27, 1998.

36. See *CTK Czech News Agency,* Prague, October 28, 1998, p. 1; and *RFE/RL Newsline—Central & Eastern Europe,* October 29, 1998, p. 4.

37. *Pravda,* October 29, 1998.

38. *SME,* August 17, 1999.

39. *Slovak Spectator,* October 11–17, 1999.

40. *SME,* December 23, 1999.

41. Ibid.

42. *SME,* January 28, 2000.

43. Eugen Jurzyca, Marek Jakoby, and Peter Pazitny, "Celkovy ekonomicky vyvoj" (General economic development), in Grigorij Meseznikov et al., eds., *Slovensko 1998–1999* (Slovakia 1998–1999) (Bratislava: Institut pre verejne otazky, 1999), p. 390.

44. *Slovak Spectator,* December 13, 1999.

45. Ibid., December 20–26, 1999.

46. Ibid., January 10–16, 2000.

47. *SME,* June 6, 1999.

48. *Slovak Spectator,* September 13–19, 1999.

49. *SME,* February 4, 1999.

50. *Central Europe Online,* August 29, 1999.

51. *Slovak Spectator,* July 5–11, 1999; *SME,* August 7, 1999.

52. *SME,* July 27, 1999; *RFE/RL Newsline,* July 28, 1999.

53. Olga Reptova, "Privatizacia" (Privatization), *OS,* Forum obcianskej spolocnosti (Public Association Forum), no. 9 (September 1999).

54. Grigorij Meseznikov, "Vnutropoliticky vyvoj a system politickych stran" (Internal political development and the system of political parties), *Slovensko 1998–1999,* pp. 57–59.

55. *Slovak Spectator*, August 23–29, 1999.
56. Ibid., December 20–26, 1999.
57. Ibid., January 31–February 6, 2000.
58. Ibid., January 10–16, 2000.
59. Ibid., September 27–October 3, 1999.
60. Ibid., September 20–26, 1999.
61. Ibid., September 13–19, 1999; *Narodna obroda*, October 23, 1999.
62. *Slovak Spectator*, January 10–16, 2000.
63. *SME*, January 18, 2000.
64. *SME*, January 18 and February 2, 2000.
65. *SME*, January 18, 2000.
66. *Slovak Spectator*, February 7–13, 2002.
67. Ibid.
68. Ibid., January 31–February 6, 2000.
69. *Narodna obroba*, February 9, 2000

dresses. The distinction is reinforced in elementary school. Boys and girls both know their roles instinctively. Normally teachers understand that and react accordingly.

Now and then, at home more often than in school, a boy will participate in cross-dressing. A girl may become more physical and take part in tomboyish activity. Parents need not become alarmed. Much of this activity is normal. The mistake is to make an issue of it.

Christian parents reinforce God's role for them when they show mutual respect for each other, when husbands assume responsibility as head of the house, and when wives contribute and carry out the role intended for them (see, for example, 1 Corinthians 7:2–5; 1 Peter 3:5–7; Colossians 3:18–19).

Motivated by biblical perspectives, parents will find great pleasure in seeing their sons and daughters grow into responsible men and women.

Helpful Family Resources

Human Sexuality: A Christian Perspective

from *The New Learning About Sex* series

by Roger Sonnenberg

Have some questions, but don't know who or how to ask? This resource helps you better understand your sexuality and its place in your life. The book addresses important topics such as the spiritual, emotional, and physical aspects of sexuality. Learn about:

- Why God created sexuality
- How sexuality should be used
- How sexuality is tarnished by sin
- Sexual orientation
- Human anatomy
- Sexuality and the single person
- Family Planning
- Reproduction
- Infertility Advances
- Sexually Transmitted Diseases
- Sexual Addictions and Problems

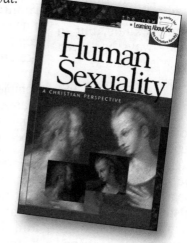

Hardback. 224 pages.

0-570-03568-6   14-2119LGN $16.99

Available through your local participating Christian bookstore or CPH at 1-800-325-3040 Shop online at *www.cph.org*

© 2003 CPH   Printed in U.S.A.   85-1802

Concordia Publishing House
3558 South Jefferson Ave.
St. Louis, Missouri 63118-3968

Good News for families

January 2003

Gender Identity

Most of us who have lived through the cultural changes of a half-century ago shake our heads in disbelief. How could we move from a society that seemingly endorsed gender differences and heterosexuality to one that not only tolerates active homosexuals, but in many ways has given them legal status?

Christians know homosexuality is contrary to God's will as well as to American standards until 50 years ago. References to homosexual behavior have appeared throughout all history, but were seldom noted publicly and have never been approved by society. The current brash demands of homosexuals are both cause and effect

for other moral lapses too. How God wants us to relate to homosexuals, as well as all people, is another topic for another time.

Rather than wring our hands in despair, we can do much to counteract the trend. Knowing how we have come to such a desperate situation today is important, but also too complex even to summarize here. We can do something about it, and it begins with the family.

Parents need to recognize and honor the fact that God created human beings male and female and for a purpose (Genesis 1:27–28). Romans 1 clearly informs us that God disapproves of homosexual behavior.

Therefore, parents are expected to support God's will for us.

Ordinarily parents will have no problem in cultivating a God-pleasing attitude and outlook. Even young babies can distinguish between male and female. They recognize higher- and lower-pitched voices and how mother and father treat them. Parents insert gender cues into the way they express themselves. Psychologists may be puzzled how little children come to distinguish male and female so early. We know; the distinction is God-created.

As they grow up, children play out their intended roles. Ultra-macho boys whoop and brandish imaginary guns while girls cuddle dolls and wear flouncy

Continued...

Subject Index

Name Index

Names in **boldface** are also cited in Subject Index.